The Marion Milner Tradition

The Marion Milner Tradition provides a comprehensive overview of Milner's eight-volume oeuvre for the first time, and celebrates her pioneering achievements both in the psychoanalytic world and in creative and scientific disciplines such as clinical and organisational psychology, philosophy, mindfulness and spirituality, management theory, art therapy, and art appreciation/criticism.

This volume considers Marion Blackett Milner through the prism of her innovative engagement with people, art, and human experience, as well as her extraordinary contribution as an original thinker and researcher within the Independent Group of the British Psychoanalytical Society. The co-editors' exploratory approach to her legacy is as open as the spirit of Milnerean 'discovery research' in defining its distinctive features. An assembly of fifty contributors were invited to interrogate the evolution of what is becoming known as the Milner Tradition, demarcating her influence on theory and clinical practice over the many decades of her life and since her death. They draw upon their professional interviews or friendship with Marion Blackett Milner, or intimate experience of her as an analyst, supervisor, or relative. Similarly, participants in global reading groups in Australia, England, Greece, Northern Ireland, the Republic of Ireland, and South Africa recount personal responses to their own exercise in action research.

The plethora of riches in this book will be of interest to both new and veteran readers of Milner's opus, as well as students and practitioners from a variety of therapeutic and other disciplines.

Margaret Boyle Spelman, PhD, is a chartered clinical and counselling psychologist, psychoanalytic psychotherapist, and organisational psychologist who has been working for more than four decades with the Irish Health Service Executive and in private practice. She is (ex officio) member of The Psychological Society of Ireland, The Irish Council of Psychotherapy, and member of the European Association for Psychotherapy. Margaret has two monographs on the subject of DW Winnicott and co-edited the Winnicott volume in this series.

Joan Raphael-Leff, PhD, is a psychoanalyst (Fellow, British Psychoanalytical Society and longstanding Member of the Group of Independent Psychoanalysts). Previously, she was Professor of Psychoanalysis at UCL and the University of Essex. In 1998, she founded and served as the first International Chair of COWAP, IPA's Committee on Women and Psychoanalysis. She is the author and editor of fourteen books and 150 single author publications. Now, in her retirement, she heads the UCL/Anna Freud Centre Academic Faculty for Psychoanalytic Research.

Lines of Development

Evolution of Theory and Practice over the Decades Series
Series Editors: Joan Raphael-Leff, Aleksandar Dimitrijević and Norka T. Malberg

---

The Anna Freud Tradition
Lines of Development – Evolution of Theory and Practice over the Decades
Edited By Norka T. Malberg and Joan Raphael-Leff

Fairbairn and the Object Relations Tradition
Edited By Graham S. Clarke and David E. Scharff

The Winnicott Tradition
Lines of Development – Evolution of Theory and Practice over the Decades
Edited By Margaret Boyle Spelman and Frances Thomson-Salo

The W.R. Bion Tradition
Edited By Howard B. Levine and Giuseppe Civitarese

The Lacan Tradition
Edited By Lionel Bailly and David Lichtenstein, Sharmini Bailly

The Klein Tradition
Lines of Development – Evolution of Theory and Practice over the Decades
Edited By Kay Long and Penelope Garvey

Ferenczi's Influence on Contemporary Psychoanalytic Traditions
Lines of Development – Evolution of Theory and Practice over the Decades
Edited By Aleksandar Dimitrijević, Gabriele Cassullo and Jay Frankel

The Marion Milner Tradition
Lines of Development: Evolution of Theory and Practice over the Decades
Edited By Margaret Boyle Spelman and Joan Raphael-Leff

The Marion Milner Tradition

Lines of Development: Evolution of Theory and Practice over the Decades

Edited by
Margaret Boyle Spelman and
Joan Raphael-Leff

Routledge
Taylor & Francis Group
LONDON AND NEW YORK

Cover image: © Giles Milner and James W. Anderson and Leon Kleimberg

First published 2023
by Routledge
4 Park Square, Milton Park, Abingdon, Oxon OX14 4RN

and by Routledge
605 Third Avenue, New York, NY 10158

Routledge is an imprint of the Taylor & Francis Group, an informa business

British Library Cataloguing-in-Publication Data
A catalogue record for this book is available from the British Library

Library of Congress Cataloging-in-Publication Data
Names: Boyle Spelman, Margaret, editor. | Raphael-Leff, Joan, 1941– editor.
Title: The Marion Milner tradition : lines of development : evolution of theory and practice over the decades / edited by Margaret Boyle Spelman and Joan Raphael-Leff.
Description: 1 Edition. | New York, NY : Routledge, 2023. | Series: The lines of development: evolution of theory and practice over the decades series | Includes bibliographical references and index.
Identifiers: LCCN 2022015852 (print) | LCCN 2022015853 (ebook) | ISBN 9781138359703 (hardback) | ISBN 9781138359758 (paperback) | ISBN 9780429433535 (ebook)
Subjects: LCSH: Milner, Marion, 1900-1998. | Psychoanalysts—Great Britain—Biography. | Psychology—Great Britain—History.
Classification: LCC BF109.M55 M37 2023 (print) | LCC BF109.M55 (ebook) | DDC 150.195092 [B]—dc23/eng/20220729
LC record available at https://lccn.loc.gov/2022015852
LC ebook record available at https://lccn.loc.gov/2022015853

ISBN: 978-1-138-35970-3 (hbk)
ISBN: 978-1-138-35975-8 (pbk)
ISBN: 978-0-429-43353-5 (ebk)

DOI: 10.4324/9780429433535

Typeset in Times New Roman
by codeMantra

Mind The Gap

Words by
Marion Milner

A Tribute To Pearl King

Music by
James O. Burger

("What is mind? No matter?"
What is matter? Never mind.") Who said this?

"Mind the gap!" shouts the mechanical voice at the Embankment
Tube station
"Mind the gap!"
I do, I did, I never have fallen between the platform and the train
I don't mind, it doesn't matter.
Or does it?

I do mind the gap between the rich and the poor.
And I do mind the gap between what I can dream of for the earth
And what we are doing to it.
Destroying the living matter on which we depend for life-
like the Amazon Forests

And I mind that I did not think
It mattered that I did not mind
When we came to the
End of the matter
So that there were
No more gaps
To mind.

Body and Mind, two sides of the same join you said?

I minded when I did not mind
That the matter did not matter any more
But I do know that it's
Out of the gaps
That new things grow.

For Beda, Astór and Saorla.

For Julian.

Contents

Figures

Acknowledgements

Mind the Gap: The poem was written by Marion Milner, aged 95, as a tribute to British Psychoanalyst Pearl King on her 80th birthday. Reproduced here by kind permission of Giles Milner on behalf of the estate. In 1998, after Milner's death, with Pearl King's encouragement it was set to music. Reproduced here by kind permission of the composer James O. Burger. ASCAP Nashville, IN 37214 USA. All Rights Reserved.

Chapter 17: 'Holding and Visceral attention': bodily concentration of an analyst under Covid-19 lockdown by Dr. Maia Kirchkheli was initially published as an article in the *British Journal of Psychotherapy* (2021), vol. 37 no. 3, pp. xxx–xxx. It was awarded the *British Journal of Psychotherapy*'s 2020 Rozsika Parker Prize (Post-Qualification Path). Reproduced by kind permission of the British Psychotherapy Foundation and John Wiley & Sons Ltd, with some additional passages on Marion Milner written specifically for this book.

Chapter 20: 'Introduction to Marion Milner's work on creativity and art' by Alberto Stefana is a shortened modified version of 'Revisiting Marion Milner's work on creativity and art', published in *The International Journal of Psychoanalysis* 2019, Vol. 100, No. 1, 128–147.

Chapter 21: 'Remembering Marion Milner' by Desy Safán-Gerard was originally given as part of a program entitled 'Marion Milner's Explorations of Creativity in Art and Psychoanalysis' featuring Emma Letley, author of *Marion Milner: The Life.* New Center of Psychoanalysis, USA April 27, 2014.

Chapter 22: Figure 22.1: Marion Milner, sketch of two overlapping jugs. Reproduced by kind permission of Giles Milner, on behalf of the estate.

Chapter 30: Figure 30.1: Cartoon by Michael Leuing, (*The Age*, 12th January 2019). Reproduced by courtesy of Michael Leuing.

About the Editors and Contributors

Editors

Margaret Boyle Spelman, PhD, is the author of two volumes on Winnicott and co-editor of *The Winnicott Tradition* in this series. She is a chartered clinical and counselling psychologist, psychoanalytic psychotherapist, and organisational psychologist who has been working for more than four decades with the Irish Health Service Executive and in private practice. Margaret, a member of the European Association for Psychotherapy, has taught widely in the areas of psychology and psychoanalysis, and has held executive positions in the Psychological Society of Ireland, The Irish Institute of Psychoanalytic Psychotherapy (where she was the director of clinical training), the Irish Forum for Psychoanalytic Psychotherapy, and the Irish Council for Psychotherapy.

Joan Raphael-Leff, PhD, is a psychoanalyst (Fellow, British Psychoanalytical Society) and academic, and heads the Anna Freud Centre Academic Faculty for Psychoanalytic Research. Previously, she was the head of University College London's MSc in Psychoanalytic Developmental Psychology, and Professor of Psychoanalysis at the Centre for Psychoanalytic Studies, University of Essex. She is the founder and first international chair of IPA's Committee on Women and Psychoanalysis (COWAP). She is also Founding Editor of the 'Developmental Lines' series, and co-editor of *The Anna Freud Tradition* volume. Her publications include twelve other books and over 150 peer-reviewed papers.

Contributors

James William Anderson, PhD, is a Psychoanalyst (Chicago Institute for Psychoanalysis) and Clinical Professor at Northwestern University. He is the Editor of *Annual of Psychoanalysis.* He has published psychobiographical papers on William and Henry James, Woodrow Wilson, and Frank Lloyd Wright, among others.

Barbie Antonis was a Consultant Adult Psychotherapist at Parkside Clinic in West London for over twenty years. She is a Trustee of the Winnicott Trust and Fellow of the British Psychoanalytic Society where she teaches and supervises candidates. Her publications include chapters on Jazz and on the Contribution of Independent Women Psychoanalysts, with a book in preparation.

Bice Benvenuto is a psychoanalyst practicing in London; founding member of the Centre for Freudian Analysis and Research; and President of *Associazione Dolto* in

Rome and a founder of the Maison Verte-UK. Bice is a Visiting professor at the New School of Social Research (NY) and Florida Atlantic University. She is the author of *Concerning the Rites of Psychoanalysis*" (Polity), co-author of *The Works of Jacques Lacan: An Introduction* (FAB), and book chapters.

Cheryl Bleakley is a psychoanalytic psychotherapist, working in private practice in Belfast, and a professional artist, with a therapeutic community background and extensive experience of facilitating the creativity of others. Cheryl is the Vice-Chair of the Northern Ireland Institute of Human Relations, and the creative lead behind the short film *The Clearing* (2019), produced by the Institute's psychoanalytically informed Art Project.

Vincenzo Bonaminio, PhD, is a training and supervising psychoanalyst at the Italian Psychoanalytic Society. He is a Professor at the University of Rome and Director of the University Winnicott Institute. He is Past Vice President of the European Psychoanalytic Federation (EPF). He is the winner of Francis Tustin Trust Memorial Prize (2001).

Michael Brearley is a psychoanalyst and author of several books. He was President of the British Psychoanalytical Society and also of the Marylebone Cricket Club. In his previous career, he was a university lecturer in philosophy at the University of Newcastle upon Tyne, and as a professional cricketer, captained Cambridge University, Middlesex, and England in thirty-one test matches.

Peter Bruggen, (1934–2018) MB ChB FRCPsych, was Formerly Medical Director and consultant adolescent psychiatrist, Hill End Adolescent Unit, St Albans, Hertfordshire, where he executed a systemic innovation for service provision. He became a psychoanalyst after a training analysis with Marion Milner. He is the author of forty+ articles and books like *Surviving Adolescence* (1986), *Helping Families* (with C. O Brien, 1987), and *Who Cares? True Stories of NHS Reforms* (1997).

Penny Busetto is a South African author whose novel, *The Story of Anna P, as Told by Herself*, won the 2014 European Union Literary Award. She is currently working on an interdisciplinary PhD exploring the 1930s archive of psychiatrist, psychoanalyst, and ethnologist Dr BJF Laubscher (head of the 'native' wards at the Komani Mental Hospital, Eastern Cape). She is due to take up a fellowship at King's College London.

Lesley Caldwell, PhD, is Honorary Professor in the Psychoanalysis Unit at UCL, and a BPA psychoanalyst in private practice in London. She is training analyst for the Independent Child and Adolescent Psychotherapy Trainings (IPCAPA) and London rep for COWAP. Her publications include *Art, Creativity, Living* (2000), *The Elusive Child* (2003), *Sex and Sexuality: Winnicottian Perspectives* (2005), *Winnicott and the Psychoanalytic Tradition* (2007), and *Reading Winnicott* (with Angela Joyce, 2011).

Donald Campbell was President of the British Psychoanalytical Society from 1999 to 2003 and Secretary General of the International Psychoanalytical Association from 2003 to 2005. Alongside his private practice, he worked as a child and adult psychoanalytic psychotherapist at the NHS Portman Clinic in London, where he served as Chairman between 1991 and 1994.

Gabriele Cassullo, PhD, is a clinical psychologist and psychotherapist working in Turin (Italy). He researches and publishes on the history, theory, and technique of psychoanalysis, and has co-edited (with Aleksandar Dimitrijevic and Jay Frankel) *Ferenczi's Influence on Contemporary Psychoanalytic Traditions* (Routledge, this series).

Carolyn Coburn is a child, adolescent, and adult psychoanalytic psychotherapist in full-time private practice. She teaches child psychotherapy and infant observation for the Child Psychoanalytic Psychotherapy Association of Australia, The Masters of Mental Health in Child Psychotherapy at Monash University, and the Child Psychiatry Training Program at The University of Melbourne. Previously at the Royal Children's Hospital in Melbourne.

Clare Crellin (1948–2021) was an independent scholar with thirty years' experience as a Consultant Clinical Psychologist and Psychotherapist with the NHS; also external examiner for psychotherapy training with Re-vision, London; and a psychotherapist and supervisor for Hospice Isle of Man.

Tessa Dalley, is a child and adolescent psychotherapist, art therapist, and clinical supervisor. Currently she is in independent practice with children, young people, and families. Previously she worked in CAMHS, an in-patient adolescent unit, the Parent – Infant Project at the Anna Freud Centre, education, and the voluntary sectors. She is the Chair of the Squiggle Foundation. She has published and lectured widely on child psychotherapy and art therapy.

Aleana Egan (b.1979) is an artist living in Dublin who creates abstract sculptures that are assembled in multi-layered constellations, in materials such as metal, wood, pigment, and fabric. Her recent exhibitions include *New People,* Konrad Fischer, Duesseldorf (2020); *Shadowy Forms,* NICC Brussels (2020); *Spitze* Farbvision, Berlin (2019); and *From Narrow Provinces,* Cample Line, Dumfrieshire (2019).

Michael Eigen, PhD, is a psychoanalyst. He has published thirty books and many papers. During the pandemic, he gives a weekly international Zoom seminar, an expanded continuation of the office seminar ongoing over forty-five years. He teaches for the National Psychological Association for Psychoanalysis and the New York University Postdoctoral Program in Psychotherapy and Psychoanalysis. His latest book is *Pain and Beauty, Terror and Wonder* (2021).

Wayne Featherstone, PhD, is a Psychoanalytic Psychotherapist and a Mental Health Social Worker working in private practice in Melbourne. He is the Past President of the Victorian Association of Psychoanalytic Psychotherapists. He also consults to the Lighthouse Foundation, which provides several different therapeutic, residential treatment programmes for traumatised and homeless young people.

Andreas Giannakoulas (1936–2021) was a psychoanalyst trained at the British Society. He later became the President of the Italian Psychoanalytical Association. His publications include *Current Trends in On-line Games for Teaching Programming Concepts to Primary School Students* and Vols I and II of *Squiggles and Space – Revisiting the Work of D.W. Winnicott((*2001) (co-edited with Bertolini & Hernadez). With Giannotti, he formed a training programme in child psychotherapy at the Instituto di Neuropsichiatria Infantile of the Univerisità di Roma LA SAPIENZA.

Shane Graham, MSc, M.Ps.S.I., is an assistant psychologist at the early stages of his career in Dublin. He has a keen interest in pathways of individual growth and the somatic experience, and is committed to balancing the application of rational and intuitive perspectives within the field of psychology.

Thanassis Hatzopoulos is a child-psychiatrist, psychoanalyst (full member of Société de Psychanalyse Freudienne, Paris, and responsible for the Greek division of the International Winnicott Association), and a poet. He works with children, adolescents, and adults and is the main translator of the works of D.W. Winnicott in Greek.

Hugh Haughton is Professor of English in the University of York. He is the editor of Lewis Carroll's *Alice in Wonderland and Through the Looking-Glass* (Penguin 1998), Freud's *The Uncanny* (Penguin, 2004), *The Letters of T.S. Eliot* (volumes 1 and 2), and Marion Milner's *Eternity's Sunrise* (Routledge, 2011).

Linda Hopkins, PhD, is a clinical psychologist and psychoanalyst in Washington, DC, USA. She is on the teaching faculty at IIPT (International Institute for Psychoanalytic Training) and IPI (International Psychotherapy Institute), Bethesda, Maryland and is the author of *False Self: The Life of Masud Khan* (Other Press, 2006; Karnac Books, 2008).

Anne Jeffs is a Clinical Social Worker and Psychoanalytic Psychotherapist working in private practice in Melbourne. She is a member of the Psychoanalytic Psychotherapy Association of Australia (child and adult) and Group Relations Australia. In addition to her private work, Anne is passionate about facilitating reflective spaces for professionals in the human service sectors.

Jennifer Johns, MD, is a retired Fellow of the British Psychoanalytic Society, a psychoanalyst, with a medical background. She has been Chair of the Group of Independent Psychoanalysts, of the Winnicott Trust, and recently of the Trustees of the Squiggle Foundation.

Angela Joyce is a Training and Supervising Psychoanalyst Chair of the Curriculum Committee and Child Psychoanalyst at the British Psychoanalytical Society. She is a member of the pioneering Parent Infant Project at the Anna Freud Centre and jointly led the child psychotherapy service there. She is Current Chair of the Winnicott Trust. Her publications include *Reading Winnicott* (2011, co-edited with Lesley Caldwell) and *Donald Winnicott and the History of the Present* (2017).

Brett Kahr has worked in the mental health profession for over forty years. He is Senior Fellow at the Tavistock Institute of Medical Psychology in London and, also, Visiting Professor of Psychoanalysis and Mental Health in the Regent's School of Psychotherapy and Psychology at Regent's University London. Kahr is also the Honorary Director of Research at Freud Museum London and, also, a Fellow of the museum. Author of sixteen books and series editor of over seventy-five further titles, his own books include, *D.W. Winnicott: A Biographical Portrait*, which won the Gradiva Award for Biography, as well as *Tea with Winnicott*, *Coffee with Freud*, and, more recently, *Bombs in the Consulting Room: Surviving Psychological Shrapnel*, and, most recently, *Freud's Pandemics: Surviving Global War, Spanish Flu, and* *the Nazis*. A Consultant Psychotherapist at The Balint Consultancy, he works with individuals and couples in private practice in Central London.

Anne Karpf, PhD, is a sociologists and writer, contributing to *The Guardian* and other publications. Her five books of nonfiction include a family memoir, *The War After: Living with the Holocaust*, and *How Women Can Save the Planet*. Her research into the radio broadcasts of Donald Winnicott was funded by the Winnicott Trust. She is Professor of Life Writing and Culture at London Metropolitan University.

Maia Kirchkheli, MD, is a psychiatrist and a psychoanalyst, a member of the British Psychoanalytical Society. She is currently in full-time private practice in London and teaches at IOPA, BPA, and on the UCL MSc in Theoretical Psychoanalytic Studies. Besides being a psychoanalyst, she has been involved in various artistic pursuits, and her main area of interest is an overlap of creativity and psychoanalysis.

Leon Kleimberg is a training and supervising analyst for the British Psycho-analytical Society, in private practice in London. He teaches different courses for candidates and postgraduate training of the British Psychoanalytical Society. He has written papers on psychoanalysis and creativity, psychopathology, immigration, and sports.

Emma Letley is a writer and psychoanalytic psychotherapist trained with the Arbours Association and practised for many years at King's College London. She is the biographer of Marion Milner (Routledge 2014) and the Series Editor of Marion Milner works (Routledge 2010–2012).

Deborah Anna Luepnitz, PhD, is on the faculty of the Institute for Relational Psychoanalysis of Philadelphia. She is the author of *Schopenhauer's Porcupines: Five Stories of Psychotherapy* and a contributing author to the *Cambridge Companion to Lacan*. In 2005, she launched *Insight for All*, which connects psychoanalysts with homeless adults in Philadelphia, where she also maintains a private practice.

Adam Phillips is former Principal Child Psychotherapist at Charing Cross Hospital, London and a psychoanalyst in private practice. He is a visiting professor in the English Department at the University of York. An essayist, first Winnicott biographer, and author of more than thirty books, Phillips was the general editor of the new Penguin Modern Classics translation of Sigmund Freud.

Andrew Malleson is a retired UK-born psychiatrist who was a member of both the Royal College of Psychiatrists and The Royal College of Physicians in Britain. He is the author of many psychiatry-related titles including *Whiplash and Other Useful Illnesses, Need Your Doctor Be So Useless*, and most recently *Coscanna: The Return of an Angry Goddess*.

Giles Milner is Marion's grandson, elder son of her son John. He and his brother Quentin grew up in Islington not far from Marion's home in Chalk Farm. He still lives in London, with his wife and two teenage daughters. He started out as a biologist, but has a thirty-year career in IT for a range of companies from blue chip to startup.

Juliet Mitchell, PhD, is a psychoanalyst, Fellow of the British Academy, and IPA and Professor Emeritus at the University of Cambridge where she established and directed a Centre for Gender Studies. She received a PhD in Theoretical Psychoanalysis at UCL. Her publications include *Women: The Longest Revolution* (1966); *Women's Estate* (1971); *Psychoanalysis and Feminism* (1974); *Mad Men and Medusas: Reclaiming Hysteria* (2000); and *Siblings: Sex and Violence* (2003).

Desy Safán-Gerard is a Training and Supervising Analyst, Psychoanalytic Center of California in Los Angeles, and is also a musician and practicing artist with a studio in Venice. Her book *Chaos and Control: A Psychoanalytic Perspective on Unfolding Creative Minds* (2018) draws on her clinical work.

Jennifer Scott, PhD, is a Senior Lecturer at the Arts University Bournemouth. She trained as an art therapist and studied architecture in London and Sydney. Her work on large architectural projects led to an interest in therapeutic aspects of design, exploring affinities between spatial aspects of Winnicott's psychoanalytic theories and architectural forms of modernist spatial understanding.

Allan Shafer, PhD, is a clinical psychologist, psychoanalytic psychotherapist, and organisation consultant in private practice in Melbourne, Australia. He also consults internationally in group relations and was associate director of the Tavistock Institute's 2019 Leicester Conference.

Alberto Stefana, PsyD, PhD, is a psychotherapist and doctor in research in human sciences. He currently works in private practice and collaborates with the Psychiatric Unit of the Spedali Civili Hospital of Brescia (Italy). He is interested in issues of clinical theory and technique, history and epistemology of psychoanalysis, and the relationship between psychoanalysis and the other sciences.

David Smith, MSc, is a psychoanalytic psychotherapist and clinical supervisor in private practice in Belfast, having previously facilitated both art and music therapy groups within a therapeutic community. David is the Chair of the Northern Ireland Institute of Human Relations and former Chair of the Psychoanalytic Section of the Irish Council for Psychotherapy.

David Tuckett, PhD, is a Training and Supervising Psychoanalyst (British Psychoanalytic Society). He is Emeritus Professor of Psychoanalysis and Decision-Making under Uncertainty at UCL. He was Former Editor of *International Journal of Psychoanalysis*; Founding Editor of the *New Library of Psychoanalysis*; and past President of the EPF. He is the author of books/journal articles in psychoanalysis, medical sociology, psychology, economics, finance, and decision-making. He is the recipient of Sigourney Award in 2007 and 2018.

Elizabeth Wolf is a training and supervising analyst of the British Psychoanalytical Society and works full time in private practice. She contributes to the development of the Independent Tradition through writing, and teaching candidates and trainees in London and abroad.

Reading Groups

Cape Town Psychoanalytic Reading group

Carol Richards; Jeanine de Villiers; Cathy Rogers; Melanie Silove; Nicolette Jordan (*all IPA, South African trained psychoanalysts*); Joan Raphael-Leff (*British psychoanalyst*)

Cape Town Interdisciplinary group

Dr Elisa Galgut (*philosopher*); Dr Coenie Hattingh (*neuropsychologist, neuroanatomist*); Dr Andrea Palk (*philosopher*); Anna Dreyer (*neuropsychologist*); Roelien Theron (*editor*); Theodor Van der Merwe (*art teacher*); Penny Busetto (*writer*).

Dublin Marion Milner Diaries Reading Group, Ireland.

Clare Crellin (*psychoanalytic psychotherapist*); Veronica O'Doherty (*psychologist)*; Aleana Eagan (*artist*); Margaret Boyle Spelman (*psychoanalytic psychotherapist*).

Hellenic IWA Reading Group, Greece

Thanassis Hatzopoulos (*psychoanalyst, SPF*); Marianthi Kalatzi (*psychologist*); Nektarios Koulos (*clinical psychologist*); Elisa Nikolopoulou (*psychoanalyst*); Marialena Spyropoulou (*writer, psychotherapist*); Nefeli Tambaki (*psychoanalyst*).

Melbourne Reading Group, Australia

Carolyn Coburn, Wayne Featherstone, Anne Jeffs, Allen Shafer (*psychoanalytic psychotherapists*).

Northern Ireland Institute of Human Relations' Clinical and Theoretical Reading Group

Cheryl Bleakley, John Boyle, Mary Cairns, Desmond Campbell, Patricia Denvir, Rosemary Drainey, Carmel McGovern, Gerry McShane, Mandy Mullowney, Janine Paisley, Phyllis Quigg, David Smith, Sue Steging, and Cheryl Towers (*all psychoanalytic psychotherapists*).

Series editor's introduction

Reader, she is indispensable!

Maybe you are like me in believing that she was just another analysand and associate of Winnicott? Or like me in knowing that she had written books about creativity, but you didn't give those enough time? Or overlooked her in trying to find some non-Anglophone, non-European authors to bring you a breath of fresh air?

In case we *are* alike, let me tell you that this collection of essays will make you confess the cardinal sin of superficiality and realise that digesting the thought, the unique approach, and the creativity of Marion Milner must have their place in the psychoanalytic core of each and every one of us.

The book will – let me embolden you right away – serve simultaneously as a sort of indulgence. While previous books in this series focused on preeminent authors whose creeds had been formed decades ago, this one is *the foundational stone for what is yet to come*. Where 'Kleinians' or 'Lacanians' have long ago established their strictly separate quasi-religious groups, recently joined by 'Bionians' and 'Ferenczians,' there is no such thing as 'The Milner Tradition.' This moment, thus, brings a fantastic opportunity to right a historical wrong, possibly motivated by gender issues, 'anxiety of influence,' or, as I have already confessed, mere superficiality. And there seems to be even more. This might be a rare moment of freshness when conceptual and historical research will be devoid of ideology, interest, passionate narrow-mindedness. One can only envy Margaret Boyle Spelman and Joan Raphael-Leff, the book's co-editors, on this almost unique opportunity.

But enough with enthusiasm. What is it about Marion Milner that makes her work the possible spring of a whole tradition?

On one level, it is the *uniqueness* of her approach and attitude. Milner can easily be the most remarkable bridge builder I have ever encountered in the history of our discipline. Her psychoanalysis is artistic, literary, curious about development and creativity, open to treating "mad parts" of our personalities, full of expertise in organisational psychology, and deeply interested in mythology, religions, and spirituality. Underneath all this, one can easily sense the coherent voice of an unyieldingly creative person (a passionate painter, who later made collages out of her old paintings), an unconventional self-questioning free thinker willing to develop only in her own authentic fashion, and, last but certainly not least, a touchingly modest and generous person, who never 'claimed her copyright.'

On another level, Milner introduced concepts, experimented and elaborated on daring clinical practices that were original at the time when she wrote about them. In this volume, four main theoretical concepts are emphasised – framing, bodily concentration in the analyst, absentmindedness, and reverie – but many contributors return to her inventive methods of self-analysis, her bid for clinical spontaneity yet constant self-monitoring; her successful treatment of a psychotic patient, and ground-breaking ideas devoted to the problem of creative blocks and ensnaring the unconscious

This might indicate an additional reason for Milner's obscure status even twenty-five years after her death. Simply put, her basic ideas were, in the meantime, appropriated in mainstream psychoanalytic thinking to such an extent that we all talk about the analytic frame, reciprocal resonance, somatic countertransferential reactions, absorption, internalised relations, authenticity, play, 'me/not me,' innate creativity... But, being intensely private as a person, Milner let people believe these ideas came from Winnicott, Lacan, Relationalists, or Bion.

It seems inevitable that this collection of essays will set things right and give Milner the place she has long deserved among the handful of original psychoanalytic thinkers. What is touching about it is that this volume mirrors Milner's approach to life, psychoanalysis, and creation. Consisting of essays, interviews, reminiscences, reports of discussion groups held on various continents, it reflects the curious, free-spirited and distinctly personal approach of Marion Milner. I feel strangely confident that she would have enjoyed and appreciated this book. And I cannot imagine that you, Reader, won't encounter in these pages the voice of Marion Milner in all its uniqueness and indispensability.

Aleksandar Dimitrijević

Prologue

Margaret Boyle Spelman

Marion Blackett Milner (1900–1998) lived and worked through the entire course of what has been called 'the Freudian century.' The esteem and affection in which she was held by fellow members of the British Psycho-analytical Society and its Institute is suggested by an incident in 1993, when she walked into a hall where Martin James, Founding Chair of The Winnicott Trust, was lecturing. One can hear on the audio-recording that James interrupted an important announcement about Winnicott's financial legacy to say: 'Ladies and gentlemen – Marion Milner!' Whereupon, rapturous and long applause can be heard.

Affection for Mrs. Milner has not translated into full recognition of her substantial and flinty contribution. In fact, her professional legacy seemed to disappear for a time after her death, with no concerted effort made to define, collate, or disseminate her work.

The present volume was undertaken to redress this deficit, and to celebrate her clinical and theoretical achievements both within the global psychoanalytic project and also within psychology, art, and even science. We set to work with several questions in mind:

- What was Marion Milner like as a person, a thinker, a clinician, and an artist?
- Can one speak of a 'Milner tradition' and, if so, what defines it?
- How can we understand her complex collaborations with Donald Winnicott?

A thinking space: Milner and Winnicott

To begin with the last question, it appears to be the case that many people have assumed that Marion Milner is of interest mainly for the light she could shine on her more famous male colleague and mentor, Dr. Winnicott. I, myself, first encountered her work as a result of studying his, during my professional training. The mere fact that she was his analysand seemed enough to inspire curiosity, and I, too, imagined she was a mere follower – an epiphenomenon. Those who did wish to read her books were likely to find them out of print. With a bit of effort, I was able to locate second-hand copies, and gradually came to understand that her collaboration with Winnicott was of immense value to them both. It was, what I have called elsewhere (Boyle Spelman, 2013b) 'a generative psychoanalytic thinking environment.' One comes to realise that even before they met, their ideas seemed to overlap. During the years of active collaboration, however, the seeds of thought germinated and took root.

It surprised me greatly to realise that while many authors had written about Winnicott (I myself was responsible for two such volumes), no one had yet written a single book about Marion Milner and her work! My hope is that the present collection will introduce her to new readers and give those already familiar a more profound appreciation.

Like Winnicott, Milner set a high premium on being herself or, as she put it, on taking possession of her own 'opposites.' As a girl of eleven, she kept a nature diary, and during her psychoanalytic training, she kept a diary of her 'misgivings.' She also encouraged students to hold on to their own *misgivings* because therein lay 'the voice of God.' However, unlike Winnicott and some other male contemporaries, Milner made a habit of acknowledging her sources and influences, among them: J.C. Fleugel, as well as Charles Sherrington, Michel De Montaigne, Sigmund Freud, Pierre Janet, Jean Piaget, and Carl Jung – as well as writers from the mystical traditions of both West and East, including Taoism and Zen Buddhism.

Milner was also wont to trawl her own depths, developing a humourous and self-revelatory style that one does not encounter in Winnicott. For her – despite carefully acknowledging sources – thinking had primacy over the thinker. Some readers have remarked on finding that an idea assumed to be a Winnicott original can be located earlier in Milner's work. For example, the trope *'me and not-me'* that we associate with his transitional object was originally hers. My impression is that their collaboration was not overly possessive/territorial. On this subject, Winnicott once sent Milner a message about a third-party query saying: 'Tell her it doesn't matter which of us thinks of it.' Of course, we don't know for sure if Milner felt exactly the same way, but my impression is that she did not regard ideas as private property.

Elsewhere, I have listed Milner's contribution to the following Winnicott concepts: *the third area of experience, personalization, the healthy and unhealthy use of imagination, transitional space, bisexuality, unintegration, play and playing, potential space, the period of hesitation in the spontaneous gesture, illusion and disillusionment, and aliveness.*

These eleven cluster concepts were lifelong themes for both, and it would be difficult indeed to determine with certainty who added which ingredient to the mix.

Environment and gender

Perhaps sensing already that Marion Milner's work was not getting its due, Winnicott made a point at the British Society of calling her 'one of the big brains of the Society' (Rodman, 1993). In the twenty-six years between his death and her own, she continued to publish including, when she was eighty-seven, a collection of papers and in her nineties her posthumously published final book. We may continue to wonder about the dramatic difference in their legacy and readership. According to Andre Green (2011) and others, Winnicott is recognised as one of two great psychoanalysts after Freud (the other being Jacques Lacan). Milner is considered a minor figure, along with the likes of Charles Rycroft and Sylvia Payne. Winnicott's works have been translated into more than a dozen languages; hers barely at all. No doubt gender was a limiting factor in the fifties and sixties even in the British Society, where women predominated. But there was perhaps also something in her own non-striving nature that kept her out of the limelight. And indeed, her biographer draws attention to a temperament that might have made ambition seem tawdry. Whereas Winnicott loved to sing, play piano, and generally show off, Milner was shy. She sometimes mentioned the emphasis her mother placed on being a good woman, good daughter, and never letting her tongue 'give offense.' There are, after all, many individuals who feel most able to maintain integrity and balance in the shadows (Letley, 2012).

Marion Milner's contributions are scattered far and wide, spanning art, and science – her interest in the scientific method is obvious in *The Human Problem in Schools*. Her interests rest in several disciplines that are not traditional bedfellows and even mutually antagonistic – the 'coming together' of interests which lived easily and harmoniously within Milner herself might otherwise require considerable effort of many normally discreet and disparate interests, forces, and disciplines.

Nonetheless, in addition to being considered Winnicott's closest collaborator, today Milner is considered by many (see Adam Phillips' interview in this volume) an important and original thinker whose contribution compares favourably to Winnicott's. Marion also holds a secure place as an important figure among the women of the independent tradition of the British Psychoanalytic Society (see the chapter by Antonis and Wolf in this volume), and was a founding member of both the Imago Group and the '52 Club.

Realising Milner's legacy

Throughout her eight books and scores of published papers, one discovers Milner's belief that 'everything is always also something else.' Believing in an innate creative process, she linked art theory and art therapy. Her imaginative techniques included use of the 'bead' memory and doodle drawings (which influenced Winnicott's Squiggle game). She pioneered the idea of writing a case history based on an analysis of the patient's art work. Milner's *On Not Being Able to Paint* is sometimes considered to be the first self-help book ever published – and one of the very best – helping countless young painters and other artists – as well as anyone trying to live authentically – to explore, rather than panic at creative impasses

About this book

The present volume presents an appreciation of Marion Milner and her corpus through personal reflections by those who knew her, or had at least the chance to interview her, as well as an engagement with her work within and outside the consulting room.

At the present time, all Marion Milner's books are in print, including *Bothered by Alligators* which appeared for the first time when published posthumously. The year 2010 saw the establishment of the Marion Milner Archive within the Archive of the British Institute of Psychoanalysis.

Structure:

With regard to structure; there are five sections in this book roughly following those of other volumes in this series entitled '*Lines of Development: evolution of tradition, theory, and practice over the decades*.' [So far these include psychoanalytical traditions of Anna Freud, Fairbairn, Ferenczi, Winnicott, Lacan, and Klein.]

An introduction before each section summarises the chapters to help the reader plan their reading.

Section I Life and legacy

This section provides the historical frame for Milner's professional work. For the first time, we have a comprehensive overview from her biographer and ten senior professional colleagues for interrogation of Milner's essential concepts and status as a significant thinker seen through personal observations of the process of growth and development of her ideas in the psychoanalytic, intellectual, and creative community in Britain and beyond.

Section II Clinical applications

Milner has written of her work as a psychologist, practicing psychoanalyst and her use of pictorial art as a form of revelation and therapy. Here, through reflections of three of her patients, two supervisees and two contemporary colleagues, we glimpse other aspects of Milner in the consulting room and her clinical legacy and its applications to psychoanalytic work under many different conditions, including Covid19-driven remote treatment.

Section III Art and creativity

Milner's creative explorations inspired many disciplines beyond artists, and art appreciators. In this section, ten colleagues with a special interest in the arts explore her theoretical ideas and creative productions, with some inspired to produce work of their own to illustrate her influential legacy in all its guises, applications, and geographic locations.

Section IV Milner's books and other endeavours

In addition to detailed commentary from clinicians and writers, the co-editors initiated a Milnerian type exercise in action research. Eight reading groups were established around the world (in Athens, Greece; Melbourne, Australia; Cape Town, South Africa; Belfast, Northern Ireland, and Dublin Ireland; Chicago, USA and London, England). Comprising over forty disciplines; each focused in these diverse places – mostly psychoanalysts or therapists, and some from other disciplines. Each focused in depth on one of Milner's eight books, and wrote up their spontaneous reactions and 'answering responses' elicited in them.

Given the Milnerean 'discovery research' spirit of this endeavour, the open-ended approach may leave the reader with a sense of inconclusive answers. Joan Raphael-Leff and I hope that this engenders a strong urge to return to Marion Milner's own writing, and in reading her at source, to discover or re-discover their own response to her singular and substantial contribution.

Section V Recollections and reflections

Here the book will provide a global treasury of intimate memories from her grandson, neighbours, colleagues, and friends who engaged with Marion Milner on her home territory.

It seems too early and may well be premature to speak of a Milnerean Tradition. However, contributors to this book allude to application of her ideas outside the consulting room and to how Milner has informed the work of allied professionals and to thinking in art and other academic branches and social systems. In sum, this volume presents an appreciation of Milner and her opus through both personal reflections and an engaged interrogation of her work in its clinical, theoretical, philosophical, creative, and artistic aspects.

Section I

Marion Blackett Milner life and legacy

Introduction to Section I

Marion Blackett Milner—her life and legacy

Before her biography appeared, Milner's opus had not received much attention in its entirety. We begin essentially with a blank canvas and assemble the conclusions of individuals who were affected by her theoretical thinking, and conversations of those lucky enough to meet her.

In **Chapter 1**, Marion Milner's biographer considers her ambivalence as a public figure—the paradox that she was intensely private but with much to contribute. Emma Letley highlights Milner's literariness, as a hallmark of the Independent group of the BPaS, and features her concepts of the frame and version of transitional space.

Next (**Chapter 2**), Gabriele Cassullo and Alberto Stefana consider indepth four concepts within Milner's thinking and usefully link them to other psychoanalytic ideas of the time, within psychoanalysis, psychology and related fields, also recognising her overlap with the thinking of the Independent group. They also include a useful exploration of how Milner imagines the analyst's body in the analytic space.

In **Chapter 3**, Barbie Antonis and Elizabeth Wolf further elaborate on Marion Milner's place among the lively women of the Independent Tradition of the BPaS (e.g. Ella Freeman Sharp, Marjorie Brierley, Enid Balint, Pearl King, Nina Coltart, Alice Balint, Paula Heimann and others). In teaching candidates, they focus on the subtle and paradoxical quality of Milner's thinking, the key ideas of 'illusion' and 'play', becoming one out of two, the essential role of the malleable environment and recognition of healthy regressions throughout life.

In **Chapter 4**, Margaret Boyle Spelman traces the intertwining of Milner and Winnicott's relationship and lives, focusing on commonalities in their view of thinking about psychoanalytic thinking and outlining the legacy of their 'collegial love'.

In **Chapter 5**, Michael Eigan celebrates his long relationship with Marion Milner which consisted mostly of written correspondence. It was a difficult decision not to include two more of Michael Eigan's papers that seem to book-end his psychoanalytic conversation with Milner: his 'Dual Union' paper and his review of *Bothered by Alligators.*

In **Chapter 6**, James William Anderson shares a verbatim account of his conversations with Milner in 1981, nominally about Winnicott, including various anecdotes about their collegial relationship. And fortunately, much about herself.

In **Chapter 7**, Brett Kahr brings to life for us the older Marion Milner, whom he knew from 1985 to 1998, in all her sensibilities and includes bits of gossip and her opinions from within the psychoanalytic community of the time. He also makes available many anecdotes and includes their private adventure in Freud's House.

DOI: 10.4324/9780429433535-2

In **Chapter 8**, Deborah Anna Leibnitz talks to Milner, amongst other things about what Winnicott thought of Lacan. The conversation begins with Milner drawing a blank on Lacan but gets around to Milner's perspective on many of her psychoanalytic contemporaries and her patient Susan and ends locating the conversation in time, speaking about Margaret Thatcher's resignation.

In **Chapter 9**, Linda Hopkins tells us about her alternative 'afternoon tea' with the almost ninety-seven-year-old Marion Milner. During this conversation, she candidly spoke of discontent with her analysis with Winnicott and told some stories she particularly wanted to be heard.

Chapter 10 is the verbatim text of a conversation between Margaret Boyle Spelman and Adams Philips, Winnicott's first biographer, who's company Milner sought. He recalls discovering many common affinities and during their Saturday afternoon sessions would talk freely. Sharing some of this, he gives his considered ideas about Marion Milner, whom he rated highly as a writer, and about her legacy and her thinking.

Chapter 1

'Joy to be hidden'

Thoughts from a biographer

Emma Letley

Milner loved to be hidden: her colleague and friend, Donald Winnicott's phrase is a very keen description of her demeanour and her way of being a biographical subject. Intensely private, she was characterised by some of my respondents as one who tended to be silent, one who would sit aside from discussions and would not put herself forward with her views. She liked to be illegible (Letley, 2014) often preferring to remain quiet. In addition, she was a clinician with few, if any disciples. A complicated situation from the outset, the question is: what is the tradition associated with Marion Milner? Is there a legacy? And, if so, what might it be? As biographer and series editor of the main texts (2010–2014), what have I learned about these questions? From the series I came to understand that Milner was a very literary person. Like many of the Independent Group analysts, she shows a bias towards the Humanities; she was profoundly attached to the canon of English Literature and her work is peppered with, timely and helpful allusions and references to Blake, Lewis Carroll, the Metaphysical Poets and Shakespeare. A look at one of her key texts, *Hands of the Living God*, shows us this penchant. Keats's 'diligent indolence' is employed to reference and elaborate on Milner's central notion of the 'unfocussed stare'; while D.H. Lawrence's words[1] underpin the text as Milner tells us that, in her work with her patient, Susan, the lines had been continually running through her head (Milner, 2011, pp. 60–61); the interpretation of certain of Susan's drawings is much enriched by Milner's referencing and examining their connection with Lady Macbeth. (ibid., pp. 234, 247, 248)

The texts in the series, re-issued with new introductory essays by Rachel Bowlby, Hugh Haughton, Adam Phillips and Janet Sayers, seemed naturally to call forth literary responses which attest to Milner's literary sensibility. Lesley Caldwell's book in honour of Milner (2000) does the same, with John Fielding, Malcolm Bowie and Adam Phillips all considering her work through a literary lens.

A literary bias is one hallmark of Independent thinking shared by Masud Khan, Ella Sharpe, Juliet Mitchell, Christopher Bollas, Adam Phillips and Ken Robinson, amongst others. Other hallmarks of the tradition are Milner's commitment to jargon free, plain language; her attention to pre-verbal experience and to bodily communication; her attitude to creativity is especially significant. In the appendix to *On Not Being Able to Paint* (ONBAP), she writes that this was a workable tool for her: 'Psychic creativeness is the capacity for making a symbol and creativeness in science is making a symbol for knowing' (p. 173).

DOI: 10.4324/9780429433535-3

As biographer, my experience, as for many who engage in life writing and most especially those who work with the biography of analysts (and, by extension, their patients, supervisees and succeeding generations of both), was one of gaps and absences. Milner's life is punctuated by silences and lost objects – the painting of 'The Hens,' the humorous image of Anna Freud and Melanie Klein fighting over the precious egg of psychoanalysis was lost for a long time: the manuscript of her last and posthumously published book *Bothered by Alligators* has never been found. Then there is the important and ever more legislated, post GDPR in UK, issue of confidentiality. The identity of Milner's patient, Susan, is not known to me (and this is the case, today, six years on from the biography) and I have not sought to find out further. Today guidelines on publication insist stringently on the consent and permission of the subject in writing – although it must be said that consent under the sway of transference is not consent at all.

My own travels with Milner started when I was in my 20s, with writing block and a burdensome Ph.D.: I read and lived ONBAP then; training in psychoanalytic psychotherapy, I read it once more; and eventually, in working on my biography, ONBAP became part of a long dialogue with Milner, the best of biographical companions. The travels continue with recent work bespeaking Milner's continued significance: Patricia Townsend's recent book *Creative States of Mind*, draws extensively on Milner's work in searching out an understanding of 'the inner processes that may underpin the artists' accounts of their experiences' (Townsend, 2019, p. 4); in writing of what she terms the 'pre-sense' Townsend draws, too, on the 'bodily nature' of Milner's relationships with her subject matter; while an important section on 'Creativity, Aggression and Destructiveness' references and develops Milner's notion, following Jan Gordon, of the need to 'spiritually envelop the object' (1950, pp. 66–67). The key Milnerite idea of the frame also has a significant place in Townsend's book delineating 'an area within which what is perceived has to be taken symbolically, while that outside the frame is taken literally.' In working on ideas of creativity, in Italy the scholar Alberto Stefana has ably taken up Milner's work in his recent paper 'Revisiting Marion Milner's work on Creativity and Art' (Stefana, 2019); while in the United States there is an ongoing interest in her legacy.

Thus, in honour in part of Milner, the Californian analyst and painter, Desy Safán-Gerard takes central Milner ideas in her book *Chaos and Control*. She echoes Milner as she demonstrates her paintings 'taking off in their own direction' underlining the role of accident and of dream in their creation. Milner, I think would have been gratified by the homage paid to her in the chapter on 'Destructiveness and Reparation: A Retrospective.'

I shall conclude with Safán-Gerard's remarks on *ONBAP* in her section on 'the meaning of creativity': 'In *On Not Being Able to Paint* Marion Milner made an independent discovery of Winnicott's transitional space, the sense of being separate and together' (Safán-Gerard, 2018, p. 245). It is, in my opinion, this creative dialogue with Winnicott that is a last mark of the tradition forming her legacy (Letley, 2015).

Note

1 'It is a fearful thing to fall into the hands of the living God/But it is a much more fearful thing to fall out of them'

Chapter 2

Some essential concepts of Marion Blackett Milner

Framing, Concentration, Absentmindedness, Rêverie

Gabriele Cassullo and Alberto Stefana

It is rather impossible to assign property over concepts among the group of Independent analysts Marion Milner belonged to, a group which included Winnicott, Rycroft, Khan, Little, Guntrip, King and others. Even so, we shall elaborate on four concepts which we hold to be representative of Milner's conception of psychoanalysis. The semantic area covered by these concepts does indeed overlap, and each concept entertains a circular relationship with the others. In fact, the reader should see them as four facets of the very same object: an object we want to get in contact with, which is the "analytic object" in Marion Milner's thinking.

Framing

Milner's reflection on the *frame* is a most fundamental contribution. The frame, as she observed, is a *constituent-constant* element of any inside/outside division. Through the frame, two different realities are established. The practice of psychoanalysis is based on a certain spatio-temporal frame: "It is the existence of this frame that makes possible the full development of that creative illusion that analysts call the transference" (Milner, 1952b, p. 87).

Milner built on Winnicott's intuitions about (1) a *set situation* (1941), which would later become the psychoanalytic *setting* (1955), and (2) the *primary unintegration* of the personality (1945, p. 139): our identity is born out of discontinuities, of gaps, which are gradually integrated, but never fully are. Milner observed that the gaps can not only be *filled* with interpretations and other constructions of meaning, but they can also be *framed.* She connected those two intuitions of Winnicott's and arrived at the idea of *framing the gap*: 'The theme of the framed gap, emptiness, seemed to have led me on to talk about gaps in one's own self-awareness, for instance, the kind of concentration that we call 'losing oneself in an activity', something that can be greatly longed for, delighted in, but which does require a safe setting, a setting that will still be there when one emerges again into ordinary self-awareness' (Milner, 1952a, p. 81).

The analytic function, for her, does not require an explanation of the content of the patient's mind, but it inevitably implies "to wait in very active present mindedness and be content with being a frame, holding the empty space if something new is to emerge, something that has never been before" (*ibid.*, p. 82). The analytic frame is a prerequisite to such a process. When the frame is interpreted, it stands-off what Bleger[1] (1967) called the *non-process* (the constant and invariable elements within whose bounds the

DOI: 10.4324/9780429433535-4

process takes place) and takes part in the analytic process. A new non-processing frame (mute, unperceived) thus comes into being. Thus, the analysis proceeds by broader framings.

Besides Argentina (Bleger, Etchegoyen, etc.), it was in France that the subject of the frame came to the forefront. 'If French psychoanalysts of the three IPA Societies ... have been reluctant to admit the extent of Lacan's influence, it is above all because of his manipulation of the setting with his introduction [in the early 1950s] of the practice of variable-length analytic sessions... Even this can be said to have had a repercussion in the frequent references to *le cadre* (the setting)' (Birksted-Breen and Flanders, 2010, p. 4).

Here are two extremes in handling the analytic frame. On the one hand, the analyst is the *guardian* of a recursive setting (Donnet, 2001, p. 169); on the other, it forbids and frustrates any desired maternal-symbiotic bond, together with its incestuous compulsion to repeat, by a sudden break (a cut, a caesura) in the frame.

In the book *The Truth in Painting*, Derrida (1978) proposes a *third* dimension and function of the frame (the concept of "the third" having been used by Lacan, Winnicott, and Milner). That is, the creation, through its thickness and depth, of a permeable space: a *passe-partout* which is neither inside nor outside, or it is both. Both Lacan and Milner conceived it as a *symbolic* space, between the imaginary and the real one. This creates a figure similar to the overlapping circles of a Borromean knot.

Concentration

In the very same year, Bowlby (1960) exposed his studies on the mother as a *secure base*, Winnicott (1960) expressed the idea of an *environment-mother*, which is taken for granted and therefore not perceived, unlike the *object-mother*.[2] And Joseph Sandler (1960) described the *background of safety* as "a definite feeling of safety—a feeling so much a part of us that we take it for granted as a background to our everyday experience" (p. 352). Such a background is created by 'the awareness of being protected; for example by the reassuring presence of the mother. I refer only to a simple background feeling which can be compared to a level of tonus in a resting muscle, and which is as different from atonic feelings of death and emptiness as a healthy muscle is from a denervated one.' (p. 354).

In this context, Milner (1960) explored what she called *body-concentration*:

> What I mean by body attention or body concentration in the analyst is this: it is a state in which the direct proprioceptive body-self awareness, which I suppose is best called the body presentation, as distinct from the body representation or body image, becomes the foreground of one's consciousness rather than the pre-conscious background. As I see it, this kind of attention in the analyst differs from the free-floating kind that, when I first practised as an analyst, was the only kind I thought appropriate and which most neurotics seemed able to manage with. It differs because it is not 'in the air'; it deliberately attends to sinking itself down into a total internal body awareness, not seeking at all for correct interpretations, in fact not looking for ideas at all—although interpretations may emerge from this state spontaneously. Other main points about this kind of attention seem to me to be

1. that it is wide focused,
2. that its object, one's own internal body perception, is inarticulate, dark, and undifferentiated,
3. that what looks like a turning away from the object and the outside world does in fact seem to result in the opposite from turning away, that is it results in an increased perception of the nature and significance of the external object, in this instance the patient,
4. that, as far as I can observe, it does seem to bring about a change in the analytic situation and freeing of the patient's material.

(pp. 239–240)

The analyst's body-concentration provides a "uterine space", where something can generate and grow. However, this can be experienced by the patient for a long time as a worthless "empty space", or a space at risk of collapsing, or of being invaded by deadly anxieties and primitive terrors, or even a *claustrum* which can sink into irreversible and eternal constriction, contrition and depression. "A cold, horrible, unfriendly, and frankly dangerous dark landscape" (Sklar, 2011, p. 18). The threats of emptiness, at this point, are experienced by the analyst as well[3]; the lifeline becoming our own breath (the original meaning of the Greek word *psyche* being *breath*), the sense of our weight, and silence (Milner, 1960). Accordingly, Milner proposes a quality of analytic listening which allows us to communicate at the level of pre-symbolic sensoriality, thus including those synaesthetic experiences which preceded the structuring of logical thought and of language (Di Benedetto, 2005).

Concentration occurs when we let ourselves be immersed into ourselves *and* into an object. It implies a merging of the boundaries, a pre-logical fusion of subject and object (Milner, 1952b). A process that implies the recognition of the sense of oneself *and* of a separated, objective reality. Furthermore, Milner's idea of body-concentration requires the sphere of the somatic and the sphere of the mental to be aligned, becoming *concentric*. This is Milner's analytical position: "A kind of deliberate filling out of one's whole body with one's consciousness … not just with … one's head" (1969, p. 49). This is an "extremely unclear, an unstructured awareness of all that is 'behind one's eyes'" (*ibid.*).

This concentration, which implies a pre-logical fusion between subject and object, and between body and mind, seems to facilitate the patient in allowing his own material to arise. By "material" meaning "what matters". But more than that—coming back to the creation of a background of safety, or inner secure base, for the patient—according to Milner (1969) it is precisely "one's own inner body awareness that takes over the role of the external mother" (p. 273). Thus, this concentration is needed in order to "fashioning a kind of psychic sphere … of one's own body image, as being the only secure place to inhabit, from which to put out feelers to the world". (*ibid.*).

Absentmindedness

In introducing Milner's book *On Not Being Able to Paint* (1950), Anna Freud described the link Milner established between absentmindedness, creativity, and psychoanalytical practice.

> The amateur painter, who first puts pencil or brush to paper, seems to be in much the same mood as the patient during his initial period on the analytic couch. Both ventures, the analytic as well as the creative one, seem to demand similar external and internal conditions. There is the same need for 'circumstances in which it is safe to be absent-minded' (i.e. for conscious logic and reason to be absent from one's mind). There is the same unwillingness to transgress beyond the reassuring limits of the secondary process and 'to accept chaos as a temporary stage'. There is the same fear of the 'plunge into no-differentiation' and the disbelief in the 'spontaneous ordering forces' which emerge, once the plunge is taken. There is, above all, the same terror of the unknown.
>
> (A. Freud, 1950, pp. XIII–XIV)

The analytic frame, and the couple's body-concentration, create a place for experiencing absentmindedness. Just like for Freud the dream is necessary in order to preserve sleep, for Milner daydreaming is necessary for creativity:

> Many of the impediments to going forward into living are the result of a failure of the child's environment to provide the necessary setting for such absent-mindedness. For it seems likely that, in this phase of not distinguishing the 'me' and the 'not-me' we are particularly vulnerable to the happenings in the inner life of those nearest to us emotionally.
>
> (Milner, 1950, p. 192)

Freud addressed this "before I was I" area by defining it *primary narcissism*: "We are bound to suppose that a unity comparable to the ego cannot exist in the individual from the start; the ego has to be developed" (Freud, 1914, p. 77). In clinical work, we usually give primary narcissism a negative connotation, inasmuch as it is imagined as a kind of masturbatory room where the self hides itself, the real word being obscured by a negative hallucination. Nevertheless, Freud also supposed that an "original reality-ego" (1915, p. 136) shall be there from the beginning, thus producing a primordial, preverbal and therefore pre-symbolic, feeling of what is real. Klein added that such an apparently objectless condition, is in fact one where the absence of the object becomes a presence.

We can imagine Milner striving to get back to that primordial contact with reality. This is a state of extreme vulnerability, in which any impingement can set in motion a displacement either towards seeking refuge into the subject and subjectivity, or towards clinging to the object and objectivity, or both, in a split state. It is an extremely unstable situation.

Winnicott echoed Freud's assertion on primary narcissism, by stating that we must "postulate a primary unintegration" of the ego (1945, p. 139). Klein added: "A tendency towards integration alternates with a tendency towards disintegration". So that, the ego responds to any danger of annihilation either by falling into pieces or, defensively, with an active splitting process within the ego, besides that of the object and the relation to it (1946, pp. 100–101).

The quest for a state of absentmindedness in psychoanalysis, therefore, stimulates disintegration anxieties in the ego, which can respond by splitting itself, the object (the analyst) and the relation to it (the analytic alliance), for giving coherence and an order to chaos. Being able to tolerate absentmindedness, a contact with a lack of meaning, is what allows a really creative process. As Winnicott learned right from Milner, "creativity can be destroyed by too great insistence that in acting one must know beforehand what one is doing" (Winnicott, 1951, p. 392).

Rêverie

All this leads us to the concentric aspects of the frame, or the "concentrated states of mind in which one creates one's own inner frame, frame of reference, as essential in all mental productivity, whether creating ideas or works of art, a state in which one holds a kind of inner space" (Milner, 1969, p. 250). Milner traced back the roots of this ability in the experience of being physically held in mother's arms and being mentally held in mind by her. This parallels the capacity of the analytic frame to work as a safe recipient for the un-integrated elements which are deposited there. We need a safe outer space in order to give form to an inner space, in which we can concentrate ourselves and experience rêveries.

Milner introduced into psychoanalysis the term *rêverie*, which she borrowed from Elton Mayo's Work Psychology, and his studies on "Revery and industrial fatigue" (Mayo, 1924, 1933; Milner, 1969). Today we can conceive those *rêveries* in monotonous work, as a mental state produced by the dissociative capacity of the mind, as a going-on-being mechanism. That is, a mental measure to preserve an inner space of freedom and agency when the individual is confronted with a frustrating or even dehumanising environment. The field of self-other-consciousness being consequently, as Janet pointed out (1889), narrowed.

However, Milner (1950) also conceived *rêverie*, which implies a fantasised relation with an object externally perceived (Milner, 1945), as a necessary process for a healthy adaptation to reality. She believed that the "me/not-me" boundary is something that the child slowly and with difficulty manages to reach. With a gradual maladjustment of the mother to the needs of the child, and the reduction of the sensory experience of subject-object fusion, what takes place is a progressive development of transitional area and the potential field. Milner maintains that the analytic space provides the analyst and patient a frame in which they can connect to a state of *rêverie*, in which the boundaries between their egos, identities, and mutual properties are temporarily suspended. In such a state, it is impossible to ascertain who is the owner of a specific sensation, an image, a thought. And, to put it in Benjamin's terms (2004), who is the *doer* and who is the *done to*.

This is Green building on Bion: "I suppose that we can say that the primordial mind is made of psychic activity rooted in the body, which is already a form of thought but without a thinker" (1998, p. 113). From the psychoanalytic matrix, *rêveries* (daydreams, sensations, images) spring, some of which are unpleasant. As Freud observed, what is unpleasant is at first put outside of the self and attributed to the other. The analyst's availability to perceive, to feel and to think unpleasant sensations and images, helps the patient in doing the same and, thus, in holding by himself his "first not-me possessions" (Winnicott, 1953).

A dyadically shared symbolic thinking is built on such sensations and images, produced during the ecstatic moments of fusion. This makes Milner a pioneer of those modern trends that conceptualise psychoanalysis as a co-construction of a semantic field rather than an imposition of meaning, coming from the analyst, on the patient's communications.

Conclusion

According to the theoretical and clinical framework introduced by Milner (also see Stefana, 2019), the analyst's task, ultimately, is to help patients achieve the ability and possibility to reflect both on the experience shared in the consulting room, and the experience of their own self. Milner considered the development of new capacities and functions of the ego essential, for patients to become able to have a complete analytic experience, on the foundation of which they can then build their present and future health, and which can be the source of new tools for their continued growth. She conceived, in this way, of a mind capable of self-observation and self-nurturing. In this analytic therapeutic process, *framing, concentration, absentmindedness, rêverie* and, more widely, the experience of countertransference (Stefana, 2017) are the clinician's most essential tools.

By following the evolutionary path laid out by Ogden (1996), it is possible to argue that, beginning with the original presentation by Freud, according to whom the task of psychoanalytical treatment was to make the unconscious conscious (or, in terms of the structural model: "where id was, there ego shall be"), over the years, thanks to the contributions of many analysts, the focus of the analytical process has been extended, progressing from the importance placed on the development of the abilities of both analyst and patient to create an intermediary zone, "the place where we live", an area of experience situated somewhere between reality and phantasy (Milner, 1952b)—or better, an area where reality and phantasy can coexist (Winnicott, 1971b)—and ultimately reaching the current conception of psychoanalysis as "a psychological-interpersonal process intended to enhance the analysand's capacity to be alive as a human being" (Ogden, 1996, p. 888), in which the analyst's fluctuation between rêverie and interpretation assumes great importance.

Notes

1 Bleger studied the symbiotic-psychotic part of the personality, which is deposited into the frame more than into the content of the session, and which becomes manifest when the frame breaks or is on the verge of rupture.

2 Freud himself (1938) described the *mother-object*:

> A child's first erotic object is the mother's breast that nourishes it; love has its origin in attachment to the satisfied need for nourishment. There is no doubt that, to begin with, the child does not distinguish between the breast and its own body; when the breast has to be separated from the body and shifted to the 'outside' because the child so often finds it absent, it carries with it as an 'object' a part of the original narcissistic libidinal cathexis. This first object is later completed into the person of the child's mother, who not only nourishes it but also looks after it and thus arouses in it a number of other physical sensations, pleasurable and unpleasurable. By her care of the child's body she becomes its first seducer. In these two relations lies the root of a mother's importance, unique, without parallel, established unalterably for a whole lifetime as the first and strongest love-object and as the prototype of all later love-relations—for both sexes.
>
> (p. 188)

The *mother-environment*, as distinguished from the 'mother-object of the child's perception', however, was first identified by Alice Balint (1933) in a seminal essay on the anxiety of *not being held in mind* and, consequently, *falling into pieces*. The loss of the object would, then, be a secondary symbolisation of the primary, unsymbolisable break in the mother-environment: the *not-framed gap* in Milner's terms. Also, Anna Freud (1967) dealt with the problem, noting that "it is only when parental feelings are ineffective or too ambivalent, or when their aggression is more effective than their love, or when the mother's emotions are temporarily engaged elsewhere, that children not only feel lost but, in fact, get lost ... children become chronic losers if they feel unloved at home or are unloved in fact" (pp. 15–16).

3 Here we may hear an echo of Keats' *negative capability* (Bion's passion). That is, the capacity of being in uncertainties, mysteries, doubts, without any irritable reaching after fact and reason. As Milner wrote in her posthumous book *Bothered by Alligators*,

> I remembered that once in the diary J [Milner's son] had asked about the letter O as meaning 'nothing' and this reminded me that I had, several years ago, quoted Meister Eckhart's use of the word 'Godhead' as 'that which contains all distinctions as yet undeveloped and is therefore darkness and formlesseness'. So here it seems it was necessary to have another look at the positive sides of emptiness, of not-knowing, of being in the dark, for J had certainly at times found something alluring about darkness, as in the tunnel on the Heath where he said his wolf goes in. Could it be that he was there trying to say something more than just anal curiosity and excitement, something more than wanting to know about the unseen innerness of the body, and where he came from; in fact, something about innerness in general?
>
> (2012)

Chapter 3

'The Pliable Medium'

Barbie Antonis and Elizabeth Wolf

Over the last decade the two of us have taught a course called the 'Contribution of Independent Women Psychoanalysts' to candidates during the course of their psychoanalytic training at the Institute of Psychoanalysis. The idea for, and then invitation to develop, this course arose from our commitment to celebrating the lively contributions of women to the Independent Tradition within the British Society. Our aim remains: we want to ensure the essential elements in the establishment of an Independent psychoanalytic identity and clinical practice are passed on to future generations. In our course we focus on nine women analysts,[1] many of whom who had not been taught before. We chose papers we believe would stimulate the candidates to discover for themselves the value of working as analysts within the Independent Tradition.

Through the evolution of this course, we discovered teaching Milner's paper, 'The Role of Illusion in Symbol Formation' (1952b), to be the most complex and challenging evening. Her paper makes one feel the paradox of not knowing, as one does during an analysis; it is accessible but we don't understand it. Some thirty years later Nina Coltart accentuated the analyst's reliance on her belief in the 'sheer unconsciousness of the unconscious' (Coltart, 1986, p. 3), unconscious communication,[2] and 'the essence of our impossible profession [which is] that in a very singular way we do not know what we are doing' (Coltart, 1986, p. 2). It is complex and hard to 'get'. The process of teaching became for us an environment that facilitated our own on-going thinking and deepened our individual identities as Independent psychoanalysts, so that Milner's ideas become part of our theoretical backbone.

In designing the course we hoped to create an environment that would provide a space or atmosphere like a 'pliable medium', taking account of the candidates' scepticism as well as their excitement, where they might discover for themselves new ways of thinking and being with their patients. The way we have done this is by holding an open seminar conducted as a dialogue with each other and in dialogue with and between the candidates, not by delivering a taught paper. We always began with biography and history and where possible, the links/connections with contemporary psychoanalysts. The personal journey towards becoming a psychoanalyst for each writer was considered, external reality always mattering for Independents. We shared our responses to the ideas presented in the paper, both positive and problematic, and we learned, with the help of the candidates' feedback, to be less protective of the authors and their ideas. To quote their feedback to the curriculum committee,

DOI: 10.4324/9780429433535-5

> there was a very open and receptive environment that allowed the group to think and 'play' with the theories and models presented in order to make sense of them… the group enjoyed this seminar very much finding it refreshing and inspiring.

This way of teaching is our expression of the fundamental Independent view that personal history and the environment must be taken into account in the shaping and development of an individual's self.

Central to Milner's thinking is *illusion*; the word illusion derives from the Latin *ludere*, which means to play. Playing with matter, playing with space, playing with reality, Milner is concerned with the full experience of illusion/play. These are key to the ideas embodied in her work: her notion of becoming one out of two, the essential role of the malleable environment and pliable medium and the recognition that there can be healthy regressions throughout life. Essential factors which are part of the process of coming to recognise a world outside oneself, not one's own creation, include bodily experiences of being separated from the loved object, and being together with it, and the repeated physical experiences of interchange with the 'not self' world such as breathing, feeding and eliminating. For the child/subject/patient there gradually grows a capacity to tolerate the difference between the feeling of oneness, of being united with everything, and the feeling of twoness, of self and object, and for this to happen, Milner highlights the factor of the capacity in the environment. She writes,

> It is the capacity of the environment to foster this growth, by providing conditions in which a recurrent partial return to the feeling of being one is possible; and I suggest that the environment does this by the recurrent providing of a framed space and time and a pliable medium, so that, on occasions, it will not be necessary for self-preservation's sake to distinguish clearly between inner and outer, self and not self.
>
> (Milner, 1952b, p. 101)

Milner suggests that states of illusion of oneness need to occur with sufficient frequency or at the right moments for the development of a sense of twoness. She also explores what happens when there is a mistimed rupture in the illusion of oneness. Milner says,

> That the basic identifications which make it possible to find new objects, to find the familiar in the unfamiliar, require an ability to tolerate a temporary loss of self, a temporary giving up of the discriminating ego which stands apart and tries to see things objectively and rationally and without emotional colouring. (Milner, 1952, p. 97) … We know boundaries exist but the child does not; in the primal state, it is only gradually and intermittently that he discovers them; on the way to this he uses play.
>
> (Milner, 1952b, p. 98)

The environment, the frame and the matter of the medium are the elements from which trust grows, that one can come back from a fused state, from loss of self.

Milner's case study of her patient Simon in 'Symbol Formation' is an example of her openness as she brings the reader right into her thoughts and experiences as they emerge organically in her consulting room. She describes the treatment of this pre-adolescent eleven-year-old boy during the Second World War. Simon had, in general, a good and loving home but 'suffered early environmental thwartings in the feeding situation' (Milner, 1952, p. 100). This showed up in difficulties he was having at school. In the sessions, Simon created a game of war between two villages, playing dramatically with fire and melting down metal soldiers. All this became the metaphor for his experience 'of complete union with a marvellous or atrocious inner object, with the obliteration of inner boundaries between the ego and the incorporated object' (Milner, 1952, p. 95). Milner felt this as an expression of Simon's transference. She recognised the significance of refashioning of self through the absorption of the inner object via the pliable medium. She saw the value of a melting down (meltdown) which provides the opportunity to modify the self; melting down allows for new integration. This is the creative flux. This refers to the process of recognising external reality.

What is a pliable medium?

Drawing on her experiences of being an artist working with materials gave Milner this metaphor of a pliable medium. She expanded on the OED's definition of medium as the '"intervening substance through which impressions are conveyed to the senses"; this pliable stuff that can be made to take the shape of one's phantasies can include the stuff of sound and breath which becomes our speech' (Milner, 1952, p. 99). We take our consulting room setting for granted as a safe space for entering into that space where we can be the pliable medium, not distinguishing ourselves from the other. We extend ourselves into the room. In the consulting room – everything about the room – the physical space, the contents of the consulting room, the total sensory qualities evoked (bird sounds, light, temperature, flowers) can become an extension of the analyst's body to be used in the service of development; joined together with our voice, tone, words, breathing, presence, we can be experienced as that medium. The room becomes the extension of the analyst, particularly for adults in analysis who can use it as a box of toys. Milner describes her discovery of this with Simon. The failure of the classical approach with the boy led her to refashion herself in the consulting room.

> I had accepted this view [Fenichel on infantile omnipotence] but grown rather tired of being continually treated by this boy as his gas, his breath, his faeces, and had wondered how long the working through of this phase would take.....But when I began to suspect that Fenichel was wrong here and that this pre-logical fusion of subject and object does continue to have a function of preparing for future action, when I began to see and to interpret, as far as I could, that this use of me might be not only a defensive regression, but an essential recurrent phase in the development of a creative relation to the world, then the whole character of the analysis changed; the boy then gradually became able to allow the external object, represented by me, to exist in its own right.
>
> (Milner, 1952b, p. 104)

Milner gives us a visual image, typical of her as someone who thought in pictures,[3] of Winnicott's theory 'The Use of an Object' (1969). Milner illustrates both his theory and the way Simon used her as the object. She was able to do this by going with and being with him in his play.

Milner recognised the necessary developmental function of regression, to go back and find new solutions, new incorporations into the self. Healthy regression is the capacity to tolerate a movement between states of illusion of oneness and twoness, as enjoyed in sex, in creation of and enjoyment of the arts, in meditation, in nature, and in psychoanalysis. The necessity for regression in healthy development is the hallmark of Milner's contribution, clinically and theoretically, to Independent psychoanalytic thinking and practice. This process facilitates growth and captures for us how we hope to make ourselves available in the analytic setting. What the patient does with or makes of the total environment (not to be confused with the total transference) is how we come to understand the patient, together with what they do or do not tell us. Our countertransference is only part of this environment. In our analytic work, we are more or less pliable or malleable depending on our own individual capacities, which are based on our own analyses, training, and life experiences. We are not infinitely pliable, we cannot take any shape, but we do have to go where the patient takes us. It is so much easier to be rigid, to think we 'know' from our theory what the patient means; so much more difficult to stay with not knowing. This includes recognising there are limitations in all of us, analysts and parents. There is no perfect analysis, no perfect parenting. These are the elements in the growth of a self, and Milner, like Winnicott, was concerned with being good enough. It is only on the basis of a thorough grounding in psychoanalytic theory that we can release our imaginative, associative and intuitive processes to move freely during a session. The analytic frame holds us and is there as a protective boundary to restrain us from indulgence. This process enables us to go on growing as analysts, as one goes on growing and developing in life through aesthetic experiences (art and music). One of our chief expressions of our creativity is in our work as psychoanalysts.

We are experiencing a new appreciation of Milner in writing this article, revisiting this paper of hers, as we do each time we come back to it. How early did she come to these ideas? Milner saw this boy during World War II, indicating the refashioning of herself in the treatment antedates the writing of this paper. It clearly antedates the publication of 'The Use of an Object', which was published in 1969. But when did Winnicott develop his ideas? This was also at a critical time in the development of psychoanalytic theory contemporaneous with Winnicott giving his paper 'Hate in the countertransference' (1949) at the Institute of Psychoanalysis in 1947 and the publication of Paula Heimann's paper 'On Countertransference' (1950). We do not know to what extent Milner got to her understanding on her own or through 'harmonious mix up' with Winnicott. Who got the ideas from whom? Milner would perhaps visualise the creation of theory with overlapping circles.

Going on growing includes having this capacity for healthy regression, to go back into an undifferentiated psychic state and to refashion the self in the melting down and reintegrating that takes place. This allows us to find new solutions and adapt to new situations. Michael Parsons develops the idea of how this psychic work can only be done when there is separation between the thing itself in reality and the representation of it in psychic reality, what he terms the positive use of negation. Parsons writes,

> The difference lies in whether negation is a fixed state to be held on to, or a mobile and flexible activity; whether it is being used to contradict ordinary reality, or provisionally to suspend it, disengaging from it for the time being without contradiction. The second makes it possible to work with the psychic representation instead of the real object, so as to come back to the real object in a new way.
>
> (Parsons, 2000, p. 183)

In our experience with our young psychoanalytic candidates, we find that these concepts within Milner's paper are utterly contemporary, powerful, relevant, modern, and enduring. Their accessibility enables them to become part of one's core.

Notes

1 Ella Freeman Sharpe, Marjorie Brierley, Marion Milner, Enid Balint, Pearl King, Nina Coltart, Alice Balint, Paula Heimann, Susan Budd.

2 'It is a very remarkable thing that the unconscious of one human being can react upon that of another without passing through the conscious...descriptively speaking, the fact is incontestable' (Freud, 1915, p. 194).

3 She speaks of herself as 'one of those people who Freud reminded us exist, people who think in pictures' (Milner, 1972, p. 246).

Chapter 4

Winnicott and Milner – recognising the legacy of collegial love

Margaret Boyle Spelman

The importance to the psychoanalytic project of collegial friendship and love is rarely conceded. Conflict and schisms get all the attention. Within the history of psychoanalysis, 'The Controversial Discussions' is an immediate example. Therefore, before the attention inevitably goes to the problematics within the friendship of Marion Blackett Milner (1900–1998) and Donald Woods Winnicott (1896–1971), this chapter concerns itself with the environment for the growth of psychoanalytic thought nurtured by their collegial friendship.

Following Winnicott's pioneering emphasis on the psychology of health, creativity and enjoyment, I contend here that the individual thinking and professional legacy of both people in this professional couple were significantly facilitated and shaped by their friendship and the intertwining of their lives: Winnicott had analysed Milner's husband, Dennis, who died of his asthma sometime after he and Marion divorced. Winnicott's biographer, Rodman, summarises some of what Winnicott was to Milner, after 1943 as:

> a colleague, a friend, [a] supervisor (of her work with [her patient] Susan), [a] provider of a home for her patient [Susan], [and] fee payer (for Susan), and [alongside all of this, Winnicott was Milner's] personal analyst, whom she paid.
>
> (Rodman, 2003, p. 135)

Our focus in this chapter is on Milner's expansions to Winnicott's thinking in the case of this patient called 'Susan', who might be seen as the analytic 'love-child' whose care Milner and Winnicott shared.

The thinking of Marion Blackett Milner (1900–1998), four years Winnicott's junior, is beginning to be given suitable attention. There is growing recognition for Milner's importance in her own right, especially since her books have recently come back into print and since 2012, availability of her eighth book, written in her nineties, the posthumously published autobiographical *Bothered by Alligators*.

Two of Milner's friends, Suzanna Richards and Nathalie Thompson, witnessed Milner's struggle before her death, to finish *Bothered by Alligators*. This seems to affirm the notion that we are just beginning to appreciate the importance of Milner as a psychoanalytic thinker in her own right and in relation to her influence on Winnicott. Only beginning then also is the journey towards understanding the nature, importance and effects on their psychoanalytic legacy of the collegial love in the friendship

DOI: 10.4324/9780429433535-6

of this couple, Winnicott and Milner. In writing this paper, my hope was to introduce balance to our understanding of this couple's relationship and to the extraordinary love for the work of understanding and healing human nature shared by Milner and Winnicott.

Marion Milner

Marion Blackett Milner (nom de plume: 'Joanna Field') enjoyed her long life and distinguished career, during which she became a mother, psychologist, therapist, psychoanalyst, author and artist. Born with the century, she kept a diary from age eleven, travelled (up to 1975), painted and continued to write prodigiously, producing apart from many articles, eight books,[1] the last at the time of her death in 1998. When Milner decided to undertake a psychoanalytic training at the British Institute of Psychoanalysis in 1940, she was already a mother, an industrial psychologist, author of three books and having received a scholarship to go there, had worked in the United States of America with Elton Mayo, author of the Hawthorne Studies. Her training analyst was Sylvia Payne and she had supervision from Melanie Klein, Joan Riviere and Ella Freeman Sharpe.

Milner's relationship with Winnicott

Milner's transference to Winnicott seems to have happened instantaneously when she heard him lecture (Anderson, 1981; Rodman, 2003) and attended his mother and baby clinics. Conversely, Marion's importance to Donald is succinctly witnessed in that she is the only contemporary to have a dedicated chapter in Rodman's (ibid.) comprehensive Winnicott biography. Their lives intertwined in complicated ways: The patient called 'Susan', whose twenty-year-long psychoanalytic treatment (1943–1963 approximately) is the subject of Milner's book, *The Hands of the Living God* (for which Winnicott wrote the Foreword), was found by Winnicott's first wife, Alice, in a psychiatric hospital. Susan lived with the Winnicott's until their marriage ended. Whilst working with 'Susan' Milner asked Winnicott to recommend an analyst for her own 'mad part' left untouched by her previous analysis. In later life, long after Winnicott's death, Milner regretted that she had taken Winnicott up on his offer to see her himself (2012). She was in analysis with Winnicott for four years (1943–1947) in her own consulting room from shortly after Susan became her patient. Milner discovered that she could not properly support Susan through Winnicott's marriage break-up whilst herself remaining his patient. She therefore stopped her analysis with Winnicott and subsequently attended Clifford Scott (Milner, 2012). Yet Milner took lifts with Winnicott to and from lectures which they attended together and he confided in her on these and other occasions.

Winnicott's thinking found and created in Milner's

Three of Milner's books (Apart from *Bothered by Alligators*) are introspective in nature. A comparison of her two pre-training introspective books, with the one begun afterwards in 1958, and published in 1987 reveals that she remains remarkably herself throughout her adult life. Milner incorporated psychoanalytic ideas into her own constant interest in her everyday experience and the workings of her mind. Whilst undoubtedly enriched by their close companionship, when we examine the trajectory of her writing over half a century, it is clear that the incredible overlap between her thinking and Winnicott's predates their friendship, her candidacy at the Institute and her awareness of his writings. In this Milner was a like-minded peer whose friendship and love provided a generative climate for Winnicott and in whose fertile reciprocity the seeds of many of Winnicott's ideas germinated.

Already as a psychoanalytically naïve 'twentysomething' psychologist, Milner thinks like Winnicott and speaks, for example, of the *'me'/'not me' distinction*. Elsewhere (Boyle Spelman, 2013b, 2013d) I have shown how her early publications prospectively expand Winnicott's later transitional phenomena. In her own right, Milner made unique contributions to existential psychoanalytic thinking through her introspective dairy-keeping. Like Winnicott she built bridges, linking the domains of visual image, art theory, cognitive and organisational psychology, psychoanalysis, English literature and Greek mythology (ibid.). To Winnicott's spatial concepts and squiggle technique Milner added use of 'bead' memory, 'doodle' drawings and Susan's prototype case of psychoanalysis through the medium of pictorial art.

The 'thinking environment' of the pair's friendship had a bidirectional influence. These English contemporaries from similar backgrounds also shared a way of thinking which sees Milner's early thinking linking to Winnicott's later concepts. This confirms the fact of Milner's influence and the reciprocal nature of influence in their theory building.

Moreover, they were both cognisant of this reciprocity. As you will note from his account in this book of two conversations with Marion Miner in 1981, James Anderson, a psychoanalyst and psycho-biographer from Chicago, shows that both Winnicott and Milner were consciously aware of the nature of their shared thinking environment and that they shared an approach that included a way of thinking about thinking. Speaking of Winnicott, Milner says to Anderson:

> I'll tell you something. The last communication I had with him. I had a student in training who was in supervision with him. And – he shouldn't have done it, of course – he sent a message to me via the student: Tell her, 'it doesn't matter which of us thinks of it.' Because I can't tell you. Do you see what I mean?...There was a lot of interchange when we talked. You couldn't say which of us had thought of something (sic).
>
> (Anderson, 1981)

From childhood Milner was oriented towards introspection and the interior life and Winnicott's 'third area of experience' is also her own first unit of inspection. The pair also shared a visuo-spatial imagination and an interest in art – stronger in Marion (Davis and Wallbridge, 1991). Both are preoccupied with the spatial concepts of boundary, space, image and form and boundary. These inform their thinking and even, as we shall see, have influenced the structure of this present chapter. Milner turned those observation skills, first honed in childhood as an aspiring naturalist, towards herself and her art. Although consciously an atheist, many Christian ideas manifested in Milner's drawings and she sometimes equates the concepts of 'experience' and 'God'. One such spatial idea which she repeatedly utters is a phrase from the bible (which she has also heard from her patient 'Susan') that one should know the 'height, breadth, length and depth of God's love'.

Winnicott's thinking in dimensions of Susan's case

One aspect of their generative influence is that Milner and Winnicott did and at the same time did not think alike. It is in this very quality of congruity and difference that Milner's thinking can be seen to expand and deepen Winnicott's. Here I will illustrate some main points of convergence and divergence in this thinking relationship through Milner's attentions to 'Susan', her patient and the 'analytic child' in whose wellbeing this professional couple was so deeply invested. Within her book, *The Hands of the Living God*, Milner gives an account of the twenty years of her professional caring for 'Susan'. We now emphasise the extensions to Winnicott's thinking gleaned from Milner's telling of it.

Holding and a personal boundary

In taking on the patient, Susan, a twenty-three-year-old woman diagnosed with schizophrenia who had received electroconvulsive therapy (ECT) three weeks earlier, Milner shows that like Winnicott, she believes that psychoanalysis can help those with boundary issues. This five-times-a-week adult analysis lasted for twenty years – the duration of childhood, adolescence and maturation with Susan eventually making the real developmental steps of entering paid employment and a long-term committed relationship.

Susan came into treatment saying that she had lost her soul and that the world was no longer outside her. Milner, who shared Winnicott's conviction that the maturational process unfolds in a holding environment, therefore allowed herself to be *used* during the long re-fusion of Susan's aggressive parts. When Susan began to conceive of this holding environment she drew many kinds of nests. As with the child's first experiences in the stage of relative dependence, Susan desires both primary undifferentiated 'wholeness/unity' and the real world of 'separateness'. She rejects Milner whilst simultaneously demanding her analyst's 100% adaptation to her in 'self-surrender'. Susan had difficulty with symbols and with the risky interplay of inside and outside. In childhood, her role reversal with her mother meant that she had poor tolerance for anything that was not real. Susan had had to keep an eye on the outside world – in fact, she could only relax her constant vigilance sufficiently to read at her Aunt's house. Susan's early experience of an impinging environment is encapsulated in her story of the fireman who had fallen and whose head was crushed by his helmet; that which is supposed to be a protective shield had instead injured and killed him.

Milner did not interpret. She preferred, like Winnicott, to wait and watch and let Susan know she was present so that Susan could find what she herself possessed. Milner tolerated 'empty-headedness' and accepted the recurrent phase of 'not-knowing' which she believed is in the rhythm of all creative activity. She managed to keep Susan to the point of describing her experience at the precise threshold between the articulate and the inarticulate, believing that thus expressing herself helps develop Susan's boundary within the transitional space. Susan's inside and outside also become interrelated through drawing as 'active contemplation'. In the analysis, for at least fifty minutes per day, she did not have to be hypervigilant and keep an eye on the outside world. Thus Susan, previously starved of the opportunity for 'reverie', was able 'to be absent-minded'.

Drawings as transitional objects

When after the sixth year, Susan began to draw, the treatment proceeded through this medium. Milner worried about the sheer volume of the drawings – sometimes ninety on a day. Milner saw these drawings as transitional objects in Winnicott's terms (Winnicott, 1953) providing continued contact with a bit of reality which was 'other' and yet completely responsive. The paper on which she drew was a readily available substitute for Susan's responsive ideal mother; it provided a reciprocal give and take on a primitive nonverbal level. Drawing offered reparation for destructive acts and a bridge between them. Milner's response to the drawings provided Susan with a mirror giving her back to herself. By drawing Susan defended against re-living her murderous rage towards her mother and communicated with those deep levels of her self-knowledge. Milner extends Winnicott's realm of the 'nonverbal, preverbal and unverbalisable' to imagery that includes all that Susan 'knew' pictorially.

ECT and Winnicott's idea of personalisation and the split-off psyche-soma

Susan's case expands our understanding of what Winnicott calls 'personalisation'. It can be seen as a case of a split-off psyche-soma. After the ECT Susan feels that she now lives only in a very narrow area on the top of her head. She feels that she has lost her background and is 'shot forward' to the monistic state of her beginning before she recognised her own subjectivity. The ECT has undone any good handling experience. Susan feels cut off from her inner world and from all memory of her relation to her mother's body. Eventually a symbol – the image of a duck – could stand for the space which surrounded and supported her.

Milner's own non-retaliatory survival serves to repair the hopelessness which Susan felt in childhood of ever having a true give-and-take relationship with her parents. Milner speaks of holding Susan in her lack of transferential hope and in her 'spikey' anger with her. Susan begins to establish a *healthy non-destructive permeable boundary*: one where what is inside will stay inside and what is outside will stay outside and yet is interrelated. Susan needs such a boundary to ensure that she will not kill Milner or 'steal' from her in the way that she and her mother did from each other. Susan must relinquish her defensive omnipotence in favour of true relating. She must live with the hate that is engendered by the disillusionment intrinsic to this process. Over time Milner's sensitive handling, her non-retaliatory survival and her welcoming of Susan's first 'me extensions'/her 'doings' are what allow Susan to inhabit her body.

Susan's drawings record the slow process of re-inhabiting her body and becoming real. Her mind/body split is exemplified by problems with her neck. As she and her mother slept together for her first fourteen years, her mother had put her arm around Susan's neck, supporting her head. This had been infantilising and intrusive for Susan. Physical symptoms of torticollis and head joggling show Susan's ambivalent feelings about living in relatedness, in her body and in the world. Perhaps related to Susan's process of re-inhabiting her body is the fact that Milner wrote a paper in 1959 towards the end of Susan's treatment, about 'primary self-enjoyment' (akin to Winnicott's 'ego orgasm'). This 'primary self-enjoyment' is a narcissistic enjoyment of the whole body which is an investment in the outer world rather than a rejection of it.

Relatedness versus omnipotence

Susan's 'creating'/'finding' herself in the world has much to do with confusion at the anal phase of psychosexual development; the omnipotent ruthless infantile Susan wants Milner to believe in her self-created environment where her turd is a baby. The non-discursive medium of drawing proves so adaptive during this, Winnicott's stage of relative dependence, because, at any single moment, it can be omnipotent/dependent and separate/undifferentiated exactly to the degree that Susan needs.

Susan struggled for years to find her own intermediate space; a place between the extremes of the 'God-like heights' of her haughty omnipotent phallic part of herself and her dependent, needy, lowly 'smelly baby urchin self'. Drawing acts as a potential space in which she can explore her possible selves.

Susan resisted becoming aware of her breathing as it symbolises her mortality. As Milner finds in 1959 it is through drawing, Susan first comes to understand that breathing takes over from the umbilicus and the womb-like state of omnipotent fantasy (as in Winnicott's account of a child case, *The Piggle* 1977). Gradually, as her omnipotent defence gives way she can then see that breathing represents life-giving interrelatedness. This is depicted in drawings in which devils and angels are interchangeable symbols showing Susan resigning herself to the hating as well as the loving part of herself, to her separateness and to the fact of death.

In Susan's case, images of ducks and babies represent the beginning of compassion and the 'bursting out sun' drawing expresses something bursting through Susan's defences against loving. In becoming a person, these drawings convey the struggle between the early forms of ego-relatedness (with depictions of the mouth/face) and omnipotent control (with depictions of the anus). Winnicott's idea of disillusionment is illustrated by images such as Susan's 'Sleeping Goddess' drawing. Milner conveys that this drawing represents premonitions of waking up from omnipotent fantasy. Similarly, the quiet non-hungry mouth contrasts with the biting excited hungry or enraged one of disillusionment.

A significant date is January 8, 1959, after which Milner finds that the rest of Susan's analysis consisted of her struggle to realise the achievements of this day. Susan's first whole-person drawing of a girl looking at her feet is reminiscent of Winnicott's much later (1971b) clinical anecdote of the baby whose seizures stopped after she had played with her toes. Susan's own 'Prussian blue and burnt sienna' painting incorporates the memory of a good mother, a new-created mother and a new-created self. It is a momentary integration of her love and hate through the medium of paint. It represents an ideal but also a real 'other', a permanent monument to the ideal.

Milner focuses on how the phrase '[l]iving, dead, nothing in between' written on a drawing at this time shows Susan's difficulty with transitional space – she has no dreamy state between waking and sleeping. Her deepest problem is denial of her urge to become 'nothing'. With great prescience, Milner states that Susan's experience of one-ness/undifferentiation will have the paradoxical effect of enhancing the sense of two-ness/relatedness. Susan now develops symbols for what her healthy self will look for in relationship.

The real Susan

Milner notes that with the development of a boundary and a transitional space within it, Susan no longer needs to cling to the idea that she has a penis with which to repair her hurt mother. She now has a heart that can bear snubs without hate or wishing pain on the other person. This growth of her concern is recorded in her prolific drawings. The dangers of separating, along with the possible destruction of one or the other, are represented pictorially – a boat in a bottle, for example. This is worked through in the repeated images of curves and hard edges and contrasting mouth experiences. Primal scene material now appears as Susan relates to people as whole objects. Transitional space is drawn as an eight-pointed star made of the overlapping of two crucifixes. Susan is realising that two separate people can come together again in a rediscovered unity in physical love-making and in many other forms of shared experience.

Form

Milner had the conviction that Susan would not be content until she found a way of expressing her strong sense of form in the world. Drawing enables an acceptance of the fact that fusion is a necessary part of the process for all creative work; that an illusion of oneness is necessary in all symbol formation and in the full recognition of the state of two-ness, of differentiation of self and not self. Susan was trying to find a fertile interplay between a state of one-ness (with indeterminate boundaries) and two-ness. Milner links this to the frame of the picture. She believes that the root of this capacity to have an inner 'frame' comes from the experience of being held in the mother's arms. She refers to Susan's picture of herself having to mind her own sore head because she was dropped by Dr. F after her ECT treatment. She considers the circle image in her drawing as the psychic equivalent of the encircling arms, with no clear distinction between the holder and the held; the holding that Susan needs to repair the splits and heal her 'de-fusion'.

Healthy oneness

In 1960, Milner gave a lecture in which she emphasised both the healthy and unhealthy aspects of one-ness and transitional space (Milner, 1987b, p. 190) forecasting John Steiner's (1993) idea of 'psychic retreat' which forestalls psychical growth. She sees Susan's drawing of three-dimensional circles referring to both the unhealthy omnipotent devil part of herself and a healthy 'oneness' to re-start or reconnect with her dependent beginnings. Milner claims that her 'primary self-enjoyment' is not a turning away from the world but enhances her relatedness to reality. Sublimation is then a reactivation of this *healthy narcissism* which overflows into objects; Susan's 'personalisation' enhances her relatedness to the world but involves the risk of retaliation from 'mother-Milner-the-world'. The only basis from which to relate to people is by re-affirming her own private space. The image upholds the paradox that getting into the centre of this circle symbolises both cutting herself off and also the wholeness of primary undivided consciousness and the mother-child unity by which to relate better to others.

Frame

Susan uses frames and diagonals to understand the concepts of duality and boundary.

Her third diagonal picture shows her growing capacity for the division of the primary wholeness and a fluid play-space at the place of contact of the two. A drawing with a permeable diagonal and curved line reminds Milner of Susan's laughter breaking up the rigidity of her face. Accepting the discrepancy between her ideal and her actual self can result in laughter. To Milner, when duality is accepted as one half of living, it may be a source of delight – a meeting place. Diagonal lines allow Susan to put things together with the degree of separation or closeness to each other that she can tolerate.

Conclusions

As, for example, in this book in their interviews with Milner reflected here in the chapters written by Deborah Anna Luepnitz and Linda Hopkins, whatever is said about the rights and the wrongs of some aspects of their relationship, it is obvious even from her own account (Milner, 2012) that Milner was uniquely special to Winnicott and that he was to her. Her writing speaks for itself.

Milner's thinking undoubtedly adds something to Winnicott's. I suggest that they shared a way of thinking and that this includes sharing what elsewhere (Boyle Spelman, 2013b, 2013d) I termed Winnicott's inherent theory about thinking, about influences and about the environment necessary to foster creative, innovative and independent thinking. Others have commented on whether an idea was Milner's rather than Winnicott's but to my mind between this pair there was never an ownership dispute.

Unlike rivalrous oedipal theories, mentioned elsewhere (Boyle Spelman, 2013), of the thinking environment and direction of influence, I suggest that, Milner and Winnicott *shared* a transitional thinking space where a permeable boundary and a safe experience of omnipotence, reigns. As with transitional phenomena, in this thinking environment, one thinker will not ask of the other 'did you find that or did you create it?' Nor would they need to ask 'did you create that or get it from me?' In the thinking space which this pair inhabited, the shared experience of thinking together itself has primacy and is generated in the fertile transitional thinking space of their collegial love.

Note

1 *A Life of One's Own* (1934), *An Experiment in Leisure* (1937), *On Not Being Able to Paint* (1950), *The Hands of the Living God* (1969), *Eternity's Sunrise* (1987) begun in 1958 and *The Suppressed Madness of Sane Men* (1987). A final book *Bothered by Alligators* published posthumously. [*The Human Problem in Schools* (1938), the results of research on the education system is not treated here, but in Chapter 28.]

Chapter 5

The Use Creativity Can Make of Pain

Michael Eigen

Thank God for Marion Milner. She was a light and support in my life, one of a number of significant presences that lit my spirit and helped see me through. We met only once, in 1975, and corresponded till she passed away in 1998.

I began reading her work in my early twenties, *A Life of One's Own*, *An Experiment in Leisure*, both under the pseudonym of Joanna Field. I never learned why she picked this name and, oddly, it didn't occur to me to ask her until this moment. I imagine fields – of daffodils, feelings, waves of life – but I am just imagining.

She seemed to me a very old lady when we met. I was not yet forty and she was seventy-five. Now that I am in my eighties, she doesn't seem so old. Still something of an archetype of a wise old woman, but it was less wisdom than a kind of airy openness. She hunted through old paintings and showed me collages she was doing. She was enjoying cutting up old paintings for collages. Her last book, *Bothered by Alligators*, confessed her maternal depression and use creativity can make of pain and emotional depths of all kinds. In her letters she told me of difficulties in her life. It may even be, at least in some small way, I was a support for her as well.

My reading her books spanned my early twenties to my late seventies and I dip in as needed to this day. What was it that held me? What first touched me as a young man was her sharing what touched her. Her early books were diaries of the most significant moments in a day, often what one might regarded as small things, shape, color, light, something atmospheric that moves one and opens depths. Sensitivity to surface that opens depth, interweaving surface-depth.

Something I sorely needed, valued and shared – psychoanalysis without dogma. How can Jung-Freud blend seamlessly? Yet in Milner they do without fanfare. So many influences feed each other without antagonisms. Colors on a palette, colors of life.

I taught the Appendix to *On Not Being Able to Paint* many years. So much packed into so little space, a highpoint of psychoanalytic writing. As in her early diaries, she associated creativity with plenitude, not simply loss, something fairly novel in psychoanalysis. So much psychoanalytic writing associates growth of symbolic processes with a sense of loss. This may also be the case. But Milner calls attention to the cup overflowing as well. The need to give expression to wondrous, full aspects of experience as well as what is missing. I published a book review of On *Not Being Able to Paint* two years after meeting Marion and another on her last book, *Bothered by Alligators*, some forty years later (Eigen, 1983, 2016).

DOI: 10.4324/9780429433535-7

Phyllis Greenacre wrote about the artist's love affair with the world. Harold Bloom wrote about the artist's love affair with creativity. I once heard Bloom speak of how Freud valued creativity, perhaps the love of his life. When Freud was old and ill, he said that when he couldn't do creative work any longer, it was time to end it, and so he did.

When I think of Milner as artist-analyst, I think of Winnicott and Bion, also artist-analysts. Meltzer, a creative appreciator of Bion, wrote of the analyst's atelier. And Bion explicitly spoke of analysis as art and the importance of psychoanalytic beauty.

In the early 1980s, I tried to pay homage by writing what may be the first full-length critical appreciation of Marion's work (Eigen, 1983, 1993). I got a shower of letters from Milner readers voicing thanks and thoughts of their own. One of Marion's close friends was deeply offended by my criticism of the term 'undifferentiation' in Milner's work. I tended to use Winnicott's emphasis on paradox, e.g., links and juxtapositions of distinction-union. Well, small bones to pick, but Marion kindly thanked me and included my suggestion in later work. She apologized for her friend not being to bear what she felt was criticism of Marion and, magically, sustained us both – or, rather, all three of us pursuing our own particular calling. To complicate and enrich matters, she concluded she must have uncritically adopted the term from Ehrenzweig, whose book, *The Hidden Order of Art* (1967) I greatly value.

So many dimensions blend and feed each other in her work, conscious-unconscious, top-bottom, in-out. In her reading of Bion she calls Bion's O, a symbol for unknown ultimate reality (in psychoanalysis, emotional reality) 0 (zero), which she allies with *sunyata*, Buddhist 'emptiness', for her creative, pregnant emptiness. And in *Suppressed Madness of Sane Men* (1987) speaks about her big toe Zen, sensitive to what every pore of being can offer.

Chapter 6

Talking with Marion Milner about Donald W. Winnicott and about herself (1981)

James William Anderson

Introduction

Knowing of this book on Marion Milner, I saw the opportunity of bringing back her voice from the past by sharing my interview with her that took place on October 12, 1981. During a six-week research trip to London to learn about Donald W. Winnicott, I spoke with everyone I could find who had known him well (see Anderson, 2014, 2015). I've regretted that I did not set out to interview Milner about herself, but as I listen to the recording all these years later, I am pleased to find we did not only talk about him but also about her.

We met in her consulting room in her home at 12 Provost Road, Belsize Park, London. She sat on the analytic couch, and I sat nearby on a love seat. According to the note I made directly afterward, she struck me as thin and graceful, "pretty old" (her age was eighty-one), and with lovely, delicate features. She dressed casually and comfortably. She wore a long blue skirt, a purple blouse, and over the blouse a white shirt, unbuttoned, and held in by a belt.

Memories of Winnicott

In a paper about Winnicott (Milner, 1978), she had mentioned her first encounter with him in the late 1930s at a public lecture. I asked her about her experience of that lecture. "It was fascinating," she replied.

> The jokes, the mixture of jokes and seriousness. Then I managed to go to his Paddington Green clinic. The same sort of thing fascinated me. The clown in him. I used to go to his lectures at the Institute of Education. I remember him coming in, like at a music hall, like a recital, like a musical comedy. It was very unusual.

Something else that struck her about him was "the concentration [he had] on the person he was with." She added, "The jokes to me were very important" and noted that a kind of "play" took place.

A memory came to her mind. Once he was coming into his clinic. There was an electric cord on the floor. "He skipped over it instead of walking around." She concluded, "There are people who are funny and not serious and people who are serious but not funny, but isn't it nice when it is joined together?"

DOI: 10.4324/9780429433535-8

She then told me another anecdote. A mother brought her daughter, about age eleven, to the clinic and explained that her husband, the girl's father, frequently criticized the girl, especially about her table manners. "He told the girl to go home and tell her father, 'I eat my peas with honey, I've done so all my life. It makes the peas taste funny, but it keeps them on my knife.'" Milner and I both laughed. I'd like to think that the girl's father laughed too.

In the 1978 paper about Winnicott, Milner, in describing him, wrote, "I think of the dark still center of the whirling Catherine wheel." I asked her what a Catherine wheel is. "It's a firework, a round thing," she explained. "When you light it, it spins round and round and round, with sparks going off. The sparks going off make it spin, so it's a fiery disc with a dark center."

"He was that image of the sparkling," she explained. "He flew out. I felt particularly in contact with him because he was open in a way. I think I chose the image [because] of this throwing of sparks."

At the time of the interview, early in my career, I was enchanted with Winnicott but also found many passages hard to understand. I commented that I saw his work as rich but enigmatic. I asked her about his writing style. "I think Winnicott was so aware of basic paradoxes," she explained. "That's why he wrote the way he did. He never forgets the paradoxes."

I asked whether he was more direct when he supervised her or was his style similar to that of his writing? "It was more direct," she said. "He'd make some tea. He'd throw out a sentence, a remark. He didn't really hold forth at length. That's the way I found it that I liked. He'd throw out a spark."

Did she recall anything specific he had said when he supervised her as she was treating Susan, the patient described in her book, *In the Hands of the Living God* (Milner, 1969)? She thought for a moment and said,

> I'm thinking of something he said to her that she told me. When she came to see him before getting the ECT. I don't think I have this in the book. He said, 'No good it could be, as good as you looked.'

(After listening to the recording several times, I am certain I quoted Milner accurately, although the meaning of Winnicott's words is not readily apparent. I've concluded he was saying that Susan, in her state before ECT, looked good and, given that, ECT could only be harmful to her.) His comment, she added, "always stuck in my mind." Susan felt as if she lost herself as a result of ECT, and much of the book describes how she became herself again during the course of her long analysis with Milner.

She added a comment of Winnicott's she found to be "tremendously fruitful" for her: "The parent's role is to be the disillusioner."

Their influence on each other

In preparing for the interview, I had noticed that Winnicott made a number of references to Milner in his writings. So, while we tend to think first of Winnicott's influence on Milner, she, it seemed, also had a significant influence on him, and I asked her about that.

What came to her mind first was the following: "He mentions the two jugs. That's what started him looking at edges and things. He said that. It's hard for me to know what influence I had on what he wrote."

She was referring to a comment Winnicott (1971b, p. 98) made in his classic book, *Playing and Reality*:

> It was at an important point in the phase of development of these ideas in me in the early forties that Marion Milner (in conversation) was able to convey to me the tremendous significance that there can be in the interplay of the edges of two curtains, or of the surface of a jug that is placed in front of another jug.
>
> (cf. Milner, 1969)

Winnicott is referring to his developing his perspective on the transitional space, in which the baby first perceives rather than conceives of an object.

I noted to her that, in his comment, Winnicott referred to her book on the case of Susan (Milner, 1969). She replied, "I suppose it's in reference to when Susan came to me and said the world is not outside her [any more], which it had been."

In the interview with me, Milner then had a second comment about her influence on Winnicott: "And my paper on a boy's play, the one I wrote for Melanie Klein's 70th birthday." She was referring to her paper, "Aspects of Symbolism in Comprehension of the Not-Self" (Milner, 1952b). She continued, "He said he'd come to see play the way I did. But that didn't exactly influence him. We both arrived at the same thing by different routes."

In that paper, she discussed regression and the abandonment of illusion. She commented to me,

> I remember a great struggle I had with that idea when I was writing the paper, that there could be such a thing. Now it's common. Then when I talked with Melanie Klein about that paper, [I remember] diffidently saying, 'I have a feeling it may be necessary to go back in order to go forward.' She agreed.... But I remember the struggle I had to get that said. It's funny.

Returning to the theme of the influence she and Winnicott had on each other, she related an anecdote. She had a student in a training analysis with her who was also in supervision with Winnicott. This was "the last communication I had with [Winnicott]." He sent her a message via the student. Winnicott had the student tell her, "It doesn't matter which of us thinks of it. Because I can't tell you." As she further explained, "There was a lot of interchange when we talked. You couldn't say which of us had thought of something."

Winnicott, Milner, and Melanie Klein

Two other anecdotes relating to Winnicott came to her mind, both also having to do with Melanie Klein.

She recalled an interaction with Klein while she, Milner, was writing the paper that was required for her to become a member of the psychoanalytic society. The paper (Milner, 1944) was about a child she treated, with Klein as her supervisor. "I'd written something, and she didn't approve of it," Milner recalled. "And this is funny. I thought to myself, 'She looks like a vulture looking out from a thundercloud.' With the hooded eyes, you know. And I was never ever frightened of her before that, and I was never frightened of her after I thought that to myself."

"And I remember telling Donald, and he said in a nice way, 'I think this is an occasion for mobilizing the forces of your personality.' I should stick to my own view. I always remember that phrase."

I replied, "It sounds like it was just the right thing from him to say to you at that point."

The central figure of the second anecdote was Winnicott's wife, Clare Winnicott. Milner said, "Clare went to Melanie for treatment when Clifford Scott [her training analyst] went to Canada." Paula Heimann told me recently. She asked [Clare], 'Why did Donald send you to Melanie?' [Paula asked because she knows Clare is] bitterly anti-Melanie Klein. Clare said, 'Oh, he didn't send me, I went.'

> Then Clare had a row with Melanie. She [Klein] was interpreting her dream, the way she did. Clare tells me she sat up and said, 'Look, that's my dream. I won't have you put your ideas all over it.' And walked out. Donald made up the breach, and she went back in order to finish her training.

"That's fascinating," I exclaimed, "I would imagine that Melanie Klein would seem intrusive at times."

Comments on *A Life of One's Own*

I had chosen a sentence from *A Life of One's Own* (Field, 1934) that I wished to ask her about. It had to do with the parent's influence on the child. It was from a section in which she talked about how the "over-receptive attitude developed." I had it in mind that she saw this as the typical "feminine stance." She clarified that that was not the case. She said it was "overdone." "I mean it's over-receptive. It's exploited femininity, as it were. I'm talking about overbalanced introversion." She noted that she herself is "an overbalanced introvert."

I read the sentence to her.

> Apparently the natural bias toward maleness or femaleness in the child can be utterly distorted by the adults around him, by the extent to which they continually draw upon him for love, or try to impose their will and personality upon him.
>
> (Field, 1934, p. 246)

"Yes," she replied, "the way a depressed mother can alter the development. It seems to me very much the child has to fit in with the mother's idea [of how to be]."

She elaborated, "I was thinking of myself probably. I had a very powerful nanny, who was tough to my brother and sister but [admitted to] spoiling me."

"So you were really sort of her favorite," I commented, "and she put much more into you, but at the same time she required a large payment from you in exchange for that. You had to be a certain way. You couldn't be yourself."

She agreed, and then she related what we were discussing to what I would call resisting the caretaker or mother. "Mother won't be able to stand it, it seems aggressive to her," Milner noted. "I'm very interested in the partially depressed mother."

As we were talking about *A Life of One's Own*, I noted that in the 1930s, when she wrote the book, it would not have seemed to her that there was a place in psychoanalysis for the ideas that were important to her. It had occurred to me that innovative psychoanalysts often find that the psychoanalysis of their era does not fit what matters to them. I asked, "Why does psychoanalysis change?" "For the simple reason," I continued,

> that people have certain kinds of experiences that aren't accounted for by its theories, and therefore new theories have to be developed. So that's an idea that really interests me and excites me. I wonder if you could tell me a little more about what it was that didn't seem to fit, that didn't seem useful to you?

"I suppose one of the things in *A Life of One's Own* was this discovery of two ways of attending, which were totally different," she replied.

> One I called wide focus. I didn't know where that fit into Freudian ideas really.... It didn't seem to me my analytic friends were aware of that which to me was so startling. The different way one could see the world from the way one intended to.

I commented, "So that was an important issue, that there wasn't that perception. It wasn't a concern of psychoanalysis [at the time]."

She replied,

> Then Winnicott came to talk about a creative way of looking at the world, which I suppose was what I was seeing as a creative way of looking at the world. The world seemed to change according to the way I looked at it. That's what I was fascinated by.

I close my account of the interview with that comment, in which she spoke of a concept that was especially important to her.

After the interview

There is a sequel to the interview. I got to know Milner better by having a second interview two weeks later and by hosting her, with my wife, for dinner at the flat we were renting. She knew that I had made the trip to London to interview people who had known Winnicott. I had been successful, as I had had meetings with Margaret Little, with whom Milner put me in contact, as well as Masud Khan, Anna Freud, Enid Balint, and others. But she was aware of how disappointed I was that I had not talked with Clare Winnicott, who was in hospital during the entire time of my trip. Milner surprised me by arranging for me to meet with Clare Winnicott in her hospital room shortly before my departure. I had Milner to thank for that memorable visit. I was moved by Milner's thoughtfulness.

Chapter 7

'What a lovely woman'

My youthful encounters with Marion Milner (1985–1998)

Brett Kahr

On 4 January 1985, as a very young postgraduate student, I had the privilege of presenting a paper at a two-day conference at Trinity College in the University of Cambridge, hosted by a student organisation – now long defunct – the Cambridge Psychoanalytical Society.

Although I had already delivered a number of papers by this point and did not experience too much nervousness at public speaking, on this occasion, however, I became quite anxious and my knees began to buckle as soon as the chairperson of the conference whispered to me, just before the start of my talk, "Brett, do you see that old lady in the front row? That's Marion Milner".

"Marion Milner?", I gawped. "But she lives in London. Has she really come all this way to Cambridge on a snowy day?"

The chairperson replied, "She has indeed. But don't be thrown. I understand she's very nice".

In spite of my trepidation, I then delivered my paper on the topic of working psychotherapeutically with schizophrenic patients, no less – the subject of Mrs. Milner's (1969) classic book, *The Hands of the Living God: An Account of a Psycho-analytic Treatment,* published roughly sixteen years previously. I spoke at some length about my treatment of a male schizophrenic patient who had suffered profound sexual abuse in childhood and whose delusional material contained many disguised references to anal penetration by an older male.

During the coffee break, Marion Milner approached me and thanked me for my presentation and told me that she particularly appreciated the fact that, unlike the previous speaker, I talked in a sufficiently clear and audible voice. She explained that, as an octogenarian, her hearing had begun to suffer; but happily, she understood every word of my paper. She also complimented me on some of the psychoanalytical interpretations that I had made during my sessions with this particular patient. Mrs. Milner's gracious and generous response to my lecture and her kindly interest in the clinical material touched me tremendously and I fell in love with her straightaway.

In the course of our conversation, I told Mrs. Milner that I had, of course, read her classic book, *The Hands of the Living God: An Account of a Psycho-analytic Treatment,* and that I had found it extremely useful. I then asked her whether the patient about whom she had written, known pseudonymously to readers as "Susan", had ever experienced childhood sexual abuse, as my male schizophrenic patient had done. Mrs. Milner looked very puzzled, as though she had not ever entertained this possibility, and she told me that she would be happy to dig out her old case notes and reconsider her clinical material.

DOI: 10.4324/9780429433535-9

For a woman of Marion Milner's age – only weeks shy of her eighty-fifth birthday – to respond in such a modest and engaging manner impressed me hugely. As a budding psychoanalytical historian, I had, at that point, already begun to conduct interviews with quite a number of the last surviving members of the British psychoanalytical community of the 1930s and 1940s and beyond, but Mrs. Milner stood out as quite exceptional. Unlike many of her more obstreperous and competitive colleagues, Milner's kindness shone through in a most sincere and authentic manner and I became a lifelong fan.

All of the guests and delegates at this two-day conference stayed overnight in student rooms in Trinity College, as the new academic term had not yet begun; and the following morning at breakfast, in the grand, sprawling medieval dining hall, I noticed Marion sitting at a long wooden table, all by herself. This surprised me greatly. Perhaps the other conference participants felt too intimidated to approach this iconic psychoanalyst. But having already had the pleasure of a brief and pleasant conversation with Mrs. Milner the previous day, I asked whether I might join her, and with a warm smile and an elegant hand gesture, she invited me to do so.

As we sipped our coffee and buttered our toast – back then no one had heard of cholesterol – in preparation for the second day of psychoanalytical papers, I expressed curiosity as to why Mrs. Milner had taken the trouble to travel all the way to Cambridge, by train, in the middle of such dreadfully cold weather. In my youthful ignorance, I presumed that most old people in their eighties would prefer to sit at home, and I also suspected that Mrs. Milner already knew everything about psychoanalysis and could not possibly learn anything more from yet another conference. But Marion smiled and simply told me that she continued to find psychological ideas most fascinating indeed and that she had certainly made the right decision to attend the conference, in spite of the uncomfortable nature of the journey in the midst of a particularly ugly British winter.

In view of the fact that I had just delivered a talk on schizophrenia and that Milner had already worked with an ostensibly schizophrenic woman in multi-decade psychoanalysis, our conversation soon veered in that direction and we talked about the cruel way in which many British psychiatrists would simply dismiss their patients with heavy doses of antipsychotic medication and would make no attempts to engage these individuals in ongoing conversations about their childhood histories or private lives.

At that point, Milner told me, with a twinkle in her eye, that, years previously, she had served as the clinical supervisor to the famous anti-psychiatrist and one-time psychoanalytical candidate, Dr. Ronald Laing, a man whose work I admired tremendously in spite of the fact that he had since developed a reputation for being a rather pugnacious individual (Kahr, 1994). According to Milner, R.D. Laing had succeeded in alienating quite a number of the older teachers at London's Institute of Psycho-Analysis, many of whom found him rather unsuitable as a candidate, but Milner explained that she rated him highly and respected his work; consequently, both she and the great Dr. Donald Winnicott championed Laing and argued that he should not be expelled from the training. Although Laing eventually parted company with the traditional psychoanalytical establishment, she remained in contact with him, and, years later, Milner (1985) even referred a patient to him, someone whom she described as an "intractable" case – in other words, a person who seemed to be very untreatable indeed. With a glint in her eye, Milner told me that Laing agreed to work with this individual but quoted a sessional fee of £60 – a sum which Milner regarded as shockingly expensive, at a time when most analysts charged no more than £10 per hour. As Mrs. Milner really wanted to obtain help for this patient, she agreed to pay Laing's fee herself.

Marion also reminisced about Donald Winnicott, with whom she had enjoyed a very long-term set of interconnections. With a huge smile on her face, she told me that Winnicott's widow, fellow psychoanalyst Mrs. Clare Winnicott, once quipped that her husband suffered from "delusions of benignity" (quoted in Milner, 1985), imagining everyone to be kindly first and foremost, rather than brimming with envy and evil.

Mrs. Milner explained that her fascination with Winnicott remained fervent across the decades and that she had become active in a newly formed organisation called The Squiggle Foundation. With tremendous kindness, she asked me to write my name and address on a piece of paper so that she could instruct the administrator to place me on their mailing list. She also engaged with my evident interest in the history of psychoanalysis and told me that she had just participated in a series of talks about the early years of child analysis, organised by Dr. Susanna Isaacs Elmhirst, and she wondered whether I should write to Dr. Elmhirst to discuss publication possibilities, as I had earlier revealed to her that, one day, I hoped to produce a book on the history of psychoanalysis. Little did I know at that point in time that, in due course, I would become a regular attendee of events at The Squiggle Foundation (and, ultimately, a Patron) and that the brilliant Sue Isaacs Elmhirst would become one of my most venerated and enlightening clinical supervisors.

As our breakfast unfolded, Milner kept regaling me with the most wonderful stories about herself and her colleagues, all related in a soft but musical voice, and I felt extremely fortunate to be able to sit at the feet of such a magnificent person. At one point, I noticed that Mrs. Milner had stopped eating her food and that she still had a full plate of eggs and sausage in front of her. With time ticking and with the first of the morning conference papers about to begin, I asked Mrs. Milner whether she had had enough to eat, whereupon she told me, very touchingly, that, owing to the rheumatism in her hands, she found it difficult to cut her food. Naturally, I offered some practical assistance. Happily, she then ate a few little bites of her breakfast to fortify herself for another long day of scholarly presentations.

I then escorted Mrs. Milner into the lecture theatre, and we navigated our way through the second day of psychoanalytical talks, most of which Marion could not hear clearly, owing to the fact that many of the presenters mumbled, in characteristic British fashion! I did my best to serve as her translator and offered little summaries whenever I could. One of the speakers, the noted Cambridge academic Dr. John Forrester, spoke at length about Marion Milner's work throughout his presentation, but, alas, she could understand very little of his paper, in spite of being seated in the front row. She gently elbowed me for some assistance, and so, I took out a notepad and began to jot down little quotations from Forrester's lecture, in which he expressed his appreciation of Milner's early book, *A Life of One's Own*, written under the pseudonym of Joanna Field (1934). Mrs. Milner beamed with delight to know that a distinguished Cambridge historian would have taken the time to read a book that she had written more than fifty years previously.

During the morning coffee break, one of the conference participants approached me, having clocked that I had very evidently fallen in love with Marion Milner. Discreetly, this woman whispered to me that, years ago, she had referred a highly autistic member of her family to Marion for psychoanalytical treatment, and, happily, Mrs. Milner cured this individual completely. As a young man, contemplating a career in the psychoanalytical community, it pleased me greatly to learn that Freudian-style treatment really *does* work and that Marion Milner might well be one of its most skilled practitioners.

As the conference drew to a close, Mrs. Milner kindly enquired if I ever came to London (as I lived in Oxford at that time), and when I told her that I did, she smiled and chirped, "Oh good, do come and visit me, won't you?" She then gave me her home telephone number. I promised that I would ring her in due course to arrange a cup of tea.

Extraordinarily, while sifting through old boxes of papers, I recently discovered my notes from that 1985 conference, held more than thirty-five years ago. It surprised me not at all that I had described Mrs. Milner as an "utterly charming and fascinating woman". But I also jotted down a few further observations at that time, namely, "Her expression betrayed a certain loneliness; her husband has been dead for quite some time, and I began to conjure up images of a single woman sitting alone, in despair". In just two days, I had enjoyed a privileged glimpse of the benign, curious, engaged, playful, and warm-hearted side of Mrs. Milner, yet I could also see the more isolated parts, struggling with ageing and with the preparation for death.

I departed that Cambridge conference feeling quite blessed that I had met such a special person who, in just a short space of time, taught me so very much, welcomed me into the fold, and gave me a master class in growing old, helping me to appreciate that if, and when, one does reach her grand age, one can still participate in the world, in spite of rheumatism and hearing loss.

I returned to Oxford and, not long thereafter, a parcel arrived from The Squiggle Foundation, courtesy of Marion Milner, containing all sorts of information about upcoming events. I felt very touched that Marion had taken the trouble to pass along my contact details to the administrator. Soon thereafter, I telephoned Mrs. Milner and arranged to visit her at her London home on Saturday, 16 February 1985, at 5.00 p.m.

*

On the day in question, I travelled by train from Oxford to Paddington Station in London and then hopped on the underground, alighting at Chalk Farm tube station, only a stone's throw away from Marion's long-standing residence at 12, Provost Road. I rang the bell punctually and Mrs. Milner greeted me with a handshake. She sported a wispy skirt and blouse, thick glasses on her nose, and very prominent hearing aids in her ears, which, I believe, she had not worn one month previously when we had met in Cambridge.

I presented her with a bouquet of flowers, although I did so somewhat sheepishly as, owing to the horrific winter weather, I could not find any truly robust floral tribute in the local shops, and the ones I offered looked a little frazzled from the wind and the rain. Marion accepted the bouquet with a sweet smile and then invited me inside her home and suggested that I place my overcoat on the banister of her staircase. She then ushered me into the ground floor lounge and told me to look outside at her snow-covered garden, while she walked down the stairs into her kitchen in order to fetch the tray of tea.

As I began to glance round the lounge, I noticed not one, but, rather, two psychoanalytical couches, and I soon came to appreciate that Mrs. Milner must have used this room for her clinical practice, although I could not be certain which of the couches she reserved for her patients. One of the couches resembled that rather an iconic piece of furniture deployed by Sigmund Freud in his consulting room on the Berggasse in Vienna, with a slightly curved back; the other seemed to be a much flatter bed with a chair parked behind. Surprisingly, Milner had placed both this couch and chair in the middle of the room, rather than, more comfortingly and snugly, perhaps, up against the wall.

I then treated myself to a closer glance at the furnishings and the decorations, and I soon became quite absorbed by her library – only two shelves of books – which struck me – a trainee bibliophile – as rather sparse. I presumed that a psychoanalyst of Milner's age and distinction would have accumulated a heaving library with hundreds of books covering every single wall.

Most of the volumes on the top shelf of Mrs. Milner's tiny bookcase boasted those familiar shiny green spines, indicative of volumes published in "The International Psycho-Analytical Library" series, a joint venture between the Hogarth Press and the Institute of Psycho-Analysis. Milner's collection included some of the works of Mrs. Melanie Klein (1932, 1948, 1961), as well as a copy of Klein's jointly authored book with Mrs. Joan Riviere, the now-classic *Love, Hate and Reparation: Two Lectures* (Klein and Riviere, 1937). Milner also possessed copies of Dr. Donald Meltzer's (1967) *The Psycho-Analytical Process*, as well as Dr. Charles Rycroft's (1968a) tomes on *Anxiety and Neurosis* and, also, *Imagination and Reality: Psycho-Analytical Essays. 1951–1961* (Rycroft, 1968b), not to mention the first edition of Dr. R.D. Laing's (1961) sturdy text, *The Self and Others: Further Studies in Sanity and Madness*, personally inscribed to his former clinical supervisor, as well as a copy of Laing's book on *Reason and Violence: A Decade of Sartre's Philosophy. 1950–1960*, co-written by Dr. David G. Cooper (Laing and Cooper, 1964). The bottom shelf consisted entirely of the twenty-four-volume collection of Sigmund Freud's writings in English.

Mrs. Milner's lounge also contained a desk, a low table with a telephone perched upon it, as well as a prominent mantelpiece, strewn with letters and invitations. I could not help but notice that she had placed my letter, confirming our meeting, on display, no doubt as a reminder. She also exhibited an invitation to attend the next meeting of the 1952 Club, a small, elite cohort of psychoanalysts who gathered from time to time to discuss their work.

As I waited upstairs in the combined lounge and consulting room, I could hear much rattling of spoons and the opening and closing of cabinet doors downstairs as Marion prepared our tea. Eventually, she began to mount the staircase, with a heavy tray in hand, and I quickly sensed that she found herself struggling with the physicality of the task, and so, I offered to help, but Mrs. Milner insisted that she could manage. Slowly and carefully, she climbed up the old wooden steps with the tray jiggling back and forth in her rheumatic hands. Happily, Marion reached the top of the stairs and then placed the tea tray on the sofa, nearly toppling the teapot in the process. With great difficulty, she then poured the tea.

Of most importance, we then embarked upon a rich and lengthy conversation. Mrs. Milner began by explaining that she had lived at 12, Provost Road, for fully fifty-two years. She stressed that, during the mid-1930s, no psychoanalysts lived in this part of London, whereas subsequently, from 1938, after the arrival of the Freud family in nearby Maresfield Gardens, the villages of Swiss Cottage, Belsize Park, and Hampstead – the three communities comprising the N.W.3. post code – ultimately became the very epicentre of British psychoanalysis. She then spoke about her house in more detail and confessed that she really needed to contract a gardener.

Naturally, we reminisced about our first meeting in Cambridge, some weeks previously. Marion explained that she had come to that psychoanalytical conference quite by happenstance. She revealed that she had really little interest in some of the papers, several of which focused on the work of Dr. Jacques Lacan, a man whom she did not rate particularly highly; but, with a twinkle in her eye, she confessed that she had always harboured a secret wish to visit the majestic Trinity College, founded in the 16th century.

Mrs. Milner then began to reminisce about some of her old psychoanalytical friends and repeated several of the same stories that she had told me only a few weeks earlier. She took particular delight in reminding me of Clare Winnicott's observation that Donald Winnicott suffered from delusions of benignity. Perhaps, Marion also struggled with benignity! I do not know.

As I sipped my tea, our conversation soon turned to books. With much excitement, Mrs. Milner explained that Yale University Press had approached her recently about the possibility of republishing some of her classic titles. But she had no guarantee that this offer would ever materialise. She told me that she possessed a collection of beautiful colour plates of many of her own paintings and she deeply hoped that someone would reproduce those in book form, although she appreciated that such a volume would be, potentially, quite expensive. Mrs. Milner did have greater reassurance from the Hogarth Press and from Chatto and Windus that they would publish her collected papers as the very first volume in a new library of psychoanalysis. This book would eventually appear in print some two years hence under the title *The Suppressed Madness of Sane Men: Forty-Four Years of Exploring Psychoanalysis* (Milner, 1987b), released by Tavistock Publications. Another book would be launched contemporaneously under the title *Eternity's Sunrise: A Way of Keeping a Diary* (Milner, 1987a) by Virago Press.

Milner then talked about her pleasure in holidays, underscoring how the little things in life – such as trips abroad – really do matter. In many respects, by speaking in this way, she certainly epitomised the Winnicottian notion of the importance of play.

Throughout our discussion, I asked Mrs. Milner many questions, inviting her to elaborate on all of the topics that she had introduced. Although most of the conversation and questions focused entirely on Marion, she did, throughout our dialogue, have the graciousness to ask about my own work and she seemed particularly interested when I told her that, a short while previously, I had founded an organisation called The Oxford Psycho-Analytical Forum, which sponsored weekly and, sometimes, twice-weekly lectures and seminars on psychoanalysis. Over the last year or more, I had invited such stalwarts as Dr. John Bowlby, Dr. Muriel Gardiner, Dr. Robin Skynner, Professor Albert Solnit, and, even, Dr. Ronald Laing to speak at the University of Oxford, an institution which, at that time, regarded psychoanalysis with tremendous scorn. Milner found this most fascinating. We also discussed my ongoing interest in learning more about the history of psychoanalysis, and she helpfully suggested that I should contact two of her senior colleagues, in particular, Miss Pearl King and, also,

Miss Charlotte Balkányi. Although I had not met Pearl King at this point, she eventually became a great mentor and, ultimately, a friend, as well as a source of inspiration who held Marion Milner in very high regard.

Throughout our discussions, I found Milner to be very liberal-minded, with a great capacity for mutual conversation. At one point, she asked me to enlighten her about the work of the French psychoanalyst Jacques Lacan. Although I have never become a "Lacanian", I had met some of the early British Lacanians, and I did my best to illuminate what I had come to understand about their very particular approach to psychoanalytical work.

After discussing my interest in the history of psychoanalysis and my fledgling work in Oxford, Milner told me that I would enjoy the meetings of the 1952 Club (a gathering which she described as "exclusive" (quoted in Kahr, 1985a)), and that I might also appreciate the discussions of the group known as "Imago", run by her psychoanalytical colleague Dr. Harold Maxwell, designed to explore a whole wide range of interesting Freudian topics. Milner explained that several members of Imago had expressed a particular fascination for the contributions of the Chilean psychoanalyst Dr. Ignacio Matte Blanco, whose work I had not yet encountered. Milner confessed that she struggled to understand Matte Blanco's extremely complicated theories.

At this point, our focus shifted to further discussion about her famous patient "Susan", whose tragic but, also, hopeful, case history Milner had described in great detail in her aforementioned book *The Hands of the Living God: An Account of a Psycho-analytic Treatment*. In the midst of our discussion, Marion stood up from her seat and showed me a whole selection of small plasticine sculptures of a pig and a zebra, which Susan had made as part of the treatment process.

Marion then revealed an important psychoanalytical secret. She explained that during the early years of Susan's sessions at Provost Road, this very psychiatrically challenged woman, only recently discharged from a mental asylum, actually lived nearby in the Hampstead home of Dr. Donald Winnicott and his first wife, Mrs. Alice Winnicott. The Winnicotts provided a secure space in which Susan could live safely and then attend psychoanalysis with Milner nearby. Marion spoke very highly of Donald Winnicott; but she described Alice Winnicott, the spouse, as somewhat "dotty" (quoted in Kahr, 1985a) and recalled that, after the couple divorced, Alice moved to Wales where she then died in isolation.

At the time of our conversation in 1985, Milner had not yet revealed publicly that Susan had once lived in the Winnicott family home. The following year, on 8 April 1986, she wrote to the American historian Professor Judith Hughes about this matter (Milner, 1986a), who then published this intriguing information in her book on *Reshaping the Psychoanalytic Domain: The Work of Melanie Klein, W.R.D. Fairbairn, and D.W. Winnicott* (Hughes, 1989).

Apparently, Susan required quite a great deal of extra-analytical looking-after in addition to her formal psychoanalytical sessions. Not only did the Winnicotts care for Susan for a period of time but, so, too, did a certain religious couple known as the Craxtons, at least one of whom worked as a minister.

Milner then reminisced most generously about the details of Susan's treatment. For instance, she told me that Susan had had to endure rather primitive electroconvulsive shock treatments while in hospital and that Susan claimed that these bodily assaults actually produced many dreadful side effects and, consequently, ruined her life. Milner agreed with Susan's assessment of the dreadful nature of primitive 1940s electric shocks.

Marion talked with affection about Susan and revealed that her long-standing patient still attended sessions, after more than forty years. Unsurprisingly, at the outset of treatment, Susan referred to her psychoanalyst as "Mrs. Milner", but, over time, she began to call her "Marion".

On the basis of my conversation with Mrs. Milner, it seemed that Susan had, in fact, made considerable progress as a result of psychoanalysis, and, in more recent years, had even managed to hold down an intellectually demanding job and, also, to maintain a relationship with a partner. At the time of my meeting with Marion, she explained that Susan had recently begun to date a priest. Marion also reported that Susan always boasted a very good sense of humour and that whenever Marion would enquire, "How's your man?", Susan would reply, "Which one?"

After many years of work, Susan retired from her institutional post, and Marion helped her to arrange for a pension. Clearly, the lives of these two women became very deeply intertwined. Marion confessed that the great American psychoanalyst Professor Harold Searles had once written to her offering his view that not only had Marion become therapeutic for Susan but also that Susan had proved to be therapeutic for Marion. Mrs. Milner told me that she certainly agreed with Professor Searles's assessment.

Milner explained that across the years, a number of psychoanalysts from overseas had corresponded with her about this now-famous case history. Although Milner had always conceptualised Susan as "schizophrenic", some American psychoanalysts had suggested that "borderline" might be a more appropriate diagnosis. Winnicott (1969a,b), however, did subscribe to the diagnosis of schizophrenia, having known Susan intimately for quite some time.

Throughout our conversation, Marion kept referring to Susan – the pseudonym used in the publication – by her real name. Whenever she did so, she apologised immediately for having mistakenly revealed the patient's true identity, but I have certainly never repeated these details and I did not record Susan's actual name in my notes. Mrs. Milner also told me that Susan, in spite of her improvements, still suffered from agoraphobia after many years and had to seek specialist treatment elsewhere. Also, Marion explained that Susan would often speak very scornfully about the lack of cleanliness of the house on Provost Road, and that she would often criticise Marion for living in such a grotty residence.

When Marion Milner and I first met in Cambridge, after I delivered that paper on the role of child sexual abuse in the aetiology of schizophrenia, I asked her whether Susan had ever suffered such experiences as a youngster. At that time, Mrs. Milner claimed not to remember and promised that she would consult her notes. During my visit to Provost Road, I asked Milner about this matter once again and, on this occasion, she told me that she *had*, in fact, reviewed her old case notes and could now confirm that Susan had succumbed to child abuse of some sort. Marion seemed most unclear as to why she had not included this information in her landmark book: a true indication of how very few psychoanalysts in the 1960s could think about the horrors of parental sadism in a clear manner.

Milner then asked for more clarification about my own burgeoning clinical work in Oxford and even revealed that one of her patients had once attended the Warneford

Hospital in Headington, just outside of Oxford town centre. We continued to speak at length about schizophrenia and we enjoyed discussing some of the psychodynamic aspects of this most severe form of psychosis.

Between the time of our first meeting on 4 January 1985, and our subsequent meeting on 16 February 1985, Marion Milner had celebrated her eighty-fifth birthday. It surprised me that a woman of this grand age would still be working psychoanalytically with patients, but Marion explained that in addition to her occasional consultations with Susan, she continued to treat three analysands on a regular basis. She then revealed that although most of her patients have enjoyed the couch, one of her current patients – a man – came to experience the couch as a sadistic object and would refuse to lie down. Milner underscored that she would often shift the precise position of her chair in order to face this man more directly during sessions.

Mrs. Milner also talked to me about some of her training patients, and she expressed concern that over the years, two candidates from the Institute of Psycho-Analysis had proved to be particularly unsuitable for training and that she had to terminate their treatments. Milner made no mention of the names of these two disappointing psychoanalytical trainees and she provided no information which would have constituted a breach of confidentiality in any way.

Milner then turned her attention to some of her London colleagues. I did not have to prompt her at all. I suspect that Marion might have appreciated the fact that a young man with an interest in the history of her profession had come to visit and that she could speak in great detail, sensing that I would listen carefully.

Mrs. Milner began to reminisce at considerable length about the controversial Indian-born Mr. Masud Khan, then only sixty years of age. Marion explained that she met Khan shortly after his arrival in England and that she had even attended his wedding to Miss Jane Shore. She lamented that Khan had become alcoholic in recent years and, also, quite sadly, that he had developed cancer and had recently had a lung removed. She had, apparently, seen Khan not long ago, after he had delivered a lecture to The Squiggle Foundation – his first public appearance in quite some time – and he seemed very pleased to know that he could still command an audience. Milner lamented that as a result of her own hearing difficulties and of Khan's vocal struggles (a sequela of his cancer), it had become extremely difficult for the two of them to engage in basic conversation.

She then spoke very fondly about Dr. Margaret Little, a fellow elderly psychoanalyst who had moved from London to Kent. I later discovered that Little (1985) had undergone psychoanalysis with Winnicott and, consequently, the two women had a great deal in common. Milner underscored that she enjoyed visiting Dr. Little in the countryside, particularly in view of Little's age and isolation, but that she could only manage the journey during the summer and not in the winter, owing to the lack of a platform at Sevenoaks station, which made walking rather more difficult. Helpfully, Marion suggested that I should hop on a train to Sevenoaks in order to interview Dr. Little (which, in fact, I would do later that year, and, as a result of that conversation, I learned a great deal more about the history of post-war British psychoanalytical politics (Kahr, 1985b)).

In addition to gossiping about Masud Khan and Margaret Little, she also shared her thoughts about Dr. William Gillespie and his wife, Mrs. Sadie Gillespie. Marion told me, perhaps somewhat brashly, that she regarded Dr. Gillespie as a dour old Scot who would always tow the line; nevertheless, the two remained in contact and she had come to learn that Dr. Gillespie had recently begun to write his autobiography.

As our conversation unfolded, Marion continued to chat and reminisce freely, regaling me with stories and anecdotes about such noted figures as Madame Janine Chasseguet-Smirgel, the distinguished French psychoanalyst, and, also, Dr. André Green, whom she dismissed as far too academic and not sufficiently clinically empathic in her estimation.

Milner then explained that in recent years, French psychoanalysts, especially those of a Lacanian persuasion, had begun to take an increasing interest in her work, not least Lacan's very own son-in-law, Monsieur Jacques-Alain Miller. Apparently, Miller had sent one of his Lacanian publications to Mrs. Milner, but she confessed that she could not understand it at all and passed it along to a colleague who spoke French far better than her. Monsieur Miller had asked Marion to consent to an interview, but she told me that she refused his invitation as, two years previously, she had made a decision not to grant any more interviews. Upon hearing this, I felt rather fortunate that Mrs. Milner had agreed to meet with me at all.

After chatting about colleagues, both British and French, Milner told me that, at present, she had become preoccupied with only one major task, namely, the completion of her collected papers. Apparently, she had only just begun to craft an introductory essay but admitted that she struggled to find an overarching theme that would link all of her papers together. Mrs. Milner explained that she hoped to finish this gargantuan writing task before too long so that she would then be able to free up far more time for her truly profound and playful passion for painting.

In the middle of our conversation, the telephone rang, and Marion rose slowly from her chair and walked towards the phone, perched on a nearby table. She picked up the receiver, and, in that characteristic mid-20th-century English manner, she announced, "722 2112", thus reassuring her caller that he or she had, in fact, dialled the correct number. Marion spoke very briefly to the person on the other end of the line, explaining that she had company and could not talk at length.

Mrs. Milner then sat down and revealed the caller to be none other than Mr. Alexander Newman, a former priest who gravitated towards psychotherapy and psychoanalysis in order to support his parishioners. Newman then went on to create The Squiggle Foundation, an organisation devoted to an exploration of the work of Donald Winnicott. Apparently, Newman had become very friendly with Milner and, also, quite concerned about her, and it seems that he would check up on her regularly, especially after meetings, to ensure that this increasingly frail octogenarian lady would have arrived home safely. Milner also explained that Alexander Newman's wife, Mrs. Miriam Rapp, often assisted her with the typing of her papers. It pleased me greatly to know that this Winnicottian couple took such an interest in Mrs. Milner's well-being.

When I first arranged to meet with Marion at her home, I presumed that I might stay for merely an hour or so, but my gracious hostess revealed no signs of fatigue and she continued to talk. I sensed that she might have become quite lonely by this point in her life and that she may have welcomed the opportunity to chat with someone with tremendous admiration for her work and with a great fascination for her professional community.

Somehow, our discussion veered towards the First World War. Milner lamented that she lost many friends and acquaintances in the Great War and that this stirred ferocious anger which, she admitted, none of her own psychoanalysts had ever helped her within any significant way. I must confess that I found this revelation rather surprising. I would have thought that psychoanalysts would have discussed warfare quite extensively, but it may be that, in the early days, practitioners focused more on the private biography of the patient rather than upon the traumatogenic impact of broader social and political explosions. In spite of the fact that I barely knew Mrs. Milner, she did inform me that, at some point, she had consulted a psychodramatist and then participated in psychodrama sessions, which certainly helped her to process the horrors of the 1914–1918 war more fully. She revealed such a respect for the discipline of psychodrama that she would, at times, recommend this method of treatment for her patients. Marion then told me that she needed to locate a good London-based psychodramatist for one of her patients and wondered whether I knew of any. I did, in fact, have an acquaintance – one of the leaders of the British psychodrama movement, whom I had met recently at a conference in Oxford – and I believe that I passed on the name of this colleague to Marion.

Thereafter, we began to chat about the Swiss-born psychoanalyst, Dr. Alice Miller, who, in the late 1970s and early 1980s, had become increasingly popular in the English-speaking world, especially in view of her emphasis on the realities of child abuse and of parental insensitivity (e.g., Miller, 1981). We talked about Miller's notion that many psychological workers enter the mental health profession as a covert way of dealing with their own depressed mothers (cf. Miller, 1979). Mrs. Milner considered this hypothesis very sensible and explained that she regarded her own mother as having suffered from significant depression, though not clinically so.

Our dialogue seemed to be unending, with no shortage of fascinating topics. But as the sun had set by this time and evening had approached, I wondered whether I should excuse myself in order to allow Mrs. Milner some rest. She, however, seemed keen to continue our chat and so I remained perched in my chair. Marion then asked me if I gardened. As I lived at that time in student accommodation, I explained that I had little opportunity for either planting or pruning. She spoke, though, with delight about her love of gardening, perhaps hoping to inspire me to do likewise.

At this point, Marion continued to reminisce about some of her old psychoanalytical companions. She explained that she would often attend painting classes with both Masud Khan and, also, with Mr. Anton Ehrenzweig, a good friend and scholar of art and music whom she met through their mutual passion for psychoanalytical theory. Apparently, Ehrenzweig, a Viennese refugee to Great Britain, attended the meetings of the Imago group along with the writer Mr. Adrian Stokes – one of Melanie Klein's long-term analysands. According to Milner, both Ehrenzweig and Stokes engaged in frequent verbal combat with one another, often in quite a rivalrous manner. On one occasion, Ehrenzweig telephoned Milner to complain that Stokes would no longer speak to him. When Milner enquired why that should be the case, Ehrenzweig revealed that he had actually told Stokes to go to hell!

Unlike many of the elderly psychoanalysts whom I interviewed at that point in time, I did not experience Marion as pathologically narcissistic in any way. Certainly, she talked about herself with pleasure, but, throughout our conversation, she continued to turn the lens onto me and took a serious interest in my work, which I found rather sweet and kind. I discussed my research post in a psychiatric hospital, my first forays into professional writing (having begun a book on the psychodynamics of schizophrenia), and my own small efforts to organise psychoanalytical lectures in Oxford. When I told her that R.D. Laing had come to speak on one occasion, Milner asked immediately whether he had arrived drunk – which, in fact, he had – thus, she clearly knew all about his alcoholism (cf. Kahr, 1994). We also discussed the psychopathology of wife-battering and other forms of domestic violence, as one of my very first patients had to endure much physical abuse from her husband. As I recall, Milner and I had a most interesting conversation about the potential role of unconscious masochism in such cases.

I believe that I asked Mrs. Milner whether she had entertained any plans to retire fully from clinical work. She told me that many of her colleagues had already urged her to set a formal retirement date, owing to her advancing age. But Milner insisted that she still had work to undertake and that she had no plans to retire in toto. She underscored that psychoanalytical work progresses very slowly indeed but that her patients do, eventually, make great strides. Marion insisted that she would remain very active in the psychoanalytical community and that, in the upcoming week, she hoped to attend a meeting of training analysts at the Institute of Psycho-Analysis, to keep herself engaged and stimulated.

As I prepared to depart Provost Road and return to Oxford, I told Mrs. Milner that I regarded her as quite an inspiring and courageous woman who had made such a huge contribution to mental health. I exclaimed that she deserved a Festschrift or some other written tribute which would examine her work in detail. She rather liked this idea, but she could not think of anyone who might have the capacity to prepare such a testament on her behalf. (Thankfully, the editors of the very volume in which this essay appears have now done so as a wonderful and long-awaited posthumous tribute to this great lady.)

I then bid Mrs. Milner farewell, expressing the hope that I would meet her again in the future. As I reached for my overcoat, which I had hung on the hallway banister, I noticed Marion's walking stick, which she kept in a bucket placed not far from the front door – a powerful reminder of her age and her physical struggles. I then shook her hand warmly, bid her farewell, and braved the cold weather of Chalk Farm.

Mulling on this very unique encounter, I felt both inspired by Marion but, also, saddened by her widowed state and by her loneliness, and I wished that I had brought her a more useful present than some unimpressive flowers. I jotted down pages and pages and pages of notes, by hand, and I concluded my write-up with the following summation: "What a lovely woman".

Several months thereafter, I travelled abroad on a visiting fellowship, but I remained in communication with Marion by old-fashioned letter-writing. I shall never forget that, on one occasion, perhaps in early 1986, I sent her a draft of a very lengthy paper that I had prepared on the psychoanalytical approach to schizophrenia – an elaboration of the talk that I had delivered the previous year at Trinity College in Cambridge. To my utter surprise and delight, Milner read this juvenile typescript rather carefully and she even took the time to write back with some extremely detailed comments.

Upon my return to the United Kingdom one year later, I registered for a weekly Saturday morning course of lectures about the work of Donald Winnicott, sponsored by The Squiggle Foundation; and to my great surprise, I discovered that Mrs. Milner also attended every single one of these talks quite regularly (Fielding and Newman, 1988). Although delighted to see Marion, it stunned me that she would wish to devote every

Saturday morning to these basic seminars about Winnicott when she had known the man personally over many decades and, in all likelihood, could have delivered each of these introductory talks in her sleep! But clearly, her affection for Winnicott persisted long after his death in 1971, and she certainly enjoyed being part of this vibrant Winnicottian community.

The other students on the course regarded Mrs. Milner as a historical object of veneration and did not dare to approach her. Rather like those conference delegates in Cambridge who left Marion sitting alone during breakfast in the great hall of Trinity College, my fellow Winnicottian seminar participants kept their distance. Indeed, young people often find very old people somewhat frightening as few have yet begun to prepare themselves for the possibility of death, at least not in a mature, well-processed manner. But having had the pleasure of knowing Marion already, I took great delight in sitting with her after each of the talks for a cup of tea. We chatted about anything and everything and I found her to be a joyful woman, full of warmth and curiosity. Throughout our association during the 1980s and 1990s, these Milnerian characteristics never wavered.

On one memorable occasion, we began to speak in more detail about the particularities of her relationship with Winnicott. Obviously, owing to our age difference and to the fact that she and I had met in a professional context, she did not tell me *everything* about her feelings towards Winnicott. For instance, I did not know at that point that he had treated her late husband, Mr. Dennis Milner, or that she, herself, had undergone a period of analysis with Winnicott and that he had actually conducted *her* psychoanalysis in her very own lounge at Provost Road – the room that I had visited in 1985 – in order to save her travelling time to and from his office (Milner, 2012), or that she harboured a very strong erotic transference towards him (Milner, n.d.). Most of that information became known to me only after I had read the unpublished correspondence between these two historical psychoanalytical figures years later, much of which will be documented in a forthcoming book (Kahr, 2021a). Back in the late 1980s, I knew none of that.

But Marion did tell me something about Winnicott which no one else had ever known or appreciated, namely, that this extraordinary king of psychoanalysis harboured a secret wish to write an operetta in the style of Gilbert and Sullivan (Milner, 1987c).

I must confess that I found Milner's musical reminiscence to be quite striking. Why on earth would Great Britain's most famous, most productive, and most path-breaking psychoanalyst yearn to be a composer and lyricist in the tradition of Sir William Gilbert and Sir Arthur Sullivan?

Milner did not elaborate much on this aspect of the man to whom she referred, rather intimately, as "Donald", having known him so well. But, in my subsequent archival researches in years to come, I uncovered a fair bit of confirmatory evidence which has supported Milner's reminiscence about this aspect of Winnicott's profound musicality (Kahr, 2021b). Winnicott did, indeed, derive much joy and inspiration from the wit and wisdom of these two magnificent progenitors of the English operetta.

I certainly cannot do justice to the significance of Winnicott's interest in Gilbert and Sullivan in this brief context, although I will, in due course, publish a study elaborating on this thematic in more detail (Kahr, 2021b); however, I can state succinctly that, in many ways, Winnicott's passion for Gilbert and Sullivan epitomised his love of play and joy and humour and wit – in a deeply serious manner – because, in my estimation, no two musical writers had ever encapsulated the seriousness of play more successfully than that pair of 19th-century gentlemen.

*

In 1986, shortly after the opening of the Freud Museum – the former home of both Professor Sigmund Freud and Dr. Anna Freud – I became the Deputy Director of the International Campaign for the Freud Museum, having chosen to interrupt my post-graduate studies for a year in order to pursue this unique opportunity to work in the Freud house and to help establish the museum in its early days. Naturally, I hoped that I might be able to invite Marion to the museum for a special private viewing.

As a young woman, Marion had attended seminars conducted by Anna Freud in the famous double-length study on the ground floor, but she had not visited 20, Maresfield Gardens, in London's Swiss Cottage, during Anna Freud's later years. Shortly after the museum opened its doors to the public in the summer of 1986, Marion did pay a visit as an ordinary tourist but, as she told me, owing to her failing eyesight, she could not see much of Freud's famous archaeological and antiquities collection in any proper detail, as she, like all the other members of the public, had to stand behind the cordon.

It brought me great satisfaction that in my new role, I could arrange a bespoke tour of the Freud Museum, just for Marion, and I even obtained permission from the head of security, Mr. Alexandre Bento, to turn off the burglar alarms for a short while and to remove the cordon in the study so that Marion could view Freud's priceless collection up close. And so, on 27 October 1986, I arrived at Marion's home at Provost Road in a taxi and I escorted her personally to Maresfield Gardens for this private viewing. Happily, Marion enjoyed herself immensely, and she especially loved walking around Freud's incomparable consulting room without any ropes to restrict her movements! Marion reminisced about having attended a particular seminar in the study many decades previously when the psychoanalyst Dr. Augusta Bonnard, one of Anna Freud's associates, delivered a paper. At that very moment, Marion brought the past back to life in such a vivid manner and she became a true messenger of the early history of psychoanalysis, resurrecting all of those wonderful, pioneering characters.

As Marion gazed at the objects in the study up close, she became particularly preoccupied with the small, lacquered Chinese statuette of an old Daoist sage, perched on the little card table adjacent to Freud's wooden desk (Davies, 2019). Upon seeing this piece of artwork, Milner (1986b) exclaimed with delight, "Oh look, he's got a little cap on". Marion's evident pleasure in this small detail of one of Freud's art objects reminded me of her whole philosophy of living, which she had outlined in her book, *A Life of One's Own* (Field, 1934), published some fifty-two years earlier – all about the ways in which we might find pleasure and engagement in tiny moments and miniscule details, thus embracing the canvas of life to the fullest.

I believe that I refrained from revealing to Mrs. Milner that this statuette of the Chinese sage, which Freud himself used to greet every day (Fichtl, n.d.), is actually a modern piece of art, not an ancient one (Gamwell, 1989), as many had suspected – unlike most of the other multi-thousand-year-old objects in the study – but, had I done so, I doubt that Mrs. Milner would have minded.

Marion's playful engagement with this little figure from Freud's collection produced a huge smile on my face. I remember thinking that, in all likelihood, many near-nonagenarians might be so jaded by life at this point that simply glancing at a tiny little statuette might have little impact; but Marion still had the great capacity to imbibe Freud's study and the objects contained therein with a lively, almost childlike, sense of wonderment, which inspired me greatly.

While ambling around Sigmund Freud's famous office with Marion, I told her that I had brought a copy of her book *On Not Being Able to Paint* (Field, 1950) with me to the museum, and I wondered whether she would do me the honour of autographing my inexpensive paperback version of her classic text. The original cloth publication bore the pseudonym of "Joanna Field" on the title page, but my edition, published in 1984 and purchased for £4.95, boasted the author's real name, "Marion Milner" (Milner (Joanna Field), 1984). To my delight, Marion agreed to sign my copy but explained that she would need to sit down in order to do so.

At that moment, she asked me whether she might perch herself on Freud's office chair and sign the book at Freud's desk! It seemed quite fitting and appropriate that this *grande dame* of British psychoanalysis should be permitted to spend a few moments in Freud's chair, and I, thus, bade her do so.

Marion then seated herself on the leather chair, specially designed by Felix Augenfeld, a friend of Freud's youngest son, the architect Ernst Freud (Augenfeld, 1974; Molnar, 1992: cf. Welter, 2012). Happily, Marion had a pen in her handbag, which she extracted, and then she began to write an inscription.

But just at that moment, a member of the curatorial staff of the museum came rushing into the study, no doubt having observed me and Marion on the security camera, and this vigilant colleague explained that owing to the tremendous delicacy of the Augenfeld chair, no one must be allowed to touch it, let alone to sit upon it. To my great shame, although I had worked at the museum for some months by this point, none of the curatorial team had ever told me that we must *never, ever* touch Freud's chair. (Indeed, the desk and chair would ordinarily be roped off, but, owing to Marion's exalted status, she and I did have special permission on this occasion to approach each object at closer range.)

I expressed my regret to Marion that I had allowed her permission to sit on Freud's chair without having appreciated that this might not be permissible. But, undaunted, Marion then kneeled on the floor and placed the book on Freud's desk and signed my copy thus: "For Brett with all best wishes and thank you Marion".

After Marion and I had explored Freud's study in some depth, the museum's convivial Press Officer, Mrs. Karen Booth, very kindly prepared a special tea for us on the unique, sunlit half-landing where Martha Freud, the *Frau Professor*, used to entertain her visitors. It pleased me greatly that my colleagues at the Freud Museum treated Marion so graciously and afforded her this unique opportunity to explore Sigmund Freud's consulting room at close range, and then, to enjoy a tea in Martha Freud's special space. I know of no other psychoanalytical practitioner who has ever received such royal treatment. During the tea, Marion spoke to me about a welter of topics, but I particularly remember her childlike pleasure in revealing that, often, during sessions with her own patients, she would "doodle" (Milner, 1986b), drawing copious squiggle-like figures on pieces of paper. I could not help but wonder whether such

Winnicottian doodling actually enhanced her capacity to concentrate on her patients' free associations or whether such activity might have distracted her.

Over the successive years, I had the pleasure of encountering Marion on several more occasions, not only at the Freud Museum, and at various psychoanalytical parties and book launches, but, most frequently, at meetings of The Squiggle Foundation. On one occasion, in 1991, I attended a lecture delivered by a very senior colleague, Dr. Martin James, a great friend of Donald Winnicott and a close colleague of Anna Freud. Marion sat in the front row, keen to hear Dr. James's thoughts on Winnicott's relationship to psychiatry. At the start of his very interesting talk, James (1991) singled out Milner for special recognition, which pleased me greatly. I suspect that the frequent Saturday meetings of The Squiggle Foundation gave Marion some important structure to her week as well as some richly deserved celebrity status.

Marion had become such a devotee of The Squiggle Foundation that the editors of *Winnicott Studies: The Journal of the Squiggle Foundation* published a special edition of this periodical in Marion's honour, complete with lovely tributes from such distinguished colleagues as Mrs. Sadie Gillespie (1988), Dr. William Gillespie (1988), and Mrs. Frances Tustin (1988).

In her final years, Milner began to lose her eyesight, and towards the very end, she became almost completely blind. In order to amuse herself, she would sit in her armchair, cutting up some of the paintings that she had made in previous years and then rearranged the segments into lovely collages (Walters, 2000). For her very last public outing, she visited Imperial College, part of the University of London, in order to study the newly unveiled bust of her deceased brother, Patrick Blackett, the distinguished physicist, who, in 1969, had become Baron Blackett, in Chelsea in Greater London.

Although quite a few of us presumed that Marion might well reach her one hundredth birthday – and she had talked to her friends and associates about the possibility of a centenary – she died peacefully on Friday, 29 May 1998, at the age of ninety-eight years, at her long-standing residence, 12 Provost Road, Chalk Farm, London N.W.3. Marion Milner may perhaps have lived longer than any other psychoanalyst in the entire history of the profession. I can think of no other practitioners who survived to such a grand old age.

As a young psychologist, impassioned by psychoanalytical ideas and keen to work in this field, and as someone obsessed with the rich history of this profession, meeting Marion Milner proved to be a tremendous pleasure and a memorable privilege. It never occurred to me that I would ever encounter someone who, as a young woman, had studied with, or fraternised with, some of the most significant pioneers in this field, including Professor John C. Flügel, one of Great Britain's very earliest psychoanalysts, who knew Sigmund Freud personally; Dr. Irmarita Putnam, who became Milner's first psychoanalyst and who had herself undergone analysis with both Professor Sigmund Freud and Dr. Carl Gustav Jung; Dr. William Healy, one of the pioneers of child psychiatry; Dr. Sylvia Payne, one of the queens of British psychoanalysis, who became Milner's second psychoanalyst; not to mention her supervisors, Mrs. Melanie Klein, Mrs. Joan Riviere, and Miss Ella Freeman Sharpe, let alone her subsequent psychoanalysts, Dr. Donald Winnicott and Dr. Clifford Scott (Dragstedt, 1998). Essentially, Marion Milner knew all of the founders and she shared her reminiscences

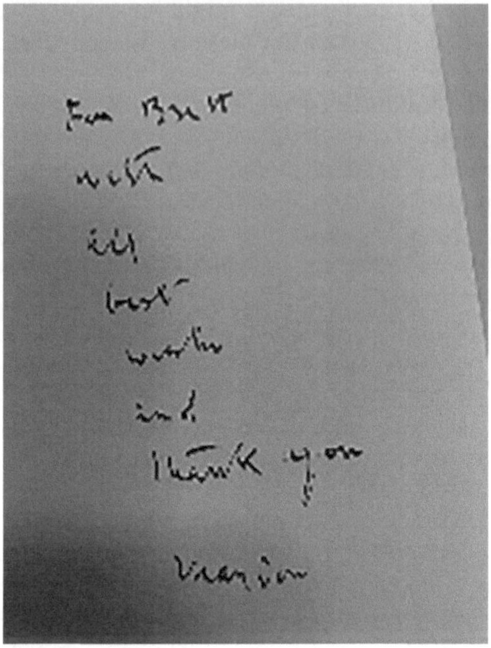

Figure 7.1 Book dedication from MM.

and the wisdom which she had internalised from these foundational fathers and mothers with a deeply open heart.

I consider myself immensely fortunate to have had the opportunity to spend time in the presence of such a truly lovely woman (Figure 7.1).

Chapter 8

Interview with Marion Milner (1990)

Deborah Anna Luepnitz

Preface

I had the pleasure of interviewing Marion Milner in her London home on November 23rd, 1990. At the time, I was planning to write a book about Donald Winnicott and Jacques Lacan and hoped to include interviews with people who had known or worked with them. I knew that Mrs. Milner was a colleague and friend of Winnicott's but wasn't aware until the interview that she had also been his analysand.

Mrs. Milner, age ninety, greeted me at the door on time, dressed smartly in slacks and a stylish vest with a red scarf, hair pulled atop her head in a pony tail. A few minutes into our conversation, she had trouble hearing me and said: "It is a *nuisance* not being able to see or hear well anymore!" I moved to sit quite close to her but worried it might feel like an impingement. She smiled warmly as if to say it was a good solution.

Before we began, she asked about my personal life and my training. She also wanted to know if I was involved in the *arts* in any way. I told her about the community theater to which I belonged, and the thrill of having recently acted in one of our Shakespeare productions. Again, this seemed to make her feel connected to her interlocutor. After the interview, she asked if I would like to see her paintings from the 1930s and 1940s. I was delighted, of course, and she led us into a room lined with dozens of canvases. We stopped first in front of a painting of two hens tearing each other apart, blood and feathers flying. Mrs. Milner said: "I like to say it's Melanie Klein and Anna Freud, fighting over psychoanalysis!"

The interview below is transcribed verbatim from audiotape. She asked that I leave out several items. Later on, she sent a short note saying: "The talk with you has in fact helped me to deal with my internal D.W., especially your remark about him being a difficult person to get angry with. Thank you."

She was later to describe their relationship at length for the first time, in her book, *Bothered By Alligators*, published posthumously in 2012.

Interview

MM: You are writing about Winnicott and Lacan. I don't know Lacan. What is it you find useful about him?

DL: It's a good question, and hard to answer in a few words, but I think he addresses *desire* in a way that no one in English or American psychoanalysis does. [pause]

DOI: 10.4324/9780429433535-10

I'm curious, having read the correspondence between the two men, did you ever hear Winnicott talk about Lacan – about his ideas or his conflicts with the IPA?

MM: No, I never heard Donald mention him, but I heard others talking about him and another fellow – Lagache – before they were expelled. It wasn't of great concern to me.

DL: May I ask what you think of Adam Phillips' book on Winnicott?

MM: I like it a lot. I think it's very good. He seems to be clear where Winnicott gets in a muddle.

DL: Yes, he doesn't idealize Winnicott.

MM: He doesn't, and I like that... Did you say you work with adults or children?

DL: I treat adults, and I also do a lot of family therapy.

M: That interests me. They do it at the Tavistock.

DL: Yes, they do some very good work there.

MM: Well, they do some very bad work, too. I sent a couple there, years ago, for marital therapy, and it was just awful – quite missing the point.

DL: Hmmm. How did you meet Winnicott?

MM: At a lecture. I was enchanted with Winnicott. He was so funny and so serious at the same time. Donald analyzed my husband. He was asthmatic, and I thought Winnicott would be the one who could do it. He came to the house when there was an asthmatic crisis. He once came to see my husband thirteen times in one weekend. And later, he analyzed me for a while, after my marriage broke up.

DL: I wasn't aware of that. I thought your analyst was Sylvia Payne.

MM: Yes, she was my training analyst, but after I qualified, I thought that Sylvia didn't understand what I saw as the *mad* side of me, and I said to Donald that I needed another analysis, and asked who I should go to. Surprisingly, he said – why not him? He thought he could analyze the mad bits of people, and I think he felt he was the only one who could do it. So this went on for a while, but it was really a disaster, very difficult, because I was already treating "Susan" [the patient Mrs. Milner describes in *The Hands of the Living God*] whom he himself had sent me, and she was living in his house. His wife, Alice, had met Susan through her work and had brought her home to live with them. When the marriage got into trouble, it affected Susan terribly, who would come to my couch and talk about how badly the two were getting on and might split up. It worried her so much she had to be taken in by a friend of theirs and brought to me in a taxi every day. I was having to hear all these things about my analyst. It was such a mistake, and I finally said I couldn't go on with it, and he said, alright, and I ended up with Clifford Scott, who said, "This is a travesty of analysis."

DL: How long did your analysis with Winnicott last?

MM: Almost four years. The thing is, we never talked about it much. We became friendly. He used to come here, to my house, and I would lie on this couch, and he would sit there. My house was between his home and his consulting room, so he came here to save me the time of going to his office; it was a kindness, as I was just beginning my practice. Anyway, we probably should have discussed more what happened.

DL: I wonder why you *didn't*. I wonder if Winnicott was hard to get mad at.

MM: Yes. But I'm also not very good at anger. Anyway, Donald always did feel bad about it. I knew that, later on, years later, he said I was a "casualty" of analysis, and that he would feel guilty about me to his dying day.

DL: Do you know what became of Susan?

MM: She rang me the other day; she just celebrated her seventieth birthday. She's been with her man for forty-three years.

DL: Was she ever mad again?

MM: Oh, no. By the way, she wasn't *schizophrenic*; I had such a row about it with the publisher. They used that word in a blurb, saying that in America, it was used more loosely. She was *schizoid*. I had to pay to get it altered!

DL: Where are Susan's 4,000 drawings?

MM: I think I still have most of them.

DL: Do you still paint?

MM: I do collages, using my old paintings. I cut them up; I'm recycling myself!

DL: Brilliant! By the way, who else was analyzed by Winnicott that you know of – besides you, and Margaret Little and Harry Guntrip?

MM: You know Margaret Little wrote a book about it; I encouraged her to do it. Also, Enid Balint was analyzed by Donald, and Masud Khan, too – but his was a disaster. He was being seen by Donald, and he really needed it. Then, he got married, and his wife got depressed and became suicidal... So Khan asked Donald to accept Jane instead of him, and Donald agreed and dropped Khan. It was a disaster. Khan never really had a full analysis with anyone else, and it was central to the rest of his problems, I think. Instead of getting analysis, he went every Sunday morning to Winnicott to edit his papers. It's beautifully done, but he was never even asked to stay to lunch. Clare didn't want him to. Anyway, he eventually had twenty cancer operations and just became worse and worse. And then he came out with that book [*The Long Wait*] that made everybody angry. I put it down. What did you think?

DL: I didn't like it. [pause] Adam Phillips and others criticize Winnicott's lack of attention to fathers.

MM: It's true.

DL: Are there analysts you know who are paying more attention to fathers in psychoanalytic theory now?

MM: Well, there is Michael Eigen in New York. Do you know his work?

DL: I do, actually, but not on that subject. I must pursue it! [pause] Mrs. Milner, Winnicott said something like, "I can't say I had analysis with Joan Riviere, although she analyzed me for ten years, and continued to do so in scientific meetings after that."

MM: Yes, Donald would say something like that. I didn't like Joan Riviere, either. She supervised me at Donald's suggestion. We didn't get on very well.

She once said to me, "Well if you don't do what I say, what's the good of you coming?"

DL: Oh, dear. Well, what else can you tell me about Winnicott during the time of your analysis?

MM: One day, when Donald left after one of our sessions, I saw that he had taken three matches and an elastic band, and made a beautiful crucifix out of them – the central match was the body of Christ, with the match bent so that the head was bowed down. I thought he was really saying something about his marriage. I thought he was telling me something about himself, don't you?

DL: He wanted you to know he was in tremendous pain. I can see how complicated this analysis must have been for you. By the way, can you tell me more about Alice?

MM: Well, I am told that before they were married, her brother, Jim Taylor, said, "She's mad, you know." But she was a good artist. I hear; I never actually saw her work. She was *fey*, I think.

DL: What did she look like?

MM: She was a bit fat when I knew her. I remember the two of them next to each other looked so odd – she, so large and he, so small. I didn't know her well. Susan was fond of Alice. But the marriage was a disaster.

DL: Winnicott's impotence is now the worst kept secret in psychoanalytic history.

MM: It's quite true, according to Clare.

DL: The first marriage, I learned in another interview, was annulled on the basis of non-consummation.

MM: I didn't know that, but he was impotent. Clare said she cured him of it. But he wouldn't leave Alice for a long time, despite it all, and Clare was so exasperated. Clare said to me he was like a wet blanket during that time. He simply would not take a stand with Alice. I said to him once, "I think you'll die if you don't leave Alice." I was afraid he'd have another heart attack.

DL: Is it the case that he waited to divorce until his father died?

MM: So I am told. His father would have been very upset about the divorce.

DL: Was Alice analyzed?

MM: I don't think so. I am told that she said she heard things – heard messages from the birds' songs. Of course, that kind of thing can be poetic, too. [pause] Well, what is it that the Lacanians have against the British school? What are the areas of difference?

DL: Well, one has to do with what they think of as a kind of reductionism on the part of object relations theory – making the early relationship with the mother determinative of adult "mental health."

MM: What do they put in place of the mother-infant bond? The self?

DL: No. They don't speak of the "self," but of the "subject."

MM: The subject. Very abstract. Do you like the idea of the True and False Self?

DL: I have to admit it's very compelling to some patients, but I don't like it. Maybe it's the capital "T" and "F." And you, Mrs. Milner?

MM: Well, I didn't like it, but I'm coming around to it a bit more. Perhaps you and I would accept it with a small "t" and small "f."

DL: Another difference between Lacanians and object relations analysts has to do with the question of sexualities. The French see the British as anti-Freudian in their emphasis on heterosexuality. The Tavi people I've spoken to talk about homosexuality as a perversion, and the perversions as though they were evil.

MM: Well, some people at the Tavi are not very good.

DL: But it's not just individuals. It's policy in the British Psychoanalytic that no homosexual man or woman can become an analyst.

MM: Is it? It really is? But there are homosexual analysts.

DL: Anyway, this is one thing that got me interested in Lacan, because the value of psychoanalysis is to go beyond conventional moralizing on the question of object choice, and of the erotic, in general. As we were saying earlier, Winnicott didn't devote much of his writing to these questions, and Lacan certainly did. At the École de la Cause Freudienne de Paris, there are no such prohibitions, and there are gay analysts who practice.

MM: Well, there are in Britain, too. [pause]

DL: Do you still see patients?

MM: I stopped two years ago.

DL: By the way, as an analyst, did you talk a lot?

MM: I talked less and less.

DL: Is there anything in particular about Winnicott that my questions haven't covered that you want to mention?

MM: Well, I might like to add that he was quite a brilliant theoretician; I still find his papers fascinating. But his clinical work was, at times, disastrous. He had problems unhooking people from the transference. He was a funny mix of conventionality and unconventionality. At Paddington Green Mothers and Babies Clinic, he'd jump over the electric fence after seeing his patients out, just for fun. In other ways, he was conventional – a bit of a Tory, I think.

DL: Yes, he wrote an article on feminism in 1967 in which he put all feminism down to penis envy!

MM: Did he talk about womb envy? I think there was a lot of that in him.

DL: Hmm. Did your experiences as an analyst in this particular community, years ago, make you feel that the men envied your creativity, your strength?

MM: I never felt like a strong person.

DL: I'm surprised. You were not only prolific, but you wrote, in *A Life of One's Own* about taking charge of your life, long before the avalanche of self-help books.

MM: But I didn't feel in control. I felt *used* by the ideas. There was something in the air, and I was writing. One is an instrument. Does this make any sense?

DL: Yes, yes... [pause]. Do you have children, Mrs. Milner?

MM: I have a son who is a physicist, now working as a Fellow of the humanities, making connections with universities in Eastern Europe. And I have two grandsons, one a biologist and one a doctor. [pause]. Well, I'll be interested in your book, and hope I'm alive when you finish it.

DL: Somehow, I can't feel the shadow of a doubt about it. [pause]. Mrs. Milner, may I ask you how you felt yesterday when Mrs. Thatcher resigned?

MM: Me? Ecstatic. Some friends came over, and we had a whiskey. And you, how did you feel?

DL: We had champagne.

Chapter 9

'Tea' with Marion Milner (1996)[1]

Linda Hopkins

In the context of interviewing people for my biography of Masud Khan (Hopkins, 2006), I wrote to Marion Milner to ask if we could meet—and she responded with an invitation to tea. This was an exciting invitation for me because I was a longtime admirer and also because she had known Khan since the 1940s. Along with Sylvia Payne, they had taken painting lessons in the late 1940s at a Polish art school, and after that she had been Khan's supervisor and then a loyal friend. Khan had helped Milner to improve the second edition of *On Not Being Able to Paint* (see Letley, 2014, p. 80) and he was personally responsible in many ways for the publication of *The Hands of the Living God* (see Hopkins, op. cit., pp. 137–138). Khan is a controversial figure in the world of psychoanalysis, but Milner did not turn on him when he fell out of favor due to his misbehavior and his alcoholism, and indeed she accepted for analysis an analysand with whom he had begun a live-in relationship, Khan thereby breaking one of the deepest taboos in the field. Milner believed that every person has internal "madness" that is potentially destructive, and she would not dismiss him as an "other." I was eager to hear what she would say about his "madness."

As things turned out, Milner at age ninety-six, a year and a half before her death, did not have much to say about Khan. But like many old people, she was eager to tell me stories. She had talked about her history with other analytic historians (e.g. Robert Rodman, Janet Sayers, Deborah Luepnitz)—but since every pairing of people is difference, I had my own experience with her. In this paper, it is my intent to give a somewhat subjective account of what she was like, at her advanced age, with me, at this late afternoon "tea."

The interview

It was a cold grey day (November 25, 1996) when I arrived on Milner's block of Provost Road. There was a row of attractive brick homes with gardens, all with white gates leading to the front walkway. Only one gate was different—it was bright red. This was number 12, the home of Marion Milner.

Milner answered the bell quickly and I saw before me an old lady, bent over and moving slowly. I was struck by her lively and sparkling eyes and by her ancient beauty. She had paid careful attention to her clothes—black pants and a rust-colored silk blouse with matching scarf. Later I learned that she was known in

DOI: 10.4324/9780429433535-11

London for her brightly colored clothing, which revealed artistic sensibility, and also suggested that she was different from the "usual" analyst who tended to dress conservatively.

As we walked into the living room, Milner showed me several oil paintings of landscapes that she had painted. Except for the paintings, her home was quite ordinary. A gas heater warmed us in the musty space just outside of her kitchen. [See Letley, Plate 13, 2014, for a photo of the room that closely matches my memory.]

It was 4:30, time for tea. The ritual that I had experienced with other interviewees in London was that the host would pour carefully prepared tea into small china cups, with the tea regularly replaced to keep it at a perfect temperature. In addition, butter cookies or other sweets would usually be served on top of a doily placed on a china plate. This tea time, however, was different. Milner asked me if I would join her in drinking whisky. Surprised but also pleased, I agreed. She went into the kitchen and brought back a tray with two small glasses that were painted with pink roses, the kind of glasses my grandmother had used for serving orange juice, glasses that must have been around since the 1940s. I was delighted to drink whisky out of those glasses with her.

As we began talking, Milner announced that she would be ninety-seven years old in just a few months and she warned me that she was hard of hearing. I actually did not find her to be hard of hearing, which surprised me, because a friend in the States and advised me to not even try to talk with her because she was too deaf.

In general, I found Milner's mind to be quite sharp. She was curious about me, filled with questions even as she was eager to tell her stories. She particularly wanted to know if I knew Michael Eigen, the New York analyst and writer, whom she seemed to adore.

In interviews for my research, I always brought a gift. For Milner I brought a box of soft chocolates and also something that I considered to be very special. It was a picture of several different kinds of red shoes arranged on shelves, a picture I had found in a magazine and reproduced on stiff paper. The picture was a reference to Milner's *A Life of One's Own* (1934) in which she described her attempt to put into words and study the "best" experiences of her day. I had remembered from a long ago read how, on two different days, her mind had been preoccupied with red shoes: first with how to find a pair that fit and then with how nice her new shoes looked all day. In her diary entry of January 11, 1927, she wrote: "I've discovered where a great part of my thought goes. I was thinking about my new frock and red shoes." This was a small part of the book, but she had put into words something that rang true to my own experience, and I had remembered the image of red shoes over the decades as an example of how ordinary things could brighten an entire day. In anticipating our meeting, I imagined that Milner would find the picture humorous and pleasing.

So I gave her the chocolates, which she liked, and then handed her the picture. She looked at me in surprise, not understanding the significance. I told her, "These are red shoes just like you described in your book!"—but she still had no idea what I meant. I now think that her incomprehension was in part a sign of her age, but perhaps also because red shoes had not been as central to her as they were to me. When I was a young woman reading the book and trying to integrate feminism with psychoanalysis, the admission of a great analyst that she cared about her shoes had been quite freeing to me. But that is *my* story, not hers. We wisely dropped the topic and continued talking. (I wonder what she thought about that picture after I left!)

We then had a short discussion of Khan, whom Milner described as "a beautiful and gifted young man," referring to him in the time before he became mentally and physically ill. (His deterioration was from the late 1960s until his death in 1989.) She quickly went on to talk about her disappointment in her analyses with Sylvia Payne and Winnicott, how Winnicott had analyzed her in her living room, the same room where she was analyzing Susan, the patient from *Hands of the Living God.* Susan lived with Winnicott and his first wife, Alice, at a time when their marriage was ending, while Winnicott was having an affair with Clare, who would later become his second wife. Milner said that the dual relationship with Winnicott was too hard for her, so she ended her own analysis in order to be able to continue seeing Susan. Most of this was news to me, but I have since discovered that she spoke about it with other interviewers, and I will repeat just a few anecdotes:

> The analysis with Winnicott went on for at least four years and it didn't really help me. I think Donald saw the same problems in me as he had in himself… [But] there was one thing he told me that I found especially helpful. It was in a session when I had been talking about my niece. She had been telling me about her friend who had a three-year-old daughter and also a new baby. The friend had walked into the baby's room and she saw the three-year-old standing over the cot with a lump of wood, as if she was going to hit it [sic]. That night, in the middle of the night, I developed angina in my jaw, and it was quite painful.
>
> In analyzing the jaw angina, Donald told me that he thought my sister had hated me when I was a baby, and that she had looked down on me in the cot with hatred. I think he is right about that. Winifred, my sister, and I are very close, so I had never thought of that.
>
> The analysis with Winnicott was a failure. Once, after we had ended, he said to me, 'You'll be on my conscience until my dying day.' But I never asked him why he said that! I think it's because there was no use of the countertransference in the analysis—that's what I needed, to find my 'madness'. I needed to experience my own aggression, which is so split off. It's linked with my sister's hatred.
>
> I envy the people in analysis now, because today's analysts know how to find the aggression and work with it.
>
> [Note: With this comment, she may have been thinking of Michael Eigen.]

[Responding to my comment that Masud Khan's analysis with Winnicott also seemed incomplete (Hopkins, 1998)]: "Yes, I agree that Masud's analysis with Donald was a failure. It was a failure because Donald couldn't handle Masud's aggression."

Rodman (op. cit.) and Letley (op. cit.) describe sexual tensions between Clare, Donald and Milner during this turbulent period. Masud Khan believed Milner was jealous of Clare. But Milner said that Clare was jealous of *her:* "Clare competed with me. I once told her, 'I could never have married Donald.' She didn't like that at all." And Milner told me that *Khan* was jealous of *Clare:* "Masud and Clare were always competing for Donald. Masud used to say, 'I can't bear Clare telling me one more time that she made DWW potent!' " It seems that Winnicott himself may have been somewhat unaware of all this turbulence. Milner told me that when she decided to end her analysis in order to see Susan: "I cried and cried. Donald said to me, 'I didn't know that you cared so much.'"

Another story from the Milner-Winnicott analysis illustrates the richness of analytic symbols, as well as the impossibility of understanding what anything "really" means in analysis. Milner refers to a session she had with Winnicott in her home:

> In one of our sessions, Donald was playing with some matches and an elastic that were here on the table. He made them into a beautiful little crucifix. There were two matches for the cross and then he bent one forward like Christ, with the head hanging down. A rubber band held it all together. He left it here and I always thought he was trying to tell me something.

This story has been repeated elsewhere with various interpretations. Milner's interpretation to me was "I think it was about his marriage to Alice." She is referring to his unhappiness, which she had heard about from Susan. I privately recalled Masud Khan's interpretation of the cross story. He had written (undated correspondence with Robert Stoller) that Milner was always looking for perfect connections, including sexual connections, and that Winnicott "knew he was crucified in a hopeless predicament [with Milner]." I thought later that Milner might agree with Khan.

Milner obviously had intense ambivalence about Winnicott. She told me that, while in analysis, she often criticized Winnicott—but never to his face, only to her friends—for inventing words when he didn't need to. And she was openly contemptuous to me regarding one of his well-known comments, made to Clare, that his greatest fear was that he would never have another original idea. Milner's opinion of this was: "What's the big fuss he [was] making? It was his omnipotence that made him have that worry."

Upon reflection, I think that Milner's discontent with her analysis in some ways reflects her psychological health. Nobody who is in touch with their "aliveness" and the depth of the unconscious mind ever feels fully analyzed. Throughout her career, Milner had valued experiences of uncertainty and change, and her adherence to this way of thinking is seen in the final story that she told me:

> Masud told me that I was one of the cases in Winnicott's book *Playing and Reality* (1971). I was described as 'someone with an unpredictable mother.' I told him, 'But Masud, my mother was totally predictable!' Then, in the 1980s, my mother told me something I had never known: that she had weaned me at four months because she had a breast abscess. So I had to think about everything in my past in a totally new way, starting again from the beginning. But one always has to do that.

Conclusion

After telling me the above story, Milner suddenly said: "I'm very tired. I must stop now." She had been perfectly alert for over two hours, but now she looked totally exhausted. I said good-bye immediately. As I walked out, filled with thoughts and feelings, I was once again impressed by Milner's red gate, which stood in bright contrast to the white gates of the other houses on the block.

As an overall impression, I cannot do better than to quote the words of Bob Rodman (2003), who talked with Miner in 1996 and on other occasions. He gives a perfect summary: "She was a beautiful woman, even in her nineties, graceful, alert and responsive, if in obvious decline" (p. 139).

Note

1 Portions of this chapter are based on L. Hopkins, "Red Shoes, Untapped Madness, and Winnicott on the Cross: An Interview with Marion Milner," *Annual of Psychoanalysis*, 32: 233–244, 2004. Those portions of the chapter are reprinted with permission from the Chicago Psychoanalytic Institute.

Chapter 10

My friend, Marion Milner

Adam Phillips

(Conversation with Margaret Boyle Spelman, London 1st May 2019)

M: Adam I've been eager to have your voice included in this book on Milner for many reasons but particularly since coming to know that you knew Marion. So could you say a little about how you came to know Milner and could you tell me a little about your time with her, what it was like to be with her and what she was like in all aspects, what it was like to be in her company?

A: Yes, I first came across her work through Masud Khan who was my training analyst. He recommended that I read her. And once I started reading her I really loved the writing and felt a really strong affinity towards it. I had never come across writing quite like that at all and so I read everything she wrote that was available. Then sometime after this I gave The Annual Squiggle Lecture [October, 1992] at the Squiggle Foundation which as you know is a Winnicott-based group. So I gave the lecture and sitting in the front row there was a rather beautiful old lady in an orange trouser suit. So at the end of the lecture this woman comes up to me and she says, with no flirtation, with no portentousness, very straightforwardly, 'I knew after reading your Winnicott book that you would look like that'. And it was rather wonderful, extraordinary because it was very direct and it was true; that is what she thought. I said something like 'Oh, what's your name?' and she said 'I'm Marion Milner'. Of course, I was astounded because she was a heroine of mine and I'd never come across her. So, I said to her 'I am a fan of your writing'. And she said to me 'Would you be willing to come and talk to me about Winnicott?' and I said 'Of course'. So, there was a period of, it may have been a year, I cannot be sure as it was a long time ago, when I would go on a Saturday afternoon, and we would drink whiskey because she liked doing that and I was more than happy to do it. We would talk freely about all sorts of things, but she did want to talk to me about Winnicott and this went on for about a year. There weren't lots of meetings but there were certainly at least 6 or 8 – it was extraordinary, wonderful and we felt an affinity for each other. As I was thinking about this interview I was remembering that there were three very striking things in this affinity: One was that Marion Milner when she was a girl wanted to be a naturalist and so did I; the first passion of my life really was birds and animals and plants and so on. So that was rather extraordinary! Then there was one moment in the first meeting when I said to her – and I can't remember what we were talking about but – I quoted something from D.H. Lawrence. I said something to her like, 'I don't know if you know this but D.H. Lawrence said "I have three ideas about

DOI: 10.4324/9780429433535-12

educating children; leave them alone, leave them alone and leave them alone"'. And she beamed and she said that's one of my favourite quotations. It was one of those things, one of those meetings. And then further on – and I mean there are a lot of things about Marion's work that I found interesting – but I was very interested in her ideas about the nothing, about emptiness, because – and I had only relatively recently started writing – my experience of writing was that there was nothing in my mind and then there was something and I wrote it. It is not as though I experienced myself as being full of ideas and thoughts. I didn't. But when I started writing they turned up. So even though like everybody else I could infer an unconscious and unconscious processes, the actual experience was that something came from nothing; Marion was very, very, interested even though she believed in the unconscious, she was very interested in the primary process. She did also genuinely have a quasi-mystical idea about 'the nothing' that we are and how things come out of that nothingness. And that was exactly my experience and it was rather wonderful. I think I felt – well, I felt a great fondness for her – but it was really an extraordinary piece of luck for me that I met her because I did feel a like-mindedness. I found the idea of something coming from nothing very heartening, and her endorsement made it realer for me. Of course, we were very different people with different backgrounds, histories and so on and so forth. And even though I loved Winnicott and was very, very, interested in his work, Winnicott was a bit too empirical and a bit too much a doctor whereas Marion would quote Blake, she was reading Blake and as you know her bibliographies are extraordinary. They are weird and wonderful; and so I felt in her presence that there really was free-floating attention. We could both speak very freely and I certainly felt that I could say anything to her and I think she felt something similar with me. And her initial agenda was that she'd had some analysis with Winnicott and she was extremely admiring and fond of him and all that – so it wasn't anything like a character assassination – but she had been left with real misgivings about him and the misgivings seemed to be about what she described as his omnipotence, his sense of himself as a kind of magical omnipotent person. And that she felt – and this wasn't her word – that there was something a bit megalomaniac about the way that he behaved. She felt that she had gotten a huge amount from him, there was no question. But she also felt but he was rather overwhelmingly omniscient; that he idealised his own intuition, as though he himself was a piece of magic. And she was wary of that, I think. She thought omniscience was the saboteur of aliveness. I think that she had felt – there were various things she told me – at one stage for example, Winnicott analysed Marion in Marion's own consulting room; it was done for reasons of practical convenience but she, at least in the period in which she was talking to me – felt that this was very inappropriate. Also, Susan, the famous patient from 'The Hands of The Living God' lived with the Winnicotts during some of the treatment. And again Marion's view then when she spoke to me was that Winnicott was rather interfering and it was as though he wanted to – as it were – get in on the act. Now clearly he had done a wonderful thing by taking her in, there is no question about that; but I think that what Marion seemed to feel, in the period of her life when I met her, was that Winnicott had been a bit of a usurping presence. And given one of the things which to me is one of the great things about Marion Milner was her capacity to 'use' – in the best sense – things and people for her own development, so she could incorporate things from all over the place. She had a very, very, strong sense of affinity and relevance and of what worked for her. I think that she felt to begin with that Winnicott was an extraordinary find – and that she could really use him in the best Winnicottian sense – and then over time that he got more from her then she got from him. I don't know how one could assess it but that was her sense of it.

M: Yes, okay. When you were speaking about your experience of writing, it sounded very like what she has written about painting.

A: Very, 'On Not Being able to Paint', for example is a great book about writing and it is also a great book about painting and about not being able to do things; she was and is in a very unique way really interested in how people make futures for themselves and how things can be allowed to unfold. I remember her saying to me once – because she was also very funny about herself, very ironic about herself and very ironic about wisdom, though she was, in fact very wise, she said to me (and she has also written about this) – she said 'When I am painting a tree I look at everything except the tree'. And I thought that was fabulous and this is probably one of the things that matters most to me about her work; she's really interested in the capacity for absorption and what it is to concentrate.

M: Might I just interrupt, as I think that you have gone on to talk about one of my next questions; I was going to ask you to speak about Marion's distinctive features. I wonder what you think her distinctive features are, in her writing, in her thinking, in her practice, in her way of being?

A: Shall I elaborate it a bit?

M: Please.

A: I think a distinctive feature of her writing is: it is written, in the best sense, in plain ordinary language. It is accessible but you also feel that she is – in the best sense – making it up as she goes along. It is literally unfolding as she is doing it. So, it is not as if she has all these ideas and she is now going to write them down for us. I am sure that that is partly true but I think that things occur as she writes and it feels like that; you feel as you read her work that something is unfolding, in her and then in you, the reader.

M: And she has written about that.

A: She has. And she is clearly working something out in the writing. It's a bit like what Keats said; 'that which is created must create itself'. *She is always creating herself.* I think that's wonderful. Also, it seems to me that the aim of the analysis is that the person develops a capacity for absorption, and for wanting to go on creating themselves. And that of course is a very, very, interesting aim because it's not about getting cured, it's about actually finding what absorbs you and being able to be absorbed, wherever that may lead. One of the wonderful things about this as an aim is that it is completely open ended. It predicts no future it simply says you have to find what absorbs you and you have to go with it if you can bear it. So, you can see with Susan that Marion is always analysing the obstacles to her capacity to forget herself; and so in her version of analysis – in my version of her version – the aim is to be able to forget yourself. It is not about self-knowledge, it's about what are the obstacles to your forgetting yourself.

M: And is that in some way to do with your connection to your surroundings?

A: Yes, I think very much so, and this presumably is where the Winnicott connection comes in, which is that you can only forget yourself if you are in a sufficiently reliable and sympathetic environment. Remembering yourself in this story is simply remembering your defences.

M: Okay, so to be in a position of defencelessness.

A: Yes, to be open, to be able to be receptive without being too anxious. To be receptive means not being omniscient.

M: So, is there anything in that that translates into her technique?

A: I think that one of the things that Winnicott implicitly suggested – and I think that Marion Milner was very good at this – is that there is a sense in which you could imagine doing analysis without there being any resistances, because the resistance is all in the phrasing. So, the art of psychoanalysis is in finding ways of saying sometimes difficult things in a way that people can hear and possibly even enjoy. Now what strikes me about Marion Milner's technique – although technique is not the right word – is that she is really not worried about 'who is doing what to whom'. She clearly believes in the sense in which the idea of boundaries is in itself a fantasy. Once you forget about boundaries all sorts of things can happen between people and within people. So, I think that she is very, very, good about this with Susan; in a sense she and Susan are the same person and they are different. And that is why it works. I don't know about this in the actual treatment because I wasn't present but it seems to me that she has *an amazing capacity to both identify and dis-identify at the same time* so that she can really be with somebody and separate; so there can be exchange and communion.

M: Okay. I wonder if you agree with Milner's description of her professional self in 'The Suppressed Madness of Sane Men' when she says that rather than going in a linear thread that she felt herself to be like a tree with several branches.

A: I think that it is a much better analogy because it is not linear and because it is recycling all the time and it's not going in a known direction. There is another very interesting thing about her work and her descriptions of analysis; that there are multiple directions. And she says that the one thing that you mustn't do in an analysis is try and cure people. And that is the point because if you drop cure what have you got? Well what you've got is the unknown quantity (and quality) of what people are capable of doing together and so it is like a whole new story about sociability.

M: So, before we leave this area of Milner's distinctive characteristics is there anything else that you want to say there?

A: Well in terms of what it was like being with her, I mean she really was fun. She was very amusing. She was very ironic. She really wanted to have a good time. She wasn't earnest at all. She wasn't worthy or virtuous in that sense. She wasn't exactly mischievous but she was certainly game for a laugh. And you could see that she backed her own pleasure. There were paintings everywhere, mostly hers and she would sometimes illustrate things by looking at her paintings. So it was very, very, free flowing. It's very hard for me not to idealize this because it was so pleasurable. And it was so – it wasn't revelatory – but it was so wonderful being with her and especially for me *then*. Because I went into the world of psychoanalysis knowing nothing about it. And I met a lot of very grim and moralistic bossy people. The good people of course were fabulous and I'd never met people like this and Marion was one of the good people. And so as a young person one gravitates to the wonderful elders.

M: She came quite late to psychoanalysis.

A: She did.

M: And it seems quite seamless the way she was and how she wrote before the psychoanalysis and then after. It's as though she absorbed it and went on.

A: Yes, it's almost as if she invented psychoanalysis for herself, then went into it and then carried on doing it. So, in a sense psychoanalysis was incorporated. Another great thing about her for me was she wasn't a sort of devotee of psychoanalysis. She was really interested in it and it was a kind of romance but it wasn't a religion for her. It was one of the things that she could use to do the things that she wanted to do.

M: Thank you, we are flying through my questions. I wanted to ask you about something: You are Winnicott's first biographer and foremost translator but you knew this woman as well. So, I thought that it is really important to get your 'take' on that relationship. The first thing that I was wondering about was about their thinking – you've touched on this already – but do you think that there was mutual influence between them because when I was first writing, I wrote as though Milner was Winnicott's analysand. And then I realized as I wrote that actually these two people were colleagues and I felt that there was a mutual influence; what do you think about that?

A: I think that is right; that it is better or truer – or whatever the word is – to think of this as like a field. That this was a very unusual group of people – and I think that Khan was part of this but of course he was younger. But I think certainly Winnicott and Milner and then Winnicott, Milner and Khan, were a kind of inter-animating group and that there was often – in Milner's sense – not many boundaries. And so they were having each other's ideas. Because you can read that though their styles are very, very different, there's tremendous overlap in terms of the basic ideas and the basic assumptions and basic enjoyments. So I think that this was a group of people with an unconsciously shared project that they were elaborating that was as it were their version of psychoanalysis. It wasn't quite object relations and it wasn't quite not object relations and it wasn't Klein but it was influenced by Klein and it was Freudian but it was a really radical revision of Freud.

M: I am wondering about the time that you met Marion Milner and if you think that there was a relationship of one sort between Winnicott and Milner and then there was the analysis that is not reputed to have gone at all well and then another sort afterwards.

A: I certainly got the sense that that was true. What she conveyed to me was that to begin with when she used to attend his Paddington Centre consultations, that he was a very inspiring and admired figure; he was very mixed as an analyst and then a very good colleague and they were kind of bound up together. But what she couldn't integrate into her relationship with him was her disillusionment. And I think that it was very tricky, partly because she was very fond of him and wanted to protect him given that he was much criticised by Kleinians. So she clearly didn't want to be adversarial but there were disillusionments. And the disillusionments went to the heart of something for her. They weren't just irritations and misgivings, they went to the heart of something crucial for her which is something to do with the real dangers of, the temptations of omniscience, of self-idealisation. Because in a way, her work, if you wanted a formula, and this isn't one, but if you wanted a formula; her work is against grandiosity. That is why it is so freeing. Because it doesn't really believe in character it believes in something else.

M: I interviewed some people who knew Marion in her last years and when she was writing 'Bothered by Alligators' she was very sad, especially around that chapter that she wrote about Winnicott.

A: Yes, I was seeing her when she had just finished that book and she asked me if I would edit it and my misgivings were that it was about her son and she had misgivings about this too. I said that I couldn't do it wholeheartedly because it was about her son, so I felt that she should find somebody else to do it. And she was very perturbed because obviously it was a real question. But the woman I met was sad but she certainly wasn't only sad and she was very alive.

M: She was sad on that issue of the relationship with Winnicott.

A: Yes, exactly. She was sad on that issue. I think, and I'm totally making this up, but I think that she was sad that she didn't have more children – but that's totally my fantasy. That's really none of my business.

M: So now we come onto the purpose of the book and thinking about Milner's legacy. But before getting into details of her legacy, do you think that she suffered a relative neglect as a psychoanalytic thinker; Winnicott's papers are always in the top ten of the PEP web and her books were out of print for quite a long time?

A: It's very hard to know because if one talks about relative neglect it is as if one's got an idea about what people should be reading. And I don't know that. My sense of this is that, and it's not that she's a cult writer, but she is the kind of writer and theorist – if she is a theorist – that appeals to very particular people. So I think that there is no way that she could be popular or be one of those strong psychoanalytic voices. I mean for me she is almost the one. For me with psychoanalytic writers, Milner and Pontalis would be my two and then Winnicott – and there are a lot of good ones. I think she's an acquired taste or she is a 'something'. You've got to tune into it. It's got to be your 'cup of tea'. But I think that for the people for whom her writing works, it *really* works. And – perhaps like you – I think she should be on syllabuses. I think that she should be taught because her work it is full of stuff. It's very unrealised in a way. It's very inspiring if you happen to be inspired by her but of course you've got to hear it first. And I think that it may be that what she has suffered from is not having enough inspiring teachers, people who could teach the text in ways that were engaging.

M: And I wonder was her work ever taught. Yeah, that's an interesting idea, just the teaching of it as a way of it getting out there.

A: Exactly. How was it disseminated? If you think about the way in which it was disseminated… I would never have read her in my training if it weren't for Khan. I would have read her out of interest but in my training it certainly wasn't on my reading list. And I had never heard of her when I came into analysis. But that seems strange when you read her because when you read her you think 'God, she's at the centre of something!' Or you think 'She is a really inspiring figure!' but I think it's in the best sense a modest project and Winnicott seems to me to be extremely ambitious. I think Marion wasn't. She wanted to be found without being exploited.

M: I wonder if it's that she is crossing genres and crossing genres that do not necessarily go together; like her ideas about mindfulness for instance which has been taken on by cognitive behavioural psychologists. And she does that and she does that in a seamless way along with psychoanalysis.

A: Yes, I think that's dead right. I think the thing about her is that she is almost too interesting a writer. For example, she also writes autobiographically. There are so many mixed genres because it's her idiom; because no one else writes like that.

M: And do you think – I mean Winnicott didn't write autobiographically and he was popular within psychoanalysis – was that too far of a reach for people within psychoanalysis?

A: Yes, I think that it is possible. In a way she might have suffered from her era – she wasn't enough of a Kleinian, although clearly Klein influenced her. She wasn't a Freudian in the sense that she was more of a mystic than a sexually preoccupied person although she writes very, very interestingly on sexuality. She's not an empirical scientist, she's not a doctor and she is quoting Blake. Well from a certain institutional point of view this is cranky stuff – she refers to the wisdom of the East, Zen Buddhism, Taoism etc. And for the powers that be – who want respectability – this is too 'off the wall'.

M: You may have thoughts on my next question: Are there lessons that she leaves for psychoanalytic practice or for our thinking or for our living well?

A: Lots, lots. And it relates to your previous point and to what you were saying because in a way that question has never been addressed properly. She hasn't been sufficiently well taught or taught.

M: The question of her lessons?

A: Yes, the question of her lessons. And my prejudiced view is that anybody interested in psychoanalysis couldn't help but get a huge amount from her writing – both by the practice of it and ways to think about it.

M: Well my final question is to see if you have something else that you want to say here or is there something that you think that I should have asked?

A: I feel like – this is an exaggeration – but we could talk for hours about Marion and I was very aware as I was thinking before the interview and this is what we were talking about: Actually, Marion was really important for me – but I never speak about it, not because it's a secret but because no one's asked me about it! And it makes me think as we talk, of the extent to which she has been radically underestimated. She has been really under-read. And there should be a course on Milner's work in every training for the people who are interested and I think that it could lead in all sorts of directions.

M: Okay, I do actually have another question: She wrote eight books. One on adolescent girls' education, one on a twenty-year case history, one on painting, four introspective diaries – this is my description – and a collection of her papers. Do you have a favourite?

A: Well I've got a lot of favourites. 'A life of One's Own' is fabulous. 'On Not Being Able to Paint' is wonderful. I think 'The Hands of the Living God' is the best psychoanalytic case history that I know and of course in 'The Suppressed Madness of Sane Men' there are so many interesting things. But I think that she is one of the very few psychoanalytic writers who make you feel that everything that she writes is interesting. Her writings may not all be equally interesting but they are always interesting.

M: And you wrote the new introduction to 'The Hands of the Living God', what was the experience of writing that like for you?

A: Yes, I was just thinking about that. It was really good because with 'The Hands of the Living God' Khan had told me about the original version of 'The Hands of the Living God': Marion turned up at Khan's flat with two carrier bags full of case notes and together they edited it into the book that we now have. And he said that it was amazing because it was very chaotic but from the moment he started reading the stuff, he thought that it was incredible. So, I knew something of the genesis of it.

M: So, Khan was the original editor.

A: Khan was the original editor… I thought that the introduction to that book was from my point of view one of the best things that I've ever written. It was partly because just in re-reading that book and re-reading all the rest of her stuff, it really recycled my interest in her work and how interesting I knew her to be. And I felt that it was really worth doing. I was really pleased to be asked and really pleased to be able to write it. Because it was a bit of a homage to her but it just also really made me realize how much there was in that case history and how much there was for me. And of course like all of these things, its long so some of it is boring as is true of a lot of great books, they have boring patches in them. But it does not alter the fact that there is so much in that book.

M: Okay, so I am glad that we got back to that and Adam, it's been a pleasure thank you.

A: Before we finish is there anything else that you want to ask me about this or that has occurred to you while we've been talking?

M: I was wondering, as you were talking about the teaching of Milner, how you might do that. I was thinking of how extraordinary 'The Hands of the Living God' is. I mean it's a twenty-year psychoanalysis using drawings and it would be a really big project, actually.

A: Yes, and that might be something that one might do at the end of a training because it's hard, it's also hard. Whereas if you start with 'A Life of One's Own' it seems to me that you start with somebody discovering psychoanalysis for themselves before they do it. Or, and, in 'On Not Being Able to Paint' – I mean it's obviously not a book to summarise – but 'On Not Being Able to Paint' is about 'on not being able to do things' and therefore it is just infinitely interesting and relevant to so many different areas of people's lives. And then you would have to get into the papers because my guess would be that with her work, if it takes, people will read everything but in order for it to take somebody has got to be able to show people, who don't take to it easily, what is good about it.

M: And I even wonder if anybody takes to it easily. There is a certain way in which you read yourself into it.

A: I think that that is right. Exactly. And maybe that's the point at which people need help; to learn *how* to read her and just how to get into it, how to be able to get into it. Have you taught her?

M: I haven't. I have spoken about Milner but not taught her. Okay. Thank you, Adam.

Section II

Clinical applications

Marion Milner in the psychoanalytic consulting room

Introduction to Section II

Clinical applications: Marion Milner in the psychoanalytic consulting room

From her diaries, we know that already during childhood Milner was interested in human experience, especially her own subjective encounter with the world (and writing about it). Then having first made herself her own subject of self-analysis and clinical scrutiny, she became an incredibly skilled, dedicated and curious clinician.

The following chapters are personal accounts, locating her in her consulting room, whether as analyst or supervisor.

In **Chapter 11**, through her own experience of training as a psychoanalyst at the British Psychoanalytic Institute, Joan Raphael-Leff provides *a mise-en-scene* for Milner's professional environment and the psychoanalytic community in London at the time in which Milner trained, worked as a psychoanalyst and remained receptive to ideas of generations of trainees that followed hers.

In **Chapter 12**, Andreas Giannakoulas tells Margaret about his enjoyment of his own third analyst with Marion Milner, and then of their subsequent friendship and endeavours with psychoanalytic colleagues.

In **Chapters 13 and 14**, two of Marion's early patients, both psychiatrists, and one also a psychoanalyst, speak both of their analyses with Marion and of their experiences with Donald Winnicott—one as a child patient and the other as a supervisee. In their verbal accounts, the warmth and holding of Milner's clinical presence was palpable all these decades later in the affection and esteem with which she is held in memory by both.

In **Chapter 15**, psychoanalyst Juliet Mitchell muses on Milner's special qualities as a supervisor in her late seventies. Referring to her original process notes, Mitchell speaks of the supervision as a true conversation, vividly remembering how Milner looked at the patient as well as listened.

In **Chapter 16**, psychoanalyst Leon Kleimberg writes about his experience of Milner as supervisor when she was in her nineties. He too found her both authentic and intimate in her approach, helping patients express their psychic experience, with an important departure from 'the here and now' technique at the time. He tells of the joys of watching Milner connecting to, and playing with, his young son [whose picture appears on the book cover].

Bringing us up to date, in **Chapter 17**, psychoanalyst Maia Kirchkheli discusses Marion Milner as her created/found companion/support during the COVID-19 pandemic, with whom she conducted an inner dialogue as she conjoined the elements of creative process, body and psychoanalysis while treating her patients remotely.

DOI: 10.4324/9780429433535-14

Chapter 11

'Access to darkly hidden powers'—the context to Marion Milner's psychoanalytic training and clinical work

Joan Raphael-Leff

Having graduated from University College London in 1924 with a first-class degree in psychology and physiology, Marion worked as an industrial psychologist and received a Rockefeller scholarship to work with Professor Elton Mayo in the US in the aftermath of his Hawthorne experiment. Two years later she returned to England, and after the birth of her son in 1932 she wrote, published and until 1939 worked for the Girls Public Day School Trust (see Chapters 27 and 28).

So, when, at forty, impelled by her personal discovery of psychoanalysis Marion chose to become a clinician, she did so as a psychologist, original thinker, and established author, researcher, painter, and mother. The British Psychoanalytical Institute was the sole available training in England. However, for a person of her multi-talented capacities it was a providential choice. Unlike many other IPA-approved training institutes around the world, from its inception it had welcomed non-medical ('lay') candidates—which provided a rich interdisciplinary mix of social science practitioners and others from literary and artistic backgrounds, with a commensurately less hierarchical and male-dominated structure.

Furthermore, it undertook introduction of Psychoanalysis to the English-speaking public—in addition to a treatment clinic for 'needy' patients (established in 1926), it housed the *International Journal of Psychoanalysis* (founded by John Rickman and Ernest Jones). And the *International Psycho-Analytical Library* (which renewed, was to publish Marion's own book) as well as Freud's newly translated Standard Edition, all printed by Hogarth Press, a home-based enterprise belonging to Virginia and Leonard Woolf.

Perhaps due to such close connections with this gender-subversive Bloomsbury group, even within the first generation of members, women held official positions of leadership, including Susan Isaacs and Marjorie Brierley, and Marion's first analyst Sylvia Payne; her supervisors Ella Sharpe, Melanie Klein, and Joan Riviere (Winnicott's analyst). Some also held professional positions elsewhere (e.g. Institute of Education; Tavistock; Cassel; Maudsley) and brought their psychoanalytic thinking to a variety of themes ranging from women's issues of abortion, menstruation, and female periodicity; the psychology of fashion; eating disorders; drug and alcohol addiction; stammering; and children's games and play.

The emerging training in child-analysis produced a flurry of written psychoanalytic contributions on developmental issues and emotional ramifications of childbearing and childrearing, education, and social change seen through prisms of mythology, anthropology, literature, and linguistics.

DOI: 10.4324/9780429433535-15

A rich diversity of 'continental' approaches added to the uniquely British combination of pragmatic empiricism and scepticism (Rayner, 1991), since, due to lack of training analysts, first-generation British candidates travelled for their (albeit brief) analyses to Vienna with Freud, or Abraham and Sachs in Berlin or Ferenczi in Budapest. Along with wartime émigrés, they brought back variations of psychoanalytic ideas and praxis that formed the foundation of later tripartite groupings, which was to affect training of future generations (only abolished during Don Campbell's presidency in the late 90s).

Marion qualified as both adult and child-analyst in 1943 and became a Training Analyst in 1946. Although she felt she had been somewhat 'rushed through' due to the war, undoubtedly this second generation[1] was exposed to the most formative experience—the turbulent '*controversial discussions*' following Freud's death in 1939 (see King and Steiner, 1991).

Over a period of eighteen months across 1942–1944, as the world descended into madness a bombs fell outside, analysts met in London to debate fundamental differences between Melanie Klein and Anna Freud, each supported by powerful women colleagues wearing formidable hats (a scene described to me by my supervisor, Paula Heimann).

Three distinct perspectives emerged from this searching debate on infantile endowment and psychic formation. Despite these differences, true to Milner's own notions on 'toleration of conflict' (published in January 1943), the British Society did not split but reached a 'Gentlemen's Agreement' (between three women) to maintain separate trainings at the Institute. From 1952, this was augmented by training Child Analysts at Anna Freud's Hampstead Clinic in Maresfield Gardens (where Marion later recalled stumbling around in the wartime black-out when her torch failed). Unusually, she maintained cordial relations with members of all schools of thought, partaking of their teaching.

Elsewhere, I defined these groupings as hallmarked by their foci: an Anna Freudian focus on *inter-structural* forces (and evolution of the ego to mediate between conflictual internal structures and accommodation to external ones); a Kleinian *intra-psychic* emphasis (an innate ego, with internally generated unconscious phantasy and narcissistic projections), and 'Middle Group' stress on the *inter-psychic* origins of the self (and emergence of the subject from 'symbiosis' to internalised self-object relations).

I proposed that the divergent melding of theory and practice evolved by these groups rested on conceptualisation of early developmental processes which in turn, dictated the corresponding maternal, and by analogy, therapeutic, input. For instance, Klein's baby, seen as instinctually driven by projected sadism and envy, was coupled with a (biologically determined) pre-conceived maternal object irrespective of her qualities. This differed from Anna Freud's baby's anaclitic love for transposable care-providers (a view she changed in the war-nurseries), which differed again from Ferenczi's infant's primitive loving relatedness towards the 'found' object (who will inevitably disappoint). His neonate was assumed to be in a state of 'fusion' rather than narcissistically self-engaged, imperiously demanding ('his majesty'), hell-bent on destruction or fused with an omnipotent (phallic) or idealising mother. I further suggested that a tacit equation between baby-carer and patient-therapist drives each treatment model and technique, including specific anamnesis, procedures, and outcome goals of the analytic relationship (see Raphael-Leff, 2013a, 2013b).

A period of consolidation followed in which the cross-disciplinary approach played a crucial role in generating theoretical change. To the Ferenczi influenced British Middle Group including Milner, the psychoanalytic *relationship* was the crucial mutative factor. Influenced by Suttie, Winnicott and fellow 'Independents' Fairbairn, Guntrip, and Balint elaborated a paradigm of an infant's mind as *inherently dyadic*, thus replacing the tacit psychoanalytic goal of 'autonomy' with lifelong 'interdependency' (Raphael-Leff, 2023).

Winnicott's domain of combined Paediatrics and Psychoanalysis expanded the Object Relations shift in emphasis from the authoritative Oedipal father as seminal influence to primacy of the pre-oedipal nurturing mother. Drawing on over 60,000 mothers and children he had seen at two state hospitals, he famously declared in 1947 at a Society meeting: 'There is no such thing as a baby!' [without a caregiver].

This Independent group of which Marion Milner was a founding member became noted for its emphasis on environmental factors, seeing aggression as a reaction to frustration and early traumata. And they stressed the mutative benefits of a benign regression within the (dialogical) psychoanalytic process (see Kohon, 1986). Soon after qualifying, Milner too realised that work with a deeply disturbed schizoid patient like 'Susan' necessitated revision of classical technique (see Chapter 25).

By the time the British Society moved in 1951, from Gloucester Place to its magnificently painted-ceilinged new home in New Cavendish Street (built in 1776, and previously the town house of Lord Mansfield, he of Kenwood House)—a new era was fermenting.

Ernest Jones' long overdue retirement from Presidency in 1945 instigated a time-limit restricting any office to three consecutive years. Sylvia Payne was duly elected President. The Institute curriculum was revised to include postwar expansions of technique. Many clinicians worked in the recently established National Health Service, in existence since 1948. Jones' three-volume biography of Freud was finally published in 1953, and the earliest of Freud's twenty-four volumes emerged (newly translated by James Strachey with Anna Freud's help and approval).

Hoping to improve society via psychoanalytic thinking, the interdisciplinary Imago Society was founded by Milner, Adrian Stokes, and others in 1954. Membership included Bion, Meltzer, Money-Kyrle, Gombricht, Ehrenzweig, and Wollheim. Marion, a founding member of the Independent group, was also invited to join the '52 Club' that continued to meet regularly at Pearl King's home (Milner's erstwhile patient and supervisee) for over fifty years, and still meets today.

Enriching, controversy infused the British Psychoanalytical Society's agenda.

In fact, in his presidential opening speech on the occasion of the 50th Anniversary celebrations (30.10.1963) Bion noted that given the 'peculiarly lonely and isolated' nature of psychoanalytic work 'lively, controversial' discussion was essential as it 'provides the growing points from which our work starts' (p. 16). And grow it did!

Winnicott's remarkable acknowledgement of maternal ambivalence negated idealised mothering His reference to similar issues of 'hate in the countertransference' (1947) paved the way for further innovation. Later, innate sociability and need for security were empirically confirmed by Bowlby's Attachment research methodology. Further research corroborated Milner's view of fusion as an illusion, and better understanding of the dual nature of unconscious constructions was to follow, when feeling hamstrung by Kleinian orthodoxy, after her ground-breaking 1950 designation of countertransference as the *useful* corollary of transference Paula Heimann 'defected' to the Independents.

As a longstanding member, to my mind what primarily distinguishes this 'Group of Independents' as it is now known, is a toleration of *not-knowing* that renders understanding and interpretations provisional. Across the spectrum of our many differences we have a capacity for what Keats called 'negative capability'. Perhaps it was this very open minded tentativeness that appealed to Marion and many others. Over the next decades, under several Chairs the Independent group consolidated its presence to become the largest group in the British Society.

The groups became increasingly insular. However, a third generation of psychoanalysts was emerging. During the heady epoch of the 1960s and 1970s social revolution was in the air we breathed. Within a counterculture of individuation, anti-nuclear campaigns and student rebellion fomented by Anti-Vietnam questioning of authority, availability of the newly invented the 'pill' liberated sexual norms, unleashing a second wave of Feminism that clearly necessitated a revision of psychoanalytic notions of 'female sexuality'. Scepticism and insurgencies grew. When I began my own training in the UK[2], 'Swinging London' formed the backdrop—a cultural hotbed of dramatic transformations in the fields of art, music, and education accompanied by flamboyant fashion and widespread use of psychedelic hallucinogenic drugs (as Milner's two patients in Chapters 13 and 14 attest). Raised consciousness was the stated goal in the 1960s and Marion Milner's passion for enhancing the capacity for inner observation fitted the times.

Meanwhile, heavily influenced by psychoanalyst Ronnie Laing (Milner's erstwhile supervisee), an 'anti-psychiatry' movement was fermenting. Questioning the prevailing orthodoxy of medical models of diagnosis, ECT, and biological treatments for psychosis it built on a paradigm shift towards *collaborative* work with patients, pioneered in the postwar years by psychoanalysts Tom Main, Wilfred Bion, John Rickman, and Heinz Foulkes instigating Therapeutic Communities, Group Analysis and Day hospitals. The first of these, the Marlborough Day Hospital was to be my new workplace. Marion's book, *In the Hands of the Living God* published during this time, reflected her own original clinical experimentation, seeking new ways of fostering 'self-curative forces' in her patients.

The quest for change also spilled over into the Psychoanalytic Institute. We candidates established a student organisation and made demands for modification of the teaching curriculum (deemed 'infantalising' and 'straight-jacketing'), as well as preliminary negotiations for a Professional Register.[3]

Due to this our training differed considerably from the heated wartime training Marion Milner experienced, and from the lava-cooled postwar version. In 1973, a fresh Curriculum Committee Chaired by Pearl King acknowledged they were conceding to pressures for change from three sources (students, seminar leaders, and 'newer educational objectives and attitudes' in schools, universities, and postgraduate institutions) (E/73). Our new training included Lecture Courses 'arranged around [contemporary] psychoanalytic topics and problems, rather than around specific contributions and papers'. Clinical Seminars and choice of Study Groups were no longer necessarily segregated by groups or level of qualification. Looking through my papers from that time, I see that our teachers included Nina Coltart, Herbert Rosenfeld, Pearl King, Harold Stewart, John Padel, John Bowlby, Masud Khan, Dinora Pines, Anne-Mare Sandler, Hanna Segal, Donald Meltzer, Betty Joseph, Henri Rey, John Klauber, Eric Brenman, Isobel Menzies, Edna O'Shaughnessy, Elliot Jacques, and others. Although she did sometimes teach on dreams and other subjects, Milner's name is not on the curriculum at this time. Many trainees came from overseas, a trend which has continued to this day.

I had several babies while training leading to my specialisation in reproductive issues, combining academic and clinical work with mothering and qualitative empirical research. My focus was on the emotional turmoil of pregnancy and early parenting. With increasing refinement of equipment neonatal research flourished and became more psychodynamic, switching focus from an individual baby to the interpersonal exchange (see Emde, 1981) which supported the dialogic view of the Independents. Frame-by-frame micro-analysis of filmed interchanges clearly demonstrated not only alert social responsiveness, mimesis, and initiation from birth but complex cross-modal reciprocity within the embodied interactional matrix, akin to Milner's evolving ideas.

Due to her longevity, Marion Milner encountered several further generations of psychoanalytic candidates and saw many innovations of theory, training procedures and technique. Into her old age she continued at times to attend select Wednesday Scientific Meetings at the British Society, where she sat quietly near the front, perhaps because of her increasing deafness. I have no memory of her intervening but on occasion when I found myself giving her a lift back to Provost Road, would animatedly discuss points on the way home.

On her 90th birthday, the Independent group celebrated Marion as a founding member whose rich multi-modal oeuvre in word and image had so expanded our theory.

This book is another homage to her extraordinary contribution to so many fields.

Marion Milner died on May 29th 1998 and never visited Byron House, the Institute's new home in Maida Vale which now houses her archive. But given her persistent

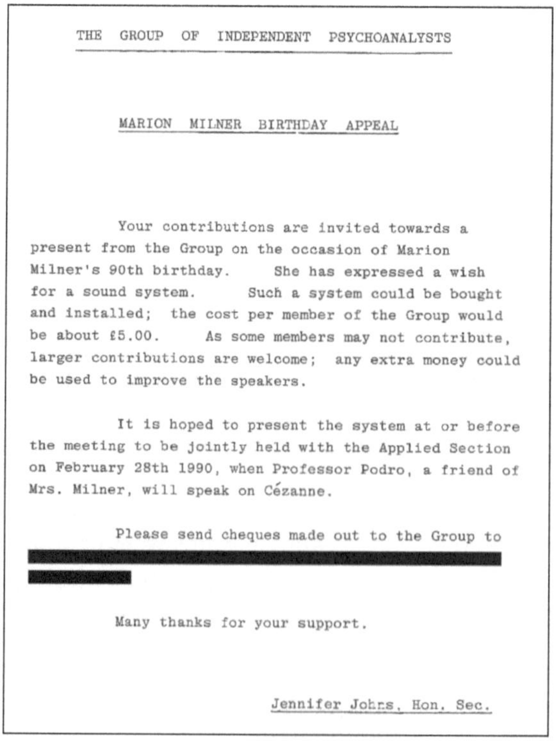

THE GROUP OF INDEPENDENT PSYCHOANALYSTS

MARION MILNER BIRTHDAY APPEAL

Your contributions are invited towards a present from the Group on the occasion of Marion Milner's 90th birthday. She has expressed a wish for a sound system. Such a system could be bought and installed; the cost per member of the Group would be about £5.00. As some members may not contribute, larger contributions are welcome; any extra money could be used to improve the speakers.

It is hoped to present the system at or before the meeting to be jointly held with the Applied Section on February 28th 1990, when Professor Podro, a friend of Mrs. Milner, will speak on Cézanne.

Please send cheques made out to the Group to [redacted]

Many thanks for your support.

Jennifer Johns, Hon. Sec.

Figure 11.1 Independent Group's collection for MM

questioning, I believe she would have been pleased that in the spirit of change, a major controversy in the year of her death (around the invited lecture by homophobic Soccarides) culminated in further revision of psychoanalytic theory, and acceptance of openly homosexual candidates in a Society which paradoxically, given its emphasis on truth-seeking and transparency, had driven some eminent friends of hers into secrecy.

Looking back on the evolution of Marion Milner's own explorations and expansion of psychoanalytic theory and practice over the many decades of her work, I would hope that similarly *wonder, curiosity* and *pliability* power the searchlight by which we continue to inquire. I trust that inspired by the courageous way she strove to illuminate minutia of preconscious experience in herself and others, further generations of open-minded analysts will exceed their own training by imaginative reverie, pursuing elusive ever-changing dynamics of imagery and bodily expressions of affect. Paradoxically, through inner dialogue and experimentation Marion Milner democratised creativity – enhancing our own access to 'darkly hidden powers' to exteriorise interiority.

Notes

1 Four of these 'generations' are represented in a book I co-edited with Rosine Perelberg, the current President of the British Society (Raphael-Leff & Perelberg, 1997, new edition, 2008).

2 On a scholarship to study in the USA I spent 1963–1964 in Alabama, to partake in the emerging Civil Rights movement. After the 1967 six-day war in Israel, with degrees in psychology, sociology and English literature, I completed my postgraduate studies there and at the London School of Economics, beginning psychoanalytic training in London in 1970, while studying autism at the Medical Research Council's Social and Cultural Research Unit at the Institute of Psychiatry.

3 Although psychoanalytic training standards were monitored by the IPA and in my day a Handbook was issued to every Associate, a strict code of ethical rules was only gradually consolidated over later years with formal Regulation negotiated by the next generation. This rests on heightened awareness of implications of the power imbalance between practitioner and client, eschewing any physical intimacy or prejudice (such as disgracefully displayed by Masud Khan, Milner's one-time supervisee, fellow artist, editor, and colleague). Importantly, to protect confidentiality, patient consent is required in any publication.

Chapter 12

'My Analyst Marion Milner'

Andreas Giannakoulas

(Telephone conversation with Margaret Boyle Spelman July, 23rd 2009, Rome)

Preface:
Having made arrangements by email to telephone him, I first spoke to Andreas about the study that I was completing for my PhD and the fact that I would like to record the call. He agreed and asked me to speak a little bit louder.

> *It will be obvious that for this interview my main interest at the time was in Milner as Winnicott's analysand. Then, in the course of the interview, that I got two pleasant surprises, and was so happy that at last I was speaking to an analysand of Marion Milner's!*

Interview

A: I would rather prefer to talk freely and then you could extrapolate what you think is useful...

M: It's just that if you give me references and things...rather than taking notes.

A: You will have to talk slowly because after my analysis with Marion I live in Rome. Anyway, well let's see. I would like to help you but I don't know in what way.

M: Alright. Actually, I did not know that you had an analysis with Marion I thought that you were supervised by her.

A: No, I had an analysis with Marion for seven years.

M: Oh, very good. That's so much better for me because I did not have anyone for my study who was analysed by Milner.

A: Marion was my third Analyst. And I went there at a time when I was already myself and analyst... And it was important because I felt totally free and I could talk freely. I never enjoyed an analysis with somebody else the way that I did with the analysis by Marion Milner. Because it was a free kind of exchange.

M: And what years were they?

A: ...Oh, it was before and after 1980...It was three or four years before 1980 and for two or three years after; 1976–1983. I was already an analyst. I was already an ordinary member (of the British Psychoanalytical Society).

M: Did you train with the BPAS?

A: Yes, I started with Rubinstein who was an analyst of the Freudian kind of tradition. And I was accepted into the Institute at that time belonging to Anna Freud's group who was I suppose, what I call 'neo-something'...Rubinstein was his name... I think he was analysed by Anna Freud. Then he died at the Vienna Congress and

DOI: 10.4324/9780429433535-16

I changed analyst and group and I went to analysis with Masud Khan. My second analysis was with Masud Khan.

M: Oh, that is very good because in my construction of things he also would be part of the Winnicott group, the family.

A: Well I qualified when I was in analysis with Masud... And then I became an associate member and then an ordinary member. But then I started to teach in Rome University and I was commuting between coming and going. My wife and two children were in Rome. We all lived in Rome. I was doing my seminars in Rome University every second week. At that time [that I] entering analysis with Marion [that] was more or less at my own request. My supervision was with Pearl King who was analysed by Marion and with Paula Heimann. Paula Heimann ...was admiring of Marion Milner... She would often say things to me from Marion's work, she knew Marion's work.

Here Andreas explained that Marion was seeing some people for their second and third analyses at that time. She was seeing Charles Rycroft in this way at that time and he was often the session before Andreas and that he therefore 'prepared the couch for him'. AG laughed at his younger self for having fantasies that Marion preferred Rycroft.

Then because my interest at that time was primarily Winnicott-focussed, I asked Andreas if he knew Winnicott and he told me that he did and that for many years he 'was one of the people who went to seminars, the encounters in Winnicott's house' and was a rather good friend of Clare Winnicott and that Clare was very good friends with Marion too. He said that they formed a 'very select group to go on with Winnicott's ideas and work' and that after he died, it included Giannakoulas's and Winnicott's friend, Martin James, Clare Winnicott, 'Kit' [Christopher] Bollas and others. It was a group that was 'starting to create the possibility' for what subsequently became the Winnicott Trust. Then he said that Clare was alien to the idea and they stopped meeting. I said that I had listened to Martin James's lecture as Chair of The Winnicott Trust in 1992 and Andreas said that Martin was brave with his discovery of premature ego development and that Winnicott acknowledged this contribution. I then asked Andreas about where I might get his own writings.

A: ...I gave some papers in England...I gave two papers in the European Federation meetings on borderline engagement and hysteric predicament and as you may know Marion was very much involved, in a very fine way, with borderline references, with fusion and de-fusion...In all my papers I use Marion's ideas and thoughts. Recently – and that's my main tribute to her – I made a film with Blake's illustrations of Job. That is the main thing that I wanted to communicate to you (laughs) because that was my tribute to Marion...

M: Okay, so you have made a film... is that film published yet, is it on release?

A: Well if you would like to know more about it, Marion when she was ninety-four she came here and she remained with us for more than a month in Rome. And (laughing) it really was like a marvellous time because every night she would say to my wife 'what are we going to do tonight' and she wanted to go around Rome like a teenager – that was Marion's way of being. But she gave a lecture at the university and it was about the sense of nonsense, you know this paper, it is in

The Suppressed Madness of Sane Men, it's about Blake's reference to Job. It is one of the main papers...And she gave this lecture at the university. It was very well attended and received but she was trying to show Blake's illustrations. They were very small slides and the people there were rather frustrated that they couldn't see what she was talking about. That was the point... it was what actually made me think about this work very many times after that. I was talking with her and saying 'What shall we do in order to present better slides for you?' Then she told me that the publication was difficult because it cost a lot to print illustrations, with the printers and editors.... And that was a starting point. Then I started to give lessons at the university on the same work of Blake and Job... Some of my collaborators and students, they managed to put ...pictures of the original illustrations on the computer, and then we started to work three years ago together with Italian television. It took a lot of time because it was very difficult to match Blake's, Marion's ideas with my own ideas about this marvellous paper of Marion's 'the sense of the nonsense' she was calling it... We were very lucky because it was a very good film director and a very good photographer and we worked together – there are twenty-one pictures – it is very nice work and I presented it when I was in England, and my British and other colleagues were very satisfied with this presentation. And I have a CD and let's see how we will arrange it because perhaps – it's not sure – but Bernard Barnett told me.... that I might like to present it to the Squiggle Foundation... I think that it is closed for the summertime but after September I will know.

M: So you are going to go to London to present the film?

A: I think so. I already showed it in a closed meeting 'The Copse' it's called. There was Mrs. Laufer and Laura Scharpf who was supervised by Marion... she was one of the best supervisees of Marion Milner – she wrote a paper on Marion...

I asked Andreas about these people and the papers and he told me that he intended to send on more information. He also said that he was preparing a book with some papers on Marion Milner. The book was also to contain a paper by Laura Scharpf and Nina Farhi.

A: You know the article of Nina Farhi. Nina Farhi was one of the best connoisseurs of Marion...more than every other person. Nina's papers were superb...the best of all of us...

M: ...And Nina also knew Winnicott.

A: Well, Nina also knew very much, Winnicott and Masud Khan. But unfortunately she died some months ago... So for the moment it is very difficult ...

But I have some of her articles because I also organised a Winnicott congress here and she presented on Marion's work...I organised three international Winnicott Congresses. They were all of them here and Marion sent me a beautiful letter which I can show you...

M: You have been absolutely immersed in their work and then brought their work to other people.

A: Well a lot of people were inspired by Marion ...and some of them picked up her ideas without acknowledging that they were Marion's ideas...including Winnicott.

M: Yes. I even noticed that myself.

A: Well when I am saying that people may jokingly say that I may have wanted to be the only one who picked up Marion's ideas but (laughs) I see that it is not only me. Even Winnicott did that. She was a very original thinker, you know. That's the destiny of the original thinker...

M: If you could pick out some characteristics that would best illustrate her thinking...

A: I think that you will find that in terms of theory, I think that she was using less psychoanalytic jargon and that made her ideas much more available outside psychoanalytic society and larger. And because of that some people felt that they could use her ideas without quoting her. Some of her ideas were very original. In terms of psychoanalytic importance and theory I think that 'the book of Susan' [is important]. I wrote the introduction to [the of] *The Suppressed Madness of Sane Men* for the Italian edition ...I am talking about Marion...Her book of Susan is a masterpiece of analytic ideas...that nobody else will ever write and include other people, all of us in their daily work with Susan...

> *Andreas again considered here if it would be possible to send me his papers but said that what is most important is to consider Marion's work and to consider it in a different way. He said that he was sorry to tell me that and on reflection I think that he was being critical here of the fact that at the time I was speaking to him because I was primarily considering Marion because she was Winnicott's analysand. I think Andreas would have considered this to be a reduced view of Marion.*

A: ...But you see *On Not Being Able to Paint* was translated here in Italy in a bad translation...My wife is a painter and as I told you Marion was here and we had a marvellous time and we want to translate the book in the right way. It took us ten years, only now we are in the process of re-translating the book in the right way, even the title was wrong... 'On Not Being Able to Paint' ...is like Freud's work on dreams. She is free associating about the images as they emerge...As far as I am concerned, after 'The Interpretation of Dreams' we did not have a single book of this kind of self-reflection, of analysis, of free association and symbolism etc... And that was a pre-analytic book of Marion's...of the other pre-analytic books there are several kinds of references...

M: ...I am thinking of the two other books she had – before training and after, one called *A Life of One's Own*...

A: Yes, and then *Eternity's Sunrise* comes later... But anyway the analytic ideas they are one by one in the chapters of *The Suppressed Madness of Sane Men* and...in the first chapter, the capacity to tolerate doubt, it's an extraordinary paper... The paper on symbol formation is one of the papers very much used by everybody but not acknowledged...Hanna Segal's work is secondary to Marion's work on symbolism etc.... Yes, it is difficult to pick just one reference from her work...on her reflection on dreams and in my comments on Job I am more or less going along with Marion but I am saying that the dream experience – in one of the pictures of Job – is a profound change that is connected with Marion's comments about dream experience. There are very many original ideas. It's difficult to put them together. Let's hope that we have another talk...

M: Yes... *(here we spoke about the fact that most of AG's work is not yet translated from Italian and made arrangements for him to email me references and then I included*:

If you think that Marion influenced Winnicott in any particular ways perhaps you will let me know those?

A: Everybody asks me that...for the moment I will tell you what is honest and much more practical and useful for all of us; to say that there was no doubt about it that there was a tremendous fertilisation between Marion and Winnicott ...and it is difficult to pick up who was fertilising whom. But I think that they were two extraordinary minds with mutual influence. That is the correct way to put it.

M: You know that there is a remaining unpublished book of hers. I think that it has got the title *Bothered by Alligators*, the one that she was writing when she died...

A: It is about her son...Marion told me...she was inspired by what she wrote when her son was a small child but that is very confidential *(Andreas was speaking at a time before the book had been published).*

M: I have spoken to two women painters who knew her when she was finishing that book and they were saying that she wanted the book to be published.

Andreas, honouring Marion, may have been uncomfortable with this as it was before the book was published – and he asked if I could write to him about that. I then thanked him and we said our goodbyes.

Preface to Chapters 13 and 14

Marion behind the couch

Margaret Boyle Spelman

This chapter and the next one, are based on my interviews with two of Marion Milner's patients: Peter Bruggen and Andrew Malleson.

Both men spent their working lives as well-published and high-profile psychiatrists. They also had links to Marion Milner's colleague and second analyst, Winnicott.

One of Milner's patients met Winnicott as his child analyst when he was newly sent to boarding school aged four years old. The other was supervised by Winnicott while himself training as a psychoanalyst and in training analysis with Milner.

It is particularly fitting that these patients appear in this book on Marion Milner as it was during my prior focus on Winnicott (Boyle Spelman, 2013a, 2013b, Boyle Spelman and Thomson-Salo, 2014b) that I first became aware of, and then progressively more interested in, Milner's own substantial contribution to the psychoanalytic project, rather than seeing her simply as Winnicott's closest collaborator.

I interviewed both these patients of Marion Milner when they were in their seventies. Excerpts of the lengthy interviews are included here not only to illustrate Milner's unique way of working clinically, but to locate her work into the context of her times.

Context

Historically, the period following WWII was also the aftermath of turbulent 'Controversial Discussions' (1942–1944) between Melanie Klein and Anna Freud (see King and Steiner, 2005) which the majority of Members of the British Psychoanalytical Society had lived through. This meant that for the next twenty-five years until a turning point was reached, each individual psychoanalyst's clinical technique and beliefs about earliest development of the mind were very much affected by loyalty to their respective theoretical affiliations. Both Milner and Winnicott belonged to the 'Middle' group, later termed the 'Independents'. Both are described here by these two psychiatrist-patients as open minded, non-hierarchical and more receptive to interdisciplinary cross-fertilisation while also disseminating psychoanalysis into other fields.

Both men were in analysis with Milner during the London's 'swinging 60s'—a time of flamboyant appearance and psychedelic hallucinogenic drugs. Both these patients speak here of their experimental and therapeutic experiences with LSD while in analysis with Marion Milner—independently of their work with her (and legitimately, at the time, within their medical community).

Furthermore, it is noteworthy that these analyses took place in an era preceding professional statuary regulation of psychotherapeutic practice. Today's regulations clearly eschew the type of intersecting multiple complex relations which Marion Milner herself found in her own analysis with Winnicott, and with one of the patients interviewed here.

In Chapter 14, this second patient also provides a poignant example of the emotional experience of parentally deprived children of Milner's class who often were sent to boarding school at a very early age. This puts her own relationship with John and her 'blindness' to 'the intensity of his anger' at separation' (Milner 2012) into a different perspective.

Through a combination of direct extracts and important facts coming from my transcripts of the interviews I will now focus on the subjective experience of these two men's analyses with Marion Milner and of their experience of Winnicott including any mutual influence or similarities that they saw between these two psychoanalytic collaborators.

I begin with Peter Bruggen. I first interviewed him on the 27th of May 2005. I followed this up twelve years later when Peter agreed to speak to me again. He met me on the morning of 8th of July 2017 at Belsize Tube Station (not far from Marion's home) and walked me back to his house where I met his wife, Joan Bruggen (also a psychoanalytic psychotherapist and social worker) before we set to work. Interestingly, at that time Peter covered much of the same ground as we had done in 2005 with slight changes of emphases here and there. Therefore, unless otherwise stated I use the first interview here.

Chapter 13

'I was her last Training Case' – analysis with Marion Milner and supervision with Winnicott

Peter Bruggen

(Conversations with Margaret Boyle Spelman: 27th of May 2005; 8th of July 2017)

Peter told me that he first saw Marion Milner for five years of five-times-per-week psychoanalysis when as a young psychiatrist in the 1960s he trained as a psychoanalyst with the British Institute. 'I started psychiatry when I was twenty-six or so as a junior doctor in a psychiatric hospital. And there was quite a bit of thinking about psychodynamics and psychoanalysis'.

She was recommended to him at the time by a few people including a consultant psychiatrist he worked with and his friend, Andrew Malleson who had already had an analysis with her (see Chapter 14).

Before Peter trained as a psychoanalyst, he had attended a psychoanalytically influenced psychotherapist and had a helpful supervision at the Tavistock Clinic as part of a group. During his time in analysis with Marion, Peter was also in supervision for approximately two years with DW Winnicott.

He told me in our second interview (July 8th 2017) that he found Winnicott's supervision of particular help when he, Peter Bruggen, was establishing a residential service, Hill End Adolescent Service, St Alban's, and was insisting that the parents or guardians make the decision about whether the young person be admitted to the unit or not. This was based not on traditional diagnosis classifications but on the single consideration category of whether the parents/guardians felt that they could or could not cope with the person in their existing environment. Bruggen said that particularly at the point where he felt that funding might be threatened, it was helpful to have someone of Winnicott's stature saying more or less the same thing as he was saying.

Peter recounted going into his supervision session and having to wake Winnicott who was asleep on the floor. He also said that Winnicott accepted that when he got too distracted Peter insisted that they come back to what he wanted to talk about as he was paying him to supervise him.

P: He [Winnicott] died while I was in supervision. I knew he had been ill and I knew how old he was. The day before the next supervision session, my secretary had a message from his secretary to cancel the next session because he had died.

So the next session I had with Marion which was at eight o'clock the following morning, was a very sad one. Because she was crying as well as I was crying, during the session. And I went to his funeral which was lovely [the first non-religious ceremony that Bruggen had attended]. I had actually met him a couple of weeks before at another

DOI: 10.4324/9780429433535-17

funeral, Michael Balint's funeral …In the yard outside we bumped into each other and said hello and he sort of screwed up his eyes and said, 'Nice things they say about you when you die'.

M: Prescient…
P: Yeah… (pause). Well, I got somebody else: The society was very good at handling that sort of thing. I saw Pearl King immediately, Pearl King was President then or became President a bit later, and had been in analysis with Marion. And I was supervised by her for a time and then...I had two other full-term supervisors, Margaret Little and Harold Stewart.
M: Marion Milner was crying; that is so much NOT what certain analysts would do.
P: I know, yes…And I mean you'd have to be pretty defended not to because she was close to the man, he had just died and I was her first patient in the morning and the first words I said to her as I lay down on the couch was 'You look so sad'. And she said 'So do you'. That was a good start to a weepy session…
M: What kind of woman was she and how was it to be analysed by her?
P: She was lovely. She was lovely and very helpful.
M: What age were you at that stage and what age was she?
P: I was her last training case and she had her 70th birthday while I was in analysis with her. I heard this from I-forget-who and I gave her a rose for her birthday the next session and she accepted that…I started in sixty-seven I should think when I was thirty-three. I finished in seventy-one or so

…Oh yes, yes, she held my hand on my last session and I was getting up and I just burst into tears again and she held my hand. That was lovely, lovely…

…

I heard her speak once… a memorial session for Winnicott of the Psychoanalytic Society and I thought she spoke very well because she spoke in pictures: She said 'I'm one of those people who thinks in pictures', and she described a 'picture' she had of Winnicott like a Catherine wheel in a village fair... But the way it was written up by the Society in their Bulletin made her sound 'gaga' – and she wasn't as she presented it…

In our second interview [at his home on 8th July 2017], Peter also told me that later on in the analysis he remembered that he was hating Milner over something which he didn't seem to remember or consider important. He said that he stood up off the couch and turned to Marion and said, 'I hate you, I really hate you'. And Marion replied 'And you know that I can take your hate'. Then later she added, 'And you must remember when I die that it is not your fault'. Peter said that he felt this was 'tremendous'.

(This incident also makes it clear that Marion was already working in a way that used the concepts that Winnicott was writing about at this time; the patient's use of the object and the analyst's non-retaliatory survival.)

…

P: I have a memory of Milner which I never confronted her about; I didn't feel the need but I believe she rang me up shortly after I stopped analysis with her. It was a funny piece of behaviour because it was nice but also it threw me a little bit. And it certainly was against the rules. I didn't mention it to her.
M: Do you think she was just reassuring herself?

P: Oh yes, I mean she was a human being, yes, of course. But some things just have to be gone through...It's hard to pursue this without getting very emotional in a sense, feeling things about love and acceptance and so on. You see the last time I saw her, I mean I saw her shortly before she died. I was actually due to see her on the day she died. She was interested in dying. We were discussing how North American Indians seem to be able to go out and just lie down and die...I think it might be possible to organise that somehow with one's psyche: Maybe she did it and maybe she didn't. I think she probably did not. But...things like that – when she said 'yes' over Martin Luther King dying, – and Winnicott uses these extremely simple notions – there's something about this; we are all in the same boat. I did feel that they were both very 'non-hierarchical' people. When I heard that her marriage had been rather a disaster and I mentioned this and she said 'oh, so you've learnt a bit of reality...'

Peter explained that two to three years after his analysis had ended, he saw Milner for four sessions 'when [he] cracked up'. After another few years he saw her again for four sessions and on that occasion he said that he was not getting through things so quickly and needed another four. He said they worked hard in these sessions and the sessions proved very helpful.

During the course of the interview Peter referred to the several 'demands' that he made on Marion during the course of the analysis. He said that the last demand that he made was several years after the therapy when he suffered a serious professional upset and his wife asked him if there was anything that he could give himself to feel better. He said that he would like to invite Marion to dinner and did. Marion agreed instead to come for a drink on a Sunday morning. Peter remembered with great fondness that they sat in the sun in the garden and it was lovely.

[Talking about his supervision with Winnicott]

P: I met Winnicott... on the stairs of the Institute of Psychoanalysis ... and introduced myself, although ...we had met once before. I said 'I am coming to you for supervision in January'. He looked and screwed up his eyes and said 'I look forward to discussing a case with you'. And that was tremendous, I thought. It was a very non-hierarchical statement about supervision.

Towards the end of our conversation Peter agreed with my summary of his answer to me when I had asked about Milner's characteristics as an analyst Peter had told me: 'fun', humaneness, a lack of hierarchy, the idea that things must be borne and a kind of deference to and an acknowledgement of reality. He said 'sometimes I wished that she'd take a strong line with me and say 'stop it!' over one thing or another'.

Peter told me that he visited Marion several times in her nineties, decades after his analysis, 'for conversation'. He felt that Marion was interested in a very wide concept of psychoanalysis. He said that he had also met her son John who was quite 'neutral' towards psychoanalysis and had not read any of his mother's writing.

Chapter 14

'Marion was uniquely placed to understand'... (analyses with Marion Milner and with Donald Winnicott)

Andrew Malleson

(Conversations with Margaret Boyle Spelman: 6th of June 2005; 3rd January, 2021).

Preface

In 2005, a few weeks after our interview, having first checked that he was happy to speak to me [MBS], Peter Bruggen introduced me to his friend, Andrew Malleson and we spoke on the telephone on the 6th of June 2005.

Andrew told me he was born in London in 1931, the second child of Joan Malleson, a celebrated GP and pioneer in women's health, who privately and very separately suffered from severe and intractable depression (she had tried ECT to no avail).

Andrew explained that he had little contact with his father, a distinguished actor and writer, as his parents separated shortly after he was born. Andrew had been seen by Winnicott as a four year old for one or two years and by Milner in early adulthood for six or seven years, with interruptions during medical training and work. In adolescence Andrew had attended a male Jungian analyst two to three times per week during secondary school holidays, from age fifteen for approximately five years. Andrew explained that his mother was interested in psychoanalysis and was friendly with both Winnicott and Milner, and paid for analysis for both her sons (and other relatives).

Interview:

M: You didn't find the fact that [Marion Milner] knew you, that she was your mother's patient or that you knew her before, you didn't find this intrusive in the experience?

A: No, not at all, I mean I think actually I found it rather helpful. My mother was a pretty difficult person, I mean difficult in so much she was very successful but she had a severe depression. I mean she had a puerperal depression when I was born from which she never really recovered.

M: Were you her first child or her only child?

A: Second child, I ha[d] a brother...nine years older than me.

... And she...I mean she put a lot of energy into her work; she put quite a lot of energy into men (laughed) – and although she was a very responsible mother I think she found it very difficult to be with either [of her sons]...[Y]ou know both of us [were]sent off to boarding school. [My brother] when he was three and I went when I was four. And she was very unavailable most of my childhood, so indeed was my father. So you know I had a lot of problems to deal with.

DOI: 10.4324/9780429433535-18

... Anyway that's how I got into analysis with Marion Milner. And I had been in analysis with Winnicott as a child... [w]hich was a very nice experience, I was about... I was at school. I think I was about four at the time.

...Yes, I was at boarding school which was in Bloomsbury somewhere and I think one of the... – probably it was the house maid who took me to see Winnicott. I don't know if it was every day but it was very frequently.

...

M: And do you know why you were going to see him?

A: Hmm...well my mother was, again Winnicott was a patient of my mother's and they were very close and you know my mother was into analysis and she knew that emotionally I wasn't having a very good time.

[Andrew also explained that at the time, his best friend in school was the son of his father's new partner and was living with and seeing Andrew's father every day and at the weekend when he, Andrew, saw him only rarely.]

M: Did you say you were already in boarding school at this stage?

A: Yes, yes. I mean I remember Winnicott as a very nice man, I mean I look back in rather amazement actually about my analysis. He had, it was near Wimpole Street, somewhere in the Harley Street direction...

...

And anyway it was a slightly mock-Tudor house as far as I remember. And he had a consulting room there and he had a store room there full of interesting toys. I remember fairly regular occasions where I was making a bonfire on one of the tables in the room which consisted of...crunching up bits of writing paper and making a pile and setting it alight.

M: You actually did set it alight?

A: Yeah, yeah, I was amazed – I mean I wasn't amazed then but I'm amazed looking back at it. The other thing I remember very well was making very long tubes of plasticine and peeing down one end and getting the urine going to the sink, I mean it was a sort of hydrodynamic exercise. Obviously I enjoyed it, anyway, it stuck in my mind. And I think in some ways it did make me, you know, in some ways not exactly easy, sexually but a lot less sexually neurotic, considering the kind of background I was brought up with. I mean I remember asking Winnicott if I could see his penis and I remember, actually I think I remember him looking a bit sort of uncomfortable about the whole thing. Which I'm not surprised (laughing)...

M: But you were at the Oedipal stage ... a lot going on then.

A: Yeah absolutely, I mean I heard my mother say that I think Winnicott had interpreted it as burning my father's hair but I'm not quite sure about that, a long time afterwards....I mean I never quite know what to make of this. I had a very, we lived in a house called Portstown Road where my mother ran a practice from, it was in the red light district in London – with two other women doctors. And my parents had more or less separated ...just after I was born and my father, I don't really remember my father being at home. And then my mother moved out too, and so [my brother] and myself were left …[W]e each had a nanny and there was the housekeeper and her husband who was a bus driver and they had two children. And the secretary and the house maid and we were really looked after by them. I mean there weren't any parents. But I was very attached to my nanny 'M' who was sweet. And then my mother felt that 'M' had had an unhappy love affair and was getting too close to me and that there was too much cuddling and things going on. And that it would be better if she was sent away and I think it was at that time that I went to school. My mother said …she made the decision with Winnicott, I mean whether that was true I don't know. I mean my mother was a fairly forceful woman and she was probably capable of brow-beating anybody into agreeing with her. But you know I think from my experiences as a child it was a big mistake… I needed somebody who was physically very close. It was the only sort of physical contact I really had.

…[More about therapy with Winnicott]

M: It was regular and frequent?

A: Yes, yes, and I remember one… incident, I think the only thing I really have ever stolen in my life. In his store room he had a kind of whistle that you filled with water and blew and it made a noise just like a nightingale. And my brother was very interested, my brother who was nine years older…than me was very interested in birds. Anyway I stole this machine, and I didn't like my brother very much – he gave me a bad time – and outside the window I would make nightingale noises with this and he would then go out hunting for the nightingale. He never found it. Anyway Winnicott was obviously quite keen that I didn't steal any of his machines and I did.

M: Did he know, do you think, that you had it?

A: I don't know whether he ever knew or not. I suspect he probably ought to have done if he didn't. But I don't remember it ever being talked about.

M: And do you remember how the sessions would go? Do you have any recollection of that?

A: Well I remember playing house a lot, he had some sort of canvass screen which I would tilt up into the side and make a tent onto a bed. Crawl into it. I remember him being very concerned that you know the matches shouldn't be near the screen and things, very sensibly. And I remember sitting down next to him and him drawing me a picture of the female genitalia with a womb and things you know with a description of how babies were conceived and how they were…born, etc.

…

M: So you were making these houses, were these in miniature or …you were you using your whole body..?

A: Whole body yes. I mean in retrospect I sort of review the whole thing in horror, I mean I seemed to have caused absolute chaos in his office. It must have been quite difficult to clear it all up.

M: That means he was completely permissive of anything you wanted to do.

A: Yeah, yeah – I mean the only thing that I ever remember him putting his foot down was not showing me his penis, actually.

M: Because lighting a fire in his office must have been quite disruptive.

A: Very, I'm sure (laughing)... [I]t was on the table. The table, you know because I did it quite a lot of times... I can remember the table quite well it had a sort of..., it was a special table which he kept for my fire. And it had a sort of charred thing in the centre of it.

M: And these fires you would make the bonfire and just watch it go out?

A: I remember watching it go out or how it went out. I mean the paper just burned. But it must have made a lot of smoke and things, you know in a house with other sorts of doctors and consultants ...I don't know how it all worked out, actually. But unless my memory is playing me tricks, I have a fairly clear recollection of it happening.

...

[Andrew chose to begin analysis with Marion when he was about twenty-four years old because he was phobic of blood and crowds, depressed and worried about himself.]

A: In fact, I was actually in a session [with Marion] when the news came through that my mother had killed herself.

[Andrew explained that his mother had spoken to himself (and his brother) on several occasions about her depression and had told him that she would wait until he was 'up and running' as an adult before ending her life.]

...

M: Will you tell me a bit about what you remember about Marion then?

A: Yeah, well I liked her a lot. I mean theoretically it was interesting because you know...

[Andrew explained that his previous therapist, during his adolescence, was Jungian.]

[A]nd obviously he very much liked themes of fairy tales and mythology and in some ways it was a rather good education in this way. I learnt a lot. But he was... obviously very comfortable with Freudian type analysis of dreams. And with Marion, although they came from very different positions she would totally accept 'the Jung' and the interpretation of a dream. She was very 'unrigid' if you like, at least she was with me – about what things meant. So they were always interesting sessions. She was nice in so much that she was very concerned that I would be in my body – you know, she would like me to lie on the couch and just sort of say what I could see for instance, which was interesting. I remember on one occasion she asked me to describe [what I saw] and I described something that was above my head and she sounded surprised and said 'Can you really see that?' Actually when I came to think of it, I couldn't; it was the window behind me and I was just envisaging what was there but I wasn't really seeing it.

M: You mean that she in some way wanted that you would feel real and [you would be] grounded if you could relate to your physical surroundings?

A: Yeah, which I think is true. So I mean I've thought about that a lot and you know thought that this was a very useful experience; you know trying to get living in my neurotic head. But, you know, actually what it was like to experience the world around one, without any interference from anything else.

...

Anyway for me as a young man I was very sexually uptight and this was, this whole thing was kind of a huge release, actually.

...

M: I'm thinking that there must be something particular to the analysis from the fact that [Marion knew] your mother, knew your circumstances.

A: Yes and I mean I find that ...teaching that you have to go into therapy and you shouldn't really have any connection with the analyst...I mean, I think it worked very well and ...I think lots of people would have had difficulty in understanding what I was talking about with my mother unless they had actually known her; yeah, and known her rather well. Because her professional side was very different to her family side, you know. If Marion hadn't known my mother probably it would have been rather bewildering to her.

M: And you were lying on the couch and was she sitting beside the couch, behind the couch?

A: Oh she would sit slightly behind to one side and smoke. She smoked an awful lot...

...

M: Yes, so I was wondering about how the therapy with Marion Milner...ended up, how did you come to finish?

A: I think...it was probably finishing and I moved onto LSD therapy...

...

M: Do you think [LSD therapy] gave you something that therapy alone didn't give you?

A: I think it probably did actually...You know just to light the 'door of perception'... You can sort of relive childhood situations and... suddenly you are presented with feelings of what it was like being a child but one has the adult capacity to find different ways of dealing with it.

M: And had your therapy with Marion finished completely when you were doing the LSD therapy?

A: I think it had finished, I mean I did see her once or twice afterwards but that was more or less as a friend really.

...

I asked Andrew about Milner and Winnicott's characteristics:

A: Yeah, if I was to be asked one thing about the characteristics of both Marion and Winnicott, it would be that they were very open to discuss any ideas [from any] way one wanted to look at them. And take the idea seriously and be able to be involved in open discussion of them... [T]his is why I think Marion was always interested in Jungian interpretation of dreams and... she wouldn't say 'oh no it's not that, it's this'. She would go along with it and say '[Y]ou know, now I can see that' and so on.

...

Oh I would have seen Marion as a serious person who would be concerned that things go well and she would...take her own professional life very seriously, her work very seriously. She would put energy and effort into it. I mean I really don't remember as a child, Winnicott, other than the fact that I liked him and of course having read bits of Winnicott and things since... I see him as a... very thoughtful serious concerned man of the human race, of human being.

...

Well... it's difficult to know if it's from them or from family things but I've always been a fairly questioning kind of physician. I hope I've brought some of their open-mindedness and generosity and also acceptance of people, whoever they are..., the whole questioning of quite a lot of medical orthodoxy.

...

I feel I got plenty out of our sessions... I am sure that I would not have survived some of what I went through without it... It's something that I think I've digested over the years, honestly. It's always continued to be incorporated into my life, in the way I feel. I mean it's difficult; not many people are fortunate enough to have a very good analyst and see them for a long time.

...

I think the traditional analyst's point of view of trying to remain absolutely neutral so that ...patients can project feelings onto [the analyst], doesn't work because no person is neutral. And it's a pretence, it's probably much better to be open and... without getting patients involved in one's own life – but to give patients enough of one's own life so that they can see that's how you would deal with the situation or might consider dealing with the situation. So ... in some way they have somebody to identify with; [someone] who's dealing with the problem – actually the more modern, useful, emotional intervention; that one can ...hope to be without symptoms and problems, you can...be reasonably successful at dealing with problems. ...This is why it's useful to have a therapist who is prepared to discuss how they might deal with the problem. And how they might feel about it and how they might deal with feelings.

M: Did you feel that Marion was like that?

A: I certainly felt that Marion was like that, yes. I don't know with Winnicott. It's too long ago.

...

Conclusion

At the time of interviews both men were in active retirement and had enjoyed high-profile careers. Both had had exposure to many types of therapy, not only personally but in the course of their work – Peter told me of the guided imagery, family therapy, brief therapy and group interventions which he and colleagues used in his adolescent service and Andrew, with an eclectic approach, spoke about the good research results in terms of therapeutic outcomes for cognitive therapy. Using Freud's criterion, one could say that both men's psychoanalysis had successful outcomes as they had been able to love and to work.

The great affection and respect of both men for Marion and her memory was evident even in the way they spoke her name. They knew of Milner's writing and keen intellect. But here they were personally grateful to Milner and wanted the opportunity to speak highly of her and to put their names to testimony vouching for Marion's concerned and boundaried warmth as well as her substantial clinical acumen and professional earnestness. Both seem to have been able to introject an enduring good and useful object as well as an enquiring mind, a lively curiosity and a helpfully open way of thinking.

The clarity of the recollections of both men so many years later bears witness to the continuing effects of their experience of analysis with Marion Milner. Each of these men, in his own way, had the retrospective indebtedness for the analyst who had gracefully maintained at times seriously challenged boundaries. And all this in the face of momentous competition in the professional environment at the time from the dramatic, seductive and instantaneous grip of LSD therapy within the therapy sector, the medical community and particularly its innovative experimenters in London at the time.

Having already written the above and shown it to him, I had spoken to Andrew on the previous Sunday which was also his 90th birthday and he told me, amongst other things, about his newly published book.

I then got an email on the following Friday, 8 January 2021:

Dear Margaret

Inspired by our conservation I have just read Marion's *A Life of One's Own.* It is such a thoughtful book. I don't think we discussed these sorts of ideas in my analysis, but they most certainly are my own. Did I come to such ideas on my own or did I quietly absorb from Marion? It is the sort of thing that is difficult to know, but one way or another, I am very pleased to have them.

Andrew

Chapter 15

Marion Milner

Thinking together... (on her supervision with Milner 1977–1978)

Juliet Mitchell

Musing, as requested, on the specific qualities of Marion as a supervisor something has become clear as this book goes to press. I will leave my earlier thoughts more-or-less intact – but the penny has dropped: as always with her work, Marion's supervision was a true conversation.

It is now more than forty years since I met Marion as the supervisor of my second training patient. We met on a weekly basis for a year in 1977–1978. Four decades is a long time ago! I immediately found that I could remember the patient we chose to work with extremely well. Marion is still vivid but the difference between the two types of memory is marked and has left me wondering...The difference in itself recalled aspects of Marion's thinking that I picked up from our discussions and interested me in those of her books which I read then and still open from my shelves. Her books are gently marked in faint pencil – again, as with our discussions, I noted disagreements as well as agreements embedded in a particular, idiosyncratic but distinctive type of exchange which characterized getting to know her. An example: when we first met she asked me if she should read (which meant absorb) the work of Jacques Lacan. I said neither 'yes' nor 'no' – we discussed whether she should or should not in a completely open-ended way. I am not sure I ever formally knew what she decided. We continued as we had begun...Marion was interested in what I knew about and as always in her work – set up an equal exchange – a conversation in the true meaning of the word.

When asked to write these few words, I was excited to so fully remember my patient and strongly wish, if she is still with us, that she would get in touch. I would write to her but do not have the address of where I hope she is living. This is an aspect of the two different memories – of Marion and our patient, I will call her 'Gilly'. I feel I know Gilly's region, her 'habitat' as one of the most beautiful places in the British Isles which for forty years I have wanted to visit – but would never do so without an invitation from her. The sensation is reminiscent of our clinical work – Marion's deep, deep interest which was always inquiring but never intrusively curious: what would Gilly tell us if we looked as well as listened. Well, looking was listening and listening, looking. Marion was grateful to Freud that he recognized some people thought dominantly in images. This was Marion's pursuit of different types of thinking.

I see Marion as one remembers someone with whom one talked open-endedly – I found her quietly beautiful in the setting of a modestly lovely room; Gilly I more than 'remember', she is with me today in the body-concentration that so interested Marion.

DOI: 10.4324/9780429433535-19

I still feel the visual image as, for once so happy, she burst into my home-consulting-room, the sun was shining golden through the windows, saying as she came: 'last night, I had a phone-call from my mother!' – she laughed with shy joy – 'I know it's not much... but it *is* wonderful'. Her mother had died tragically when she was six months old.

Thinking back today on this training supervision, I realize that I learnt from Marion that counter-transference and transference were a permanent and ever-present feature of what she crucially called the 'frame', the necessary, indeed essential, boundary – that she wrote about in *Not Being Able to Paint* and experienced Donald Winnicott, her own brief quondam analyst and subsequent colleague, as lacking.

Yet when I once asked her advice for a seriously ill friend, she referred me to Winnicott for help. Having talked to Winnicott, I realized that Marion had suggested him exactly the treatment she most disagreed with him for practicing. She disagreed with how Winnicott both himself housed and/or visited patients at home (they called it 'management') yet she knew that this was what was needed in my friend's case. However, as though in unspoken but utterly usual dialogue with Marion, in this instance, Winnicott when he discussed it with me decided that was *not* the path he recommended! Looking back, I have a feeling that was so familiar to me throughout that year: although advising the opposite, they were both right and one had to think differently to decide what was best.

For this reminiscence I looked back at my still extant process notes, my own thoughts about Gilly and myself and Marion's typically egalitarian sharing of the reports she had to submit on my work. I had one abiding take-away recollection of Marion saying that Gilly had 'insufficient narcissism'. I puzzled and puzzled and could not re-discover what she could have meant. Narcissism was not a concept that featured much either in the notes on Gilly or in Marion's books. Today it is being re-visited with a general assertion that enough narcissism is essential for survival and a re-working of the concept as a syndrome by such practitioners as Gwen Adshead. I myself have recently highlighted for students the overlap of 'negative' narcissism in the work of Herbert Rosenfeld and Andre Green. I realized it would have been suited to the roughly 'borderline' status of Gilly.[1] But I knew this was the wrong line to pursue.

Still dissatisfied, I was about to leave it at that when I re-read a footnote I had completely forgotten in *The Hands of the Living God.* I need to quote it at length as it stands as a centre-point for these recollections.

Marion wrote, paraphrasing Herbert Marcuse:

> In 1956 I read Herbert Marcuse's *Eros and Civilization* (1956). I found that he puts forward a thesis, based on a theoretical analysis of Freud's basic concepts that seemed to point in the same direction as the ideas that were evolving out of my own clinical experience. Marcuse is especially concerned with how Freud's new concept of narcissism, in 1914, pointed the way for a new orientation; for, he says, whereas narcissism, as usually understood, contains the idea of a withdrawal from reality, it is now becoming connected with the idea of oneness with the universe and a fundamental relatedness to reality; thus it may contain the germ of a different relation to reality, a state in which the libidinal cathexis of the body (body ego) may become the source, reservoir, for a new cathexis of the external world. Sublimation then begins by a reactivation of narcissism, which somehow overflows and extends to objects. (p. 272n)

I now recollected that I had radio discussions with Marcuse about his book[2] and this interested Marion. Now, with a sense of relief as great as the sudden-ness of understanding, I have remembered why Marion had said this about Gilly's lack of narcissism and why it was so pertinent. Gilly had a wonderful appreciation of nature but needed to sublimate this so that there would be more narcissism which would release in her body-ego an openness to a wider creative reality. This helps me today with the toddler and its sibling on whom I work. Recollection upon recollection is coming back to me – a few months ago I was 'discussing' in my mind with Marion what I had read of Rachel, her own training case with Melanie Klein in 1943. She would have been interested to think about siblings with Rachel. After her supervision she felt a strong need to find her own way on her own. I have never needed that with Marion – our conversation is always there 'to be continued'...

Notes

1 When I told Marion that a clinical group at the Institute of Psychoanalysis to whom I had presented my work had declared she was 'unanalysable' Marion was adamant 'how could anyone who dreamt as Gilly dreamt be unanalysable?'. Now I think her rejection of this opinion was part of her wider concern with what is 'reality'. See the quotation below on 'narcissism'.

2 Four 'in conversations' for the Australian Broadcasting Company. Marcuse was in La Jolla, California and I was in London where the BBC co-ordinated them – if I remember rightly!

Chapter 16

'A meaningful encounter' – my supervision with Marion Milner (1990–1993)

Leon Kleimberg

I came across Marion Milner in her paper 'Psychoanalysis and Art' (1987) in the late 1970s and met her personally in the early 1980s. The simplicity and 'realism' of the agonizing search for the soul and identity remained the same.

The Marion I found in the consulting room as a supervisor was the same Marion that I found in the soul-searching paper that I was so impressed by.

She was in her early nineties when I brought to her a severe case of perversion, that was turned down by younger colleagues as unanalysable or too difficult to treat, and without any signs of doubt or anxiety she engaged with me in working with this patient, criticizing me for not allowing his illusions and idealizations to be expressed enough, due to my constant 'here and now' interventions.

She reminded me immediately of what I had perceived in her work in the past that had made me come and look for her guidance. *Our fragility is our strength!*

She opened my eyes to another aspect of our work as psychoanalysts. By letting patients express themselves and be themselves, we can try to find stories within stories and see images within the verbal communications (Kleimberg, 2019).

Over the course of the next three years of fortnightly supervision, I suppose my own personal search for meaning made me receptive and ready to take in Marion's own explorations with the self and identity and to be ready to take this approach to clinical work.

Marion had a great respect for the need to accept illusions and idealizations in patients and people, not only as protective devices but also as necessary stop-overs in the developmental life cycle.

So she made me understand that identities can only be found and developed in the context of the free expression of illusions and personal stories.

To access that, she said, frames and parameters, paradoxically had to be firmly established so a 'gap' was created where they could express themselves within the self and with the other. But gaps only emerge if we have boundaries; once we have them, we can get lost within them again.

Her focus on the gap invited in the patient a search for the self and the other in a creative but chaotic context and invited him or her to bridge the gap between internal reality and the external one.

She had a great belief that only with anger and aggression these boundaries between self and other could be formed and she showed me this by coining the phrase 'In order to love we have to hate'. Hate will bring separateness between self and other and in

DOI: 10.4324/9780429433535-20

the gap created in the separateness, illusions, identities and selves can be formed and shared.

The awareness of the fine balance between creating a space within boundaries and allowing illusions, personal stories and mergers or fusions within that space has remained with me with conviction until today.

Marion was a shy person but with a special beauty. The beauty of her soul would transcend the simplicity but elegance of her physical appearance. She possessed a distinguished aura within an ordinary and simple presence.

She was very capable of being intimate and authentic with a special zest for life. She could be an adult one moment and a child the next. Towards the end of our work she asked to meet my family and young son. Watching her connecting and playing with him was a joy. Drawings, paintings, doodles and chocolates were their shared language.

We always sat in chairs in her consulting room for supervision, but when my family was invited to pay a visit we sat on the (analytic) couch! (see the cover photograph). Marion's interest in my son's artistic development ended up years later with his attending with his sister the Hampstead School of Art where she herself was still remembered.

The greatest clinical confidence she disclosed to me, which influenced the way I saw aggression ever since, was that she was not happy with her analyst Donald Winnicott for not analysing her anger sufficiently. 'He did not analyse my aggression and hatred enough. He was very creative but not always disciplined'.

It was an important revelation from someone who came across to me as so calm and composed!

Getting her clinical 'Weltanschauung' was an important departing moment from a mechanical application of the 'here and now' technique so popular at the Tavistock Clinic and British Society of Psychoanalysis in those days. Sometimes, she made me aware that the totality of the process is more important than its parts, and, that the opening up of psychic experience is more relevant than pinning it down.

There was always a way of being with her that left also space for me to be!

She showed me her art work with incredulity and humour and showed me one painting with two chickens in it saying that it was 'Anna Freud and Melanie Klein arguing'! Aware of my South American background she gave me a journal of the Uruguayan Psychoanalytical Association containing one of her articles in Spanish.

Sadly, in her last years she was resigned not to continue living for much longer because of her inability to read! In her ordinary and realistic way, she said to me 'Leon, there is no need to go much longer as I am losing my sight and I can't read any more'.

Maron Milner's humility, simplicity and profound sensitivity in the way she related to me personally and professionally are invaluable legacies to my continued process of learning and growing from/in Psychoanalysis.

In sum, I came to London looking for a myth and ended up finding a substantial and real person with lots of talent and humanity to share.

Chapter 17

'Holding and Visceral Attention'

Bodily concentration of an analyst under COVID-19 lockdown[1]

Maia Kirchkheli

Ils ne mouraient pas tous, mais tous étaient frappés.

(La Fontaine, 1678)

[Although all did not die, all were affected (The animals stricken with the Plague).]

Marion Milner, my created-found companion

This chapter emerged from my clinical experience of working psychoanalytically by remote contact during the pandemic of COVID-19. In many ways, it has been an extraordinary experience when the whole psychoanalytic world moved overnight from a physical consulting room to a virtual one. During analytic listening, in the absence of bodily togetherness and in the presence of mutually heightened anxiety about physical survival, I turned my attention inwardly towards the interior of my own body and made a spontaneous gesture of doodling. These two moves mental and bodily, both unintentional and unconventional to my analytic training, restored my psychic aliveness and facilitated the process of analytic holding.

But how could I talk about that to other psychoanalysts?

It was in this moment of solitude that I realised I must have already been engaged in an internal dialogue with Marion Milner, an artist and a psychoanalyst, whose writings conjoin creative process, body and psychoanalysis in a unique way. 'She would surely understand the significance of being alive and open to modifications of one's own clinical technique in the service of providing the conditions for what is needed to be received', I thought. Her book *The Hands of The Living God* (1969) is a testament to that. It describes her case of Susan, an adolescent girl diagnosed with schizophrenia, whose description of her own state was that 'she had lost her soul' (p. xix). The book is replete with Susan's doodle drawings. Emerging out of the analytic process, these in many ways depict the core struggle for psychic survival that severely tested her analyst's own capacity for psychic aliveness. Milner began to discover that 'What I said was often less important than my body-mind state of being in her sessions' (p. 42).

Gradually, Milner became preoccupied with how to justify psychoanalytically the change of her technique. This is a hallmark of her way of thinking: experiential truth prevails over a given framework; a thought is bigger than its concept[2]. This ethos so central to creative living resonated with my own search for meaning that could bridge the gap within myself between new and old, unknown and known, self and the other, inarticulate and articulate, body and mind.

DOI: 10.4324/9780429433535-21

Milner allowed me a creative meeting of two sides of my identity in these unprecedented times. This invokes my first encounter with her books some years ago when I moved to England and was living the loss of all that was familiar, going through an identity crisis. I managed to survive psychically through drawing and painting on a daily basis while embarking on a personal analysis. I heard Marion Milner's name for the first time from my supervisor, Barbara Antonis. After carefully listening to my thoughts about the experience of surrender to the ink and paper from which the feeling of existing emerged, she pointed out to me that I reminded her of Marion Milner's ideas. Milner's book (1950) *On Not Being Able to Paint* was given to me by a fellow trainee as a token of her admiration for my ability to paint. Her own personal study of psychic blocks to creative expression reads like a journey full of observations and experiments which Milner undertook during her training analysis with Sylvia Payne. Her reflections that psychic creativity stems from our inner being as a need for self-realisation through self-expression made me feel understood. As I read through the book, I was overjoyed to discover such a courageous companion held in my hands. It took me a few more months to encounter Milner in my own analysis when I heard my analyst's response to my spontaneous gesture that only after he had accepted my version of him, I was prepared to surrender to what he had to offer. It is in accordance with Milner's thesis developed in her classic paper The Role of Illusion in Symbol Formation (1952). She observed that her child analysand Simon's clinical progress was followed by her modifying the technique in terms of becoming more in-giving, allowing herself to be used like a *pliable medium*. It is another original concept of hers born out of a creative intercourse between the artist and psychoanalyst in her. She observed how toys enabled Simon to settle in the process of playing and to become freer. Just like paint was a medium for her to recreate her emotional self. Milner realised that at that point in his development, Simon needed not so much to hear interpretations but to be allowed to use his analyst as a medium, similar to the way he used the toys. This acceptance of his regressive move in analytic sessions ushered into a new progressive phase where the school incorporated Simon's spontaneous gesture, a photography club, and made it possible for the boy to begin to comprehend a 'not-me' aspect of himself.

This creative me-not-me back and forth movement is the common thread to her writings and echoes my own ongoing journey of self-realisation as a newly qualified psychoanalyst. What a delight it gave to me to discover that Marion Milner was *indeed* my analytic great grandmother!

Recently, I have yet again re-found her in times of struggle for psychic survival. I think her internal presence has held me in my courage to remain open and to surrender to my body-self. To describe this particular experience, I will be using Marion Milner's concepts such as *framed gap* and the analyst's *concentration of the body* which I further conceptualise as 'visceral attention'. I consider it as a corporal counterpart of 'evenly hovering attention'. While an impetus to elaborate this concept came from the specific experience of doing psychoanalysis by remote means, I believe it has a wider implication for an analytic technique in the ordinary psychoanalytic setting. Visceral attention is to be located in an area of psychic survival that is part and parcel of doing psychoanalysis especially in phases when not knowing prevails. The chapter explores an analogy between visceral attention and doodling to hold the analytic process on a nonverbal level. The blank paper and blank inside of the body stand for the 'framed gap', a negative space for a new thing to emerge.

In the moment...

Each morning, I sit in my consulting room next to the phone and in front of my laptop.[3] I wait for the call. This is now my new place in the space that is familiar but feels unfamiliar. I stare at the empty couch with an empty chair behind it – an absent couple. I see the loss. I am anxious, frightened and overall too agitated for feeling the loss, but I see it out there lying on the couch. It is almost as if there is no time for mourning. It is psychic surviving that I am doing. It is going-on-being that matters (Winnicott, 1956).

Telecommunication is an inevitable sensorial deprivation and feels like being torn away from an analyst mother's body. You have not entirely lost her, there is a voice. You know she is alive but you do not know when the two of you will be reunited. There is a traumatic rupture of the illusion of union. The physicality of the illusory space has been lost and sound becomes the only envelope to hold the dyad. But there are many other sounds: technical, human, animal that interfere with the line. Yet silence is also feared: is the other still there? This coupled fear of intrusion and absence feels too noisy and too silent almost at once. Parsons (1990) wrote about the need for the negation of ordinary reality, for psychic reality to be allowed in the analytic session. We are in a situation when disengagement from external reality equates with denial. If we stay in touch with it, external reality takes over. I can tell you how it feels: *it is too real to be real.* It is surreal. I stopped dreaming at night. Psychoanalytically speaking, I could not represent this experience because of the loss of the intermediate space between inner and outer from which creativity and imagination derive and where meanings are created (Winnicott, 1971b). There is no overlap of the two but disconcerting fusion. What happens when this is a state of mind of the analyst?

I was sitting at my desk on an audio call with my patient. Before I knew it, I reached for a pen and began to doodle. My hand drew lines while my mind followed my patient's anxious discourse. Doodling has become a part of my listening, something that I usually do when being with myself. Now whenever my hand is searching for a pen, I just surrender to it. I pay hardly any attention to what I am doodling. What matters is that somehow this automatic activity helps me to focus more fully on my experience with patients. I have realised, however paradoxical it may seem, that doodling in the process of listening enhances my psychic receptivity and availability.

Virtual analytic encounters

Mira dreamt that she was being chased and beheaded: 'now, it's only our heads that could meet', she tells me; a disembodied encounter. Her unconscious is also saying that the traumatic separation of our bodies leads to a loss of her link with her own body. A psyche-soma rupture within herself. She has a developmental need to be in my bodily presence in order to be in-dwelling in her own soma (Winnicott, 1949). It is indeed the body that became the principal character in dreams, in my view, as a response to the premature loss of the maternal body. The loss of the physicality of the analytic space has exposed the fragility of mental space.

Amadea has recurrent dreams of being cut open and left with her insides exposed. She was trying to stitch her own tummy.

P: You cut me open and abandoned me!

How to stitch the rupture? How to repair the loss of the holding frame? I wonder. The weekends have become unbearable and a source of anguish.

P: I don't know how to plug this void.

She is right. It is not the broken frame that we need to repair. For her the room represented my body that she would enter and feel safe. She does not yet have a psychic awareness of boundaries that hold her. She wants to get back into my body. It was the emergency C section. She was not ready to come out, to be born. She did not initiate the separation. Amadea is in agony as she feels she is falling forever in this void. My voice is the only proof of my existence and therefore of her existence.

The long silence on the phone lacks substance. I don't have nonverbal cues to gather the affective communication. At times I draw on my intuitive knowledge of the patient.

P: It is so different to be silent now. I feel abandoned, left on my own.

Amadea draws my attention to a new element of the experience that needs to be accepted and acknowledged. Her nonverbal presence cannot be the same. It does not feel the same because we are not in the same space. I feel anxious and wonder how to hold her without using too many words that would serve to reassure, to negate the silence rather than transform it into meaning. At times of prolonged silence when it feels I am too deaf to hear, I notice that it has become a part of my technique to tell her that it is not clear to me where she is at. In part, it contains mutual anxiety. 'You have not given up on me, you are still looking for me' responds the patient. It also has a more anxious connotation: 'you are not dead'.

This time, during the long and anxious silence, I turn my attention towards the interior of my body. I hear my racing heartbeat, something is moving, curling up inside me; it is tight. Then it all unfolds, and my lungs feel free. I get hold of the baby within myself. The baby screams! I feel it is an impossible task to distinguish whose scream it is, mine or my patient's. Instead, I draw my attention to imaginative holding. I surround my arms around the internal baby and stay still. Next, I remember Edvard Munch's painting of a screaming man – a silent scream. Then, I hear myself saying:

A: The silence that screams.

There is an immediate affective response:

P: I am just remembering my favourite object on your bookshelf. It is a deer and her baby feeding on her.

My gaze has found the dyad on the shelf that Amadea is missing. Now imaginatively she is here with me in the consulting room.

A: They are attached by a piece of land. They constitute an inseparable unit.
P: They are? I always thought that they were separate, and you put them together, so that she could be fed.

The poignant recognition of the work my mind has done. The feeding couple has been reconstructed, and with it, the representational capacity has been recovered. I feel warmth within my body.

Philip is talking to me over the phone. There is a noise down the line. He pauses and says:

P: It is a helicopter.
A: I can hear.
P: You do? Through the phone?
A: From the sky.
P: We are under the same sky!

The illusion of being in the same space has been recreated if only for an instant. The joy of proximity! This exchange feels profound against the background of the loss of the couch, the mother's lap (Winnicott, 1949). Philip, who speaks to me from his car, drives around his neighbourhood to try to park in the same spot. Today he feels dislodged: even the parking space cannot be kept! This time there was another car parked there, and he was raging. Next thing he complains about is the pain in his back. His back is missing the couch. He insists that he just wants to stretch his body. I imagine a baby slowly waking up in his cot in the presence of the mother.

Acoustic hyperactivity and holding

'Under the same sky' or 'on a piece of land' – what my patients have been trying to recreate is the common holding space that allowed some degree of illusion of physical togetherness to be established. Winnicott used the notion of holding to conceptualise the importance of maternal arms. Mother through holding gives her baby bodily warmth and framing structure, while imaginatively perceiving him/her in her mind. At this early stage of human development, mother's psycho-somatic presence is fundamental for her infant's survival both physical and psychic. The concept of holding reflects this dual property, which has transpired to be so relevant during the loss of physical union. I noticed that the need for holding was especially acutely expressed by regressed patients who were psychically fused with me, re-living this early phase of psychic development and ordinarily needed silent presence in the room. It was the physicality of the room with its sensual dimension of smell, temperature, light, small objects that constituted the essential element of analytic experience. During this phase of analysis, an analyst is the background and the room is the foreground. This mode of being is necessary to be worked through in its own time, before such patients can gradually move towards more separate psychic existence. This is crucial for the development of mental space that can survive separate bodily existence.

One of my patients told me: 'if you are human, you must be affected too!' I would like to reflect here on how I have been affected and what I have learnt in this mutually disturbing situation marked with the loss of the shared room in the context of existential uncertainty.

Milner wrote about the importance of the gap that is framed (Milner, 1952). The frame marks off outside from inside, and what is inside needs to be taken as a metaphor. Analytic sessions are framed in space and in time. During the period of working by remote means, what has been lost is the spatial frame, and we rely on the temporal one. We cannot be together in the same space, but we can be together in the same time-gap. Thus, the nature of holding has changed. The room has been replaced by the technology. What was around us is now between us. There was an abrupt shift in which the physicality of togetherness was lost. Sound is now only perceptual real, the only flesh linking an analytic dyad. Hearing becomes hyperactive like a hypertrophied organ to compensate for the lack. The question I pose is: how is this change in frame and in perceptual impoverishment affecting my analytic listening?

> First of all, I am both wary and weary of hyperactive listening. It is anxious and results in acoustic overload that is exhausting. I have found myself unusually tired and frustrated. Only when I began to direct my listening to the interiority of my bodily space did I recover something essential to my analytic work. It felt almost like re-finding my own body, perceptually recovering its depth.

Visceral attention

Milner spells out what I am grappling with in her paper 'The concentration of the Body' (1960):

> What I mean by body attention or body concentration in the analyst is this: it is a state in which the direct proprioceptive body-self awareness, which I suppose is best called the body presentation, as distinct from the body representation or body image, becomes the foreground of one's consciousness rather than the pre-conscious background. *As I see it, this kind of attention in the analyst differs from the free-floating kind* that, when I first practiced as an analyst, was the only kind I thought appropriate and which most neurotics seemed able to manage with. *It differs because it is not 'in the air'*; it deliberately attends to sinking itself down into a total internal body awareness, not seeking at all for correct interpretations, in fact not looking for ideas at all – although interpretations may emerge from this state spontaneously.
>
> (pp. 239–240 my emphasis)

Milner understood the importance of this bodily attention in particular when working with patients suffering from early maternal deficiencies. These patients lack a sense of in-dwelling in their own body, and she observed that they need 'to achieve an intuitive awareness of an unanxious mother figure contentedly anchored in her own body and in happy communion with it' (Ibid. p. 240).

Regressed patients benefit more from this kind of state in the analyst which must mainly be transmitted on unconscious to unconscious level than from verbal communication. As Milner describes, it is a total letting go of thinking in ideas, to achieve unmindfulness. The object of this attention is: 'one's own internal body perception, [that] is inarticulate, dark and undifferentiated', the inner unknown. That is why I choose to call it a *visceral attention*, and rather than contrasting it with the attention *in the air,* I consider it as the nonverbal aspect, the corporal counterpart of free-floating attention. It is through concentrating on our bodies that we free our mind to attend to the primary process and widen the scope of our receptivity. In other words, the mind surrenders to the body, and it is a mindful body that listens.

Previously, I might have been using this type of attention as part of my listening. However, it was more of an unaware drifting within me due to relaxation than an act of immersion. Recently, it seems to have been my own anxious state that accentuated the need for the active awareness of inner holding. In the face of impaired analytic frame and the loss of my patients' bodily presence, I must have lost the sense of safety to carry on with what is so fundamental for analytic listening: surrendering to one's own unconscious, the unknown within myself. The inner analytic frame of mind was also shattered. Therefore, I actively had to carry out the process of holding, something that goes unnoticed in the usual analytic situation. When reflecting on what I did, I think I gave up the patient in the external world and *willingly* attended to my own inner body-self. Paradoxically, it resulted in re-finding my patient. Milner writes:

> What looks like a turning away from the object and the outside world does in fact seem to result in the opposite from turning away, that it results in an increased perception of the nature and significance of the external object, in this instance the patient.
>
> (Ibid. p. 240)

To describe this state would be to say that I would follow my internal body contours, as if I was drawing my own bodily frame. In fact, I am creating the missing boundary between the inner and the outer realities with my attentive inner gaze. Moreover, Milner observed that this mooring of one's attention within the sea of one's own body, a visceral attention in my words, 'bring(s) about a change in the analytic situation and freeing of the patient's material' (Ibid. p. 240).

As the brief clinical encounter shows, it freed my patient's mind to the point of re-finding an object that stood for our togetherness. The memory of feeding deer, a mnemic image (Freud, 1900) of a satisfying feeding situation, restored the much-needed illusion of safety that is necessary for a symbolic work of analysis to be carried out. Milner, whose lifelong preoccupation was the creative use of a meeting of mind and body, points out that it brings the affective changes in the analyst's mind. In my experience, it certainly engages the mind to perceive the very essence of our vitality. It feels like a journey within one's own internal organs. This must be reminiscent of our visceral being, what it might have been like to be in the mother's womb so close to her organic aliveness. Is it not also about the importance of the analyst's body awareness in re-finding the missing body of the patient? The analyst's voice that stems from the visceral space must carry the mark of its origin and potentially enable patients to reconnect with their own bodies. It might also be an attempt to frame the unbound immaterial uncertainty by focusing on its counterpart within ourselves that is framed by our own bodies.

Freud (1923) stated that the conscious ego 'is first and foremost a body-ego' (p. 27) to emphasise that the thinking ego is underpinned by a double perceptual reality. That it is the interface of the inner and outer realities. Attention is the function of the ego that is the principal tool we use whose deepest feelers can distil the information needed for perceiving a mental state of another human being.

Some Considerations for Technique

When Freud (1912) outlined his recommendations on analytic technique, he referred to his earlier paper in 1909 in which he stated a fundamental rule for clinicians, a counterpart of free association. There, he suggested examining the case of Little Hans, recounted by his father without trying to understand the case at once, but first of all to be open to be impressed and '...give our *impartial attention* to everything that there is to observe' (p. 23 my italics). Later, Freud (1923) gave a more comprehensive summary:

> Experience soon showed that the attitude which the analytic physician could most advantageously adopt was to surrender himself to his own unconscious mental activity, in a state of *evenly suspended attention*, to avoid so far as possible reflection and the construction of conscious expectations, not to try to fix anything that he heard particularly in his memory, and by these means to catch the drift of the patient's unconscious with his own unconscious.
>
> (p. 239)

Botella & Botella (2005) elaborated the concept of regredience, the analyst's regression towards more primary mode of functioning to represent something inarticulate in an analysand's psychic material. However, their emphasis is on the evolution of the representation. The under-focused aspect remains to be how to do it. How to surrender to the unknown, give up the area of secondary elaboration and get closer to a primary mode, to inarticulate in Milner's words. Perhaps, in part, it is so because as Milner (1950) put it 'We are trying to talk about a process which stops being that process as soon as we talk about it' (p. 161).

Our own personal analysis equips us with an intimate practice of surrendering to our own unconscious in the presence of the other. Through the process of internalisation of it, we continue self-holding in the physical absence of the other, and it becomes the background matrix of our mental space. The challenge arises in circumstances of intense anxieties in the analyst caused by the major life events such is the current COVID-19 pandemic. In my understanding, the capacity for visceral self-holding is a fabric of being a psychoanalyst which is hardly noticed like our breathing and heartbeat that gets consciously registered when disrupted. The anxiety of psychic survival disturbs this body-mind unit that holds us, and we need to attend to its awareness or active restoration. Visceral attention through in-dwelling in our own bodies comes as a part of the technique that is available to facilitate holding the self and the other.

It is my contention that albeit the scale of it may vary, in every analysis, there is a phase dominated by uncertainty in which analytic listening confronts us with a high degree of anxiety that threatens our psychic survival. I believe that every analyst is familiar with the experience that might last for weeks and is characterised with the sense of despair and frustration in an analytic pair with the concomitant pressure on the analyst to make sense, to do something about it. Coltart (1993) called it a *phase of bafflement* in which all that is needed is a 'perpetual bare attention'. She borrowed the concept from Buddhism to highlight the quality of profound 'opening of oneself to another person'. (p. 182)

Milner's emphasis is on analyst's own body and how to achieve this bodily attention. It is, in part, to challenge the mystery of it 'just happening'. There is an aspect of active engagement using the will to create the frame of mind to hold the attention inwardly and wait. The mysterious component, the passive aspect is about having no control over the outcome of a meeting of the mind and the body which initially is represented by a metaphor of gap.

In this light, the technique of listening consists of active and passive components. The will performs an active turning of the attention to the interior of the bodily self that I argue is crucial for achieving a state of free-floating attention. Only the attention that is anchored in the body can freely float. When I grasped this paradox, I have realised that visceral attention has a rhythmic quality to it perhaps thanks to its closeness to breathing; it submerges into the body and emerges out of its depth.

The will and visceral attention create a frame of mind, a mental psychoanalytic room that holds the analytic dyad. Milner delineates the limited function of the will that 'has to wait in very active present mindedness and be content with being a frame, holding the empty space if something new is to emerge, something that has never been before' (1952, p. 82).

The framed gap: blank paper and visceral space

I suppose that doodling is the part of body concentration on paper that is the framed gap. Being also an artist, Milner studied the importance of the surrender to the body in the process of painting. It is a kind of deliberate filling out of one's whole body with one's consciousness, so that one perceived whatever one was trying to paint with a whole body attention, not just with one's eyes or one's head (Milner, 1969, p. 48)

I wonder whether doodling has an additional freedom: it is aimless. It is not about a drawing an external object but one's inner feeling state. It is more about the process that is primary in its mode than a product; more of a mental gesture than an artistic expression. What it succeeds in is giving form to something inarticulate within us. It certainly helped me to achieve the unanxious enough state described by Milner and reconnected me with my patients. Perhaps, my unconscious search for a blank page to doodle derived from the need for a negative surface where representative activity could be recovered and representations could begin to emerge. The blankness of a piece of paper must have allowed the attention to be held. Perhaps unmindfulness is akin to a 'no memory, no desire' state of mind that Bion (1967) recommended. Ultimately, visceral attention denotes the quality of an analyst's engagement with one's own corporeality which in its perceptual presence hardly leaves room for memories and desires to take over. For perception-consciousness and memory are mutually exclusive (Freud, 1896). One of the ways to be devoid of one's own memory and desire is to give up a mind via 'some sort of active direct feeling contact with a primary body awareness' (Milner, 1960, p. 235).

As I took more interest in these free-flowing drawings, I have detected the pattern in the process itself. I would begin with a dot unfolding into a spiral which then took on a quality of life of its own. It is as if the first circular lines engaged my eyes and my hand in a way that followed the inner search for forms. I have also noticed that in fleeting moments, I would see that these various bends and loops were shaping into something familiar. Challenging to be articulated, this nonverbal process is reminiscent of the experience of utter concentration during 'a cloud journey' I would take with my five-year-old daughter as a part of home schooling during the lockdown. Whenever I perceived a bunny or a bear amongst swimming clouds, I wished she could see it before it disintegrated into a shapeless white.

Gradually, I began to see the theme in my doodles. Some depict dreaming human bodies with their eyes closed emerging from the background. I am wondering whether I have unconsciously been recreating the physicality of togetherness with my patients (Figure 17.1).

Figure 17.1 Sleeping figure. Kirchkheli.

However, most of the doodles are seashells... seashells cast ashore evoke Tagore's (1912) poem 'On the Seashore' quoted in Winnicott (1966):

> On the seashore of the endless worlds children meet...
> They build their houses with sand, and they play with empty shells.

Doodling must be a type of playing through which I recovered transitional space where empty seashells are created-found objects (Figure 17.2).[4]

Figure 17.2 Empty seashells. Kirchkheli.

And maybe, I have created and found an acoustic container, the framed gap that receives the sound: if you put your ear close enough to a seashell you hear the waves whispering about its unknown inhabitant…

Notes

1 This chapter is an expanded version of an article initially published in the *British Journal of Psychotherapy* (2021), vol. 37 no. 3, pp. xxx–xxx. It was awarded the *British Journal of Psychotherapy*'s 2020 Rozsika Parker Prize (Post-Qualification Path). It is reproduced by kind permission of the British Psychotherapy Foundation and John Wiley & Sons Ltd, with additional passages on Marion Milner.

2 It is a title of Milner's painting that I have seen in the entrance hall of the Institute of Psychoanalysis.

3 This paper was written in June 2020 when emerging out of the first national lockdown due to the pandemic of COVID-19. In July, I presented it to the British Psychoanalytical Society. At that time, there were no published papers on the subject, which accounts for the lack of relevant references. I have chosen to preserve this 'lack' which is the loss, as the birthmark, partly represented in the structure and the spirit of the paper.

4 Roussillon (2010) uses a term trouvé-créé (found-created) for Winnicott's conception of primary creativity. It is more accurate to say créé-trouvé (created-found) as Winnicott's baby finds what s/he has already created.

Section III

Milner

Art and creativity

Introduction to Section III

Milner: art and creativity

Clearly, there is some overlap among sections. Within these next pages, we relate more specifically to Milner's own answering activity. And this section too consists of answering 'activity', some inspired by reading group discussions to Milner's experimental drawings, her paintings and her writings about art and creativity.

In **Chapter 18**, Lesley Caldwell (who published a book *Art, Creativity, Living* dedicated to Milner in 2000) considers Marion's contribution to ideas of creativity, symbols and illusion. Caldwell gives the history of Milner's paper 'The Role of Illusion in Symbol Formation' (1952). She makes connections between Milner's thinking and that of others, including Winnicott, while showing Milner's distinctive contribution to art, creativity and psychoanalytic technique.

In **Chapter 19**, Hugh Haughton who has had a long-standing and deep relationship with Milner's work writes about her as a writer, as an artist and as a commentator on art and art history in her writings. To him, Milner's art is as original in its form as it is in its reflections. More so than Freud, Milner was part of a dialogue between psychoanalysis and art in the mid-20th century, by her participation in the Imago Group and her placing *On Not Being Able to Paint* in the art theory conversation.

In **Chapter 20**, Alberto Stefana gives us an in-depth introduction to Milner's work on creativity and art. He shows us how Milner's thinking evolved through creative lived experiences within her own relationship with art. He highlights two concepts with Milner's process of fusion: *fantasy (*only in internal reality can two separate items merge into one); and *illusion (*a fantastic relationship with an object perceived externally). Marion's presence in psychoanalysis in Rome and within the psyche of many Italian psychoanalyst is also evident within this chapter.

In **Chapter 21**, fellow artist and therapist Desy Safran-Gerard writes about her own experience as artist and gives us insights into Marion's way of thinking and influence on her. She describes the mutual enjoyment when in her annual visits to London she and Marion shared their experiences of artistic 'mischief' and ideas about the role of accident in art.

In **Chapter 22**, Jennifer Scott also examines Milner's artistic insights in 'The role of illusion in symbol formation' (1952) and 'Psychoanalysis and art' (1956). She notes how through the idea of cadenced cycling between the mental states of diffusion and definition Milner extends existing psychoanalytic formulations of art as substitution and reparation to include exploratory motivations towards the undiscovered. Scott situates Milner's thinking within her artistic community namely Ben Nicholson and

DOI: 10.4324/9780429433535-23

Cedric Morris, citing overlaps of experimental 'free' drawing, unconsciously interchanged body-parts, and mixing the 'visitation of the gods' with everyday objects, potentially used to explore human relationships.

The last four chapters in this section bring subjective responses to reading Milner's books particularly concerned with art, imagery and creativity—*On Not Being Able to Paint, The Suppressed Madness Of Sane Men,* and *The Hands of a Living God.* These impressions come from members of diverse reading groups around the world.

In **Chapter 23**, Aleana Egan, an artist, gives us something of her own long-standing personal response to Milner's writing as it manifests in her thinking about art and within the art itself. She highlights 'aquatic' references in Milner's work of being submerged until the tide turns for creativity to occur, linking these to her own thoughts during lockdown (in Spring 2020).

In **Chapter 24**, Wayne Featherstone, Past President of the Victorian Association of Psychoanalytic Psychotherapists in Australia, gives a succession of subjective 'pearls', including a dream, seeded by reading Milner. He uses his own introspective and self-analytical skills—taking the example of Milner who used herself in this way all through her life—to parse his experience and delve into its meaning.

In **Chapter 25**, writing on behalf of the International Winnicott Association Hellenic Group, psychoanalyst Thanassis Hatzopoulos elaborates on differences between Freud and Milner's approaches to art and the creative process. He cites Milner's triple axis of interpreting images, as drawn from art works, based on child analysis drawings and processing personal lived experience.

Finally, in **Chapter 26**, the last in this section, David Smith and Cheryl Bleakley convey in words and her own newly created images, their reactions to having read *The Hands of the Living God* with the Northern Ireland Institute of Human Relations' Clinical and Theoretical Reading Group in Belfast. They liken Milner the analyst's piecing together 'a highly complex, multi-dimensional picture' of her patient 'Susan', to Milner the artist's care and creativity in putting together her collages.

Chapter 18

'Milner and the origins of creativity'

From symbolism to symbol formation and illusion

Lesley Caldwell

Milner's important paper 'The role of illusion in symbol formation' first appeared with the title 'Aspects of symbolism in comprehension of the Not-Self', a special issue of the *International Journal of Psychoanalysis*, a festschrift for Melanie Klein's seventieth birthday (1952). When it was published in book form in *New Directions in Psychoanalysis* (1955) it was shortened and retitled with one of its former sub headings, that section then becoming *Illusion and Fusion* (p. 85). In the collection of Milner's papers *The Suppressed Madness of Sane Men* (1987) the missing sections were restored under the heading *Postscript* and included material from her main case, that of Simon, a second case, Ruth, and a response from Klein to Milner's second draft.

The first title itself had already gestured at a different canvas in its mention of the Not-Self, a formulation not associated with Klein, and surely a reference to Winnicott's paper on transitional objects, given in May 1951, which, considered by both editors and author for inclusion in that same IJP volume, seems to have been finally abandoned by mutual agreement.

The significant addition of 'illusion' to Milner's second title, introduces a concept elaborated by her and by Winnicott in the years preceding this publication but, again, not a notion associated with Melanie Klein or the Kleinians. Though referring to Klein's 1930 paper on 'The importance of symbol formation in the development of the ego' and its claims for the ego's early development, the identification of one object with another as the basis of symbolism, and symbolism as the basis of all talents (including sublimation), Milner offers a more complex view of the process of symbol formation than Klein or the other authors she cites by amplifying one aspect of Ernest Jones's argument in his paper on 'Symbolism' (1916). Both Jones and Klein stress loss and fear/anxiety as the major reasons for the infant's shift of interest from the original primary object to a secondary object, emotionally felt as the same, but, for Jones, though symbolism originates in prohibition, it does not only derive from it: there is also the need to establish a relation to reality in 'the easiest possible way' (1987, p. 84).

In this Milner saw Jones recognising a need to endow the world with something of the self, that is, a wish to establish a relation with reality, and while he, together with Hans Sachs and Otto Rank, summarises this process and the resulting equivalence as 'only a symbol' (in Milner, 1987, p. 84). Milner is interested in this symbol in and for itself, as an original form of expression, a part of prelogical thinking that gathers in the need for an inner organisation, and the establishment of identity in difference.

DOI: 10.4324/9780429433535-24

She questions their primary emphasis on symbol formation as an essentially defensive activity aimed at avoiding conflict and unease, since such a view overlooks the newborn's curiosity and interest in the surrounding world.

Her consistent interest in illusion, shared with Winnicott, but also embracing the word's wider history and its importance to the English Romantic imagination, lead her to insist on a much wider, more generous understanding of symbols: initially grounded in the body as they may be, for Milner they go well beyond that equation to be considered as part of the creative process. Milner's paper also provides the opportunity to observe a particular clinical approach to interpreting the body and its contents current at that time but extended through the theoretical differences Milner proposes and deploys.

Drawing on the art critic, Herbert Read's query, 'Is the symbol only derivative or is it an original form of expression?' (Milner, 1987, p. 86), she favours the newness and aliveness of the creative process and the enrichment offered by a symbolic capacity. Her conviction of the value of this emphasis was arrived at through the clinical work she reports with Simon, together with her thinking about her own drawing as somehow enabling a freedom between hand activity and mental organisation. But these are also the years when her long term patient, Susan was bringing large numbers of drawings to every session, so this paper carries the distillation of her ongoing thinking about her own activity, together with her work with at least two patients who pose questions regarding the roots of the self and its origins in a creative encounter with an environment.

In her report of Simon's 'a game of war between two villages' (pp. 86–91), Milner begins with a typical if somewhat unexpected statement for a clinical paper, 'Moments when the original poet in each of us created the world for us', moments she describes as 'when the imagination catches fire and a whole subject or skill lights up with significance' (p. 88). Simon's game involves his bombing a village of people and animals where Milner was a villager whose role was to save the toys from being destroyed. Her initial interpretations addressed bisexual conflicts in relation to her and to his parents, and to men and women more generally, but she also related his play to the school and its unsatisfactoriness, making the symbolic parallels between the entry into knowledge and the desired, but forbidden entry into the mother's body.

Milner had been particularly struck by the different tones her patient adopted towards her and towards the toys. At the beginning of a session he was bullying and head-master like towards her, but as he played with the toys this would change so that he would become able to speak to her in a friendly, considerate way. She related this to his being able to do what he liked with the toys, which she came to understand as his use of a *pliable medium*, outside himself, with which he could do what he wished. In turn this seemed to enable a different relation with her, and with himself. The play with the toys was 'something half way between daydreaming and purposeful instinctive or expedient action' (p. 92) which from her own experience of her free drawings she related to how moving the toys changed the parameters of the village. Once she had made a mark on paper, it inevitably provoked new associations, 'the line, as it were, answers back and functions as a very primitive type of external object' (p. 92).

Milner then describes a shift two months after the session she had described in detail where she observes that the boy's bullying tone had gone. This she linked to an external event: the school had agreed to allow the photography club with which Simon was involved to have meetings in the school. It was not the school's first accommodation of the boy and his difficulties but Milner thought that this decision incorporated 'an acceptance of a bit of his own spontaneous creation' (p. 93) which, in its turn, changed his relation to the school.

Milner regarded Simon's play with the villages and with his analyst over many months as play both about his relation to the not-me-ness of the world of school and to the original difficulties: a dad away at war, a new brother, London being bombed (Milner's own area and house had suffered) and the loss of his woolly rabbit, the lost transitional object. The transitional object is the quintessential object that is and is – not me – the baby can do what he likes with it, it is both an object and a relation that can further the illusion, initially provided by the maternal holding environment, that there are no clear boundaries or variations in the existence or non-existence of body boundaries. Gathering together the extended meanings of the transitional object Anne Alvarez says 'For Winnicott the transitional object carries the meaning of that which as yet is not the other and that which is and is not the self' (Alvarez, 1976).

Milner saw Simon discovering the boundaries of the self through exploration of the boundaries between him and his analyst, and theoretically she argued for this as *the* exploration, enabled through illusion, of necessary states in the development of object relationships which supported her own contention that oneness is the condition for two ness. To her the environment initially facilitates this oneness by the recurrent provision of a framed space and a pliable medium where no decision is necessary about what is self and other. And Milner commented that there would sometimes be a quality of beauty in the setup of fire and light Simon created in his play which she sums up as 'it was my imagination that caught fire' (p. 96).

For her the establishing and awareness of objects have to precede any attempts at repairing them, and drawing on her own work she further proposes that to find new objects a temporary loss of sense of self has to be tolerated and that the idea of the dissolution or existence or non-existence of body boundaries is significant in the making of art: it reproduces states that are part of everyday experience in healthy infancy...

Her interrogation of her creative activity in the forties and the fifties, especially her interest in her relationship with the basic tools of drawing, the line, the outline, the frame, colour, rhythm, form, space, action (in the sense of vitality), areas associated with manuals about how to paint, and with painting and drawing itself, were approached through what she herself produced, together with that wider interest in illusion which was further deepened by her exchanges with the critic Adrian Stokes, both of them passionate about art and psychoanalysis. All these contributed to challenging an approach to the world as originating in deficit and compensatory activity.

Her postscript to *On Not Being Able to Paint* further discusses the creative process in relation to the external world:

> Observations of problems to do with painting had all led to the idea that awareness of the external world is itself a creative process, an immensely complex creative interchange between what comes from inside and what comes from outside, a complex alternation of fusing and separating.
>
> (p. 171)

For her, a capacity for reverie involves an abandoning of any insistence on a rigid separation between me and not-me, albeit, in her introduction to the Routledge reprint,

Janet Sayers proposes that the book is best thought of as an investigation of the creative process and its vicissitudes in which Milner focuses on her own images as a way of getting to herself and her different states of mind (2010).

In taking up her work, Michael Eigen proposed that the notion of 'undifferentiation' with which she had originally worked, should be abandoned in favour of an arena where making a distinction between me and not-me becomes irrelevant. In that arena, which Winnicott calls 'transitional', *Me and Not Me can be accepted as coexisting.* It is an arena where the development of the creative process is above all something new, alive, containing life itself, where the pressure of the creative process exists for its own sake, not as a backward looking attempt at reparation (as proposed by Klein). Milner pursues the internal and external conditions necessary for this throughout her work.

In his tribute to both Milner and Winnicott, the art historian Michael Podro (2000) explores what gives painting its specificity, its own life, so that it actually matters. The difference between representing the world and imbuing it with the feeling necessary for it to be art regards how affect and thought relate, and he describes how the painter has to relinquish the external details of the subject, take it into herself and reconstruct it in the painting, that particular overlap of inner and outer worlds Milner herself endorses:

> Painting goes deeper in its roots than restoring to immortal life one's lost loves, it goes right back to the stage before one had found a love to lose… what the…innovator in art is doing, fundamentally, is not recreating in the sense of making again what has been lost (although he is doing this), but creating what is, because he is creating the power to see it. By continually breaking up the established familiar patterns…he really is creating 'nature' including human nature.
>
> (p. 161)

> Milner was also interested in the more internal aspects of the frame, or the "concentrated states of mind in which one creates one's own inner frame, frame of reference, as essential in all mental productivity, whether creating ideas or works of art, a state in which one holds a kind of inner space" (Milner, 1969, p. 250). For her such a capacity derives from the experience of being held in the arms of the mother and it is recreated in the particular creative illusion of the transference. Following her personal search into her inability to paint, she suggests that it is exactly in these moments of primary 'madness' that every man creates new symbols that attribute a personal and subjective meaning to the reality just built, in as much as: "the substance of experience is what we bring to what we see, without our own contribution we see nothing"
>
> (1950, p. 33)

As respondent to Ernst Gombrich, Milner took up an idea of his which resonated with her work on symbol formation where he had emphasised art as primarily an act of creation, insisting that 'substitution precedes portrayal and creation precedes communication'. That is, the art work, first and foremost, involves the encounter between artist and materials at a particular moment, though of course its symbolic value as a communication about something else may also be there. Milner concluded,

> Ernst Gombrich makes a strong case for seeing art as having to do essentially with the very basis of our interest in anything beyond the primary objects of instincts. In fact, it (art) not only uses symbols, it creates symbols.... it brings about what Gombrich called "the basis of civilisation"
>
> (1954, p. 411).

Her emphasis is on 'this deliberately fostered getting in touch with not just hidden wishes but with a different way of functioning and a way of functioning which is essential if something new is to be created' (1987, p. 214). It is not on what is symbolised or the unconscious wishes informing it (pp. 211, 214) but on what is created and its links with 'the alternation of ego states, this interplay between the articulate and inarticulate levels of functioning as basic in all creative activity' (1969, p. 293). Milner, like Winnicott, emphasises the link between art and the more ordinary forms of creativity available to all. The title of her chapter 6 of *The Hands of the Living God,* 'Attention to the threshold between the articulate and the inarticulate', echoes this. What is important is how different forms of functioning are made evident in what constantly presents itself in the consulting room.

Milner (1960) states that:

> My own clinical experience does lead me to agree with the idea that the ability to find objects with whom relationships can be made does depend on the previous existence of a recurrent state of unity, one which comes originally from the mother-child fusion. Also that this feeling of unity is not a projective identification resulting from splitting a pre–existent ego, but is the result of recurrent awareness, in feeling, of an undifferentiated state of no separation, a state described by Masud Khan ... in terms of 'a pre-stage of infancy development where ego and id themselves emerge from an undifferentiated matrix of energic potential structure'.
>
> (1960, p. 238)

Within the illusory setting established by analysis, the analyst accommodates the patient's need for a type of experience which, at the start, may not have allowed as a healthy enough process of development. As Stefana claims, Milner 'functions as an environment-mother described by Winnicott, being a psycho-physical presence – and as such, a support – capable of experiencing the absence of sense, without the compulsion to attribute meaning to it, capable, in other words, of observing, and letting the patient discover that she is there (Stefana, 2018).

In conclusion, Milner's contribution to the debate fifty years ago was distinctive and it remains highly pertinent to present debate about art, creativity and psychoanalytic technique because it makes the relation between internal and external world not merely a condition of symbolising an internal development, but it takes seriously the sense of urgency that drives us to live and emphasises that both living and art spring from the wish to be a participant and not a bystander of one's own world, whether alone or with others.

Chapter 19

'The Chosen Medium'

Milner's art

Hugh Haughton

With *A Life of One's Own* (1934) and *Experiment in Leisure* (1937), Milner established herself as a writer before she became a psychoanalyst, so that when she did become an analyst, she was a very special kind of analytic writer. Also a keen artist – in *On Not Being Able to Paint* she calls herself a 'Sunday' painter – when she wrote about art, as she often did, this informed her whole exploration of the aesthetic. In *A Life of One's Own*, she tells us that she'd drawn and painted from childhood, and in adulthood she attended week-end classes with Cedric Morris (the teacher and portraitist of Lucian Freud) as well as with the emigré Polish painter Marion Bohusz-Szyszko (in a painting group which included her fellow-analyst Masud Khan). In later life she also held an exhibition of her own art in London in 1971, as well as making collages out of her earlier paintings.

These first-hand experiences as a painter and writer gave her contributions to the psychoanalytic study of visual art in *On Not Being Able to Paint* (1950) and elsewhere a unique authority and inwardness. Milner found her vocation as a writer in *A Life of One's Own* when she started writing about her own diaries – the kind of writing anyone might do – and the thematic driving force of *On Not Being Able to Paint* is that it is an exploration of the kind of painting 'anyone might do'. Her own art-writing remains overtly autobiographical or testimonial, revolving around her own diary entries as well as her 'free' or 'doodle' drawings, and diary-style commentaries on art by herself or others. Later in *The Hands of the Living God* (1969), her pioneering combination of case history, memoir and revisionary psychoanalytic theory, she offers a comparably inward account of the drawings and paintings of a patient called Susan, and a candid account of her countertransference, creating a sustained biographical narrative that combines post-Winnicottian art therapy and speculative aesthetic theory.

As in all her writing about visual art, her stance is searchingly autobiographical and about the role art-making and art-viewing plays in all our lives rather than the lives of Leonardo or Michelangelo. She intuitively follows the principle of Walter Pater, who said 'the first step towards seeing the object as it really is, is to know one's own impression as it really is' (Pater, 1980, p. xix). In *A Life of One's Own*, she describes her impressions 'in front of a Cézanne still-life' of 'green apples, a white plate and a cloth' as she gradually becomes aware 'the colours were coming alive'. She returns to Cézanne in a chapter on 'Paintings as Making Real' in *On Not Being Able to Paint,* where she quotes him inviting us to 'Descend with the painter into the dim tangled roots of things' (Milner, 1950, p. 29). In all her writings about art she too descends into

DOI: 10.4324/9780429433535-25

the dim tangled roots of painting and viewing, inserting the artwork into the place of Freud's dreamwork, and viewing it as part of the continuity of psychic life.

Freud opened the door for psycho-analysts to talk about art – with his speculative, biographically-slanted essays on Leonardo and Michelangelo, in particular – but, though he was an inspiration to the Surrealists, he didn't reciprocate their interest (vide Dali) and wasn't touched by the Post-Impressionism of Cézanne or what John Berger calls 'The Moment of Cubism', as Milner clearly was. In fact she was part of a much larger intellectual moment or movement in the middle years of the twentieth-century when a number of British post-Freudians and post-Kleinians, became caught up in a dialogue between psychoanalysis and art. Deeply personal as her approach is, it was part of a larger contemporary project, involving many other major players, particularly Adrian Stokes, who after several years of analysis with Melanie Klein, brought psychoanalytic thinking into play in his prolific reflections on visual art and artists, including *The Quattrocento* (1932), *Michelangelo* (1955) and *A Game that Must be Lost* (1973). In 1951, the poet and art critic Herbert Read published 'Psychoanalysis and the Problem of Aesthetic Value', while in 1952, Ernst Kris published *Psycho-analytic Explorations in Art* in 1952, and Anton Ehrenzweig *The Psycho-analysis of Artistic Vision and Hearing.*

Shortly afterwards in 1954, Stokes, Milner and others founded the Imago Group, which met weekly to explore the relationship of psychoanalysis and art. The group included Ehrenzweig (later author of the influential 1967 *The Hidden Order of Art*), the hugely influential art historian Ernst Gombrich (author of *The Story of Art* and *Meditations on a Hobby-Horse*) as well as the philosopher Richard Wollheim (author of *Art and Its Objects*), among others. In this maelstrom of theoretical speculation, there is a case for seeing Milner's provocatively titled *On Not Being Able to Paint* as offering the most brilliantly heterodox post-Freudian investigation into the creative process that we have. Ehrenzweig told Milner that his *The Hidden Order of Art* was 'triggered by his reading and reviewing' it, and it was also reviewed enthusiastically by a bevy of influential analysts, including W.R.D. Fairbairn, Michael Fordham, D.W. Winnicott, and Masud Khan, as well as having a Forward to the second edition written by Anna Freud and generating an illuminating correspondence with Adrian Stokes.[1] Whatever about being able to paint, this confirms Milner could certainly *write* about painting in a way that transformed psychoanalytic approaches to art. Writing in the wake of Post-Impressionism and what John Berger calls 'The Moment of Cubism', Milner offers an account of the mimetic process in non 'realist' terms as a response to the inner, subjective world as much as to the outer, objective world.

Nicola Glover has argued that Milner and Winnicott broadened 'the scope of traditional Kleinian aesthetics', emphasising 'the importance of a *psychoanalytic creativity* – the role of creative and aesthetic experience' in both patient and the analyst' (2009, chapter 6). Commenting on some of her 'free drawings' of 'Earth', she suspects that 'painting goes deeper in its roots than restoring to immortal life one's lost loves, it goes right back to the stage before one has found a love to lose' (1950, p. 79).

Though like Klein, Milner's view of 'psychic creativeness' is rooted in the experience of early infancy, she argues that 'there is much evidence to suggest that this function of art as restoring lost objects, is in fact secondary; and that the primary role is the 'creating' of objects, in the psychoanalytic sense, not the recreating of them' (Milner, 1950, p. 187). In the chapter on 'Painting and Living', she develops an account of the 'artist in us', and integral to her account of the work of art and artists is this sense of there being 'an artist' in everybody, related to our capacity for 'symbolism' and the 'symbolic' thinking she sees as embodied in the artwork. Her discussions of aesthetics, unlike Freud's and Klein's, are focused on the production of forms and indeed on form itself, both the medium and the created object.

She conjures wonderful names for her drawings – 'Ape in the Garden of Eden', 'The Angry Parrot', 'Skeleton under the Sea' – and those of her patient Susan, like 'Duck Exploding' or 'The Coiled Snake' – giving them an identity like that of gallery paintings, and offering detailed morphological and symbolic interpretations of these enigmatic objects comparable to Adrian Stokes' readings of Donatello or Freud's of his patients' dreams. Her democratising work is not about geniuses, so much as what Blake called 'the Poetic genius' in all of us.

In *Eternity's Sunrise* (1987), an exploration of travel diaries, drawings and memories, she begins by pondering the 'tangled mass of fragmented images' she finds in 'the cave of memory' on her return from touring, in an attempt to understand what meant most to her in four tours of Greece, as well as travel to Italy and the Holy Land – whether they are 'the public moments, the seeing of places listed in the travel brochure' (including classical temples, churches, and works of art), or 'small but private moments', and the relationship between these different kinds of experience' (1987, p. 5). In the course of this unprecedented psychoanalytic travel book, she tries to untangle the meaning of some of her own paintings like 'The Goat and the Chapel' and 'The Gardener and the Frog' (which she reproduces) as well dwelling on a series of epiphany-like encounters with public artworks that struck her with peculiar force and intimacy. They include a mosaic of Christ Pantocrator from a monastery in Daphni, a mosaic of the Mother and Child in Torcello, the 'Virgin and Gypsy' or 'Tempest' by Giorgione in the Accademia in Venice, as well as a Madonna and Child by Masaccio – all paintings with both a religious and familial dimension, which elicit Winnicottian as well as quasi-mystical speculations from her about infancy, the body, and gender. Setting these images against each other in a one-off exhibition within the text, she finds 'the same look of speculation, surmise, half-seen possibilities' or 'consciousness on the verge of a leap forward' in the eyes of Giorgione's 'gypsy' and the Byzantine Christ in Daphni, saying 'whatever they meant for whoever made these works of art at different times and places', 'they were undoubtedly saying something to me in this second half of the twentieth-century' (pp. 50–51). Commenting later on 'The Bathers' by Seurat in the National Gallery in London, a painting she says she had 'loved for years though had never thought why', she notes that while it is another 'perfect summer day', as in so many Impressionist paintings, all the figures are 'all in their different ways deep in reverie' (her primal subject), and that there's a 'small halo of light' behind the outline of the boys' skins and that one boy's hat makes 'a circle within a circle', so that 'the inner, smaller circle is part of the outer larger one, yet each maintaining its own identity' (p. 173). 'Whatever it meant to Seurat (consciously), she says all this evokes in her the sense of 'a meeting of mind and body in a deep self-sensation that can bring transformation, a kind of resurrection' (comparing it to Piero's Resurrection in San Sepolcro).

Milner's readings and interpretations of artworks like these make no claim to be 'objective', but then her whole stance towards art is that involves a counter-point or synthesis between the objective and subjective. Her essay on 'Psychoanalysis and Art' of

1956 is probably her most systematic, objective-looking review of the field, and closer to an official 'paper' than most of her avowedly personal reflections on psychoanalysis or the arts. The essay takes its bearings from Freud, Ehrenzweig, Stokes, Klein, as well as thinkers like William James, Herbert Read and Jacques Maritain, but as it develops it morphs into an extraordinary commentary on William Blake's *Illustrations to the Book of Job*, 'a work of art which combines the vision of two poets' (1987, p. 173). Offering attentive psychoanalytic interpretations of each of Blake's pictures, Milner reads the double artwork as if it is, not a symptom, but a work of psychoanalytic theory, embodying the idea that 'the unconscious mind, by the very fact of not clinging to the distinction between self and other, seer and seen, can do things that the conscious logical mind cannot do' (p. 214). It ends with her own answer to the question 'What is art?', based on 'a guess that has grown out of my own experience in using the method Freud invented for observing unconscious processes'. Answering it (and the 'Answering Activity' is one of her key terms), she invokes 'the capacity of the conscious mind to have the experience of cooperating with unconscious depths, by means of the battle to express something with the chosen medium'. This emphasis on the transformational 'medium', unlike Freud's, is akin to Christopher Bollas 'transformational object', and lies at the heart of her psychoanalytic interrogation of the subject.

Milner writes as a practitioner in *On Not Being Able to Paint*, as a therapist in *The Hands of the Living God*, as a tourist and gallery visitor in *Eternity's Sunrise* and in 'Psychoanalysis and Art' as a commentator on Blake's *Illustrations to Job* for her most focused theoretical treatment of the subject. Blake figures in all her books as poet, painter, and authority on creativity and gave her the title for *Eternity's Sunrise.* His notion of 'the Poetic Genius' in everyone is one she embraces with dialectical subtlety and sophistication. Milner aligns herself not only with psychoanalytic predecessors but with the English visionary tradition embodied in Blake, offering not only a psychoanalytic interpretation of Blake but an exhilaratingly Blakean version of psychoanalysis as life-writing and art-writing.

My own encounter with Milner grew out of my own overlapping investment in poetry and the visual arts on the one hand and in psychoanalysis on the other. I first got to grips with the productive sibling rivalry between these forms of writing as the editor of *The Uncanny* (2004), for the New Penguin Freud, a volume that included many of Freud's most compelling explorations of art, including 'The Creative Writer and Daydreaming', 'Family Romances' and his speculative biographical essay on Leonardo da Vinci and a memory of childhood. No other psychoanalyst has been as hospitable to daydreaming (or what she calls 'reverie') as Milner, and my Freud introduction led naturally to me writing an introduction for a new edition of Milner's *Eternity's Sunrise* (2011), the crowning volume of her work both on diaries and the visual arts. I had been a reader of Milner since first encountering *On Not Being Able to Paint* many years earlier, but I found this late book about the potentially mind-opening experiences of leisure, travel, art, memory, and psychoanalysis a mind-opening artwork itself. Indeed, each work of Milner is both an experiment and a record of a journey that's still unfinished, both a travel diary and a meta-diary reflecting on earlier work.

As noted earlier, Milner made a series of collages out of her own cut-up earlier paintings in later life. In a sense this is also how she treats images, symbols, artworks and drawings in all her hybrid texts. Milner's *oeuvre* works at a cross-roads between psychoanalysis, autobiography, and aesthetics, and is as original in its own form as in its reflections on the central role that forms of art play in our lives in helping us negotiate what she calls, following the philosopher George Santayana, 'the suppressed madness of sane men'.

Note

1 See Janet Sayers, Introduction to *On Not Being Able to Paint* (London: Routledge, 2010), xliii–xlv.

Chapter 20

Introduction to Marion Milner's work on creativity and art[1]

Alberto Stefana

Introduction

This chapter outlines the thinking of Marion Milner as psychoanalyst and painter and examines the issues of creativity and art. Milner, as a result of personal research on the inability to paint, came to believe that the creative artistic process, intended as the creation of new symbols that attribute a personal and subjective meaning to the newly created reality, occurs during moments of "primary madness" (of illusion of unity, of pre-logical fusion between subject and object), making it possible to have a relationship of reciprocity between internal and external reality. In such a process, the aesthetic experience of the artist at work plays a key role. Using Milner's ideas about the creative process as a base, I investigate links between psychoanalysis and the unconscious processes in symbol formation and artistic creation, showing that Milner's work is still relevant to clinical psychoanalysis today.

Creativity and art

In 1938, tired of her own drawings that seemed more like accurate copies of external reality, Marion Milner began her study on how to learn to draw. This research and subsequent reflections upon her drawings she eventually used as a kind of internal dialogue, even in the analysis she started in the same year with Sylvia Payne (Sayers, 2002). Milner believed it might be interesting to try to draw something without any conscious intention and was shocked to discover, almost by chance, that sometimes it is possible to execute sketches or drawings, allowing eye and hand to be free to do exactly what they wished, without the conscious seeking of a preordained result, without the inclination to draw "something". Milner, thus, began to look at drawings in the way Freud approached dreams, and she realized that in implementing this "free" method, as she termed it, moods and ideas, represented by the signs of the pencil on paper, could emerge, and that these, on a conscious level, seemed totally absent. Therefore, free drawings were permeated by the shape of emotions and pure thoughts (conscious and unconscious) of the one who produced them. Milner conducted an analysis of her drawings and of her own mental processes that accompanied these creative experiences.

It became clear to Milner that painting is deeply connected to the problems of distance and separation between subject and object, and she realized that the edges of objects in the reality of nature are not so fixed, clear and compact as "reasonable"

DOI: 10.4324/9780429433535-26

and reassuring common sense would want: "When really looked at in relation to each other their outlines were not clear and compact, as I had always supposed them to be, they continually become lost in shadow" (Milner, 1950, p. 18). Behind this certainty of the existence of borders, Milner saw a defence against the fear of being crazy, "fear of losing all sense of separating boundaries; particularly the boundaries between the tangible realities of the external world and the imaginative realities of the inner world of feeling and idea" (p. 19).

Such creative experiments, which resulted in her book *On Not Being Able to Paint* (1950), were inspired to some extent, as she herself said (Maclagan, 1992), by her seeing Grace Pailthorpe (also a psychoanalyst) and Reuben Mednikoff's joint exhibition of paintings at the Guggenheim Jeune Gallery in London between January and February 1939. Their work, which was defined by Breton as "the best and most truly Surrealist of the works exhibited by the British artists" on the occasion of the International Surrealist Exhibition in London in 1936 (Walsh and Wilson, 1998), featured extensive use of automatic drawing (Montanaro and Stefana, manuscript in preparation). Furthermore, it is in Milner's free drawings that the squiggles of Donald Winnicott (1971a; see also Stefana and Gamba, 2018) are deeply rooted (Stefana, 2018).

The process of symbolization

According to Milner (1952b), symbol formation is preceded by an identification of a primary with a secondary object, whereby the latter is different from the former in reality, though they are equivalent from an affective point of view (of course this affective equivalence does not mean that the subject actually confuses them). For clarity, it should be noted that by primary object we mean the object, or that part of it, to which the child initially relates. It is in this primary object that the subject tries to find a representation of his moods, the acquisition of which would remove the need to abandon these feelings. The secondary object is another piece of the world (a person, a work of art, etc.) that becomes significant as a result of the process of symbolization.

There are two concepts to which Milner refers when reflecting on this process of fusion: fantasy, because only in internal reality can two separate items merge into one; and illusion, implying a fantastic relationship with an object perceived externally. Milner (1950, 1952b) understands illusion as a necessary tool for a healthy adaptation to reality, and not at all as a failure in the adaptive process (here Milner anticipates some aspects of Winnicott's transitional phenomenon concept). Indeed, she argued that the existence of boundaries between "me" and "not-me" is not known innately but is something that is experienced even though one might not be aware of it. The acquisition of this knowledge is in fact a slow and painstaking process for the baby:

> our inner dream and outer perception both spring from a common source or primary phase of experience in which the two are not distinguished, a primary 'madness' which all of us have lived through and to which at times we can return.
>
> (Milner, 1950, p. 33)

Thus, Milner grounds her notion of illusion in the sensorial experience of fusion between self and object. As the mother steadily becomes less attuned to the needs of the baby, the development of transitional phenomena and potential space will take place, and it is in this context that mental space, alongside the space for playing and symbolizing, is created. Here Milner implies the necessity of maintaining a degree of illusion.

What brings the infant to shift its interest from the primary to the secondary object is either the actual loss of the object or alternatively the existence of an internal conflict which forces the child to transfer its attention and invest in another object in order to protect the primary from its own (the child's) aggression, and itself from guilt feelings (Klein, 1926, 1930). According to Milner, premature ego development—due to a childhood in which primary omnipotence had found too little space to develop—inhibits the capacity for symbol formation. Having seen the need to establish object relations, Milner identified not only the need for reparation (Klein) but also the need to endow the external world of aspects of the self (Jones, 1918) that make it familiar as the basis of this process of identification. Milner sees this process as the only possible way to understand the world.

The imaginative concentration

Beginning in the 1930s, Milner began to think about Zen Buddhism and the mystical traditions of both the East and the West in an attempt to learn more about methods to produce changes in consciousness by means of concentrating on the inner awareness of the body. In this way, she came to support the need for a particular type of imaginative focus (active and immobile at the same time), a contemplative action that enriches the outside world of certain qualities matching the subject's own (Milner, 1956). Such a state of deep concentration is a sensory experience in which you create a space, a kind of womb from which something new can be born. Focusing on this creation of an imaginative illusion is ecstasy: the emotional experience of searching and finding a substitute, the familiar in the unfamiliar. Being in such a state of ecstasy is like being in touch with one's own overwhelming ability to create the world. In this sense, we can say that "Art creates Nature", that is:

> By suffusing, through giving it form, the not-me objective material with the me-subjective psychic content, it makes the not–me 'real', realizable. (…) So what the artist (…) is doing, fundamentally, is not recreating in the sense of making again what has been lost (although he is doing this), but creating what is, because he is creating the power to perceive it. By continually breaking up the established familiar patterns (familiar in his particular culture and time in history) of logical common-sense divisions of me–not-me, he really is creating 'nature', including human nature. And he does this by unmasking old symbols and making new ones, thus incidentally making it possible for us to see that the old symbol was a symbol; whereas before we thought the symbol was in 'reality' because we had nothing else to compare it with. In this sense he is continually destroying 'nature' and re-creating nature—which is perhaps why the depressive anxieties can so easily both inhibit and be relieved by successful creative work in the arts.
>
> (Milner, 1957, pp. 228–229)

What Milner tells us is that the poetic genius hidden in all of us, the one that "creates" the outside world, discovering something familiar in what is unknown, needs a particular kind of imaginative concentration, a contemplative widespread attention that enriches what one recognizes as a particular quality of one's self. This concentration within the self and within the body is not to be seen exclusively as a regressive movement, but also, if not more, as a pre-logical subject–object fusion, as well as a body–mind fusion (Milner, 1960, 1969).

The experience of the artist

An essential part of the personal affective experience of the artist at work is contained within the artist's body. In this regard, Milner argues that in order to achieve balance and stability one needs to create a relationship of reciprocity between the bodily rhythms of the subject and the person who so dedicatedly and lovingly cares for this body. Moreover, it is equally important that there be a possibility of reciprocal exchange between the individual qualities of the chosen medium of expression (see Rayner, 1991). The psychophysical rhythm of a person immersed in creating a work of art, whatever it may be, is unique and unrepeatable. It is the source of life that animates true works of art, those creations that are an externalization, through lines and colours (in the case of the painting), of the uniqueness of the artist's own psychophysical structure. Milner (1957) tells us that the psychophysical organism of everyone has an intrinsic rhythmic potential that can acquire a more stable order with respect to the belief in an either externally or internally imposed order (the conscious planning mind).

More generally, we can say that:

> what the painter does conceptualize in non-verbal symbols is the astounding experiences of how it feels to be alive, the experiences known from inside, of being a moving, living body in space, with capacities to relate oneself to other objects in space. And included in this experience of being alive is the very experiencing of the creative process itself.
>
> (Milner, 1957, p. 227)

This attempt to preserve experience is the unconscious attempt to recreate the relationship with the primary object that was lost, either because of the unconscious aggressive feelings aroused by the separation from the not-me, or because transience is a characteristic of the emotional experience. Let us be reminded, however, that the primary function of art is not the recovery of lost objects, but the "creation" of new ones. So in a certain sense, the artistic process could be called "narcissistic", "because the work is done 'to' the painting, and not 'with' the painting. If, instead, the painting becomes 'the other'—having desires and demands of its own—there can be a transcendence of the preoccupation with the self" (Safán-Gerard, 2018, p. 6). Then the artist can engage in a true creative act of creating an object, experiencing him/herself at the service of the work and making communication between them possible—"the artwork now has a life of its own and the creator can interact with it" (ibid.).

The bodily experience—more specifically those interests invested in the various stages of psychosexual development (the oral, anal and phallic stages)—plays a key role in generating those symbols that everyone uses in the creative process. This is what is meant when we say that metaphors originate in the body.

Some considerations of aesthetic experience within artistic creation

A key element in psychic creativity, defined as the ability to form a symbol for the emotions, is the necessity of finding the familiar in the unfamiliar or vice versa, with similar results. Fulfilling this requirement allows the author of the symbol to overcome natural fears (the unknown being inherently disturbing), to gain knowledge of the reality of detachment and separation, with all of the accompanying anxiety, and to establish object relations. This process is made possible by the basic identifications which "require an ability to tolerate a temporary loss of sense of self, a temporary giving up of the discriminating ego which stands apart and tries to see things objectively and rationally and without emotional colouring" (Milner 1952, p. 189).

This mental state of deep and harmonious interaction between internal and external, me and not-me, subject and object, in which the variations in the perception of existence or non-existence of the boundary of one's body play a key role, involves the feeling of enclosing the whole world (both good and bad objects) inside one's own body (Milner, 1950, 1952). Milner (1969) called that feeling "a sea of undifferentiated being" (p. 29).

It is during this "aesthetic moment" that the viewer of the work of art identifies with it and dissolves completely into it. It is clear that the anxiety that the subject feels in these moments of immersion into creative depths is an integral part of the creative process; therefore, it should not be avoided or denied. On a perceptual level, the subject must be able to arouse a contemplative, extensive attention, implying a kind of deconstruction of the mind's conditioning, which opens up the possibility of having a more complete experience of both one's own self and the external world, to "actively" abandon oneself to the moment.

According to Milner (1956), the creative process, resulting in a cancellation of the separation between subject and object (a separation upon which logical thinking is based), takes place within the context of the gaps in our mental activity on the surface: "it must be clear to anyone who looks inward that our mental life does progress with a movement rather like a porpoise" (p. 195), where there is a cyclical sequence of immerging and re-emerging with respect to the surface of the water, or more precisely the border between the conscious and the unconscious. Milner (1957) considers that "the logical terms in which the capacity for symbol formation is thought about are perhaps less important than the pre-logical" (p. 217).

Creativity cannot simply be attributed to the mental state, defined as "a sea of undifferentiated being", but it is strictly tied to the continuous oscillating between the state in which the ego of the child (and then of the healthy adult) is not yet differentiated from the surrounding external world, and the state characterized by the surface mind activity, in which things and the self are grasped separately (Milner, 1956). Such cyclical alternating is in part passively experienced, but it is also used actively with the intention of producing something. But for it to take place within the subject, a situation is needed that makes it possible to surrender to reverie and to the illusion of oneness, a context that is offered by painting, both to the artist and the consumer (Milner, 1957). Therefore, what needs to be reached or recovered is a mental state resembling that of childhood's dual union, where the self and the not-self are not very distinct, because only in these mental states is it possible to experience creativity (Spitz, 1985).

Milner (1952b, 1956) opted to characterize art as a bridge between inner reality and outer reality, where the boundaries merge and not without getting a bit confused. Therefore, art is a method that allows the adult to escape the mortal sterility inherent in a fixed and exclusively "objective" perception of the world. This can occur because art makes the illusion of unity and a pre-logic fusion between subject and object possible, allowing a relationship of reciprocity between internal and external realities. Crucial to this process is the role of the surrounding framework. Its goal is to guarantee that all that is represented within it is not an objective reality but an illusion; in this sense, what we perceive inside the frame has to be interpreted symbolically, as a metaphor (a way of knowing and communicating), expressive of the psychic reality (Milner, 1952a).

It is obvious that, through the use of an expressive medium, artistic activity allows one to experience the act of creating an object. (If one's emotional development during childhood went reasonably well, this is actually a re-experience.) Milner (1952b, 1956) tells us that the expressive medium, being flexible, allows itself to take the form of one's own fantasies. But the expressive medium is also something which, in all likelihood, the artist tends to idealize to a great extent. Only if the artist loves this medium to the extent that he can become sensitive to its real qualities and potential (and, therefore, take full advantage of the pliability of the material) will the object created live up to the idealization. From what has been said, it follows that artists can only be ambivalent towards their medium; they love and hate it and fight it constantly.

The creation of something new, and not the original subconscious wish symbolized by the object created, is the most important aspect of every work of art (a new piece of the external world that through the process of symbolization has satisfied the primary need for unity, shifting interest onto the real object). The artist moulds his own private experiences into a new form that can be incorporated into the social world of art, creating symbols that let the inner life leak through. In this way, the artist reduces, without completely removing, the gap between experience itself and the linguistic and visual means of expressing feelings. The work of art, via the "form" through which it has become visible, represents the vehicle of communication for the feelings of the artist. This means that the symbols already discovered by the artist acquire full meaning (for him/her) (Milner, 1952b).

What Milner wants us to understand is that:

> the unconscious mind, by the very fact of its not clinging to the distinction between self and other, seer and seen, can do things that the conscious logical mind cannot do. By being more sensitive to the samenesses rather than the differences between things, by being passionately concerned with finding 'the familiar in the unfamiliar'.
>
> (Milner, 1956, p. 214)

What can be deduced from Milner's works is that in life there are moments, recurring and circumscribed, found both in children and adults, where there is a temporary renouncing of differentiation, where boundaries dissolve and Aristotelian logic loses its meaning. Milner (1950), following her personal search into the inability to paint, suggests that it is exactly in these moments of primary "madness" that every man creates new symbols that attribute a personal and subjective meaning to the reality just built inasmuch as "the substance of experience is what we bring to what we see, without our own contribution we see nothing" (p. 33).

To conclude, we can ask ourselves, along with Marion Milner (1956), what is art?

> Can we say that it is to do with the capacity of the conscious mind to have the experience of co-operating with the unconscious depths, by means of the battle to express something with the chosen medium? If so, then perhaps it is true to say that the measure of genius in the arts is linked up with the extent to which the artist does succeed in co-operating with his unconscious mind by means of his medium
>
> (p. 215)

As we have determined, it is within such a concept of art and artistic creation that the aesthetic experience of the working artist plays a key role.

Some implications for clinical psychoanalysis

In Milner's vision (see also Stefana, 2011, 2014), the psychophysical health of a subject rests on his/her ability to pass with ease from a state in which fantasy and reality, self and not-self, inside and outside are not clearly distinguishable one from the other, to a state in which separateness is recognized. However, before such an alternation can take place, it is necessary for the subject to experience a good enough environment, one that functions as a protection from outside intrusions and allows the subject to feel a sense of security, to be able to indulge in fantasies without having to seek refuge there and reject an "external" reality that is too painful; otherwise there is a risk of a premature and, thus, defensive development of the ego, which would trigger an inability to move from one state to another, creating an excessive concentration either on the logical and external world or on the pre-logical and internal world. The result in both cases is a sinking into psychopathology on the part of the subject. In this way, for a person entering into psychotherapy, the resumption of the psycho-emotive developmental process often emerges from being able to fully experience an undifferentiated reality, the basis upon which the resurrection of one's own body and one's own personality and the acceptance of subjectivity and reality will rest. Obviously, such an illusion of unity must be temporally limited and cyclical, or rather must alternate with a state of duality, if one does not want to risk a pathological loss of contact with reality (delirium). It is curious to note that here Milner did not differ from classical psychoanalysis in its insistence on dualistic thinking, or rather that there are two discrete ways of thinking and seeing "one characteristic of infancy and one of adulthood, and that they are as distinct and distinguishable from one another as a painting is from the world around it by its frame" (Turner, 2002, p. 1071). The originality of Winnicott's conception of the transitional object actually lies in the overcoming of this "polarization of distinction and merger" (Eigen, 1983, p. 424) "into transitional space where one-ness and two-ness can coexist and one can inhabit both inner- and outer-world reality" (Marks, 2014, p. 95).

The potential space about which Winnicott (1971b) speaks—possessing a somewhat visual connotation, as Milner had noted—corresponds to the transition from a state of unity to a state of duality, or to the dialectic between the experiences of fusion and separateness (Hernandez and Giannakoulas, 2001). Thus, it becomes clear that potential space "defines a field where emergent processes of both self and object occur, and where transitions between the intrapsychic and the intersubjective take place" (p. 159), a passage that leads to experience. With the progressive development of transitional phenomena and potential space, mental space will come into being, as well as the space to play and create symbols. We can see here the hypothesis of the necessary maintaining of the illusion—which Milner conceives as an essential means to a healthy adaptation to reality, rather than as a failure of adaptation.

According to Milner, it is within the illusory situation created by analysis itself that the analyst must encounter the patient's need to have the kind of experience that in the initial developmental phases was such that it could not lead to a healthy enough process of development. The analyst, thus, plays the role of environment-mother (Winnicott, 1963), being a psychophysical presence—and, as such, a support—able to experience the absence of sense (the void linked to the abandonment of reassuring logical thought is potentially a space where anxiety and terror can lead to an irreversible depression) without feeling the necessity of attributing meaning to it, learning to wait, observe and allow the patient to understand that he/she (the analyst) is there. The primary task of the analyst is, therefore, that of creating and maintaining a setting—either mental or concrete-formal—by means of which he/she can provide the patient with a type of relationship, a situation of "total active adaptation", progressively waning in adequate fashion, so that it may become an environment good enough to satisfactorily meet the needs of assuring separateness and promoting integration (Milner, 1969).

The experience of fusion (which can be either between the self and the object, or between a new and an archaic situation) requires the subject's profound concentration, the "quality" of which will influence how good the result is. In therapy, when the patient focuses on the creation of an illusion (a state of concentration that we can often either visually perceive, in that the patient can, for example, change his/her facial expression, posture, speech, etc., or notice through countertransference), the analyst gains nothing from interrupting such creative acts and getting the patient to re-emerge from his absorption. In fact, it could prove useful for the analyst to awaken his/her own imagination in an effort to grasp important aspects of the patient's pre-verbal communications, his attempts to communicate particularly important experiences that he/she is living through. What follows is that the analyst must allow for a lapse in his/her own Aristotelian logic by paying attention to the patient's concentration. This also proceeds from the concentration in the body (not only in the head, which would coincide with logical thought) of the analyst: a state in which the direct proprioceptive body-self awareness, regarding the relationship taking place in the here and now of the session and linked to the observation of one's own thoughts, without forcing them, can facilitate the move from the pre-conscious background to the conscious foreground, in both patient and therapist. This psychic and somatic concentration, even though appearing at times as a distraction, seems to help the patient to allow his own material to surface and helps the clinician understand, share and experience it. This concentration in the self and the body should not only be viewed as a regressive path, but also, if not mainly, as a pre-logical subject–object fusion, besides a mind–body fusion, as Milner underlined (Milner, 1960, 1969). It is important to note that Milner was not referring only to the simple concentration of the body-self, but also to the working through process, making reverie (Bion, 1962) possible.

The Italian psychoanalyst Mario Bertolini maintained that the concentration to which Milner was referring could be seen as

> the psychic state of the analyst who ends up abandoning him/herself to the surprise of being in contact with and of sharing in some of the modalities of the patient's psychic life, those communicated in the *hic et nunc* of the transference and counter-transference. This self-abandonment allows the therapist to refrain from asking the patient or him/herself the reason behind the thoughts. The therapist receives the feelings of transference in a kind of psychophysical continuity that is relatively indeterminate and undifferentiated with respect to the patient. He/she operates by patiently working through this psycho-physical state (...) The material the analyst works on is the form of what he/she feels: this form allows him/her to imagine that what he/she feels in the body is not a purely physical sensation.
>
> (Bertolini, 2001; quoted in Stefana, 2017, p. 138)

In short, in a therapy or analysis, archaic situations of bodily functioning exist, referring to earlier times, in which the precariousness in the continuity of the self can be experienced, situations in which the analyst, in the dynamics of the therapeutic relationship, must: first, allow him/herself to be engulfed by the patient's functioning processes; second, be able to recognize this experience as related to the patient's functioning processes; and third, be able to form thoughts around such experiences (Milner, 1952b, 1960, 1969, 1973; Bertolini, 2016). Let us imagine that the analyst, at a particular moment in a session, realizes that they have been imitating the patient's breathing pattern, instead of breathing according to his/her own normal rhythm. What do they think of this breathing pattern, of this need to be totally taken over in one's body by the patient, in order to form thoughts about the experience? Such a state of fusion could represent a base upon which to contemplate something, a previously "unknown thought" (Bollas, 1987b). We are dealing here with a pre-symbolic catalyst to the symbolization process.

This is because the continuity of the self necessitates another person, who can provide the base upon which to make use of one's own psychic apparatus, starting from that point in the process in which the patient finds him/herself.

Note

1 This chapter is a shortened and slightly modified version of "Revisiting Marion Milner's work on creativity and art", Alberto Stefana (2019), *The International Journal of Psychoanalysis*, 100:1, 128-147, copyright © Institute of Psychoanalysis reprinted by permission of Taylor & Francis Ltd, http://www.tandfonline.com on behalf of Institute of Psychoanalysis.

Chapter 21

Remembering Marion Milner (from 1981 to 1998)[1]

Desy Safán-Gerard

I am grateful that Emma Letley has written Marion Milner's biography and that Milner's contribution to psychoanalysis will be more widely appreciated. I am also happy that I realize I can hold so clearly in my memory the magical conversations Marion and I had over the years. It was the book *On Not Being Able to Paint* that enticed me to write to her in 1981, which led to my visiting her that same year. She used her own experience with painting as a way to explore alternatives to the educational methods that do not take into account the extraordinary power of the mind.

I visited her again in London in the summer of 1988 and then almost every other year after that. She was more interested in her recent collages and sculptures than in discussing her ideas about psychoanalysis. She complained that she was not altogether clear in her head to answer difficult questions about her collected papers, published by Tavistock as *The Suppressed Madness of Sane Men* in 1987. That turned out to be untrue – at ninety-two she was still very sharp and witty and had an irreverent and refreshing sense of humor about the current controversies in psychoanalysis. With her interest in states of fusion, un-differentiation and soft boundaries between self and other, Milner finds her place with Winnicott, Balint and others in the object relations Middle School, now referred to as the Independents.

I treated myself that summer of 1988 to her other most recent book, *Eternity's Sunrise*, published in 1987 by Virago Press in London. This is the third book of a trilogy that spans over fifty years on the general theme of leisure and the capacity for joy, a theme largely ignored in psychoanalysis. These were written as diaries about the daily events that most affected her.

She distinguishes between responding to an experience with one's mind or, as she puts it, "with one's bones" and she is determined to get to the latter. Possibly representing a vestige of her Christian childhood, she calls these special moments of feeling "beads" and attempts to find the common thread in these experiences. She has to start with an image in order to get to the feelings. She quotes from her own diary, "Oh, that dreaded moment of starting to write in the morning, how I keep forgetting my own discovery that I must start with an image, that is the way in. I should have known that I would forget it…" (p. 29).

Marion gives evidence of her commitment to moving beyond the world of reliable knowing and is determined to find the necessary steps to create the stage for "nothing" so that "something" new may appear. This was familiar to me because I would suggest to a new analytic patient that free association meant that he or she had to create a stage for nothing and wait until something would appear. "Feeling something

DOI: 10.4324/9780429433535-27

in one's bones" and "being behind one's eyes" are metaphors Milner used in her quest for awareness as opposed to living only in one's conscious mind. She writes about the "answering activity" referring to the dialogue with her unconscious mind that results from her opening herself to it. A thread in her writing is her ongoing, relentless attempt to keep that communication open.

The paradox of the answering activity is a feeling of partnership, "...of plugging into a presence, an active 'something' that is both 'I' and 'not I' and which gives me the feeling that I am not alone." She claims that it is not only "the good internalized object" and is clearly trying to broaden Kleinian concepts to make room for a feeling that goes beyond confidence or well being. She writes about praying for an answer from her unconscious and this praying frees her from egocentric preoccupations. "It is like suddenly remembering to open a kind of little trap-door inside and finding a great expansion of spirit" (p. 51). These were ideas I had toyed with, especially with regard to the inspiration phase of a creative project.

Some years earlier, during my clinical training at UCLA, I discovered that my art teacher, Keith Finch, was self-taught and that is why he never used the academic language that takes you away from the unconscious mind that one needs to have access to. He had found ways to help his students experience their creative potential and had been suggested to me by artist Marge Oderberg, the wife of Phil Oderberg, one of my professors at UCLA. A group of four trainees had been invited for coffee and dessert at their house, which contained an impressive art collection. It was in front of a De Chirico desolate landscape that I suddenly felt, "What the hell I am doing with my life! I *have* to paint." I asked Marge if I could come to her studio to experiment with paints and she suggested her teacher to me.

I take this opportunity to tell you how my involvement with painting began because I am often asked this question. I also take this opportunity to write and honor Keith, because, as you will see, he and Marion were kindred spirits and I am lucky to have had them in my life. The first time I attended Keith's class of about six students in his Los Angeles studio he suggested that I explore with a pencil held vertically to the pad of paper as if it was land that I was walking through. "Don't lift the pencil and don't be afraid of crossing the lines," he said. After doing this, some spaces were created and he suggested that I fill them up with watercolor paint. He would come back a while later and suggest to go back to the exploration with the pencil, drawing on top and across these areas. This created new areas that could be colored and this could be done on top of the previous colors once they dried so that new combined colors were appearing, resulting in an increasingly complex design. I found this to be very exciting. He then told me, "Desy, now you have to do 200, 300, of these because you have to discover your line and you *are* your line!" In the ensuing days and months I could not stop exploring with pencil and colors in the way Keith suggested and brought many examples to him. He said to me, "I didn't really mean 200! But I am happy you have become caught!" I even did them under a large table where psychology interns at Children's Hospital in Los Angeles would meet to receive mandatory instructions on how to fill out insurance forms. In one such boring meeting I had all twelve of us interns drawing on a pad in this way, under the table, and passing it around. These are the kinds of experiences I would bring to Marion and she not only enjoyed hearing about my mischief but also would respond by telling me of similar mischiefs of her own.

It is at this time that my dual commitment to psychology and art began – my life would forever be split between these worlds. After I started to work with Keith, I decided that Tuesday afternoons, the time of Keith's class, was sacred and should not be interfered by my clinical training at UCLA. Years later and in my own Venice studio I tried to share with others what I had learned through painting. I worked with a group of five people interested in becoming freer with their creativity. I designed several exercises, some of which included music since music was always and still is my first love. They were to start a drawing and after five minutes move to the next person's drawing around the table and continue this drawing trying to capture the spirit with which it was started. They would move like this around the table and then discuss their reactions in front of the drawing they had begun, especially the negative ones when the other people had failed to capture the spirit of their drawing. At times, the reaction was positive when someone in the group had added something unexpectedly beautiful to the beginning drawing. In this case, it was gratitude to be acknowledged and responded to in this way.

On one occasion the participants were engaged in a free painting. One of them had told me she had had to quit several art schools and later, art classes. In front of the free painting and after a while of improvising she exclaimed in disgust, "This is where I have to quit!" I asked her to tell me why. She said, "It is off, it doesn't have any harmony or balance." I asked her to tell me if there was anything in it that she particularly liked and, reluctantly, she pointed to a small area, the size of a dime. I asked her to put aside her judgments for a while and work exclusively in this area she liked. When I came around to her after some time, her area of interest had become a bit larger and she didn't have that sour face anymore. At the end of our time together, she was almost finished with a beautiful abstract watercolor. The problem of balance and harmony that so haunted her at the beginning could now be addressed. She finished the piece the following session and she was beaming, "The very first piece I have ever done that I really like!" she said.

I would tell Marion about experiences like this and she would talk at great length about premature judgments and how deleterious they are to the creative process. She always had some suggestion or some enlightening memory of her own.

Early on, while still painting with Keith, I wrote a paper entitled "The Role of the Accident in the Creative Process." A couple of years ago I wrote an extension and elaboration of that early paper entitled "The Creative Process in 4 Large Paintings: From Mistake to Mistake." By projecting slides of work in progress I showed how the mistakes lead to new developments and deserve to be welcomed. I discussed the early paper on accidents with Marion – we saw eye to eye about this since we both valued and used accidents in our work. It makes me sad that she didn't get to see in these large canvases the creative potential of mistakes because I wasn't working on large canvases then. I know she would have loved to see evidence on a large format for an idea that permeated so much of her writings.

Her sense of humor, always refreshing, was evident in her writings and in her letters. I have saved a set of aerograms that she wrote to me from the eighties and nineties that I treasure. In 1983, she explains why she had to say NO to an invitation from Marion Salomon to come to give a seminar in Los Angeles: "I have to keep my summers away from intellectual pursuits," she wrote. She was happy, instead, that her Los Angeles friends Joel and Jean Sanville had gone to visit her in London. In 1984, she complains that she is feeling bogged down by many domestic problems that don't allow her to paint. She also complains that the publisher of her collected papers wants her to find the connecting thread in her psychoanalytic writings. She writes, "...and I cannot find that damned thread!" In another letter she tells me she is going to try the thread method I had suggested and was using at the time – to paint with a thread dipped in black ink. She also complains that she must have written to me about my migraines but she is afraid that she is too "dotty" now to remember if she did or not. In 1990 she apologizes for the difficulty I may find in understanding her handwriting and she is right, because her handwriting had become quite illegible. She ends that letter writing, "I hope you can read this. I can't!" In another later letter, she writes that she is snowed down trying to make some kind of order in fifty-eight years. I realize that the wish to leave things in order is something we all may experience when the end is near. Nowadays, I feel besieged by that need and I am trying to find a home for my collection, starting the archival process necessary for that. I have even hired someone to help me with this daunting task.

The last time I visited with Marion she came down with me to the narrow and tall front door to wave me goodbye. I was already across the street and I could see her lovely face smiling and her waving her hand at me. Suddenly a deep sadness overtook me as I sensed this might be our last encounter. Unfortunately I was right. That face at the door will be always etched in my memory.

I brought a print of a portrait I made of her and a still life she gave me when we exchanged paintings. I have had this still life, which I treasure, hanging in my office since 1988.

21.1 Portrait of Marion Milner by the author.

Note

1 Given as part of a program entitled 'Marion Milner's Explorations of Creativity in Art and Psychoanalysis' featuring Emma Letley, Ph.D. Author of *Marion Milner: The Life*. New Center of Psychoanalysis, April 27, 2014

Chapter 22

'Jugs, Mugs, and Goblets'

Comments on Marion Milner's artistic insights

Jennifer Scott

I would like to begin this chapter with words from Marion Milner herself:

> 'moments when the original "poet" in each of us created the outside world for us, by finding the familiar in the unfamiliar, are perhaps forgotten by most people; or else they are guarded in some secret place of memory because they were too much like visitations of the gods to be mixed with everyday thinking' (Milner, 1987b, p. 66).

Milner's work claims the creative power of the everyday illusion in the actions of everyday life. Milner revivifies the power of illusion through a psychoanalytic lens, which also informs the experience of making art. Milner's malleable intermixing of art practice, art theory and psychoanalysis yielded insights into the ways in which people and objects become mixed up as a way of finding oneself in the world, and how this is experienced and expressed in art. However, the value of Milner's insights is generally overlooked outside a psychoanalytic context. This application of psychoanalysis to art uses a couple of Milner's essays from the 1950s, "The role of illusion in symbol formation" (1952) and "Psychoanalysis and art" (1956). By taking her theoretical work and applying it to the still-life paintings of Milner's contemporary Ben Nicholson this essay explores the mixing up of objects and people in art. The evident implication being that we use objects to explore our human relationships. The choice of Nicholson is no coincidence since he was a long-time friend of Adrian Stokes. Milner was a member of the Imago group set up in the 1950s by Stokes and Roger Money-Kyrle to discuss the intersections of art and psychoanalysis. Cedric Morris, who ran the Benton End art school which Milner attended, was a member of the Seven and Five Society together with Nicholson in the 1920s.[1] Accordingly, Milner was more than likely familiar with the art of Ben Nicholson.

During the 1950s, Milner sought to emphasise the value of an oscillating mind-set to art-making; between a diffuse manner and an exacting manner. These two mind-sets derive from experience and theory, the theory being broadly Kleinian. In tandem, Milner discusses the way in which once valuably present objects, now absent, through loss, suppression, fear, etc. are symbolically recreated in another object that may be quite dissimilar to the original object or person. However, this dissimilar object emotes the same charge as the original object for the person creating the symbol.

Early childhood play disclosed important insights into artistic process for Milner, where "[t]he identification of one object with another is described as the forerunner of symbolism" (Milner, 1987b, p. 62). Milner develops her approach to the process of creating symbols through substitutions primarily from Melanie Klein and Ernest Jones

DOI: 10.4324/9780429433535-28

(ibid), also paying homage to Rank's formulation of identification underlying symbolisation with a regressive and infantile means of adaption to reality. For Milner, Klein's concepts of dread and fear of loss drive substitutions (p. 66), while repression and loss are important for Jones. Milner revisits the process of substitutions and symbol making as "a regression in order to take a step forward" where innovative identifications are made (Milner, 1987b, p. 63). For Milner, there is a danger of psychic sterility if the seemingly ungainly infantile mental functions are denied creative existence in adult life. Crucially, the symbol and the original object are one and the same in infantile thought and persist as an important aspect of artistic experience. Therefore, there are two senses of the symbol, being either clearly separate from the reference object or indistinguishable from the reference object.

Milner's interest in what made this dissolution of distinctions between object and subject possible in adult life had an important relevance to the artistic process. For Milner, the mitigation of distinctions underpinned the process of substitution that contributed to the ability to form symbols. The ability to collapse the division between subject and object enabled a new object to be equated with the original object, while retaining a further independent physical character. Both familiarity and unfamiliarity reside in the substituted object. Milner had sought to extend existing psychoanalytic formulations of substitution, involving repression and loss of things residing in the past, with exploratory motivations towards the new and undiscovered. Milner described "a word needed for the emotional experience of finding the substitute, and it is here that the word ecstasy may be useful" (Milner, 1987b, p. 65), which expresses the delight involved in identification and a recognition that extended the emotional and mental cognition of the outer world. Milner finds support for these ideas from the art world, where Herbert Read thought that "art is finding (rather than seeking) new symbols to signify new areas of sensibility" (Milner, 1987b, p. 156, 1987a, p. 77). For Milner, substitution and symbol making are a way of *personally incorporating what is unknown into the known world* and not purely retroactive as inferred in the words loss and suppression that had been the hallmarks of Klein and Jones.

Milner discussed the "tremendous significance that there can be in the interplay of the edges of two curtains, or the surface of a jug that is placed in front of another jug" (Winnicott, 1974, p. 115) in the 1940s. Peter Fuller has noted the importance of Milner's artistic insights and republished a sketch of two jugs by Milner (Fuller, 1988, p. 134) (Figure 22.1). The suggestion of a slang term for breasts encoded in Milner's

Figure 22.1 Marion Milner, sketch of two overlapping jugs [also published in 1980 in Peter Fuller's *Art and psychoanalysis* (Fuller, 1988, p. 134)]. Reproduced by kind permission of Giles Milner, on behalf of the estate.

two overlapping jugs emphasises the importance of early infant developmental experiences to mature cultural experience. Additionally, the relationship between the dissimilar objects of breasts and jugs is emblematic of a shared symbolism. Milner's concern with the intricacies of creative thought embedded early infantile experience in laying down fundamental components for the creative process. In the essay *Art and Psychoanalysis*, Milner discusses the importance of *a cyclical oscillation between two fundamental mental processes* as foundational to a rich creative human existence (Milner, 1987a, p. 88). Here, Milner interrelated Blake's series of illustrations on the Book of Job where

> ...a process is here going on which undoes the over-fixed separation between self and other, self and the universe. Thus, it seems that having once achieved the sense of separate existence, it is then necessary to be continually undoing it again, in a cyclic oscillation, if psychic sterility is to be avoided.
>
> (Milner, 1987a, p. 88)

The importance of a cyclical oscillation between two fundamental mental processes is foundational to a rich creative human existence.

Milner's jug image insinuates the overlapping of two mental processes as connected but separate in a manner that recalls Winnicott's potential space. Winnicott emphasised self and other, whereas Milner focused on the differences of mental appreciation between the definite and the diffuse. The diffuse state originates in very early infancy, while the definite or articulate develops with the growing sense of the separateness of self. It seems to me that Milner's observation of a cadenced cycling between the mental states of diffusion and definition allow for a temporary dissolution between the familiar and unfamiliar, which appears to be the basis for a process of symbolic substitutions in art.

Nicholson

Nicholson's art ranged from high intellectualism of his white reliefs to still-life compositions during a career that spanned from the 1920s to the 1980s. Nicholson's artwork characteristically mixed up divisions between abstract and representational, framed vs living object, form and material object, art and the common place, inside and outside, thought and material, and surface and depth. This practice of interchange between art and life was discussed by Nicholson writing in 1941 explaining that

> [t]he geometrical forms often used by abstract artists do not indicate, as has been thought, a conscious and intellectual mathematical approach – a square or a circle in art are nothing in themselves and are alive only in the instinctive and inspirational use an artist can make of them in expressing a poetic idea.
>
> (TGA 8717.3.1.12)[2]

Nicholson's poetic idea of the circle echoes Milner's different objects that nevertheless share a sensibility or similarity of emotional impact, which Milner emphasised by quoting Ernest Jones's "identity in differences" (Milner, 1987b, p. 63). Additionally, Nicholson's objects of jugs, mugs and goblets take on illusionary facets due to the manner of their abstract representations, alluding to human aspects. This aspect of Nicholson's work is emphasised by his use the epithet of "alive" or "living object" more than once in relation to his art. Nicholson refers to the living object in a letter to Adrian Stokes on 20 May 1963.[3]

> I am very keen on the idea of my paintings, reliefs or whatever not merely viewed 'as a kind of picture', they should be a kind of OBJECT and one which takes part in this life of whatever it is – in fact a living object.
>
> (TGA 8816.239)

Since art is not animate, this animation of the inanimate is another form of substitution that uses illusion as a form of continuance of something lost in a different form, aligning with ideas that derive from Jones and Klein.

Nicholson's still-life paintings during the 1950s used the table top as a location for the placement of jugs, mugs and goblets. These objects reveal a core of maternal material when seen as substitutions of animate objects for inanimate objects. Nicholson's table top scenarios, which could include the abstract white reliefs of the 1930s as well as the more recognisable post-cubist still-life painting theme in the 1950s, can be considered, to some extent, as a recreation of elements of his relationship with his mother, who died when Nicholson was twenty four (Kite, 2009, p. 156). Kite's examination of an interchange between Nicholson and Stokes inferred that Stokes detected a psychoanalytic dimension to Nicholson's use of table. Nicholson, writing in 1941 for the Horizon publication, described the table thus:

> In painting a "still-life" one takes the simple every-day forms of a bottle – mug – jug – plate-on-table as the basis for the expression of an idea; the forms are not entirely free though they are free to the extent that each object can be seen as many viewpoints as you wish at one and the same time but the colours are free: bottle-colour for plate, plate-colour for table.
>
> (TGA 8717.3.1.12)

Nicholson commonly interchanged elements, such as colour or texture, and inferred substitutions of rectangles for tables. Nicholson connects his 1930s white reliefs as "scrubbing the much scarred kitchen table" with his experience of his mother (Kite, 2009, pp. 156–157). The objects and elements of the reliefs are not necessarily inert but recall a memory of presence, imbued with emotional potency. Jugs are very much part of this table top scenario, and their presence might symbolise an illusionary depth beyond the everyday object.

Nicholson's complex density of mugs, jugs and goblets and other paraphernalia that is suggestive of Milner's uncommon mixing of the "visitation of the gods" with everyday objects. Furthermore, Nicholson's art uses inanimate objects in his still-life paintings in a way that infers body parts that recalls Milner and Winnicott's discussion on overlapping jugs. Nicholson's frequent subject matter of objects such as jugs, mugs and goblets necessarily prompts images of breasts, faces and mouths. Nicholson, of course, is one example of a plethora of artists' depictions of domestic objects during the mid-20th century, as well as indeed in other centuries. Conspicuously, Nicholson was an artist directly connected to many of Milner's stated artistic influences, such as Herbert Read, Kenneth Clark and Adrian Stokes (Milner, 1987a, p. 77, 1987b).[4] Further to this, Nicholson's art during the 1950s can be used to illustrate Milner's ideas through the focus on spaces of interchange, reciprocity in the practice of free drawing, substitutions or interchanges between abstract elements, and concepts of framing. Paintings that illustrate these aspects are *1947, November 11 (Mousehole)*, *1945 (still life)* or *1946 (still life)*.

Both Milner and Nicholson described the requirement for free drawing in somewhat similar terms during the 1950s. For Milner, the act of playing was something between day-dreaming and purposeful action. Playing was not confined to childhood but was associated with Milner's appreciation of what was happening in her own process free drawing (Milner, 1987b, p. 69). Milner describes an interactive or reciprocal activity of play or free drawing where "the line as it were answers back and functions as a very primitive type of external object" (Milner, 1987b, p. 69). Peter Khoroche noted a reciprocity or free drawing in Nicholson's drawings in Italy and Yorkshire in the 1950s (Khoroche, 2008, pp. 61–62). According to Khoroche, Nicholson, when spending an intense three weeks of drawing from life in Tuscany in 1950, "Nicholson realized that he had to be free when creating one work of art out of another" (Khoroche, 2008, p. 62). Nicholson was responding to certain elements of architecture that caught his attention and in the process creating something new. In addition, Nicholson pre-prepared a series of pale washes on the paper for drawing and then chose one paper to interact with his set drawing task. The interaction between wash and pencil has a similarity to Milner's line that answers back. Khoroche describes Nicholson's drawings of this period as involving

> The omission, the selective emphasis, the touch of humour, the reordering of the motif into a rhythmic whole, the play of geometric roofs against the organic trees and hillside, the unconcern with illusionistic accuracy, are by now recognizable hallmarks of Nicholson's coolly romantic draughtsmanship.
>
> (Khoroche, 2008, p. 68)

The theme of creating something between the paring of presence and absence, geometric and organic, illusion and accuracy are the same elements that Milner describes in various ways in the case study of the boy playing, where two villages are at war (Milner, 1987b, pp. 66–68). This similarity appears to be a validation of Milner's insights into artistic practice.

The work of both Milner and Nicholson insinuated a reflexive insight into complex spatial compositions. For Milner, the experience of art was reciprocal between art and artist/viewer, as well as being contingent upon the interface between conscious and unconscious processes (Figure 22.2).

In a similar vein, in the 1950s Nicholson consciously examined his early paintings from the 1930s that unconsciously produced a complex spatiality. During the 1950s,

Figure 22.2 Ben Nicholson, *goblets*, 1962, Etching, wash and graphite on card, 330 × 260 mm. Kettle's Yard Collection (photograph by author, 2014).

he considered the unconscious processes involved in these paintings as containing a certain amount of intellectual rigour (TGA 8717.3.1.12). The specific painting Nicholson recalled was *Au Chat Botte* (1932). Nicholson's recollections appear to bear out Milner's instinct that the experience of making art involves both conscious and unconscious processes and infers that a deep creativity results from such an interface.

The resulting insights into this comparison between Milner and Nicholson demonstrate that there can be an illusion of a relation to an external object (the symbol), and this external object is also a part of the internal world. Milner draws attention to the perception that someone may have of what is internal and external to the self and observes this area of human experience as a series of complex interactions that include spatial experience as both tangible and imaginary. The coalescence of a spatial imaginary overlaying concrete experience in the work of both Milner and Nicholson gives insight into how art is performed in both is creation and reception.

Notes

1 Andrew Causey, 'Seven & Five Society (act. 1919–1935)', Oxford Dictionary of National Biography, Oxford University Press, Jan 2014 [http://www.oxforddnb.com/view/theme/96398, accessed 9 June 2014]

2 *Tate Gallery Archive* TGA 8717.3.1 Ben Nicholson correspondence.

3 This letter was also quoted for similar reasons by Stephen Kite (2009, p. 161) with an architectural focus.

4 Nicholson was a part of the world in which Milner interacted, though not directly connected. Any similarity between approaches and mind-sets is therefore not unexpected. However, these interconnections show a way of looking at Nicholson's art that is psychoanalytically informed, yet not as a form of personal disclosure. By applying Milner's insights to Nicholson's work, a multi-perspective indeterminacy of values come to the fore.

Chapter 23

Scrappy observations

Aleana Egan

This project of self-discovery laid out by Marion Milner will always be relevant although it feels particularly prescient to the times we are living through now. What I find so resonant in Milner's work is her making something out of her 'own material', felt from the inside. She communicates universal concerns with a methodology of her own making through an investigation of her internal facts. As an artist everything can change very quickly from something to seemingly nothing and I admire how Milner writes about protecting this liminal space. To protect it is to hold mute and not name. The following text is a subjective gathering of impressions gained from a close reading of Milner's texts. The accompanying images of artworks made within the last ten years, although not explicit in their reference have been imbued by the permissive qualities of openness and hope that I have felt through reading her work (Figure 23.1).

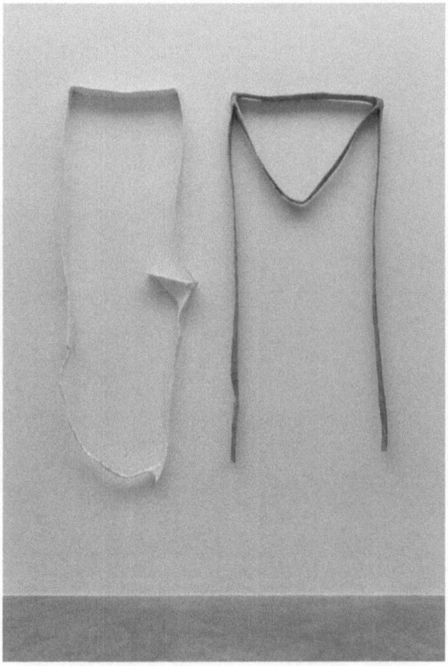

Figure 23.1 Made boats.[1]

DOI: 10.4324/9780429433535-29

In 2019, Margaret Boyle Spelman invited four of us to re-read the diary-form books: *A Life of One's Own*, *An Experiment in Leisure*, *Eternity's Sunrise*, and *Bothered by Alligators* in chronological order. We were to meet at intervals and discuss our thoughts on them. I had a longstanding interest in Milner's work and was enthusiastic about the opportunity of deeper study through re-reading. At the end of the day's discussion, we briefly mentioned our different impressions of what we had gleaned Milner was like as a person. It strikes me now as interesting that we did not give even more time to these impressions. This feeling for the author comes through when the text has a porous nature. It allows the reader to imagine in between the words. I have always felt the company of an author when I go through a period of reading their work as something additional to the texts themselves. They are present in the imagination during the interludes between reading, floating beside me.

In the case of Milner, I feel her to be an encouraging and benign presence, always with a route out of whatever narrowness I have found myself in. It is the duality of her tone; intellectually rigorous, challenging and also tolerant and open to spirituality, in its broadest sense, that led me to a deep engagement with her work. There is no strict division between hard and soft, unconscious and conscious, legible and illegible (Figure 23.2).

Masts and funnels (outline)

These sentences appear in a strange stream of consciousness sequence about an old woman who, due to eating tinned salmon, dreams that she must find seven metals to melt down in order to make a gong. These metallurgically infused dreams are so powerful that, rather than go mad, she obeys the voices from her unconscious and embarks

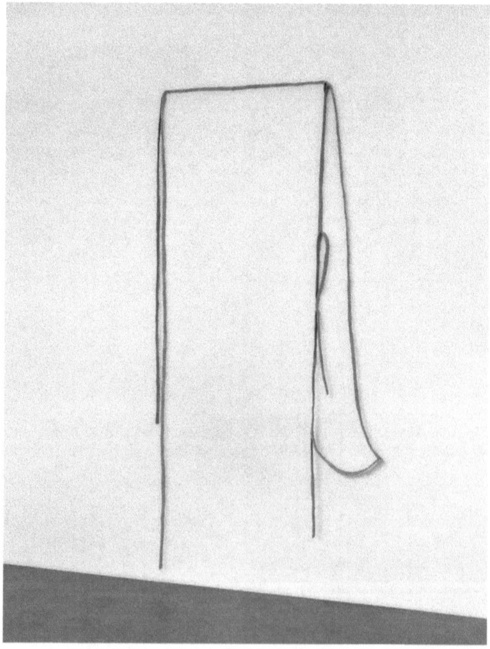

Figure 23.2 Masts and funnels.[2]

upon this material-shifting mission. In her last book *Bothered by Alligators*, the impetus for which is a diary that she kept during the early years of her son's life. Contained within this diary is a storybook written and illustrated by her son John when he was seven years old. Looking back and studying his drawings in her nineties, Milner has her years of clinical, and her own creative, experiences to draw from. She talks about what she calls 'verbal symbols' of the words 'wet' and 'sand' which are given pictorial prominence in his drawings. This is a tender yet rigorous form of looking back that generates multiple meanings for her, that is not without its difficulties.

She thinks the bridges in these drawings were inspired by a trip to Tower Bridge in London. John was curious about the tidal aspects of the river Thames; she remembers them talking about the daily influence of the moon penetrating into the heart of London. He had wondered about the stretch of sand and mud they saw between the water and the shore. She recognises his interest in gravity from all the hanging apparatus. 'Firmly defying gravity with these strong hooks'. In a chapter entitled 'Outline and The Solid Earth' in *On Not Being Able to Paint*, Milner appears to have a moment of epiphany whereby she connects the perception of outline as fact and traces an emotional need to de-lineate objects within the material world.

Outline is mentioned in relation to the subject of boundaries. The space between inner and outer. Milner travelled (with her husband) to America in the 1920s, where they spent time in Los Angeles with their friend Jan Gordon. Gordon had discussed the subject of outline as being, visually, the most 'unnatural' thing in nature. Milner repeats this anecdote again in the next chapter of the book. I wonder was that by mistake or just that it was very significant for her. It seems to me to represent the introspective world of dreams and that of an outer reality, and throughout her books she is trying to keep the veils between the two open which inspired me (Figure 23.3).

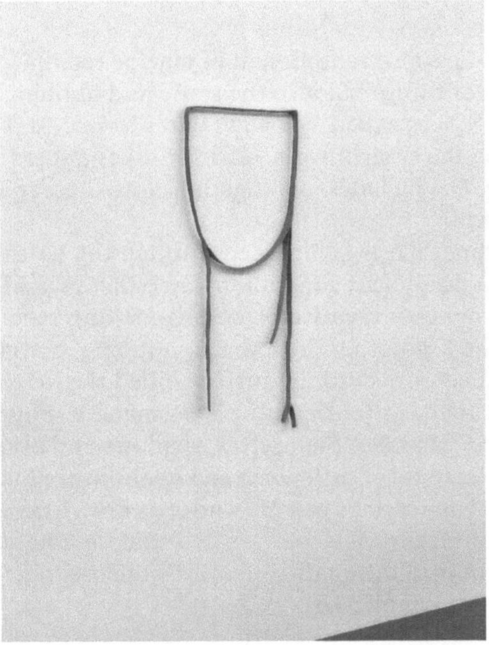

Figure 23.3 Plumb.[3]

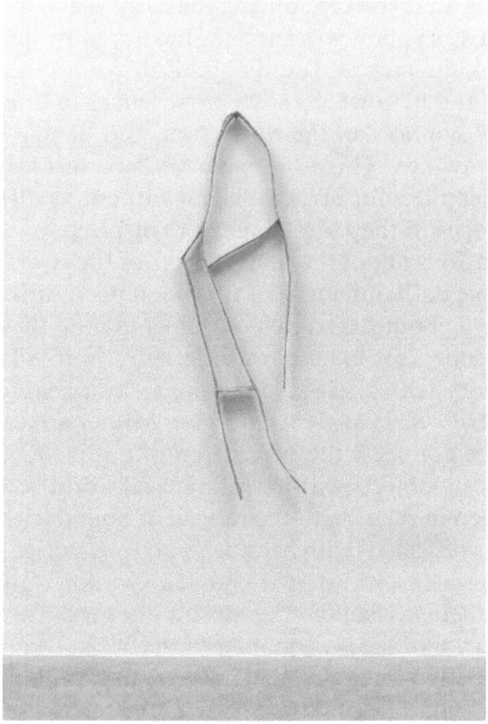

Figure 23.4 May Levitt and her daughter.[4]

The pulley systems are also reminiscent of marine references and the push and pull of nature: the action of things but also the static and bobbing. The shape of the outer world, what Adrian Stokes called 'Showing outer form… stabilising an inner content as outer shape' (Janet Sayer writing on Adrian Stokes quoted by Letley in her biography of Milner). *Alligators* includes investigations into the fragments of her own fallible memories of her parents.

The generational line that is summoned through the writing of the book is meandering and curious: a non-linear summoning up of her own history through her son's. An ongoing part of my own creative process is making relief shapes out of strips of cut cardboard and then sculpting them through taping, cutting and gravity. Over the years, I have painted colours onto the surface, filled the joins with filler, cast them in bronze and covered them in fabric and papier-mâche. (Figure 23.4) These hanging sculptures are outlines in and of themselves, shadows and also questions.[4]

I'm caught up by the sense of difference and relationship I read from the subtle variations of shapes and wonder if it's just me who feels how different each one is. Through Milner I learnt the phrases: '*what the eyes like*' and '*to hold the bones gently*', both of which express something of the quality I feel through making these and it is something I aspire to feel more of (Figure 23.5).

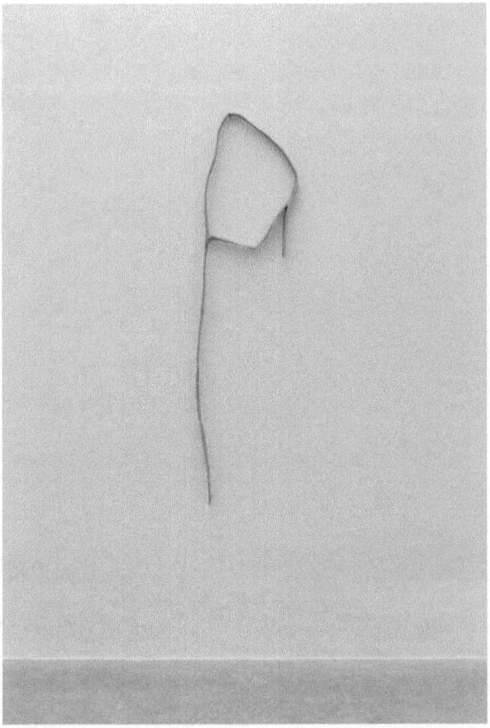

Figure 23.5 Silent tree.[5]

Oceanic (free ideas about the sea)

From the uneven sand steps of Salterns in Dorset, the writer Mary Butts learned from a young age about shape and colour. In her 1937 book, *The Crystal Cabinet: My Childhood at Salterns*, she describes how this natural coastal environment gave her a sense of the 'likeness, difference and something of the inward being of each separate thing'. Perhaps these early experiences in an oceanic climate helped to form the raw rigour that she brought to her work.

Milner emphasises the oceanic; an attempt to stay bleary within, rather than coming up to a sharp narrow point on the exterior. Her preference is for the inchoate and partial. It is like she is suggesting that something new can come from the qualities inherent in the not-fully formed. I started to notice the sea and water references in Milner's writing. Milner's treatise to the oceanic over the sharp-pointed focus.

Her perfect logic supposes that the more you focus on a sharp-pointed single area the more likely you are to leave the area around it in the dark. I am reminded of a repetitive sea dream I had for a period of time when I moved away from the sea to a land-locked city. My heart sank when I came into consciousness as being submerged under

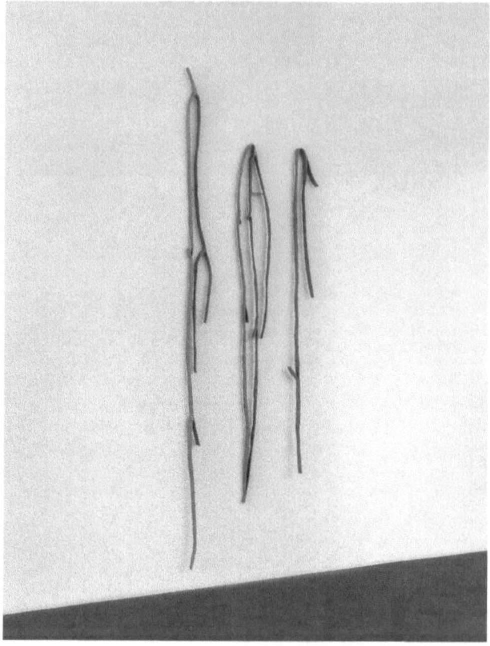

Figure 23.6 Swaying reeds.[6]

the sea was bright vision and paradoxically comforting: not drowning. The element of water and the colours within were inseparable: the colour was the water and the water was the colour. (Figure 23.6)

Milner writes about lowliness and reeds. Swaying reeds. She writes about letting go and being submerged into the lowliness of existence, only then can the tide turn and for creativity to occur. These aquatic references in Milner's work made me think of a non-hierarchical view of life's surfaces and substances – I had a thought in lockdown (Spring 2020) whilst doing the washing up, that if only I could value each wet, slimy, greasy, sticky substance on its own merits – to be curious to its structure and resistance to what I was trying to perform on it, to not only try and get rid of it quickly and finish the task.

This echoes with Milner's ideas about embodying and ritualising feelings of negativity and inferiority, to really feel into them. Milner is asserting that this feeling for the oceanic is a way of attending to the self and our capacity to take in art. If we can be open and take things in from 'behind the eyes' and with the body by 'holding the bones gently', we can experience life expansively and avoid a pre-emptive gathering of knowledge and reason. Then art and life can continue through the layers of the self and embed themselves deeply within so that resonance can occur. Layers of meaning felt.

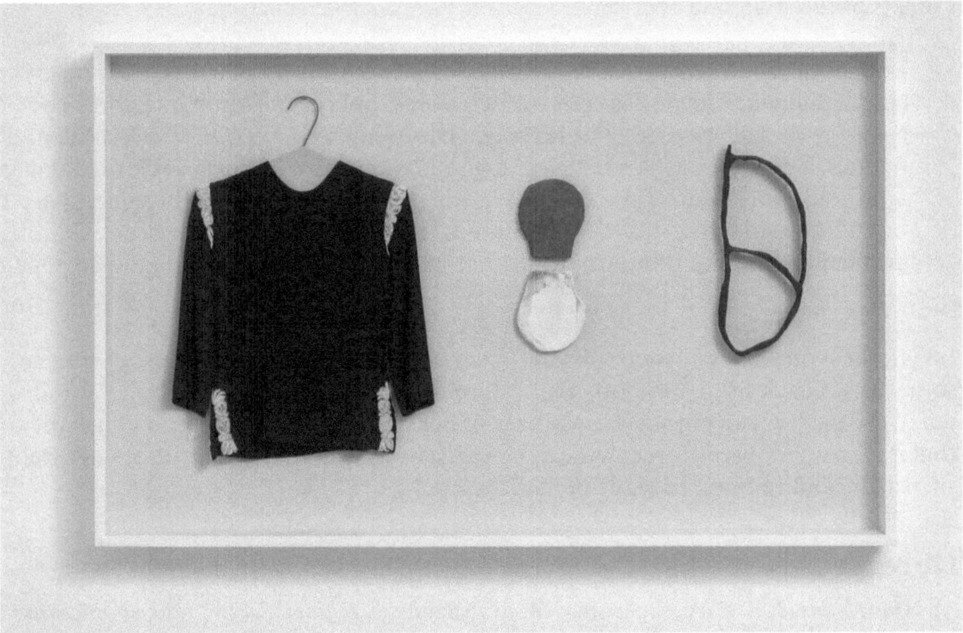

Figure 23.7 Free ideas about the sea.[7]

Outfits (personal style)

I find this image of Milner (in *An Experiment in Leisure*, p. 203) wandering around the shops, piecing herself back together by way of looking and imagining through clothes a deeply generative one. She explains that this activity is an antidote to the sense of being overwhelmed by others after social interactions. The stance of clothes hanging and displayed when they are not yet embodied, and how this enlivens her. (Figure 23.7) The attention in the body and out of the body, living in a city and taking in its shapes and traces of emotion. There is something in the bridge between what is pictured through the written word and then thought out as sculpture: scale, material, construction, colour, texture and recognition of components. An imagined disjointed sculpture through text, resonance and action.

These are essential components of art: human detail and decision making. The image of a woman browsing in a shop brings to mind 'Au Bonheur des dames' by Emile Zola; the novel of modern Paris through the invention of the department store. Balzac described the department store as a 'poem to trade'. I imagine Milner wandering around London shops in 1937 and wonder about the details of it; was she window shopping or touching and interacting with the garments and shop-keepers?

In the late 1970s in a new suburb of Paris, Annie Ernaux describes the liberating aspects of the shopping centre:

> Fountains and benches were arranged under a canopy of glass. Soft-lit arcades contrasted with the pitiless glare of window-displays and shop interiors. The boutiques were side-by-side with no space between them, so one could come and go without a door to push or hellos and good-byes to say. Never had clothes and food appeared more beautiful – accessible with no distance or ritual to negotiate. The boutiques with their playful nicknames, la Froquerie, la Carterie, la Djinnerie, granted a childlike impunity to the act of poking through merchandise. One felt ageless.

In Milner's four diary-form books she is persistently re-describing her experiences. In some senses each book envelops the last; re-assessing what she has thought and written in the past. As an enthusiastic reader of her work I feel this sense of continuity and that it is an ongoing resource that can be rediscovered again and again, always yielding surprising and relevant threads of association.

Notes

1 *Made boats*, 2017 Card, tape, filler, Modroc bandage, pigment, Jesmonite, acrylic paint 145 × 128.5 × 9 cm
2 *Masts and funnels*, 2019 Untreated bronze 277 × 125 × 4 cm
3 *Plumb*, 2019 Untreated bronze 106 × 40 × 4 cm
4 *May Levitt with her daughter Helen*, 2018 Untreated bronze 135 × 36 × 3.5 cm
5 *Silent tree*, 2018 Untreated bronze 112 × 26 × 3.5 cm
6 *Swaying weeds*, 2019 Untreated bronze 255 × 62 × 6 cm
7 *Free ideas about the sea*, 2019 Fabric, tissue, pigment, gesso, card, plaster
[All artwork images by Aleana Egan. Courtesy the artist, Kerlin Gallery and Konrad Fischer Galerie].

Chapter 24

'A Deeper-rooted Kind of Knowing'[1]

Wayne Featherstone

The dream

I am tempted to say that it all began with a dream but, in truth, I think the dream gathered it all together and thrust it under my nose.

As usual in a dream, there was a somewhat vague setting in which details sprang into life, depending on where one looked. Suffice to say, the action was set in an old Victorian terrace, perhaps in East Melbourne. Similarly, it was not clear what I was doing there at first, but I became involved in a group effort, contributing to painting a canvas that ultimately mutated into a mural occupying one whole wall of a very large room. There were a few other people around; people observing, people going about their own separate business, and some invisible presences observing and conveying approval at various intervals. Attention to the mural swelled out of the dream and absorbed me, occasionally relenting so that I could step back, observe the whole, and register the next move: a state of complete absorption wherein attention bore down or drew back for a wider perspective, as if my mind imitated a microscope.

An abstract pattern of charcoal hatchings emerged first. The overall distribution and composition of forms evoked assent, pleasure, and a hunger for more. Then, stepping further back, vegetative patterns and themes appeared: a kind of Celtic tree of life, faintly resonating with Beardsley, with Art Deco themes. Tendrils unfolded and pressed with the irresistible, insistent development of life finding a way, writhing into empty spaces, into the unknown. A certain passion gripped me as I realised that it was not really my instinct, nor my conscious judgement, but rather something unknown that lived itself out through me and determined what spaces were occupied, as well as what forms took shape within them. And, all the while, those invisible, incorporeal observers silently conveyed assent as something behind my sternum greeted each decision and each development with a twinge of pleasure and approval. The invisible ones spoke through the body.

Then an imperative impulse arose, demanding that I raise a hand to draw, despite knowing very well that I possessed a complete lack of talent when it came to sketching. However, without conscious decision and without hesitation, I began to trace forms. Something bypassed conscious intent and control as forms arose from an obedient hand. What arose? Multiple blotches, like those on the coat of a jaguar, emerged first. Each called out of obscurity other forms, a personal fauna and pantheon, and they all took their place among the tendrils that writhed into places still empty in the mural.

DOI: 10.4324/9780429433535-30

There was no hurry and there was no stillness; but there was deep satisfaction, a sense of composure, and a knowledge that, though the mural was approaching completion, there was still more to be added, as well as a distinct pleasure in being part of that process. Pleasure: not so much in determining final form or outcome, as in recognising the rightness of the unfolding process.

***

Wherein the navel of the dream?

Two days go by, two days of sober consideration and conscious evaluation of the dream. Associations click into place, silently and softly: with a sensation that subtends the bureaucratic, intellectual compulsion to put dominoes in a row, to assemble a bald, disappointing, uninspired, but allegedly informative, box-ticking account of what to make of it all; to slowly build up a composite awareness of the origins of the dream.

First, there is concern for a friend I will visit Sunday afternoon, emerging from lockdown: a friend who is fading before my eyes as a once-great mind becomes ever vaguer. Then there's a wider perspective with the realisation that my own mural is approaching completion and the judgement of the heart that says it unfolds with a kind of sober ecstasy, a feeling that asserts rightness. Unlike the perverse, rampant Spring portrayed in *The Lord of the Rings*, this is not a choking caricature of fertility. This is an aesthetic necessity: balance and life following the Pied Piper of satisfaction, a kind of holy disorder that is somehow devoid of any hint of chance.

More remove, and there's Bion and Blake, each observing in their way. But I demur and re-cast Bion. These forms are not simply the stripe on the coat of the Tiger that is Psychoanalysis. These are emergent meanings inscribed on the coat of an ambush predator: not one who stalks the night primarily, but one who can drop down from above at any moment, especially in the shift from light to dark and back again. This is a crepuscular predator. This is the work of blessed Apollo and ardent Dionysus, married in a dance from the East. And there, twirling and unfolding beyond those masculine intellects, Milner learns to surrender her hands to inner forms and unconscious intent. Milner learns to paint. Blake applauds; Bion nods acceptance. And they all follow the rhythm of Shiva's gestures, Shiva's footfall. This is not simply a dance of death, of dissolution, or even of creation. This is the terror and ecstasy of our world asking for our love. In the end, some words emerged from memory: *the force that through the green fuse drives the flower* (Thomas, 2003, p. 90).

As Blake asks in *The Tyger, what immortal hand or eye/can frame thy fearful symmetry?*(Blake, 2004, p. 125). And then, as if from nowhere, there's Wallace Stevens, urging our imagination to push back against reality (Stevens, 1951, p. 36). And we answer: *surely that must be our own imaginations, surrendered to a will beyond the world and in defiance of orthodoxy and fixity.* And who stands behind Stevens? Mary Shelley, asserting we are all monsters. And so on, all the luminaries, poets, and philosophers, in an infinite regress, in a hall of mirrors that only becomes indistinct when eyesight loses acuity, when vision fails because of distance or multitudinous detail. Is there any choice for us beyond knowing that the world speaks into our spirit, asking to be celebrated, asking to be given form? I explore that notion in one of my own poems:

Silent Sonata:

After unseasonal rain in morning early
in flickering silence
juvenile honeyeaters come
to delouse the pendent
nectarine leaves from beneath
where insects congregate
for shelter
the tree shivers with them
till
in silent agreement
they're gone
and the eye yearns
to conjure them back again...

The Task

Hence, I am attempting to record a fleeting and temporary rustling in a tree that will go on till the spirit flies away: namely, the evolution of a psychotherapeutic identity. Inevitably, the account invokes some of my influential ancestors who, as Harold Bloom contends, I had to misread to become the kind of therapist I was destined to become (Bloom, 1973). This is a composite tale, and while its telling was seeded by reading Milner, there are many poets and other psychoanalysts, as well as some philosophers, who are pressed into service in the telling. It's a tale of working free of 'mind–forg'd manacles' (Blake, 2004, p. 128) many of them are taught and insisted upon; others self-imposed out of timidity, a need for certainty, or an excessive reverence for one's elders.

Why is there a line around everything?

A friend of mine, one of Australia's premier poets, has several times recounted a question asked by one of his grandchildren: 'why is there a line around everything?' Now, I have never been able to draw, let alone paint. Nor have I ever had any real ambition to be able to paint, or even to produce a passable sketch. Long ago, I reconciled myself to stick figures. Why, then, did reading Marion Milner's *On Not Being Able to Paint* incite such a profound sense of satisfaction and intrigue as I delved further into it? Many months have now passed since I first encountered her text (2019), so there's been time to allow that experience of reading to percolate through the unconscious. In part, what emerged from the process of digestion was the dream recounted earlier. But something else emerged also. The reading seeded another development, somewhat like a grain of sand that initiates the development of a pearl. That process began to clarify itself as a genuine and pressing object of curiosity when our small writing group began to investigate the question, 'what kind of therapist are you?' And it has continued to challenge because the pearl is still forming, still revealing influences from multiple sources in concordance with Milner's insights. It involves the attempt to see oneself, the world, and the therapeutic encounter, unencumbered by stale, off-the-shelf preconceptions.

Milner said,

> …to draw the line of one object with fully felt awareness of the line of a neighbouring one and of the patterns of space that they mutually created between them, seemed as potent an act as laying a wire across the terminals of the battery; and the resulting flash seemed to light a new world of possibilities. Presumably it was fear of these new possibilities which caused such a compelling narrow focus of attention in which it was only possible to attend to one thing at a time.
>
> (Milner, 2010, p. 14)

What a difference four decades make?

In March 1978, I found myself in the Baillieu library attempting to answer a question set as an essay topic for a subject of the social work degree I had recently commenced. There it was, a daunting and tantalising question: 'What Are the Similarities and Differences Between Counselling, Psychotherapy, and Psychoanalysis?' Anna Freud's *The Ego and Mechanisms of Defence* was duly located on the shelves and, shortly thereafter, I decided that I knew 'what I wanted to do when I grew up': a somewhat belated development in my case. A training in psychoanalytic psychotherapy beckoned. But at that point, another process also gathered momentum: the process of conceptually drawing hard lines around objects, processes, and even the concept of 'the subject.' Now that's not an uncommon educational outcome. Nor is it altogether inappropriate. But it is something that I have spent forty-two years attempting to recover from.

The first significant seed of recovery was probably planted in 1985, in the middle of training, when my trajectory of learning seemed to be all about forming clearly drawn, individual lines. I read Donald Meltzer's *Dream Life* that year, and a contrary trend got underway, though it took thirty-five years to fully manifest (Meltzer, 1984). Even in those early years, I harboured a sneaking but inarticulate suspicion that the conceptual frame of the practice I was being initiated into felt very much like drawing stick figures.

Why?

I think it was because earlier in my education, I had been entranced by the musical, polysemic, and expressive rather than denotive characteristics of language: how poems celebrate something that they can only point to. How they create worlds: rich worlds of conceptual, embodied, and emotional complexity. To live with and inside a poem is to live within multiple, overlapping, interactive, and even contradictory lines of force within a sacred space. Louise Glück has intimated that it is also to live within a created world that reveals, like an X-ray or like an injection of radioactive dye, the lineaments of another's mind (Feit Diehl, 2005, p. 183). In terms borrowed from Jessica Benjamin, most of the psychoanalytic theories occupying my mind in those days seemed to be all about a 'doer and done to.' And, try as I might, there always seemed to be something that eluded me: something unsatisfying about that perspective, even when I began to consider dynamics within a liminal space conceptualised as a recursive interplay of T⇔CT. Thirty years after that encounter with Meltzer's book, I posed a question: 'The Analyst in the Poem, the Poem in the Analyst: Where is the Poet to be Found?' and then attempted to formulate an answer in a PhD thesis. The poem, I concluded, was a co-created 'text,' which both analyst and analysand alternatively became immersed in or interacted with. The putative poet lives and composes between them: an entity that is neither one nor the other, nor even anything 'personal' in the usual sense of the term.

Being hidebound, or not

One of the most repugnant statements that one can hear in a professional setting is, 'I am a Kleinian.' The same is true whether the therapist announces herself as a Freudian, a Jungian, a Winnicottian, a Kohutian, a Lacanian, or a Bionian. They are all deformities of authentic, complex, lived identity. It might be more acceptable to say,some spark of what I sense is truly mine, of what I am becoming, is to be found in the energy created when I short-circuit Klein with Winnicott, or Kohut with Lacan, and so on: or, better, some more complex interaction of sparking across multiple perspectives.

That sort of conception is almost acceptable, but not quite, because it still references the life of the mind as if it were simply co-terminal with the intellect. Escape from that impasse is impossible unless one believes that the whole body and nervous system is a listening ear; or unless, like Bion, or Ferro, or Ogden, we believe that there are real subjectivities – not just imaginary apparitions – in the consulting room that are not entirely ours, nor anyone else's exactly. Nonetheless, they are equally as real as our own fictions of self. And besides, it is not entirely up to us to assert what we are: the others with whom we interact mostly signal that to us. Milner advocated the adoption of a wider, more open lens in viewing phenomena. I needed to broaden my conceptual focus to include the contributions of philosophers and poets, as well as a diverse selection of psychoanalytic theorists to locate my identity as a therapist, without being left unable to see the wood for the trees.

Woods and trees

Gaston Bachelard, when contemplating the phenomenology of forests, said: 'In the vast world of the non-I… forests reign in the past…' (Bachelard, 1964, p. 188). Often we say that in therapy, we 'tame' some portion of the forest and convert it to use as tillable land. Yet, always, the forest stretches on unendingly before us, though we imagine there is some quiet, still point; some glade within that is sacred, where all is known, and nothing rankles. We need to imagine, as T S Eliot avers in *Little Gidding*, that there is a still point, which renders the bewildering dance of phenomena bearable (Eliot, 2002, p. 177).

Hence, like Bachelard, we '… sense the concordance of world immensity with intimate depth of being' (Bachelard, 1964, p. 15). And that induces reverence. It's a reverence that does not partake of omnipotence – that bogeyman of psychotherapy – but rather an acceptance of the way we are formed and exist in continual motion while we dream of stillness. Milner described painting as '… a sensory organic language rather than an idea language' (2010, p. 111). She also spoke of 'framed emptiness' (2010, p. 121). Throughout *On Not Being Able to Paint*, the iron of her thought struck light and flame on the flint of my curiosity about what it is I am doing when I work as a therapist and, most of all, who I am, and who I become, as I am doing it.

In her peroration, Milner speaks of experiences in learning to paint and claims that they '… distinguish the visual arts from the literary ones… [and]… throw light on [the] specific problem of how to express… [ideas]… in graphic rather than in literary form' (2010, p. 124). I'm not completely in agreement with the first part of that assertion. The potency of framing conditions, rhythm, the interaction of competing forces, alternation of immersion and interactivity, co-creativeness and inter-penetration of self and object, blurring and definition of self-and-other boundaries, multiple significations (polysemic language), embodied responsiveness, among other considerations, are all important in the study of literary forms; and most certainly also in conceptualising the art and the practice of psychotherapy.

Being seduced by reality

During training, while I was being supervised on my major training case, I was fortunate to have a supervisor who occasionally employed an unforgettable turn of phrase. One of her favourites was, 'you know you are always being seduced by reality.' She was referring, of course, to my inveterate habit of retreating into concreteness, and reasonableness, rather than facing the challenge of 'unreasonable' psychic reality. Thankfully, I did learn. But, since then, I have realised that the problem is much greater than either of us knew at the time. Beyond the initial fear of losing grip on consensual realty that Milner identifies as a fear of experiencing a world without hard lines and boundaries, lies a variously ecstatic and terrifying aesthetic confrontation with co-creation, as Donald Meltzer and Meg Harris Williams attest (1988).Part of the terror derives from an inevitable confrontation with the experience of something/someone unknown 'writing' our 'selves' into existence: unless, of course, mutual defences are erected to extinguish the experience. The original Greek form of the word 'aesthetic' emphasised perception through the senses, as did Immanuel Kant's later usage of the term. It is in that sense that I embrace the idea of a psychoanalytic aesthetic: that is, without recourse to judgements of beauty, or of terror as in the Romantic conception of the sublime, but with a strong emphasis on the embodied nature of communication. I advocate for a clear recognition of the fact that our sense of self is an aesthetic construct that is engendered within a boundaried space of relationship: with others, and with the world. Relationships within that space are mediated by embodied experience.

Other viewpoints

Gaston Bachelard (1964, p. xii) argues that the poetic image is 'referable to a direct ontology' and that 'at the level of the poetic image, the duality of subject and object is iridescent, shimmering, unceasingly active in its inversions' (1964, p. xv). One of the implications of those inversions is that we do not control a therapy, despite our illusion of presiding over an unfolding process,[2] because we are only conscious of a small portion of what is going on: within us, between us and others, or between us and the world. Like the philosopher who realises that 'forces are manifested in poems that do not pass through the circuits of knowledge' (Bachelard, 1964, p. xvii), we, as therapists, are changed within therapeutic interactions in ways that we cannot predict or control but must surrender to. The mere fact of being immersed in a process during which we remain equally as susceptible to, and available to influence as the analysand proves to be, is as important as anything else we might say about the psychoanalytic method.[3]

Bodily presence counts because it constitutes an experiential field that operates as a constant backdrop, a filter, and as a determinant of what can be thought and spoken. As therapists, the highest function we are capable of in therapy is to be present, and to accede to being affected in ways that don't always fit neatly with our 'go-to' concepts: projection, projective identification, etc.; or into preconceived and cherished value and belief systems. As Ferro and Ogden indicate in their different ways, the 'characters' that emerge on stage in the therapeutic discourse signal shifting states of mind that form and transform like clouds, or lower ominously like hulking mountains.[4] We are co-creators of those ephemeral but influential figures, as well as embodied presences affected by them through the awareness of those dynamics, however fleeting. Awareness of our own subjectivity may become vague. I explore that thought in another of my own poems:

On the way:

Today,
this heavy, solder-grey sky
and there,
in wetlands before the racecourse,
a pool of weepings project their origin.
Here,
in the locale of I,
in the fiefdom of Macedon
under the aegis of the Real,
passing headlights blur.
Later, the sun,
like a lucent moon cut adrift
to wander in daylight,
traverses a gap between
banks of cloud bulked like the mountain.
Unclear, unclear.
And the mind that registers all this
hardly less temporary
than the rain, than that
obscurantist, ostensible moon.

Bachelard coined two terms – *resonance* and *reverberation* – to describe the process of mutual influence created by the intersections of others and our selves, or between ourselves and the world at large. He said, 'In the resonance we hear the poem, in the reverberations we speak it, it is our own. The reverberations bring about a change of being' (1964, p. xviii). Furthermore, 'the exuberance and depth of a poem are always phenomena of the resonance-reverberation doublet' (1964, p. xix). This notion of dynamic and mutual influence could be expressed thus: resonance⇔reverberation. And where have we encountered similar attempts to represent a reversible, recursive dynamic? Consider these examples: PS⇔D (Bion) or T⇔R (Ferro). Meanwhile, ahead of us in fact, the literary arts have devised their own means trying to conceptualise the phenomena of subjectivity arising in the encounter of self with other, or in the interaction of self and world. Everett (Vic Web) cites as examples Wordsworth's *spots of time*, Emerson's *moments*, and Joyce's *epiphanies*. But perhaps the most intriguing example is Gerard Manly Hopkins' distinction between *inscape*, defined as 'the unified complex of characteristics that give each thing its uniqueness' and *instress*, defined as 'the force of being which holds the inscape together or the impulse from the inscape which carries it into the mind of the beholder' (Everett, 1988).

Sacred space and transformations

I wondered for a long time why I tended to intuitively conceptualise therapeutic situations in spatial terms: in terms of intermediate space and complex, overlapping lines of force. That is, in terms of experiences involving recursive dynamics and mutual influencing. Then I became familiar with some of the basic tenets of neuro-psychoanalysis, such as those enunciated by Antonio Damasio (2010). Once I absorbed his ideas about the centrality of body mapping processes in the construction of a sense of self, so much became clear. I found echoes of these insights in Milner's work, though her book was ostensibly focused on the pragmatic task of learning to paint. She spoke (2010, p. 11) of feelings determined more by a sense of touch than by the sense of sight, and of feelings conveyed by spatial configurations (2010, p. 13), and of the realisation that we are much more mixed up with objects than we like to imagine (2010, p. 12). Adapting one of Freud's dictums, Mark Solms has recently described feelings as the body's demands on the mind to perform work (Solms, 2015, 2020). Art does not really imitate science. Nor does science imitate art. They fundamentally echo each other's conclusions in another key, and via different vocabularies.

Dreaming up the self

Almost imperceptibly and by degrees, I was led into a world of overlapping conceptualisations originating in very diverse disciplines and fields of experience. One of the very few constants that persisted was the way that creativity consistently took centre stage as a measure of the health of the therapeutic process. More precisely, therapeutic co-creation and transformation assumed the role of bellwether signatures of progress. In his introduction to the 2014 Kindle edition of Bachelard's the Poetics of Space Richard Kearney asserts that 'poetics is about hearing and feeling as well as crafting and shaping...' (Location 96 of 5233), and, as seen above, Milner obviously concurred. She also said

> ... it had not as yet become apparent that the very problem so insistently trying to draw attention to itself was something to do with achieving a relation to the inevitable 'otherness' of what is outside one, to the reality of the solid earth.
>
> (2010, p. 24)

I came, thereby, to a situation where phenomenological philosophy spoke into one ear and poetry into another, while psychoanalysis – at least the psychoanalysis practised by Marion Miller and those of her ilk – paid respect to both. In response, I could not shake the memory of Wallace Stevens' anthem for the 20th century, *The Snow Man*, wherein he spoke of the need to remain open to the 'nothing' that it is the world unsignified, and the importance of eschewing projection into the world of our own fictions (Stevens, 1990, pp. 9–10).

Those encounters led, inevitably, to questions about how to separate self and other, self and world. Reflection on Stevens' 'nothing,' which invites comparison to Bion's 'no-thing,' emphasises the need to tolerate the gut-wrenching realisation that the world is quite indifferent to us; and that we are compelled to 'push back' against its tyranny through imagination, as Milner also discovered (Stevens, 1951, p. 36). Neuroscience concurs. The mind operates as a predictive engine rather than being a simple registrant of perceptual information.

Elsewhere, in speaking of her experiences of using colour, Milner said,

> So here was a meeting of the conscious inner eye and the blind experience of colour which resulted from the willingness to watch and wait. And it was a meeting which neither destroyed the dark possibilities of colour nor dimmed the light of consciousness; in fact it produced a new and vital whole between them, and one which seemed to glow up from the depths of one's existence, like the light in my sketches which had flooded up from the earth.
>
> (2010, pp. 28–29)

She also quoted the philosopher, Santayana, who asserted that, 'Perception is no primary phase of consciousness: it is an ulterior function acquired by a dream which has become symbolic of its own external conditions, and therefore relevant to its own destiny' (Milner, 1988, p. 32).[5] At that point, memories of other philosophic observations began to accumulate. Kearney paraphrases Bachelard again: '... poetic words... are not comparisons but transformations' (2014 Location 244). And, again, '... images are more demanding and rewarding than ideas' (2014 Location 263). And, finally, '... image is a four-way relationship between author, reader, text and world' (2014 Location 288).

Where have I heard this before?

Immediately, I was reminded of Winnicott who believed that, oftentimes, the power of communication resides more in how we speak, and that it also behoves us to ask why we speak. That is, he questions whether we genuinely need to interpret rather than allow the patient to find his own way to a realisation (Winnicott, 1971, pp. 101–102). I was struck, also, by Antonino Ferro's assertion that the analytic space allows for the metabolisation of emotion within a particular and specific field: one wherein, *ad absurdum*, literal and 'everyday reality' is excluded. Under those conditions, the characters that emerge onstage, in the field, in the unique analytic space, are conceived of as being co-created entities involved in a mutual process of transformation of experience.[6] Nor could I shake consideration of Thomas Ogden's *analytic third* (Ogden, 1994, 2004a), which, in his schema, initially subjugates both subjectivities in the analytic encounter so that they need to struggle to emerge from its shadow. All going well, they both ultimately emerge from subjugation and are mutually changed by the experience.

To what end?

And what is the end of all this seeking? T. S. Eliot famously observed that we often arrive back at our beginnings only to then recognise them for the first time (Eliot, 2002, p. 209).

However, in the context of psychoanalysis and of psychoanalytic psychotherapy, we are obliged to be somewhat more concerned with outcome, and with the ongoing viability of the subject, than is implied by such abstruse but emotionally satisfying realisations. In that spirit, we can perhaps allow our phenomenological philosopher a final set of observations. Richard Kearney, in his introduction to the 2014 Kindle edition of the Poetics of Space, records Bachelard's belief that imagination constituted a 'laboratory of the possible', and that both 'reverie and poetry … give a future to the past' (2014 Location 215). He highlights Bachelard's assertion, in apparent agreement with Milner, that '… Images are more demanding and rewarding than ideas. They give logos to perception' (2014 Location 264). Milner, for her part, said, '… this idea of there being no fixed outline, no boundary between one state and another, also introduced the idea of no boundary between one self and another self, it brought in the idea of one personality merging with another' (2010, p. 29). And that was long before Ogden or Ferro came to similar conclusions.

Whose 'reality'?

On closer examination, what is central to all these perspectives is a recognition of the permeable and mutable nature of identity (self and other), as well as the apparently contradictory process of growing to be more ourselves, as Bion (1977) and Bollas (1977) have both suggested, not only through the digestion of experience – interpersonal experience especially – but also by making one's way in the world and 'making something of it'. Shakespeare, the master who 'invented' the human according to Harold Bloom (1999), told us that *the poet's pen… gives to airy nothing/A local habitation and a name.* So, too, does the therapeutic encounter, given certain conditions, including the provision of a 'sacred,' protected space and respect for mutual creativity.

Likewise, both painting and poetry, in their different ways and by somewhat different means, speak a language whose yield is greater than what can be conveyed by words designed to communicate concepts, or by rigid theoretical system building. They speak a language directed to and responding to whole, embodied, and mutable beings. Milner attained that insight via her explorations of her blockages to her desire to paint. Phenomenological philosophy and many canonical poets could not agree more with her conclusions.

Arrival or waystation?

So, where does that leave me as a therapeutic practitioner? I am left nodding assent to Bion's notion that a psychoanalyst must, among other things, function like a poet (Bion, 1990, p. 17). Milner would presumably argue for a painterly perspective. Either way, little understanding accrues unless there is respect for the fact that therapy is a mutually creative and transformative process, which will not thrive in an atmosphere of strict adherence to the 'mind forged manacles' of orthodoxy and received wisdom. What's needed, I think, is an (almost) naive openness to what evolves during the process; even, or especially when, it does not fit into preconceived categories. My own evolving psychotherapeutic identity only began to feel like a convincing and lively enterprise when, as Milner discovered in learning to paint, one line of thought was pursued with a '...fully felt awareness of the line of a neighbouring one and of the patterns of space that they mutually created between them...' (Milner, 2010, p. 14).

Notes

1 A phrase used by Marion Milner (2010), p. 142.
2 I refer particularly to the argument advanced in Donald Meltzer's *The Psycho-Analytical Process*: one that is clearly countermanded by his later work. See footnote 8 above (D. Meltzer, 1979).
3 I say this, of course, while acknowledging that there is also an alternation between immersion and interaction, just as Laure Ryan describes (Ryan, 2001).
4 Bezoari and Ferro (1992, 1999); Collovà (2018); Ferro (1992, 1999, 2002, 2004, 2005, 2006a, 2006b, 2009a, 2009b, 2011, 2018); Ferro and Basile (2009); Ferro and Bezoari (1992); Ferro and Civitarese (2015); Maxwell.
Hart (2003); Ogden (1985, 1994, 1997a, 1997b, 1998, 1999, 2002, 2003, 2004a, 2004b, 2005a, 2005b, 2007, 2010).
5 Santayana: *Little Essays,* quoted in 'The Suppressed Madness of Sane Men' p. 32.
6 Antonino Ferro. See footnote 15 above.

Chapter 25

'What sort of Mrs Milner is she?' Thinking the experience mostly in words

Thanassis Hatzopoulos

for
International Winnicott Association Hellenic Group
Marionthi Kalatzi (*psychologist*), Nektarios Koulos (*clinical psychologist*), Elisa Nikolopoulou (*psychoanalyst*), Marialena Spyropoulou (*writer, psychotherapist*), Nefeli Tambaki (*psychoanalyst*), Thanassis Hatzopoulos (*psychoanalyst*).

Standing before a work of art, Freud tries to interpret the reasons of its influence on the recipient, the impression and the energy that it creates on him and his psyche. He links the pleasure that derives from the work of art to interpretation, that is, the words that he uses to express what he feels towards the artwork. So, the source of pleasure in this relationship is his ability to say in words what he feels.[1] He takes this relationship even further by writing that the artist intends to induce the recipient to the same psychic state-constellation as the one from which the creative impulse arises. This aims to bring to light an understanding in the reader or viewer, "like any other event of mental life"[2] as Freud notes in the same text. Interpretation is the expression of the contact point with the artwork: without it he cannot approach the "emotional activity" of either the artist or the recipient. Why though, he continues, couldn't the artist's goal be communicated and understood in words, like any other event of mental life? Here Freud once again sets what is appropriate, that words need to be the means of communicating and understanding every event of psychic life, including the one between the artist and the recipient of the artwork as well as the one between the artist and the artwork during the creation process. The focus is always on words in the *function of psychic life* during creation or communication with the artwork. However, even if this is what we seek, psychic life passes through words only in part, and we often assume that this is not the biggest part, since images as well as sounds – in their own language – remain active as ways of psychic functioning throughout life.

In reading her works, our group noticed that Marion Milner notes, probably with relief, that Freud leaves room for those who, like her, think in images. And that even if Freud's approach to the work of art gives priority to speech and words, to interpretation, nevertheless he poses as the basis of mental life (and psychoanalysis as well), the dream and its function. As she says:

> Freud not only noticed the articulating tendency of our observing mind but also found that ideas coming from the lower layers of the mind, like our dream visions,

DOI: 10.4324/9780429433535-31

> tend to be inarticulate; [...] and not only our night dreams but also our day dreams have this elusive quality
>
> (1987, p. 158)

And of course dreams operate by including action and dramatization which seem closer to the reproduction of picture-sound-action, enabled and repeated by the techniques of cinema; however, there are dreams in which a simple image captures the psychic activity without passing through action, by the way of a still but vivid image, which the French call *tableau vivant*. Often these dreams, though simple in their composition, are so crucial in the scene direction of the still image that they overflow with meanings.

Milner works on the process of this image with diligence and insistence and takes it as far and as deep as she can. It is not only that she uses it in the test of reality and the overall development of the ego.[3] The perceptual and sensory elements offer her a solid field of investigation and search for their mental transformation and representation, which extends to the three axes set in her course, as they seem to appear later in her writings.

The first axis[4] is understanding and interpreting the image, the image that she draws upon from art works, as it holds an emblematic place in her texts, especially in William Blake's Job. The second axis involves the image based on drawings that she uses in child analysis, attributing meaning to whatever the child suggests, "as if" and in the place of free association, in parallel with play (action) and the transference relationship. The third axis has to do with processing personal experience, from recording outside impressions to the psychic registering of physical sensations in unique moments which she calls "mystic". These three axes obviously interact since their contact points lead to a more creative use from her.[5] What she is most interested in, passing from one axis to another, is nothing less than the underpinnings of psychic life as they reflect on the liveliness of feeling.[6]

However, from this point of view, image becomes a limit, possibly the closest to consciousness, which allows her to dive into the deep, something that Milner is utterly preoccupied with. In all her texts, her attention is steadily directed there; to the area where the subject merges with the object, to that part of the psyche where random sensations circulate with relative freedom[7] before they become registered and connected to consciousness. This earliest structure of images concerns Milner throughout the process of symbolization and she uses them in a unique way of comprehending the relationship between subject and object and through it, the structure of the subject itself. She even examines images for the way they are articulated in shapes, lines and colours, so that the unique psychological rhythm of the person making it emerges (1987, p. 230). While emphatically concerned with image (maybe because it offers her and us a "safe" canvas), Milner also seeks whatever exists beyond and behind the image, looking for traces closer to the original formless core, presented with even more indirect signs and always involving preverbal areas.

> Freud did allow that people like me, who think mostly in images, do exist. But I did wonder why he mentioned only optical memories; why not also auditory, kinesthetic, or even olfactory ones, all of which must play an essential part in mental activity before the advent of speech.
>
> (1987, p. 59)

The toddler's attainment of language by decoding and using a blend of sounds that makes their given acoustic environment seems to us an amazing effort even though we have been through that ourselves.[8]

Facing this original formless horizon from which the psychic as we know it is formed, Milner begins her exploration not by approaching what Freud thought as the (his) basic exception in relating with art, namely music, but *the area from which art emerges*, on the edges of communication – an area containing its own "language", notes that become a common human Esperanto in which anyone can be immersed in the depths before and beyond any national linguistic structure. Milner writes on music: "Perhaps music is the nearest of all the arts to communicating what can't be communicated" (1987, p. 277). The language of music, as preverbal foundation of every language which is reached afterwards, has a universality that is difficult to approach with other terms and functions in an area where rhythms and sounds could possibly take the position of linguistic signs. Each infant and toddler decode them in order to reach and enter the language of their own environment.

To clarify the functioning of sounds, Milner needs to talk about the areas within the child and the adult where an oscillation between consciousness and the unknown emerges on rhythmic bases.

> He [Freud] says that the mystic feeling is explained by our rational surface mind's capacity to visualize the inarticulate images of the depth mind, and his central point is that the creative process takes place in these gaps in our surface mind's activity. He goes on to point out *how these rhythms of the mind can be seen as a series*; it ranges from the rapid oscillations of everyday thinking and perception to the slower cycle of waking and sleeping and to the even slower double rhythm of the creative activity in which the submerged phase may be sometimes extremely protracted.
>
> (1987, p. 196, our emphasis)

Sleep and the orgiastic experience are only two of these so common moments where rhythm requires a time-factor (1987, p. 224) on the basis of which it organizes such experiences:

> For the desire for the primitive rhythms, such as sucking, free bowel movement, babbling, masturbating, may all be reactivated when the adults sets himself the task of surrendering the conscious control of movement of the hand while still going on moving it.
>
> (ibid)

Here though lies the difficulty to include, name, and process what is characterized as "mystic" or elsewhere as an "absent-minded phase". This happens because "It is only by surrendering the ego to absentmindedness, to the chaotic flow of mental images that the fragments of the self – those 'isolated bits of experience' – can fuse in a new pattern" (Ellmann, 2011, p. xvix).

However, in this pendulum movement that can only happen if only someone primarily accepts the situation of "uncertainties, mysteries, doubts" we find ourselves close to what Keats describes as "negative capability", to name the "definite emotional relation to the unknown, to the x factor; it involved a willingness to face destruction, for the unknown may always contain hidden sources of disaster".[9] This means that every man as well as the clinician reaches the sources of destructiveness in their life where both hatred and love are rooted, with all its complexity.

Milner always uses her own way of approaching her themes, the Other and the Self. Thus she comes to realize the way she herself operates:

> The reason why I did not at any time make the attempt to express what I saw in terms of conventional psychoanalytic concepts was that I wanted to keep rigidly within the bounds of my own actual observation, to try as far as possible to forget everything I had read, everything I had been told, and to assume nothing that did not emerge out of my own direct experience.
>
> (2011, p. 159)[10]

This very personal way of hers, relying on her own direct experience (despite the fact that during her quest she submerges herself in the imaginative and auditory preverbal grounds of experience, clinical or otherwise), in the end justifies Adam Phillips' saying about her in his introduction to *The Hands of the Living God*: "Milner uses psychoanalysis not to articulate something but to make articulation possible" (2011, p. xix).

On the other hand, according to Maud Ellmann in her introduction to Milner's *An Experiment in Leisure* "Her writing remains speculative, tentative, open-ended" (2011, p. xviii) precisely because this experience arrives to us through her texts in words. Furthermore, during her process of trying to make expression itself possible, words and their value become something more than a tool of metabolism of "the Real" of the experience, in their connection with the body and with others, which she tries to keep alive.

> I had continually found that I must try and give names to my experiences, it was only by trying to find words for it that it seemed to grow; but when I found words, I must let them go again, never cling to them or they would become a dead thing.
>
> (Milner, 2011, p. 139)

So the symbolization process which may begin from recognition of differences, from their connection and distinction among sounds and shapes, forms, colours, acoustic and optical images, leads words to be the foremost means of conveying experience in the way that analysis itself has chosen:

> The analytic rule that the patient shall try to put all that he is aware of into words does seem to me to imply a belief in the importance of symbolization for maturity as well as for infancy it implies the recognition that words are in fact symbols by means of which the world is comprehended.
>
> (Milner, 1987b, p. 105)

To the end of her life driven by this obsessive effort to transform into words all kinds of experience she has been concerned with, she declares her faith in words, in their transformative and metaplastic value, in the way they change and give form to anything that is formless or ugly. Moreover, as we know, the Greek word for beautiful (*omorfo*) indicates something which has a form, and so the aesthetic pursuit of Milner herself, even with painting, is registered in her attempt to give form, to beautify what is within and outside the human psyche.

Notes

1 "Nevertheless, works of art do exercise a powerful effect on me, especially those of literature and sculpture, less often of painting. This has occasioned me, when I have been contemplating such things, to spend a long time before them trying to apprehend them in my own way, i.e. to explain to myself what their effect is due to. Wherever I cannot do this, as for instance with music, I am almost incapable of obtaining any pleasure." S. Freud, *The Moses of Michelangelo, S.E.* vol. XIII, p. 211).

2 "What he [the artist] aims at is to awaken in us the same emotional attitude, the same mental constellation as that which in him produced the impetus to create. But why should the artist's intention not be capable of being communicated and comprehended in *words*, like any other fact of mental life?" (S. Freud, *ibid*, p. 212).

3 "Surely he [Freud] is here saying that the image, in all its functions, is the essential basis of our psychic existence, since he is saying that it is this which makes reality testing possible, and therefore makes possible the whole development of the ego" (Milner, 1987, p. 58).

4 "After this I began to use Blake's series as a kind of handbook for trying to understand blocks in psychic creativity" (Milner, 1987, p. 9).

5 "Thus the context of the free drawings seems to me to illustrate not only the anxieties associated with 'creative capacity', but also different ways of thinking about that capacity – and thinking about it in terms that are derived from those various bodily functions which become the centre of interest at different stages of infantile development" (Milner, 1987, p. 217).

6 "What the painter does conceptualize in non-verbal symbols in the astounding experience of how it feels to be alive, the experience known from inside, of being a moving, living body in space, with capacities to relate oneself to other objects in space. And included in this experience of being alive is the very experiencing of the creative process itself" (Milner, 1987, p. 227).

7 She also "dares" to entitle a text "The ordering of chaos" (1957), insinuating the chaos before organisation.

8 We know that in the different languages the infant hears different rhythms of lingual articulations.

9 *Life and Letters of John Keats*, by Lord Houghton, in Marion Milner, *An Experiment in Leisure*, Routledge, 2011, pp. 104–110.

10 This Milner's quotation sounds similar to D. W. Winnicott's ideas. She articulates in her own words the same position with D. W. Winnicott, for instance in a letter to Anna Freud.

Chapter 26

'A Womb of One's Own'

Holding hands, mutual muddlement, and the so-slow finding of feet in Marion Milner's creative clinical cradling of 'Susan'

David Smith and Cheryl Bleakley[1]

> *Throughout our lives we are pregnant with our lives, pregnant with unborn selves and psychic babies, including thoughts, feelings, attitudes, modes of experiencing. A pregnancy that never stops, no matter how many births. Gestation does not end. The real question is can it begin, to what extent, with what quality?*
>
> Michael Eigen, *The Therapy Womb* (2017)

Introduction

This chapter draws on the complex, challenging encounter of a clinical and theoretical reading group, comprised principally of experienced psychoanalytic practitioners, with both Marion Milner's text and Susan's drawings, which together form the remarkable illustrated account of a long-term psychoanalytic treatment, *The Hands of the Living God* (1969). A number of pieces of original art work emerged out of the synergy of the creative process underpinning the co-creation of this chapter.[2]

Given that one of the most striking features of the book is the way in which Milner holds herself so productively within a facilitating internalised community of analysts, poets, and artists, and that the account itself is written in part as 'propaganda' (p. 459) for the benefits of living therapeutically in community, there is something fitting about the idea of a community of therapists turning their collective attention to a close reading of the book. Milner's unflinching gaze and steady tone, authorial but never overly authoritative, make great demands upon the reader. And the sheer volume of richly detailed, often very disturbing clinical material, ensures that the reader actually *experiences* something of the often unbearably uncomfortable and seemingly interminable process which is being opened out with such unsparing honesty. For this is essentially an account of an analyst struggling, for a very long time, to bear the madness and to understand the perverse needs of a deeply disturbed young woman, who requires of this fledgling analyst nothing less than a complete re-evaluation of the very theory and technique with which she is (as Milner herself comes to understand) ill-equipped for the task in hand. It is a tortuous and at times torturous struggle, pioneering in its nature, which requires deep introspection of Milner, and what is remarkable is the way in which she refuses to take the option of writing off Susan as unanalysable in her psychosis; instead she concerns herself with trying to come to terms, very painstakingly slowly, with her own misgivings and shortcomings, in the process adapting both her own theoretical understanding and her technical stance in order to bend to, and meet, the very particular needs of this singular patient (Figure 26.1).

DOI: 10.4324/9780429433535-32

Figure 26.1 *'To hold in myself a blankness, an empty circle, emptiness of ideas'* Cheryl Bleakley.

The makings of an artist-analyst

In a book that is full of powerful, often very disturbing images, perhaps the most haunting picture of all is the description of Susan's mother, as a baby, clasped tightly in the arms of her own dead, emaciated young mother.

Alongside this comes the image of Susan herself being prevented from walking for the first two years of her life by an overly fearful mother, anxious at both the physical and emotional dangers associated with her daughter finding her own way in life. And these two images seem to combine to reflect something of the immense personal struggle in which Milner herself is engaged throughout the sixteen years of her five-times-a-week analysis of Susan – sixteen years which constitute the formative professional years of this recently trained and newly qualified psychoanalyst.

Susan's analysis begins in 1943 and takes place in a bombed-out London that is deeply damaged on many levels, including psychological, by the devastating, uncontained hostilities of the Second World War. The outbreak of the war has coincided with Sigmund Freud's death, meaning that psychoanalysis itself now has a towering dead father figure to manage in terms of its own ongoing development, and has its own fierce battles raging in relation to both theory and technique, in the Controversial Discussions. Melanie Klein, Anna Freud, and Donald Winnicott will emerge from this period as the living psychoanalytic gods, in relation to whom Milner must somehow paradoxically both situate and separate herself, if she is to complete the key developmental task of truly coming into her own as an analyst.[3]

Milner (p. 26) allows herself to entertain increasingly uncomfortable doubts from early on in the treatment as to whether analysis can be of any use to Susan: '...or at least the only kind of analysis that I thought I knew how to give her'. A firm believer in the primacy of creativity, and the notion of art for art's sake, Milner makes the uneasy discovery that she has no such faith in interpretation for the sake of interpretation. She works tirelessly with the material presented by Susan, but slowly comes to understand that her transference interpretations are essentially ineffective in terms of relieving Susan's paranoid anxieties and reducing the guilt with which this deeply troubled young woman is so burdened. Similarly, Milner comes to understand that her early, repetitive, and at times overbearingly insistent focus upon unconscious phantasy, envy, and aggression is not helping to stimulate any process of psychic growth or movement within Susan. In fact, it dawns on Milner that her intensive clinical strivings are actually contributing to a transference deadlock – a therapeutic stalemate which is only reinforced by the analyst's counter-productive insistence on talking in terms that she comes to realise are essentially meaningless to Susan, a patient who attempts to protect any scant, hard-earned psychic equilibrium by doggedly refusing to recognise any notion of either unconscious wishes or an internalised phantasy world.

Repeatedly frustrated in her attempts to bring psychoanalytic thinking, in terms of split-off and projected internal part-objects, to bear on Susan's tormented, persecuted state of mind, Milner (p. 27) finds herself forced to confront the limitations of both the theoretical and technical models which underpin her analytic enterprise: 'I was forced to try and re-think some of my basic concepts for the analytic work with her'. In other words, it's very much back to the drawing-board for this artist-analyst, who intuitively understands (without knowing, at all, where this will take her) that this impasse calls on her to make full use of her own creative resources, to see what both analyst and patient between them can make out of this most unpromising clinical encounter. Winnicott, a steady, holding presence in the wings for both Milner and Susan, serves a vital containing function throughout this very long and horribly uncertain phase of the analysis – with Milner suggesting that it is only his [Mr X's] belief in its ongoing viability which 'kept us at it' (p. 30). And Winnicott's suggestion, in referring Susan, that 'the main treatment would be that he and his wife were providing her with a home' (p. 3) seems to feed into Milner's growing understanding of the central importance in this case of the provision of a secure holding environment.

Of course, just because Susan does not, for her part, *believe* in the unconscious, does not prevent her unconscious from *getting in on the act*, so to speak, in a way that allows Milner to make good use of it, in terms of her perceptive and sensitive discernment of what it is that Susan needs from her. Though it will be a full seven years into the analysis before Susan's drawings will gradually begin to help Milner get a fuller picture of what might be required of her in order for the consulting room to realise its potential as a facilitating environment, the analysis is punctuated throughout with often bleakly illustrative dreams and day-dreams – including one dream that she reports upon waking up from a sleep on the couch itself. One of the earliest reported dreams, from 1945, is of a baby that cannot be born (p. 28). And this is followed, in 1947, by a dream (p. 63) in which Susan is beginning to have a baby, and finds herself deeply conflicted, and dreadfully frightened, over what to do with it. Seeing this as a reflection of Susan's terror at the prospect of an internal dynamic unconscious, with a life of its own, and with a firm sense of Susan as the baby that cannot be born (and that in some sense has never been able to fully emerge into the world), in turn helps Milner (p. 28) to adapt her focus in response to Susan's unconscious cues: 'Thus the problem of how to find a setting in which she would feel it would be safe to be born into separate existence seemed to be becoming the central one in the analysis, as I saw it'. A much later dream (p. 446), in which a woman gives birth to a baby which is not yet ready to be born, and has to be taken by Susan into her own womb, is received by Milner as an instructive communication of Susan's need for the analyst to contain her premature interpretations; holding her tongue, Milner learns over the course of the analysis, is to be one key aspect of the holding environment.

All the time working, and very much held, within a solid analytic frame, Milner responds to Susan's needs by putting her creative energy into gradually developing what essentially amounts to *a psychoanalysis of her own*. Parsons (2001, p. 609) underlines the originality of Milner's thinking, suggesting that her introspective study of both painting and of her own self set her on course for a meeting of minds with Winnicott, and that Milner's early fascination with 'in-between' spaces was to find 'a natural convergence' with Winnicott's emerging ideas about transitional spaces. Phillips (2017) describes Milner as having to some extent already *invented* psychoanalysis for herself before she ever went into it, suggesting that she was always going to find her own distinctive way of working – making *use* of a variety of theories in order to enrich and expand her perspective, rather than allowing herself to be constrained by restrictive affiliations. Milner's far-ranging curiosity and the wide focus of her attention are reflected for Phillips in what he describes as the 'wild and weird and extraordinary' bibliography for *The Hands of the Living God*. Having successfully established several lives of her own, as (amongst other things) an artist, a writer, and a mother, Milner came into psychoanalysis with both a confidence in a primary creative drive and a trust that the hidden areas of the self can be relied upon. This *faith* of Milner, in her own self and in the unseen, innate forces of growth by which we are lived, underpins her capacity to make 'unusual use of her own subjectivity' as a theoretician (Parsons, 1990, p. 413), and her willingness to let herself be used by Susan, and to become, in Milner's extension of Khan's phrase, a 'servant' of 'the process working towards the patient's self-cure' (p. 1).

'The As-Yet Failed Poet of Herself'

Milner's analytic vision, like that of many of her colleagues in the Middle Group, is informed by a deep affinity with the English poetic tradition of Milton, Wordsworth, and Blake. She shares with Winnicott, described by Farhi (Giannakoulas, 2015, p. 65) as 'a consummate poet of human nature', a poetic sensibility; both analysts write in a richly allusive style, characteristic of poetry, which stimulates personal associations in the reader. Searles (1970, p. 194) ascribes a rare poetic beauty to Milner's own richly creative writing, which itself received critical acclaim from Auden and Spender. And Milner's very distinctive, radically personal invention of a psychoanalysis which is very much her own, dating as far back as her first book, *A Life of One's Own* (1934), is described by Olson as a 'poetic unventing of analytic methods and ideas' (p. 1008).

In his introduction to *The Hands of the Living God*, Phillips (2010, p. xx) suggests that Milner's approach to analysis

> ...makes the so-called patient the as-yet failed poet of herself; and this is, indeed, the gist of all Milner's extraordinary writing. For Milner growing up is akin to an artistic vocation; it is the struggle to articulate, not necessarily to resolve, one's abiding conflicts in the process of personal development....

Within the consulting room, the nurturing of creativity is central to this struggle, and, for her part, Milner (p. 60) explicitly underlines what she calls 'the central issue [for Susan] of finding how to make contact with, and come to believe in, the creative source within herself'. Milner, who writes elsewhere (1952, p. 184) of 'the original poet' in each of us, creating the world around us, credits Susan with what she calls a 'poetic intelligence' (p. 257), with a drive to express itself pictorially in the thousands of drawings which Milner receives from Susan with wide-open arms. She attributes to what she sees as Susan's poetic thought a level of perception and symbolisation which crucially goes beyond that which is permitted to the patient's rigidly controlled conscious awareness.

Unbidden poetry, like the repeated spilling of her tobacco, is tentatively welcomed by Milner as an interesting contribution from her own unconscious, which she allows to usefully draw attention to itself. One beautiful example of this is the D.H. Lawrence poem[4] which provides Milner not only with the title of the book, but also with a powerful poetic metaphor for the holding which lies at the very heart of her analytic endeavour. Milner makes use of the poet's lines, recurrently and rhythmically pushing to be heard, to help herself to crystallise her preconscious understanding of the very complex impact on Susan of her childhood experience of a maternal holding which was paradoxically both inadequate and vital. Milner emphasises elsewhere in the book (p. 294) 'what perhaps the poets have always known', and here (p. 60) underlines the slow work involved in making analytic use of such knowledge: 'But even when I remembered the words it took me a long time to bring myself to see the implications of it, and to turn poetic symbolism into a discursive prose statement'. Milner's faith in the wisdom of the poets is echoed by Bollas (2015a), who suggests that there is more illumination to be found in poetry than in psychiatry when it comes to trying to understand schizophrenia. 'After all', he writes (p. 197),

> they [the poets] have learned how to descend through the layers of our past, to mesh the sensorial, imaginary, and symbolic, in such a way as to convey our unconscious knowledge. Perhaps poets come close to the mental intersections experienced by the schizophrenic.

Bollas sees a striking similarity between the way poets think and write about self-experience, and the schizophrenic thought process, both of which are characterised by high concentrations of meaning into single words.

In keeping with the pleasure that Milner the artist took in putting together collages, here Milner the analyst and writer seems to relish piecing together, both laboriously and creatively, a highly complex, multi-dimensional picture of Susan, richly illustrated by a diverse, eclectic range of references not only to the various poets, but also to Huxley's prose, Ibsen's drama, Greek mythology, nursery rhymes, philosophy, mysticism, and the Bible. With her belief in the usefulness of poetic imagery in illustrating states of mind, Milner is both informed and in some sense *held* in her work by generations of poets – drawing on the wisdom of Shelley, Marvell, Auden, and above all the vision of Blake. She takes inspiration and strength from Keats' notion of *negative capability*[5]: '...that is, when man is capable of being in uncertainties, Mysteries, doubts, without any irritable reaching after fact and reason....' For her part, in one of the uncanny parallel processes which characterise the book, Susan, as the analysis progresses, is also able to make healthy use of literature in order to find truths of her own, in her reading of Proust and Shakespeare. And in a very moving late passage (p. 401), this woman who for so much of her life, and at such great cost, has had to protect herself from facing into the pain of all her accumulated sorrow, is able to introduce and to some extent entertain the theme of loss, by quoting a couple of lines from her recently deceased mother's favourite poem, by Byron.

A collective reading of *The Hands of the Living God* proved to be quite an experience in itself, somehow mirroring the by turns invigorating but deeply unsettling journey which Milner is depicting in her account. A strikingly diverse range of strong, conflicted thoughts and feelings was stirred up in response to the book, with a powerful sense of the members of the reading group finding themselves drawn into a difficult enough *experience* of having to sit for an uncomfortably long time with Susan's madness, the mutual muddlement of patient and analyst, and Milner's own long-term not-knowing.

Taking the plunge into the Abyss: the reading experience

This is not a book for dipping into, but rather one that seems to demand that the reader joins Milner in taking a 'plunge' into the dark abyss of both Susan's dreadful years of 'blackness in mind and heart' (p. 421) and Milner's almost unbearable struggle to 'hold in myself a blankness, an empty circle, emptiness of ideas' (p. 280).

'Plunge' is a word which features both in D.H. Lawrence's *The Hands of God*, and elsewhere in Milner (1950, p. 155), where she describes 'moments in which there is a plunge into no-differentiation'. Indeed, it proved to be very difficult and anxiety-provoking for the group to immerse itself fully in Milner's long spells of merger with Susan in her madness; joining with the analyst in her at times alarmingly confused and disturbing fusion with the patient seemed to provoke a certain claustrophobic anxiety, a fear of drowning or of endlessly sinking perhaps, characterised by an urge to differentiate oneself from Milner by putting in some reassuring distance between reader and author (Figure 26.2).

A lot of faith in the unseen process is called for in the reader, together with reserves of containment which to some extent reflects the remarkable feat of analytic holding which Milner is describing. Milner is containing the madness of a very deeply damaged young woman, who is struggling throughout with suicidal despair and murderous phantasies which are often directed towards young children; reading the book underlines the simple but important truth of just how disturbing and frightening it is to face into, and sit with, mental disturbance, without (to paraphrase Keats) 'irritably reaching after' a judgemental, impatient, or all-knowing attitude. The reader is brought face to face with a series of fundamental technical and theoretical dilemmas, and made to wonder about boundary issues and the very nature, purpose, and aims of psychoanalysis – provoking a lively discussion in the reading group, as to whether the patient is helped in therapy more through insight or through the emotional experience of being held. Again, Milner's emphasis on taking loving care of the patient, in line with Winnicott's (1986, p. 112) belief that 'cure at its root means care', is one that can generate a certain anxiety in the practitioner-reader. And notably strong feelings were stirred up in response to the issue of mutual dependency between patient and analyst, to a certain extent mirroring both Susan's ambivalence and Milner's own misgivings in relation to the analysis. At the same time, members of the group were also very stimulated by the book, taking heart and inspiration from it, reflecting the emphasis placed by Searles (1979, p. 195) on the engagingly constructive impact of Milner's writing:

> Not only is the author herself highly creative; the reader of her book gets many creative ideas which her book itself does not contain and which he had never been able to have before. Milner's book fosters one's own creative thinking.

Milner's handling of Susan's drawings

At the heart of both the analysis and the book itself are Susan's drawings and paintings. In one of the uncanny parallel processes which characterises the analytic relationship, Susan begins, spontaneously and unprompted, in 1950, to bring in 'doodle' drawings at the same time as, unbeknownst (consciously, at least) to her, Milner is preparing for the publication of her own study of free, unconscious doodling (*On Not Being Able to Paint*). Without ever appearing to be overwhelmed, Milner receives piles and piles of drawings from Susan – over 4,000 in a six-month period. Milner accepts not only the drawings that Susan brings in to share with her in the session, but also those which she brings in to leave with her. There are times when Susan brings in ninety images one day, followed by 'a huge batch' the next – far more than Milner is possibly able to process at a time. Still she continues to receive them, and to contain her own not knowing what she is to do with them, or to make out of them, filing them carefully away. After the eight-week Summer break, during which Milner receives a huge number of letters from her patient, Milner accepts a 'holiday box' (p. 215) which Susan brings in, containing several hundred drawings. Two defining characteristics of the hands of the living God that Susan has discovered in Milner are their receptivity and their capacity for holding. (Figure 26.2)

With a quite touching sense of mutuality, this receptive, accepting stance of Milner's in turn facilitates what quickly becomes a huge creative effort on Susan's part to put her analyst increasingly in the picture, in terms of both her fragmented state of mind and her very particular therapeutic needs moving forward. And there is a sense for Milner that Susan, through the drawings, is beginning to make contact both externally with her analyst *and* internally, with different aspects of her own self. Milner is able to bring thinking to bear on what is a deeply disjointed communication – vast both in its sheer volume and in its complexity; in very characteristic fashion, she compounds a variety of diverse readings of what Susan might be *doing* with the drawings – seeing them, at different times and in different ways, as reparative, placatory, defensive, restorative, bridge-building, affirming, and transitional. In keeping with her overall analytic approach, Milner is always adding to, and extending the possibilities

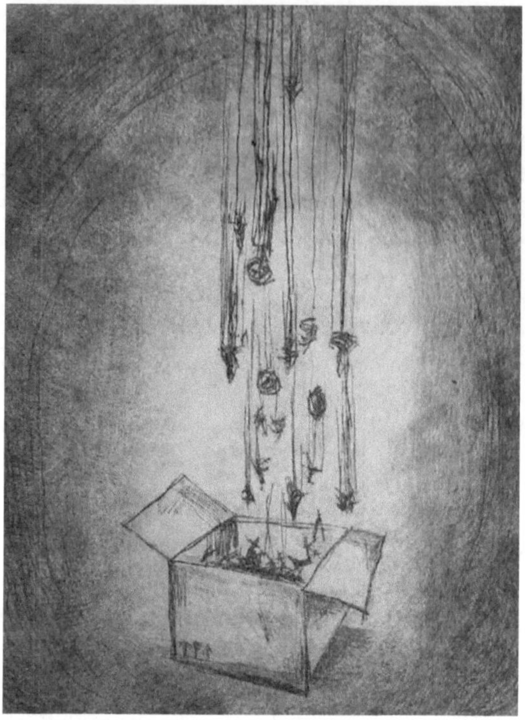

Figure 26.2 'The Holiday Box' Cheryl Bleakley.

of what might be going on, rather than narrowing down the possible meaning into reductive certainties. She sees Susan as laying down a vital foundation in her drawing for making contact with 'deep levels of self-knowledge' (p. 268), developing in the process her own visual language for communicating with Milner, but is also alert (p. 269) to the aggressive component to the drawings: '...the flood of drawings partly intended to drive me mad as she felt she had been driven mad'.

Milner, crucially, sees the artist in Susan; she believes in a creative drive in this very damaged young woman that has carried her through so much in life, and shares Ehrenzweig's (1967) faith in the notion of 'the work of art as the receiving womb and place of integration and rebirth' (p. 464). Very open to what she cannot see, and cannot yet understand, Milner intuits that Susan is somehow trying to work out, through the drawings, her ideas about her own creative process, and what she needs in order to get in touch with the innate creative force within her. Milner's slow pondering of the drawings helps her to formulate more clearly her own growing sense of what it is that Susan's maturational processes require from her in terms of the provision of a secure and facilitating therapeutic environment. And there is a very human, maternal aspect to all of this, with Milner the mother (who is well practiced, by this stage in her own life, in receiving her young son's art work) instinctively and sensitively aware of the importance of her acceptance of the drawings, and of Susan's healthy gratitude for a corrective emotional experience that stands in stark and vital contrast to her childhood experience of a deeply traumatised and preoccupied, rejecting mother who, with the words 'Don't tell me – it will kill me!' (p. 7), implored her young daughter *not* to put her in the picture about her sexual abuse.

Milner is honest about the unsettling effect which Susan's drawings have upon her, outlining the often complicated and confused feelings which they induce in her, as with the very powerful, post-ECT image (Figure 100) which she draws the night before her first meeting with Milner – a drawing, incidentally, which Susan herself has carefully held on to (through several changes of address) for a full nine years before feeling safe enough to bring it into the analysis:

> ...the impact of this drawing had been so intense that I had been unable at first to bring myself to concentrate upon its meaning. It produced such a complex state of feeling to do with tragedy and anguish that it seems I did not really know what to do with it.
>
> (p. 277)

Milner the author is retrospectively shocked at what she describes as her 'cavalier treatment' of this drawing, which she has inked over in order to see it more clearly; she understands her action as exemplifying the danger of the uncontained analyst imposing meaning in response to struggling to see the full picture: 'I was to remember this action of mine as a warning of how too great enthusiasm for the clarity of a verbal interpretation can also, at times, disastrously distort what the patient is experiencing' (pp. 277–278). But even in her muddled and at times anxious holding of these very fragmented drawings, Milner has a strong sense that she is holding open a vital link between patient and analyst, in the process modifying so much of Susan's deep disturbance:

> ...I saw her as, through her drawings, constantly creating a bridge between me and herself, a basis for communication, since I believed her drawings did all have meaning potentially; even if I did not as yet understand more than a small part of them I had at least made the attempt to relate them to what had been going on between us during the years. Thus these so many bits of herself that she had given me had, I thought, been modified by my capacity to see her as a whole continuing person, even if she could not yet see herself or me as that.
>
> (pp. 267–268)

The vast majority of the images which Susan produces are characterised by a primitive quality, with a flat, colourless feel to them. For the most part pre-symbolic in their nature, they typically lack balance, harmony, rhythm, perspective, and consistency, and tend to be very fragmented; ungrounded and unlinked, their relation to one another is often very unclear, reflecting a deeply fragile, fearful sense of an inherent opposition to any coherence or even connection. This schizophrenic quality ensures that the drawings are very difficult to read, and requires of Milner both tremendous patience and a great capacity for containing her anxiety as regards not knowing where she stands within what Bollas (2015b) characterises as a 'psychotic minefield'. Bollas, outlining what he terms 'the art of schizophrenia', describes the development of an idiom in which the patient's thoughts and fears are encrypted, suggesting that the patient who finds the analyst trustworthy will begin to pass on certain 'notes' in the analysis, indicating what the encryption is. Viewed from this perspective, the task of the analyst is 'to learn another language, another idiom', and Milner's challenge, in receiving so many visual pointers from her patient, is to become a skilled and sensitive translator of Susan's mysterious and highly personalised pictorial idiom – a view which Milner herself arrives at: '...I came to see them as my patient's private language which anyone who tried to help her must learn how to read – and speak' (p. xxi). Milner at one point refers to the 'jigsaw pattern' of Susan's illness (p. 409), and she works her way laboriously and painstakingly, piece by enigmatic and often disturbing piece, through this most complex and puzzling 4,000-piece jigsaw – with nothing left out of her characteristically wide-focused consideration.

Searles (1970, p. 193) suggests that the central theme of Milner's book is the gradual development of a whole and human body-image:

> As the years go on she comes, step-by-step, to inhabit her body fully, to experience the range of human feelings, and to experience herself as a real person in a real world. Late in the book we find abundant evidence of the patient's becoming born into the world, out of a preceding oneness with the analyst.

Indeed, one of the most striking features of Milner's analytic approach is the consistent attention which she pays to the patient's physical presentation, in which so much of Susan's emotional suffering is painfully embodied. Milner emphasises (p. 463) the central importance of the integration of body and mind, fantasy, and reality:

> ...the fantasy of a womb can, and perhaps must, become a kind of psychophysical reality, something that has to be first found (at least for very ill people) in the analytic room, and then introjected into their own bodies, becoming identified with their own body awareness from inside, and thus coming to form the true place from which to live.

There is a growing sense, as the analysis progresses and the relationship deepens, of analyst and patient combining through Milner's steady receptivity and Susan's developing creativity to forge and hold together what becomes a solid *body* of work out of so many fragmented drawings. Alvarez (2018) makes a distinction between the patient who is *undrawn*, as opposed to *withdrawn*, and in this sense, Susan's existential crisis could be thought of in terms of not only the Louis MacNeice (1944) refrain 'I am not yet born',[6] but also in the sense of 'I am not yet *drawn*'.

Something of Susan's own gradual emergence, bodily and emotionally, into the world seems to get mirrored in the way in which her art-making edges its way slowly into the analysis. After an initial seven years with no trace of the drawings to come, the ensuing flood of images are all produced at home, and brought, ready-made as it were, into the consulting room; seven months on comes a point at which Susan paints in the waiting room before a session, before finally, in 1957, towards the end of her analysis, she seems to manage to integrate the act of drawing with the analysis itself, and actually starts to draw in Milner's presence. Over time, Milner has a sense of Susan finally beginning to awaken to, and face into, her own tragic loss (as depicted in the deeply sad faces of figure 42), whilst there's also an impression of something more three-dimensional and symbolic developing in Susan's drawings, which even come to include a certain intricacy (as in figure 41), and colour, at times. Milner recognises the importance of Susan's struggle, through her drawing, to achieve an image of herself, and provides a facilitating, receptive environment in which Susan, so wary of symbolic thinking, is able, over time, to begin to find, explore, and develop symbols of her own.

Though there are times when Susan herself cannot bear to think of the drawings which she produces, and is horribly frightened of where her own creativity might take her, Milner, for her part, maintains a consistent, detailed scrutiny, and is able, crucially, to hold them in mind, and return to them in her own mind again and again. Milner's appetite for understanding and her capacity for reflection, sustained over such a long period of time, are quite staggering. And more than once she undertakes the huge task of reviewing every single one of the drawings. For her part, Milner is constantly approaching the drawings from different angles, turning them around both literally and metaphorically in order to redescribe them by trying out new layers of meaning from a different perspective. She holds on to the drawings, housing them in her own home, tracing some, attempting to draw others from memory, viewing and reviewing them constantly – firm in her belief in the continual and multi-determined fertilising aspect hidden in both the act and the content of Susan's drawing. A powerful example of Milner's wide-angled focus comes in the distinctively creative fusion of images drawn from biology, nursery rhyme, and Susan's own personal symbol of the containing cup, which combine together to inform her instructive take (p. 457) on what she describes as the most mysterious (in terms of mood) of all the images, *The Sleeping Head and the Egg* (figure 141):

> It seemed to me now that this could be seen as a picture of a new kind of womb that Susan knew that she must create within herself, a task she knew about when she drew it……[.] So, just as we had seen the slow evolution of her attempts to create the image of her actual womb, as a physical possession, so also this drawing seemed to be about her struggles to reach that higher level of psychic containment from which her new self can grow.

Elsewhere in her writing, Milner (1952) makes reference to the 1899 W.B. Yeats poem, *Aedh Wishes for the Cloths of Heaven*, and this prompted the current authors to wonder, and to try to imagine, what Susan's own version of this poem might sound like:

> *But I, being mad, have only the fragments of my mind;*
> *I have placed my fragmented images into your hands;*
> *Handle carefully because you handle my soul.*

Postscript

> *An only life can take so long to climb/Clear of its wrong beginnings, and may never;*[7]
>
> Philip Larkin, *Aubade* (1977)

'And some time', writes Seamus Heaney in his 1996 poem *Postscript*, '*make* the time……' [italics added], a point emphasised by his subsequent description of the human condition as 'A hurry through which known and strange things pass…..',[8] a phrase which resonates poetically with Milner's notion of the unconscious forces by which we are lived (p. 35). And this *making* of time, of so much reliably consistent time over such a long period, is a crucial element of Milner's compassionate analytic intervention. For without all that time taken, reflecting the devoted patience which Milner shows towards Susan, there could be no slowing down, no sustained wide-angled focus, no steady holding through all of the unbearable blackness and barely tolerable blankness, no careful finding of softly treading feet, no trusting handing-over of those thousands of visual fragments of a broken soul, and no creation of the womb-like conditions which eventually allow for Susan's gradual emergence and re-entrance into the hurried and traumatised world around her. It is only with time that Susan is able to so-slowly internalise both the therapeutic relationship and the analytic process itself. And it is this unhurried process of internalisation, together with Milner's faith in the transformative potential of Susan's powerful creative drive, which combine to underpin Milner's tentative belief (p. 458) for her patient, moving forward, 'that she will find that she has installed within herself the womb-like crucible of the analytic room enough to be able to go on growing, both spiritually and mentally'.

If Milner's book stands as a testimony to the way in which the process of writing provides a facilitating cocoon for creative psychoanalytic thinking, the authors came away from this challenging group experience with a heightened appreciation of the benefits of working in community, of reading collectively, and with some sense of the reading group itself as a generative womb – a source of what Phillips (2018) refers to as 'imaginative vitality'. To read Milner is to be left with a powerful impression, to paraphrase Winnicott (1945, p. 140),[9] that 'we are poor indeed' if we limit ourselves to a narrow theoretical and technical perspective; for Milner's wide focus and psychoanalytic creativity enable her to develop *a psychoanalysis of her own* which is greatly enriched not only by the diversity of the threads of analytic thinking which she weaves together, but also by the unique, expansive collage she makes out of the artistic, poetic, bodily, spiritual, mystical, mythological, biological, philosophical, oceanic, biblical, and musical elements which she gathers together along her singular way.

Notes

1 The authors are hugely indebted to the members of the Northern Ireland Institute of Human Relations' Clinical and Theoretical Reading Group for their invaluable collective contribution to this chapter: John Boyle, Mary Cairns, Desmond Campbell, Patricia Denvir, Rosemary Drainey, Carmel McGovern, Gerry McShane, Mandy Mullowney, Janine Paisley, Phyllis Quigg, Sue Steging, and Cheryl Towers. The group met monthly for six months to discuss the book.
2 Two of which, by Cheryl Bleakley, are included here.
3 Though Milner is very much associated with the Middle, or Independent, Group, and was very close to Winnicott, she was also supervised by Klein, and close enough to Anna Freud for the latter to contribute a foreword to *On Not Being Able to Paint* (1950).
4 D.H. Lawrence: *The Hands of God* (1932).
5 *Letter from John Keats to George and Tom Keats*, dated 22 December 1817.
6 'Prayer Before Birth' from Collected Poems by Louis MacNeice (Faber & Faber), reproduced by permission of David Higham Associates.
7 Philip Larkin, 'Aubade' (1977, Faber & Faber Ltd.), reproduced by permission of Faber & Faber Ltd.
8 Seamus Heaney, 'The Spirit Level' (1996, Faber & Faber Ltd.), reproduced by permission of Faber & Faber Ltd.
9 '...we are poor indeed if we are only sane'.

Section IV

Milner's books and other endeavours

Introduction to Section IV

Marion Milner's books and other endeavours

This book is the distillation of a rich creative endeavour involving over fifty contributors, some of who were new to Marion Milner's work. True to the spirit of Milnerean 'discovery research' we instigated an exercise in action-research of reading groups around the world who focused in depth on one or more of her books. A few of these appeared in the last section, and others in this. As noted, the section divisions in this volume are broadly in line with those of other books in this series [Anna Freud, Bion, Fairbairn, Ferenczi, Klein, Lacan, Leowald], and particularly with the Winnicott volume. However, Milner's extraordinary legacy spans many separate disciplines - psychoanalysis, industrial psychology, pedagogics, art therapy, artistic practice and criticism, etc. Although Milner's diverse interests existed naturally within her, within these pages we make an expedient distinction between those which belong within the psychoanalytic consulting room in Section II, Art in Section III and, given their wide-ranging nature of her eight books, many of Milner's pursuits are included here in Section IV with an emphasis on her as a psychologist and writer.

We begin with Milner's only book written as a working psychologist, *The Human Problem in Schools* (1937). Ostensibly an account of Milner's research within these schools, it really makes a pioneering exploration of what is needed of a psychologist in girls' secondary schools. Milner's research is relevant from many perspectives, including general social history and the history of psychology.

In **Chapter 27**, Shane Graham, psychologist, considers this application of psychological ideals and in **Chapter 28**, Margaret Boyle Spelman gives a detailed description of Milner's account of this research project which was essentially Milner writing the prescription for a discipline which did not then exist: applied educational psychology.

In **Chapter 29**, Claire Crellin extracts from and collates the responses of a Dublin-based group who recorded their conversations on Milner's four diary-type books, *A Life of One's Own*; *An Experiment in Leisure*; *Eternity's Sunrise* and the posthumously published *Bothered by Alligators*. The author/participants contribute different standpoints: Clare Crellin from a Jungian psychoanalytical perspective, Veronica O'Doherty from a mindfulness and Buddhist perspective, Alena Eagan from an art and sculpture perspective, and Margaret Boyle Spelman from a Winnicottian psychoanalytical perspective. As Milner wrote diaries from age ten until her death at ninety-nine years of age, these books constitute probes into different phases of Milner's life cycle.

DOI: 10.4324/9780429433535-34

In **Chapter 30**, four members of the Australia Reading Group based in Melbourne wrote up their responses and associations on reading *The Suppressed Madness of Sane Men*.

The next two chapters hail from different reading groups based in Cape Town, South Africa, both responding to reading *On Not Being Able to Paint*. The first group in **Chapter 31** are home-grown psychoanalysts, members of South African Psychoanalytical Association (SAPA) [the first psychoanalytic society accredited by the International Psychoanalytic Association (IPA) on the African continent, and recipient of the 2020 prestigious Sigourney Award for 'increasing the reach of psychoanalytic thought for people with histories of apartheid, racism, and trauma in South Africa through clinical, applied, and community work']. In **Chapter 32**, the second, interdisciplinary group brings quite different considered responses to the same book, which are thoughtful and thought-provoking.

In **Chapter 33**, James William Anderson gives an account of reading *The Hands of the Living God* with students at Northwestern University Medical School in Chicago. Marion Milner kindly agreed to engage with their questions and her answers are reported verbatim.

Chapter 34 concludes this section with Milner's last book *Bothered by Alligators*. Angela Joyce and Tessa Dalley bring their own child-oriented expertise to bear on the drawings and writings of Milner's young son John. They then note how in daring to follow her associative processes, Milner's 'immense propensity for introspection' subverts her initial purpose of producing a 'help book for parents'. Through courageous self-analysis, she confronts the 'inevitable limitations' of her own parenting and their sources in her own childhood losses and 'alligator kind of love'.

Chapter 27

The Human Problem in Schools

A refined application of psychological ideals

Shane Graham

Introduction to Psychology courses often teach the history of the discipline as a series of paradigm shifts – schools of thought whose popularity ebbs and flows as a function of emerging ideas, opinions and data points. As a relatively new field of study, psychologists have yet to identify a core fundamental theory with extensive explanatory value, as Charles Darwin did for evolutionary biologists, or Albert Einstein for theoretical physicists. Consequently, over the course of the 20th century, several schools of thought vied for hegemony within the minds of psychology faculty members. Psychoanalysis was largely usurped by behaviorism, which made way for the cognitive revolution. Each paradigm's epoch instilled different (and at times opposing) values, beliefs and practices within the psychological community. For all of their utility, a paradigm can also insulate a community from appropriately investigating socially important problems, because the problem in question is not readily reducible to the "puzzle form" – it cannot be stated in terms of the conceptual and instrumental tools that the paradigm provides; the proverbial baby is thrown out with the bathwater.

For a discipline such as psychology – a "soft science" – this is a pertinent risk. Plato's allegory of the cave comes to mind – bound by paradigmatic concepts, psychologists are led to hypotheses derived from mere shadows on the wall. As difficult a challenge as this short-sightedness is to overcome, a diligent investigator committed to working toward the ideal of truth can do so by adopting the scientific attitude – a commitment to open-minded investigation. In the abstract, this may sound like a simple commitment; in reality, it is much easier said than done. One should not underestimate the normative power of communities subscribed to (or possessed by!) particular sets of ideas, as was the case among "hard" psychoanalysts or behaviorists during the 1930s (and indeed, much of the 20th century). This leads to why Marion Milner's *The Human Problem in Schools* reads not only as an exemplary example of an investigator embodying the open-mindedness of the scientific attitude but as a personal triumph.

Milner's approach to her topic of investigation is wonderfully balanced. It draws on an impressively broad range of theory and mixes research methods; yet it never oversteps into making definitive claims, remaining acutely aware of its own limitations. On the one hand, several empirical psychologists (such as Spearman, Thorndike, and Allport) are referenced throughout the study, and their influence can be felt in Milner's commitment to applying quantitative data analysis methods where possible. Her application of statistics allowed for an objective framing of the kind of problems

DOI: 10.4324/9780429433535-35

that existed within schools, which allows for her later consideration of what contribution a psychologist can make toward the problems at hand. Yet (by some definitions) the core subject of investigation for a psychologist is the subjective experience, and the essence of this subjectivity is lost in the reductionism of quantitative methods. In order to mitigate against such reductionism, Milner responds by applying qualitative methods in equal measure, with much of her consequent observations informed by Carl Jung, arguably the period's pre-eminent authority on the individual's inner world. The result is a holistic approach to psychological investigation that successfully integrates concepts and approaches that many of Milner's contemporaries would have considered to be mutually exclusive; for example, Part IV of Section II, 'A Chart for Classification…', comfortably leads to 'Interest in Intuitive Experience'. Her marrying of approaches – qualitative and quantitative; rational and empirical; analytical and intuitive – leads to a nuanced snapshot of the schools that she is investigating, and the girls studying within them. The approach is multi-dimensional, acutely aware of the external social systems (family/classroom/peer) that the students exist within, all the while never losing sight of the girls' individuality and world of inner experience. The investigation's pragmatic recommendations are tempered by explicit acknowledgment of their own limitations: statistics can conceal individual differences, and there are limits to the rational investigation of "unique systems", i.e. human subjects. This objective and prudent amalgamation of approaches, drawn from a sweeping body of literature and instruments that were available to Milner at the time, is a stellar example of the adoption of the scientific attitude.

Great credit is due to Milner for the apparent even-handed application of appropriate theory and techniques within the investigation, unclouded by paradigmatic prejudice. To fully grasp the extent of the credit due, it is important to consider the publication in context – published in 1938, the influence of the behaviorist movement was significant in psychological circles, and their rejection of the world of inner experience as a subject of investigation was in vogue among leading research psychologists at esteemed institutions. We are graced with the advantage of hindsight and contemporary acceptance of the fundamental limitations of radical behaviorism. Milner was not afforded such graces, and as a psychologist tasked with a research project, her decision to buck the behaviorist trend – while not rejecting its methods – is extremely commendable. It resulted in a comprehensive research study that reads (aside from the odd anachronism) as though it could have been published today, rather than eighty-plus years ago.

Indeed, throughout the book, the reader is likely to be struck by evidence of Milner's intellect and progressivism, which makes her writing feel of our time (or alternatively, ahead of her own). There is discussion of phenomena – including sex, divorce and suicide – that were likely still taboo for much of 1930s England. There is a nuanced framing of psychological factors and mental health disorders as matters of degree, rather than dichotomy – an approach forgotten by many DSM-toting psychological practitioners during the mid- to late 20th century. There are also instances of Milner's speculative thoughts aligning with contemporary theories that would not be integrated into psychology for decades (particularly systems theory and the mind-body connection). In some unexpected cases of reverse symmetry, *The Human Problem in*

Schools also delivers moments of social commentary that unquestionably still apply to today's world. Perhaps the most pertinent is worth quoting in its entirety:

> ...if the schools cannot provide [all children] with a sense of being some use, there is the possibility that we shall get more and more young people, when they leave school, feeling so tired of not being able to find a place for themselves that they will overbalance either towards political extremism, with its artificial exaltation of ideology and the obliteration of the individual, or toward neurotic pre-occupation with themselves.

Could there be a more concise reflection of today's (Western) societies, with their increasingly partisan politics and social media influencers? In retrospect, the statement is portent and demonstrates Milner's awareness of the inner lives of her subjects.

Ultimately, *The Human Problem in Schools* displays Milner's character – her steadfast open-mindedness, her commitment to maintaining the scientific attitude, her progressivism, intellect and insight. The research itself is a stellar example of a careful psychological investigation. Several of the issues that it identified (including attention issues, staff fatigue, and effectively managing significant variance of within-class ability levels) are still found in classrooms today; the practical implementations suggested in Section IV (such as streamed classes, development of extra-curricular activities, and parent-teacher meetings) are now commonplace in many modern schools. But the true object of focus here is the excellence of the author behind the research. Milner was committed to viewing more than just shadows on the wall.

Chapter 28

Marion Milner

A many-branched psychologist at work

(*The Human Problem in Schools*)

Margaret Boyle Spelman

This chapter is included in this volume for a comprehensive treatment of the Milner tradition. *The Human Problem in Schools*[1] has a very distinctive psychological quality which – while integral to her whole career-self 'Marion/tree' – sets it apart from Milner as a psychoanalyst, thinker or artist. It is based on the only publication that Marion was commissioned to write as a working psychologist. The study is a description of Milner's work as a psychologist in a school setting, at a time before psychologists worked in schools. It gives a brief overview of Milner's work across psychology and enquires as to what might be the most appropriate work for a psychologist in secondary schools. It draws a portrait of Marion's contribution to clinical and industrial psychology and sees her aiding the development of another nascent discipline – educational psychology.

Background

As newly-weds, Marion and her husband spent the years 1927–1929 in America after she had won the Laura Spelman Rockefeller Memorial Fellowship. During this time, Marion, based in Boston, worked as an 'industrial psychologist' (now known as an 'organisational psychologist') at Western Electric. She was an investigator to the National Institute of Industrial Psychology headed by Elton Mayo, who led the landmark Hawthorne Studies in Philadelphia. During her stay in the US, Milner also had her first experience of psychoanalysis with a Jungian, Irma Puttman, as recorded in her second book, *Experiment in Leisure* (written under the alias 'Joanna Field').

In November 1933, nearly four years after Milner's return from the US, at a conference of Headmistresses, it was decided that the Council for the schools of the Girls Public Day School Trust – then the largest organisation for providing teacher training and higher education for girls in England – would employ an experienced woman psychologist to complete research; Milner was selected. There were new providers of secondary-level education in Britain at the time, and it was, perhaps, felt that this psychological approach would give the Trust an 'edge', distinguishing it from its competition as an innovative organisation.

Much of the enduring contribution of this study is the clear and intimate view it yielded of psychical, social and educational daily life, and of the female experience in 1930s Britain. And it gave this from the perspective of both adolescent girls and their adult female educators. Simultaneously, it gives us a view of a gifted psychological

DOI: 10.4324/9780429433535-36

'experimenter'. The research's nominal objective was to discover what adolescent girls needed by way of education to equip them for their adult lives and positions in society. However, it quickly became clear to the industrial psychologist Milner that there was a more fundamental research objective to determine how a psychologist should be best employed within a school setting.

Milner tells us that her work began in January 1935. She details the 'impossible' catchall first brief proposed by the Head Mistresses to the Council, which – aside from her outlined objectives – requested that she attend to issues of Staff Mental Health; visit all twenty-five of the Trust's schools for a minimum of a week; allocate time in her afternoons for vocational advice sessions with students; provide lectures in psychology to the parents and staff in all the Trust schools; research the exploration of optimum physical health and conditions, teaching methods and subject mix. Milner responded with a counter proposal, a much-reduced subset of objectives that were eventually agreed on as her brief. Ultimately, she visited seven of the Trust's schools for the study, giving one lecture to the parent and staff bodies at each.

The following headings in this chapter consider each of Milner's book's four sections and their subsections in detail.

First statements of the problem

Our contemporary 'evidence-based' practice is presciently discussed here as Marion emphasises the importance of basing findings on facts, rather than impressions. She describes the plethora of assumptions and misunderstandings surrounding core issues, including the aims of education, the nature of child and adolescent psychology, human development, personality and intelligence. She wonders about the appropriate measures and methods of investigation and asks what the measurable 'products' of education are. Are they examination success, athletic prowess, or perhaps rates of academic titles acquired, or divorces or nervous breakdowns in later life? In doing this, Milner indicates the importance of questioning everything as the essential first step of scientific investigation.

From the outset, Milner, a serious scientific investigator, is quick to note her own biases and expresses misgivings about the compromises to scientific rigour made in the applied setting of her method. For example, there is no means of controlling for the varying degrees of frankness; some teachers had nothing to say as they were 'satisfied or mostly satisfied' and some declined to be interviewed. Milner also observes that as well as the rules of behaviour differing from school to school, the attitude and approach of staff to putting a girl's name on the 'difficult' list differed significantly from teacher to teacher, and responders were left to their own definitions of 'difficult'.

Consequently, Milner devised a questionnaire in order to precisely formulate staff member's opinions for every girl that they taught. It yielded useful data but was found to be too onerous and was discontinued. Milner may well be dealing with sensitivities amongst staff members when she notes again here that there could be no statistical comparison between schools; the emphasis in the study was on description and discovering the uses of a psychologist. Milner is also emphatic that the study aims to make a small start in describing the problem areas in school life – beginning with identifying the psychological constructs that when measured will pick up salient individual differences.

Psychological techniques of observation and measurement

Section II provides the real richness of this study. It is the longest section and has eleven chapters. This must in part be due to the subject's complexity, but it is also because of the amount of interesting verbatim samples of the girls' responses that are included as an integral part of the production of Milner's central scientific concern here, 'The Chart'. The Chart is a theoretical framework, including all the most pertinent psychological constructs based on what Milner comes to recognise as the 'laboratory artefact' of a 'perfect adolescent girl' – a girl who has achieved 'optimal growth in all areas'. It is based on a notional 'perfect personality', a girl who achieves optimum scores when measured against each of those factors which account for most individual difference. Milner attempts this while also acknowledging the unique nature of each person. It is against the chart – in the absence of norms (so sorely felt by scientist-practitioner-Marion) – that any individual girl's balanced growth or healthy adjustment is measured. And it is by reference to this chart that an individual girl's standing relative to her peers could be considered. The production of the Chart within the later part of this section is preceded by an account of conceptual, methodological and statistical difficulties, limitations and the theoretical soul-searching that informed Milner's ultimate choices of influencing theories.

Intelligence testing

First, Milner discusses the subject of intelligence test instrumentation. She details economy of time and effort to be a key reason why group rather than individual tests were included. The purposes of testing were to collect information about capacities, and to make group/form comparisons. The OTIS Group Intelligence Scale, Advanced Examination Form A was used with all the girls in each school in forms from Upper III to Upper VI. This allowed the Index of Brightness (IB) to be used, which was derived from the OTIS score and allowed a comparison to be made between the score of a particular girl and the average for all girls of a similar age.[2]

Milner asked for the staffs' evaluation of these test results asking mistresses to write 'too low' or 'too high' against the name of any girl judged to be inappropriately placed. Re-tests of the 'too low' girls were completed and where scores improved, the second IB score was used. 'Too high' estimates were treated differently and taken to mean that these girls were not working to the best of their abilities and, therefore, underestimated by staff – this is where Milner saw the focus of her work.

Milner's results indicated that amongst the seven investigated schools, the percentage of girls who had little chance of passing the School Certificate Examination was between 9.5% and 19.5%. The median IB for those who passed was 155, and 170 was for those achieving university matriculation. Milner considered that this use of the intelligence test scores was a means of measuring the wasted and misdirected energy of the girls and staff. In this instance, she mentions the waste that there is in trying to prepare girls over five years for an examination that they will never pass. The results were also used to produce tables showing the distribution of intelligence within a form. Milner discusses a group of four girls who passed despite the odds and the implications of the measures put in place to achieve this. It was also possible to show that this was a skewed population for intelligence; there were girls who were of 'below average intelligence for the school' who were of average intelligence in the general population.

Interviewing as a measure and an intervention

The entire study then focuses on two groups: Girls described by two or more teachers as 'Difficult', and a teacher-identified 'Satisfactory' group consisting of class captains and those girls whom teachers deemed to be satisfactory. The former were interviewed for forty minutes, the latter for twenty. Milner succinctly examines the advantages and drawbacks, as well as her rationale for choosing her particular measures. She discusses two types of interview: the vocational guidance interview, where specific characteristics are investigated, and an unstructured clinical interview intended to reveal the interviewee's preoccupations. Milner also stressed the importance of capturing the possible range of temperamental qualities, qualities of interest and emotion.

Milner found a suitable method for interviewing in schools when she adapted Smith and Gulpin's Hypothetical Situations Method using picture postcards. She created the test herself, putting together a set of forty postcards showing different kinds of people in a variety of situations. At interview, the girls were told that a study was being made of 'the different kinds of things that people are interested in'. Interestingly, she found the girls to be so little practiced in reflection that they hardly knew their own preferences. The postcards allowed the girls express their general attitude to life and their dominant preoccupations. These were considered in the light of whatever could be discovered in the interview about home and school life. The remainder of the interview was based on the Preferences Questionnaire, where the girls were invited to elaborate on leisure pursuits, family members, vocational plans and what they had written.

Data

Milner then gives many examples of verbatim responses to the postcards, showcasing a variety of interests, fears and preoccupations. She illustrates how responses might often require follow-up or intervention, e.g. showing the need of a parent interview. Milner also explains how the emphasis in this study was the *discovery of facts with no attempt at remedy*. However, in several cases, the experience of simply being listened to brought about improvement. Individual girls' results were reported to form mistresses, and the results in general format were reported at staff meetings. If suggestions for treatment were obvious, they were communicated, but Milner always reminded staff – and the book's readers – that the aim of the study was to *illustrate* the general method of the psychological approach. Milner realised in the course of the study that all staff needed to have *a system* by which they could readily systematise their own knowledge of the individual child in respect of environmental influences, individual differences, capacity and 'bent'.

Milner next gives her attention to the discussion of the theoretical basis for interpretation of the material and considers two psychological principles: *that there is no simple cause-and-effect relation* and *one must account for the 'total situation'*. She also mentions the interactive effect of one individual difference on another.

Unlike the 'static' situation with adult workers, by virtue of growth and development, Milner considers the child's situation to be different and more complex. She summarises the challenge in terms of Jung's thinking: The individual should be considered in terms of the inward or outward direction of her interest – with a further distinction being made as to whether the interest is in physical experience or in feeling and knowing, and whether this is by intellectual or intuitive means. Developmental factors must then be layered onto these considerations – here Milner speaks of Susan Isaac's idea of different periods of mental growth, and Jung's hierarchical classification of sensation, feeling, intuition and thinking in successive stages, which build towards complex integration. In this section, she is consciously influenced by Jung, Isaacs and Spranger, and Milner's future interest in psychoanalysis is already apparent. She describes the stages of psychic growth from birth to late adolescence and outlines the shift first from bodily problems to emotional ones, on to an interest in knowing and finally to abstract relations.

The Chart

Milner then considers the rating of individual girls on a sliding scale of psychological factors in 'The Chart'. The Chart is Milner's main focus and also classifies the girls' interests; she demonstrates its usefulness in understanding and helping individual students. She introduces the 'laboratory artifice' concept: a profile that represents 'optimal growth' in all aspects of being. With the Chart, Milner initially seems to have succeeded in her attempt to find a way of systematically expressing observed individual differences.

However, Milner soon observes the merely descriptive and statistically limited nature of The Chart, and the need for norms by which comparisons with others of the same chronological age could be made. She then switches her attention from concerns of methodology and the scientific method to a consideration of the unconscious and how whole aspects of one's relation to one's surroundings may include underdeveloped functions and conscious and unconscious aspects. Consequently, Milner explores the necessary conditions for the growth of interest to move from one level of development to the next, observing that a particular level of satisfaction (neither too low or too high) is required in order for a child to progress from one developmental level to the next. She shows the need for a figure in the child's environment with whom they can safely test the submissive and assertive/aggressive aspects of their personality.

The 'B' form and the 'Difficult' group

Milner then discusses what she terms 'the problem of the "B" form'. The 'B' form – there was no reliable testing in place – was a streamed class comprised of girls *perceived to be* less able.

One can immediately see a difficulty here, especially when realising that emotional difficulties often manifest as apparent intellectual limitation. Milner is also writing at a time before 'the philosophy of difference', learning styles or the psychological effects in the classroom of congregation, segregation and stigmatisation have not yet been properly explored in the literature. Nevertheless, the subtle, reciprocal nature of classroom exchanges is not lost on Milner; nor is the value to all in the classroom of the mixed ability nature of groupings.

Milner gives examples to show how the experiences of the school day involve complexly integrated skills and require constant adaptation; experiences present differing problems for the differing biases in individual development: There are girls who develop their need for power indirectly through learning. They are good at the inward-focussed emotionally receptive and submissive aspects of the school day; the sitting and listening part. These girls find asserting themselves directly in the social milieu of the classroom very difficult so that being made a prefect or completing a maths problem on the blackboard, for example, may feel nightmarish since they work better with intellectual knowing than the intuitive 'quick' knowing of the 'give and take' of social situations. At the same time, Milner notices that when teachers need assistance, they always prefer the help of a girl from the 'B' form and she knows that this points to certain as yet unidentified superior skills.

Milner explains to the educators of her time how the complex integration gets established in the first place. She knows the importance of the environment and suggests that for the child to grow in interest from one level to the next depends on their experiencing enough – not too much and not too little – *satisfaction appropriate to their age*; the child who receives too little comfort and security at the earliest time will continually hark back to this unmet need in later years. She gives the example of thirteen-year-old Ida who had feeding problems in infancy and who mentions food six times in her essay. This example also pointed to another principle in understanding behaviour; that the tendency to hark back to the deprivation was alluding to a difficulty in the current situation. Milner also shows the difficulty with too much satisfaction experienced at an early stage in the case of Susan, thirteen years, who feels it is alright to respond to the teacher with 'I wasn't listening'. It transpired that Susan was in need of 'psychological weaning' from her mother.

Milner says that it is easy to glean from observation what attitude and pattern of relationship, assertive and submissive impulses, was set up in the experience of toilet training; the mother of Liz who was extremely uncontrolled said that she had a 'splendid nanny' and was 'frightfully well behaved'.

As a prelude to discussing the development of a balanced 'two-sided personality' (both introverted/submissive and extroverted/assertive), Milner offers a mix of research findings and psychoanalytic theory while she gives fascinating examples to show the effects of very early experience on a person's impulse management. She says that to assert oneself and submit oneself, one needs someone who is willing to be stronger and someone willing to be weaker than oneself; a person with whom one can test reality and safely exercise one's submissive and assertive aspects and learn how to use one's power in a controlled rather than destructive way. Milner says that it is sometimes helpful to think of the sides of her chart, the submissive-receptive left-hand side and the right-hand assertive-expressive right-hand side as being two sides or aspects of the personality. Then, if we think of the concept of emotional age, it seems that different levels may grow at different rates within the two halves of the personality, certain degrees of maturity on both sides. She gives the example of the successful business man becoming like a dependent baby when he comes home and as soon as fatigue forces him to rest. She suggests that all of us find one kind of response easier than the other. And she uses a phrase that she uses often in the study – 'it is as yet impossible to say' – in relation to knowing if the individual biases are due to inherited constitution factors or early experiences.

Adolescence

Milner also observes that such biases seem to occur equally in men and women, but that the preferred method of responding to experience seems influenced by the physiological rhythms of reproductive life. The nature of mature forms is not known, she says, but what little is known is important in the life of the adolescent at school; in the girl, the physical and emotional changes of puberty seem to rouse conflict between submissive and assertive attitudes. She says that the upheaval at puberty manifests differently in girls and boys, with physical energy diminishing and internalising in girls, and increasing and externalising in boys: Girls may become 'dissatisfied, passive and lazy', and boys may show aggressive behaviour. Milner says that a 'tom-boy' may feel her tendency towards an introverted attitude to be dull, terrifying and disturbing; she may find the idea of her own femininity (and pregnancy) repellent, as it seems to be a giving up of her own will. Preoccupation with the female 'mother' role at the time of writing is apparent – for example, Milner mentions that over the course of her experiment, several parents wondered if training in gymnastics would make childbirth more difficult for their daughter. She suggests in such cases that psychological factors should be considered rather than the physical ones of developed musculature – in other words, the girl's individual development should be prioritised over her perceived social role.

Milner further noted that some children associated submitting one's will with the idea of death, and the fear of it. Nesta, for example, is a potentially brilliant student according to staff, whose work had 'gone off'. Nesta's father had just died, and she found the idea of submitting her will became bound with a fear of death and a repugnance to the idea of childbirth. Milner observes that for some, this awareness of conscious submission to inner forces is never realised, as some individuals live on the level of physical comfort. Others experience awareness with no conflict, but a third group with potentially rich, two-sided personalities, may build up resistance against such internal forces. She gives the example of Olga, who was aware of the power of inner life, was beset with irrational fears and resisted her very successful demanding father who had wanted her to be boy. Milner postulates that Olga's denial of any knowledge of astronomy or the stars was her repudiation of the very lofty ambitions that her father held on her behalf.

Milner speaks of two aspects of the personality – the implicit (what one is to oneself) and explicit (what one is to others) – and the importance of a consideration of how a girl such as Olga might integrate the submissive and assertive aspects of her personality. The inner life may be rich and varied with the impulse to overt achievement being slight, as with artists, poets and scholars – or it may be the other way around. She also draws our attention to the fact that there is a greater value given in society, school and elsewhere, to the outward-going impulse and to what is 'objectively knowable'. Great leaders and men of action must rely more on perception than reflection. Two people of similar mental calibre may then find personal expression in very diverse ways. And though the middle ground inhabited by most requires both implicit and explicit, the genius in one direction is no less an achievement than genius in the other. Milner observed that a significant proportion of the 'difficult' group were markedly inward turning and dissatisfied with themselves because of it, striving after the explicit type of success while failing to understand the meaning of their own gifts.

Anxiety

Milner turns her attention in a new chapter to the subject of the overanxious child. Anxiety featured commonly among the 'Difficult' group. She says that it has been shown in humans and animals that when an impulse or need is frustrated, the blocked energy spills into primary emotion. The kind of response will depend partly on temperament, bodily conditions and the character of others involved. The typical assertive emotion is rage (hostility from a frustrated need for power) and the submissive is fear (anxiety from frustration in the need to submit). These two develop a complex relation to each other in the adult personality.

Using Pierre Janet's idea of feelings of inferiority as the lowering of 'psychological tension', Milner alerts us to the difficult-to-study implicit response of the capacity to concentrate on external events reducing as the need to turn one's attention inward grows. Then, it is the need that is felt, rather than a feeling of power. Here, Milner alludes to the fact that she has strayed into psychoanalysis, saying that the area has the advantage of keeping close to the 'observed fact' but the disadvantage that its terms are likely to seem crude and far-fetched to the layman and consequently cannot be used as 'convenient instruments of thought'.

Milner then discusses 'one-sided ways of dispersing anxiety'. One can escape the tension of anxiety or feelings of inadequacy in many ways: through physical experience, emotional experience, intuitive experience, intellectual experience or by a social function or creative work. This discussion is rich in ideas and case examples. Milner shows how through vocational choice the needs of inward- and outward-turning tendencies may be fulfilled successfully with growth to a higher level in inner awareness and greater integration of implicit and explicit aspects of the personality. In keeping with her later preoccupations, Milner considers how the conditions necessary for anxiety, depression and emotional responses can give way to understanding and imaginative and creative work. She ends with a discussion of the implications for treatment.

Choice and personal profile

Milner speaks of Temperament and Vocational choice; knowing what you want is an expressive act integrating inward- and outward-turning aspects of the mind. Here, Milner shows her 'industrial psychologist' colours speaking about a 'job analysis' when the psychologist seeks to find out, by studying the worker in relation to the work, what particular abilities and qualities of personality the person who succeeds possesses, though beyond the scope of her study, Milner thinks that matching a girl's character to the demands of any occupation could be considered in terms of the changing adjustments noted in the Chart.

Milner then discusses the mechanism of projection as another way of escaping the emotional experience of need. By working with children or animals for example, one may integrate a feeling of need with a feeling of power; a doctor, a nurse, a teacher, a social worker. But, Milner warns, a 'Mary who wants to be a Martha' may not have all the suitable qualities and may need the deeper satisfaction of a more contemplative life. She recommends occupational suitability to be considered in terms of the amount of outward-turning tendency and assertiveness a child displays (amongst other factors).

Norms

In Chapter 10, Milner speaks of the need for 'Norms' of behaviour. The preceding chapters, she says, were an attempt to find a descriptive terminology in which the differences between children can be observed and discussed. She states that no study of the individual is complete without a comparison of behaviours with others of the same age and social background. At the time of writing, Milner can only lament the as-yet very limited capacity to make such comparisons, and cautions that when dealing with behaviour, it is wise to consider what it means to the child herself.

Chapter 11 deals with the subject of statistical comparisons. Milner stresses that the postcard sorting task was only a descriptive test, and that the information it yielded and the subsequent interpretations were not conclusive. She next considers the comparison between the interests of the 'Satisfactory' and 'Difficult' groups. She finds that there is some statistical evidence of the underlying conceptual validity, the Chart. Some of the girls in the 'Difficult' group liked physically exciting experiences, considering anything quiet or contemplative as 'dull' or 'miserable'. Others liked only the quiet experiences, and not of the exciting ones. The 'Satisfactory' group typically liked both the quiet and exciting experiences. Milner, thus, produced a table of classification: In the difficult group, disliking quiet was mentioned fifty-six times amongst sixteen girls; in the satisfactory group, it was only mentioned four times amongst thirteen girls. On the other hand, 'liking quiet' was mentioned thirty times by the satisfactory group and only twenty times by the larger difficult group. Ten out of thirteen 'satisfactory' girls enjoy quiet where only six out of sixteen 'difficult' girls do.

One might expect that the love of quietness reflects an introverted attitude, but according to The Chart, satisfactory development involved a capacity to function in both introverted and extroverted ways. This suggests that 'satisfactoriness' indicates an emotional both-sidedness, supporting the thesis underlying The Chart – a well-developed personality functions in either an inward-turning or outward-turning way, according to the needs of the situation.

The function of the psychologist within the school: section III

After Section II, the experiment is summarised in the question: 'what is the function of a psychologist in schools of this type?' and Section III is concerned with answering this question. After the innumerable activities for a psychologist to undertake in schools that were suggested at the onset of the study, Milner developed a discussion of the psychologists' possible contribution under six headings. These include techniques for the study of individual differences, the potential pragmatic application of results and technical concepts as useful instruments of thought. She posits that the psychologist offers a point of view and can be a mirror to assist staff and pupils to reflect (publicly and privately) upon daily experience.

Under the heading 'Facts about temperament', Milner expresses disappointment about the low degree of validity and reliability of the test instruments available to her. She reflects on the utility of descriptive studies (such as her own), stating that progress could hardly be made if a psychologist were to wait until all instruments were perfect before investigating a topic; therefore, what is required is an elastic system of classification that relates the ever-expanding descriptive discoveries of the psychologist to the problem of schools.

Milner's work as an industrial psychologist

In the second chapter in this section, under the heading 'Some Aspects of Cause and Effect in Work Efficiency', Milner discusses investigations that were conducted by the

Western Electric Company, where she had worked in Chicago. Under the heading 'Results of the Feeling of Personal Futility', Milner observes that the Western Electric Company research division ultimately posed two core questions:

1 Do the work conditions in a modern industrial organisation make people suffer from feelings of personal futility?
2 Or do the whole conditions of life in a modern industrial city predispose workers to this feeling?

Milner posits that the same questions can be asked of school life and consequently explores the feeling of futility in schools, concluding that every girl in school needs to feel that she contributes in some way and plays a social function. School should provide each girl with a sense that they matter to others. However, Milner notes a core obstacle to this process: With societal traditions being upended, there is a loss of certainty and security that accompanies the widening of opportunities for the girls.

Speaking of 'Freedom and Change', Milner explores what has become known as 'organisational change management'. She quotes Mayo and Whitehead and says that while the child needs stability, there is often also a need for change. The challenge to the modern school in such a situation is to ensure that cohesive social bonds bind people together as a group during change. Milner recognises that change causes 'strong emotional attitudes', according to individual differences in temperament; the conservatively minded often sees nothing but the possible disintegrative effects of change and feels compelled to keep things as they are. The radically minded wants to change everything as quickly as possible. Amongst school staff, there are these two attitudes, and everything in between – particularly on the subject of 'freedom'.

Milner quotes Susan Isaacs' idea that the child is not 'free' but under the influence of a primitive conscience or superego; he needs routine and stability and parents and educators stronger than him and who represent an ordered world of values which are firm while age-appropriate to his psychological needs and capacity to understand.

A sense of belonging

Freedom for what? Milner quotes Whitehead who found that in industrial populations, there is a desire for a shared attitude of self-expression and engagement with 'worthwhile', meaningful activities; to exercise personal initiative and choose the type and form of one's contribution and stamp the group with a character it would not otherwise have; to have the satisfaction of personal adventure in social activity. The business of growing up is about discovering one's contribution to the group. The problem is not the same, Milner tells us, in a school population as is in an adult one. Due to time constraints, it was not possible during the study to find what contribution each girl was making to her friends-group. However, it was clear that a significant number of the 'difficult' group had not achieved this. Ultimately, all school groups confirmed the fact that social activity is a fundamental human need. Social groups concern not only physical closeness but also the immediate pleasure in exercising social skills and sentiments and which, importantly, are logically ordered in terms of an ulterior purpose.

Thoughts are not things

Milner enlarges on Piaget's concept of egocentricity and its wide application to difficulties in school: We are not born knowing that thoughts are different from things. We learn this through experience, while in the meantime a child can be as frightened of an imagined dragon as of a real one in pre-logical thinking. For a rational thinker, an idea is provisional and must be tested in order to be validated. But a child does understand the need for testing. Piaget calls this 'egocentric' thinking, and we never completely outgrow it. Milner reminds the reader that we think egocentrically in dreams, reveries or when tired or emotionally stirred. And when driven by egocentric thinking, one does not recognise that other people have thoughts and feelings different to one's own. We only remove ourselves from egocentric thinking by expressing our thoughts to others, and then listening to their challenges. Milner gives us Mayo's idea that a person's cooperation can be more easily won by listening than by talking.

In the next chapter, Milner considers 'A point of view' that only the psychologist brings. As an example, she speaks about the investigation of free-willed intention. Piaget observed that when asked 'Why do trees have leaves?', children frequently answer 'Because they want to'. Accordingly, the sun shines because it is kind and wants to warm us. This intentional thinking is also found within the field of anthropology; primitive man looks for intention, benevolent or spiteful; the wrath of the sun could only be appeased by human sacrifice. The passage from childhood to maturity involves the discovery of the existence of impersonal laws. Thus, man finds that in the case of nature, he must quietly accept its indifference towards him. Though with respect to society, we are still not convinced of this, and we lapse into old ways of thinking when faced with new difficulties: We are liable to look for the cause of our troubles in the evil intentions of an 'other' person or a group – whether the Jews or the Kaiser, the Capitalists or the Bolsheviks. We have accepted nature's indifference towards the individual but still consider some societal changes to be personal affronts and try to control social happenings by direct command.

Motivation

Milner next considers our great faith in the power of exhortation. We believe that we can simply command people to stop 'unacceptable' behaviours. Milner observes that the American Child Guidance Movement is a result of a realisation that a great number of our actions are not deliberately willed; therefore, we cannot goad children into 'moving [their] ears when [they] have not learned how'. Consequently, when a child is brought to the clinic, she is asked to tell her own story, and the parents and teachers are asked for theirs so that the psychologist can discover what forces are at work. Thus, rather than appealing to the child's will, the psychologist attempts to give the child a different kind of experience.

Milner then considers Mary Follett's perspective on the issue of control in business management. Follett posits that individuals cannot change by being intellectually convinced, but by achieving the desired mental attitude. Often in school, improvement does not result from deliberate effort as is implied on report cards – often the child does not even know why they are doing something. A dramatic demonstration of the limitations of voluntary conscious effort is given by the output records of the

Western Electric Company Test-room in the closing weeks of an experiment, when The Depression was at its height in 1932. Facing imminent lay-offs (and subsequent near-starvation), workers could have eased their financial difficulty by raising their output in the remaining weeks of employment, but output levels fell violently during these weeks. Milner tells us that one of the workers explained workers' 'total situation and their adjustment to it' some weeks after she had left the firm; 'we had lost our pride'.

Milner considers that all behaviour has meaning, and rather than looking at the consciously willed intention behind behaviour, the psychologist looks on the behaviour as purposive; they want to find what function a behaviour serves. For example, doctors found shell-shocked men in WWII to be caught between high ideals of courage and loyalty, and instinctual fear. Rather than malingering, they existed in a blind struggle to escape intolerable emotional tension. Milner found that one of the girls, Adelaide, was in a comparable situation in school.

Milner then speaks of 'The Psychological Mirror as an Aid to Reflection', giving a psychological theory analogous to an economic theory that suggests that peoples' political views depend on their material circumstances, rather than their capacity for reasoning; we believe what it is to our advantage to belief. If we have tried to develop beyond the given code, our psychological and philosophical beliefs are determined by the kind of psychological adjustment that we have made in our lives. Therefore, the discussion at a school staff meeting on the subject of discipline is determined less by logic than by the need of the individuals to defend their psychological way of living. Because of emotional preconceptions, one is not able to believe that a person might not want to hold a position of responsibility, while another may believe that it is morally wrong to impose authority on a child. It is these preconceptions, these differences in temperament which make opinions so different, and which often makes the pooling of experience so difficult in a team.

Section IV – Psychology as a resource

In Section IV, Milner explores Practical Implications. She writes up a list of recommendations and it is as if she wishes to leave a resource pack to prove the worth of psychology for the teachers she has worked with, while also moulding, de novo, a starting place for future educational psychologists. Milner then considers the psychologists' role in testing hypotheses. Staff commented during the experiment in the schools that they knew what the problems were and wanted to know what to do about them. Milner emphasises both the need for reflective thinking on the problems, and the formal statement of the problems in reaching a solution: A deadlock is often undone by asking the right questions to put the 'felt difficulty' into words, and by stating the problem in different terms. This is the first step (Section I). Collection of data is the second step (Section II). The third step (Section III) is to evolve a theory, a hypothesis (possible solution) to fit the facts. The fourth step is the testing of the theory to see if it works; this step was not part of this experimental project, as it would take considerable time due to the plethora of variable factors.

Milner posits that it is easier to test results in industry than education, perhaps true at the time given that industrial psychology was more developed, and Milner was pioneering a foray into the educational setting. She suggests that the nearest approach to a scientific testing of the validity of the hypotheses offered would be a later follow-up of the girls interviewed to observe if there had been any change in the girls' relationship with particular members of staff as a result of the diagnosis offered and exploring how the change had affected work and behaviour.

Milner considers a possible modification of the teacher-taught relationship. She states the dilemma of any social community in relation to the school social unit; how can individual needs be accounted for in such a way as does not leave staff and girls feeling lost and without support?

Next, she gives suggestions to indicate possible developments within the existing system. She says that the difficulties are well known and not peculiar to these schools, e.g. ensuring tasks are graded to capacity; the difficulty of giving children enough bodily movement, allowing for difference in speed of response and for capacity to change activity-type quickly.

She outlines difficulties affecting staff; where punishment is abolished, the reliance for classroom control is on the teacher's personality. The modern teacher, Milner comments, falls between the old method of 'sit-still-and-listen' and the more recent 'find-out-for-yourself' learning method, when it is the situation rather than the teacher which is the determinant of the child's behaviour, and the idea of adult repression of children is taken too literally. One general conclusion had emerged for this experiment which was the blurring of two distinct but essential aspects of learning: repetition and drill coupled with insight and capacity for exploration; the latter is a matter of growth and not usefully controlled by the clock. There was also a feeling that staff were expected to force learning on children, and in this the teacher was often up against an already established (by experiences at home) resistance. Milner points out that as long as parents feel compelled by economic circumstances to demand academic performance from their daughters, this false relationship will exist. One way to lessen the falseness was the Howard Plan – a dividing up of the timetable into a semi-modular structure, giving the girls at least a small amount of choice in what they study and when. This has been shown to have a beneficial effect on the class atmosphere but is difficult to timetable.

Milner then gives 'Some Practical Implications of the Principles Discussed' and defers first to the greater knowledge of the educators, suggesting that she is only attempting to give weight to demands already made by Head Mistresses, e.g. for examination reform. She then illustrates possible ways in which the discussed principles might be embodied. As well as getting a global impression of Milner's approach, one will see from the suggestions below that Milner was trying to be discerning, to swim rather than drown in the ocean of possibilities presenting themselves as contenders for the emergent role of a working educational psychologist. Her suggestions include: greater contact between school and parents; ways of helping girls to deal with their emotional problems (including sex education, dramatic work, mixed staff and a hobbies period); further ways of taking into account individual differences in ability (including the use of intelligence tests in entrance exams, a 'practical' form, 'B' form consultations); ways of assisting discipline and concentration (including training in the art of discussion, cultural individuality amongst 'houses', privileges of citizenship, two form leaders in each form); ways of reducing fatigue for staff (including recognising intellectual limitations of certain children, abolishing numerical marking, economy of time spent dealing with difficult girls, teaching girls to work more independently); promoting educational and vocational guidance; and cumulative record card, medical examinations, a school leaving report and a careers mistress.

Conclusions

My own experience working in educational psychology in Dublin schools in the early 1980s shows that Milner's work has stood the test of time. Many of the items from Milner's recommendations list in Section IV were to be found in the 1980s schools' systems. The method of testing, of interviewing students, teachers and parents and ultimately reporting back with recommendations was part of my work and that of my colleagues. Thus, the approach and methods devised by Milner were still being used fifty years on (and with the greater range of standardised tests and norms that were in her professional yearnings).

Marion Milner, like her colleagues, Susan Isaacs (who is the series editor of Miner's book) and Ruth Griffiths (author of the Griffiths Infant Scales), is a pioneer in psychology; she was sought for this project because of her existing reputation. It seems particularly poignant, writing during the COVID-19 pandemic, with its similarities as a milieu for researching, writing and publishing, to consider how Milner's work, completed on the cusp of WWII, may have been overshadowed by the contemporary circumstances of an evacuating London, with England in a state of emergency on the eve of war. Despite some good reviews, attention to its published results seems to have been interrupted.

Today one might well consider answering a very sad 'no' to the questions that Susan Isaacs asks in her foreword to the book; whether the spiritual fruits of civilisation can be saved from the disrupting pressure of material complexity; and if human beings can stand the strain of social and economic relations; or of the top-heavy burden of learning and scientific technique.

Milner's misgivings from the outset about the study's statistical and methodological limitations as well as its experimental and preliminary nature attest to her own adherence to the scientific method and her role as a scientist-practitioner. From the outset, she is at pains to list the limitations of statistical extrapolation and the methodology used – e.g. the terms 'difficult' and 'satisfactory' are not operationally defined; rather the teachers are left to their own idiosyncratic definitions. Also, some teachers will not mark anyone as 'difficult' as they feel it reflects poorly on their teaching etc. As she embarks on this study, this astute 'scientist-practitioner' psychologist is aware of its statistically limited, descriptive nature, as well as its important, vital and excitingly innovative aspects.

Milner's research is relevant from many perspectives, including general social history and the history of psychology. Close readings of the text might yield interesting findings; changes in language (there is reference to 'stupid girls' and 'over-developed girls'), in assumptions about gender and ability, in considerations of general intelligence, female intelligence and social roles. It becomes particularly clear when reading the book (and the educational aspirations commonly held for girls at the time) that Milner and her colleagues are in a small minority of pioneering women who write and pursue professional careers.

It is obviously the 1930s when Milner speaks of 'the problem of the "B" form'; the basis of this grouping is problematic for Milner as a psychologist: There is streaming in place and it is common knowledge and, therefore, stigmatising within the school that the 'B' form are the form who have been perceived as less able. Nowadays, there is a move away from congregated, segregated and stigmatised groups. Rather the reciprocal nature of the exchange and the value to all – including those of significantly high ability – of mixed ability groupings is better understood.

Milner managed to find a way of beginning in these unchartered seas. At the beginning of her study, Milner immediately saw that the system within which an educational psychologist would work was overrun with assumptions that were not in conscious awareness. She could see that there were established ways of thinking about all aspects of the second-level education system for girls which needed to be unpicked, examined and discussed before they could begin to be operationally defined in preparation for study. She overcame the difficulties and negotiated the social aspects of the study's environment wisely. When there was no suitable test, she adapted and devised one. When there were no norms, she extrapolated appropriately. In a time before electronic databases, she was acutely aware of appropriate global literature and able to apply it. Milner displayed an enviable facility for interpreting, systematising and summarising data.

In the absence of computer graphics or statistical software packages, Milner effectively displayed her findings visually: One can only wonder what sophisticated statistical manoeuvres she might have completed with appealing and colourful images today.

Milner's study never got the follow-up investigation that she proposed for it. Despite good reviews at the time, the lessons to be gifted from Milner's account of her study into what a psychologist can do in schools and from this snapshot into education and female life in the 1930s remain as yet unpacked.

Notes

1 Milner's book derives its title from *The Human Problem in Industrialised Civilisation* written by the world-renowned Australian industrial psychologist, Elton Mayo, with whom Milner had worked during her stay in the US. And the fact of this title choice shows the intersection here of her varied experiences in different domains of psychology.

2 Milner explains that all the IBs (Index of Brightness) quoted in the book are inflated (the average score for an English twelve-year old is ninety-nine when for an American, it is eighty) as they are calculated using American Norms, since there are no British ones for most age categories. This did not matter so much for this test where the scores were used for 'within population' comparisons. Milner also explains that the score achieved by older girls who finished earlier than the allotted time period are underestimations.

Chapter 29

'Diaries over a lifetime'

The diary work of Marion Milner: *A Life of One's Own; Experiment in Leisure; Eternity's Sunrise; Bothered by Alligators*

Clare Crellin

[Reporting a conversation between *Clare Crellin, Veronica O'Doherty, Aleana Eagan*, and *Margaret Boyle Spelman*.]

Introduction

Marion Milner published four books on the psychological work of diary-keeping, *A Life of One's Own*, 1934, published under her pseudonym Joanna Field; *An Experiment in Leisure*, 1937, also as Joanna Field; *Eternity's Sunrise A Way of keeping a Diary*, first published in 1987; and *Bothered by Alligators*, published posthumously in 2012. The books covered most of her ninety-nine-year lifetime and almost the whole of the 20th century.

In 2019, a small group of interested people in Dublin agreed to read the four books, each of us keeping a diary of our own thoughts, and feelings as we read. In October 2019, we met to share our impressions. We hoped that our method of reading the books and coming together for a day of second-level reflection would be consonant with Marion Milner's own approach. This chapter records our explorations and conclusions.

The author/participants came from different perspectives, Clare Crellin from a Jungian psychoanalytical perspective, Veronica O'Doherty from a mindfulness and Buddhist perspective, Alena Eagan from an art and sculpture perspective, and Margaret Boyle Spelman from a Winnicottian psychoanalytical perspective. These different standpoints converged and diverged as we spoke, listened, and built on what each person said, merging as we explored further.

Although we did not structure our conversations around themes, several significant themes emerged. These included the uniqueness and value of her diary work, her courage and motivation, her method in the diary writing, her process, her development as a person and as a writer/researcher, the physicality of her writing and thinking, the importance for her of art, creativity and expression, the function of pictorial and word images, the links with psychotherapy, and the influence of her two analyses and her training in psychoanalysis.

We spoke of each book in turn chronologically. The following is an attempt to recreate the 'beads' of the day and their surrounding thoughts to reflect as closely as possible on the experience of our coming together.

DOI: 10.4324/9780429433535-37

Conversation

A Life of One's Own

MARGARET: This pioneering book, started by a twenty-six-year-old woman in approximately 1926, might belong to a genre now, but it didn't then.

ALEANA: Her narrow and wide focus is the main thing I got from it.

CLARE: I was struck by her struggle for an authentic sense of self. At the same time as Jung is working on individuation in his Red Book, she is on her own journey of self-exploration through diaries.

VERONICA: I thought of the culture of the time, pre-the concept of feminism, pre-the surge of interest of the seventies in Buddhism. Her place as a woman would have been restrictive, yet her thinking is not restrictive. There is a depth of what we would call today 'insight' meditation, where one pauses and stops to use what is going on with one's thinking process and thoughts. From all the random moments she describes, she is trying to work through aspects of her own self, asking: Is this working for me? Is this good? Is this bad? What can I learn through this? This is parallel to the road that the Buddha took as he walked around India.

MARGARET: She thought she was going to be a naturalist, interested in the world around her (*An Experiment in Leisure* Ch 1), then she steps inward, putting the focus on herself.

VERONICA: She says: 'I want to feel that I have lived, but what on earth do I mean by that?... I want ... to feel every part of me vibrating with it' (pp. 23–24). It's a mindfulness-based concept.

ALEANA: Losing her sense of self with other people (pp. 22–23), and then realising that she can release into this and get value from it (pp. 89–90). What isn't successful is just as important as the stuff that would progress her. The book is a journal of an exploration which involved 'doubts, delays and expeditions on false trails' (pp. 13–14).

CLARE: For her the act of seeing was more important than what she saw (p. 53). When she gets into more descriptive accounting of things, she pulls herself back and moves the focus inward.

MARGARET: She is watching the habits of her own mind rather than mind in general.

CLARE: And she is finding out about the mind's chatter. She's trying, from that, to capture something else that's going on that's tripping up her life.

VERONICA: We call that the 'default mode', which is how habits of mind bring us back to ways of thinking that are destructive in our daily life. I think she is trying to capture that in herself.

MARGARET: And having captured this automatic mind or 'blind thinking' in her writing, she is then in a different place, as she is looking at them (pp. 127–129).

ALEANA: It's not about discarding them. It's about living with both.

MARGARET: And bringing them back under her own observations. I think she is a young woman getting caught between wanting to be fully in life and knowing that there is something in her that can change these 'gestures of the mind', influence her own experience (p. 110).

VERONICA: She is advocating two ways of looking at the world, with a wide lens and with a narrow questioning, more self-perceptive lens (pp. 105–107).

ALEANA: And not dividing the inner and outer which would cause you pain and difficulty.

MARGARET: She watches herself and is willing to share talking at one stage about killing herself, and laughing at herself thinking 'there, they'll all be sorry then' (pp. 119–120). There's a generosity in her spirit and bravery in putting all this down on paper at that time.

ALEANA: At the same time being Joanna Field, or those girls might not like it.

MARGARET: Yes, she had a book on schools coming out at the same time.

VERONICA: She says, 'I discovered with deliberate speaking of my thoughts to myself in words, they lost their obsessive quality' (p. 138).

CLARE: Isn't that what makes therapy work, as opposed to thinking that doesn't see itself?

MARGARET: As well as the idea of ego-centric or blind thinking, she talks about our resistance to seeing the other within ourselves and to seeing the opposite of what we thought was there (pp. 158–159). Before this she talks about relaxing, about putting parts of herself out like feelers, almost like embracing an experience rather than resisting it (pp. 73–75).

ALEANA: Yes, it seems so important the way she talks about the body and about clothes as well. Looking at clothes, going around shops, thinking about these identities can put her back together (*An Experiment in Leisure* p. 203).

MARGARET: Just before chapter fourteen, she describes: 'experiencing the present with the whole of my body instead of with the pinpoint of intellect' (p. 178). It's interesting that this chapter is called 'Cart-horse or Pegasus?'

CLARE: She says that 'thought is not simply a cart-horse to be put between shafts like in an academic world sometimes, but a Pegasus alighting suddenly beside me from places I had no knowledge of' (p. 189).

MARGARET: And the thought 'I want nothing. I am nothing' (p. 107:1) changes the experience. Suddenly everything had the brightness of a newly created world. In the next chapter (Ch V111), she talks about the effect of the other on her, the effect of individual people who are in her company.

CLARE: That that seems important for therapy, the opening to another person. She says: 'I could recognise another mind and yet want nothing from it' (p. 197).

ALEANA: I have written NB by 'I was taken to see some sculpture, a form of art which I had always found rather puzzling, but this time I discovered that, by keeping very still and forgetting everything I had been told, I could slip into a world of dark tensions and stresses and strains that forge themselves into an obscure but deep satisfaction. I felt it in my bones and in my feet and in my breathing' (p. 191). Every museum should have that instead of a plaque trying to explain an artwork. That opportunity can be missed if somebody feels there is something to 'get', one thing to understand, what she is saying is to experience it wholly, physically and intellectually.

MARGARET: Later she talks about watching and waiting, active passivity (p. 207:1). The experience and the reaction were in every part of her. At the same time, it's about balancing. Being widely aware fosters a life of consciousness rather than a life of natural impulse (p. 208).

An Experiment in Leisure

In this book, written close in time to *A Life of One's Own*, Marion Milner looked at hobbies.

MARGARET: It originated from a desire to think about how she spent her leisure time, and from her feeling that this is a matter of identity. Is she seeking acceptance of all parts of herself? The leisure is the acceptance and accommodation of the other within oneself.

ALEANA: She says she read further, 'led by a curious remote sense of intimacy in these scrappy observations' (p. 3), valuing them by her feeling towards them. Later she says: 'What is most intimate to us is also that which most eludes our grasp, the source of life inside you, the thing that lives you, that possesses you' (p. 179). 'All we can do is wait quietly and watch for images' (p. 222). Images are important in this book.

MARGARET: Her detective hunt seems to be to find the things she cares about, the images that remain with her after sifting through and finding what matters to her.

VERONICA: And it's about desire. Should you give in to your desire or not?

MARGARET: She talks about submitting to an alien force which wished to destroy you, that she could feel as a part of herself.

CLARE: She is moving into a deeper and darker place in herself. We see this in the sea and diving images. I am curious about her discovering a desire not to do the thing one most wants to do.

MARGARET: Is it connected to wishing to submit to an alien force?

VERONICA: Well, are the things she wants to do really the things *she* wants to do?

ALEANA: That's the crux.

MARGARET: It's two aspects, the image of killing the god, the ego-centric blind part, and the idea of 'I am nothing. I want nothing' (p. 40). The other part wants to be one with nature, and by virtue of giving everything up, to have everything.

VERONICA: There's more depth than in the first book.

MARGARET: She has already written the first one, so she is in a different place.

CLARE: Her experiences now are richer, more painful, darker. The spectrum is growing. As she continues to practise internal self-observation, more of it becomes available to her. It's the sheer practice that is widening and deepening.

VERONICA: You need more time with this book. There are references that you want to look at, read and re-read. She is leading you on another journey.

MARGARET: For her, God and the experience are the same thing, the one above and the other within. She was in analysis with a Jungian analyst at this time.

CLARE: Her stories. Amazing!

MARGARET: So much of her imagery is of nature, and some of it looks very cruel, but it is man's delight in others' pain that she sees as evil.

CLARE: I thought about the transitional aspect in the story of the upturning of the sea, and the translation of metals. It struck me that here was Jung's theory of archetypes, the idea that thoughts in formation will clothe themselves in appropriate forms. She says: 'My sole concern was to borrow forms … by means of which my own obscure pre-occupations could deliver themselves' (p. 110). She is experimenting with the idea of the dynamic force of images, and images as a precursor to thinking.

ALEANA: And that's one of the manifestos to experiment in this book. To live is to experiment.

VERONICA: At the bullfight, she felt almost exalted as if it was a religious experience. She is questioning her own morality.

MARGARET: Sunday after Sunday this drama is enacted. 'That one final truth of life, the certainty of death. ...Fears must be faced, not hidden away' (p. 118).

CLARE: She is looking *at* in order to look *in*. She talks about how, by engaging with death, you are somehow looking into life.

MARGARET: The death of the bull is called the moment of truth.

CLARE: It seems to me that she's asking: what is the truth that this is the moment of? Then later in this book, she talks about a different aspect of destruction, about the image of a fire that does not destroy but creates life itself, primordial fire.

ALEANA: Maybe, by being hard on herself, she marshals things rather than their being destructive.

VERONICA: The ability to face the finality of our lives has a profound effect on how we can lead our lives. It is interesting that we are discussing this book in a different way from the other book. It is more challenging to discuss.

ALEANA: ... because it envelops the other book within it.

VERONICA: She refers to negative capability when trying to recapture childish memories 'I could only recapture this sense if I let my mind flow away from the facts to whatever images occurred to me' (p. 149).

MARGARET: And she talks about expression, the value of expression.

CLARE: In this book, she places art as essential.

ALENA: ... and as vital sustenance.

CLARE: She says that her preference is for visual images, but she weaves equally vivid images with her words.

VERONICA: She believes that Yeats was right, that the forms in which man expresses his sense of being alive, are a powerful force for change, though in a different way from any deliberate attempt to get things done. This changes men's hearts.

CLARE: This gives so much importance to the role of the image in the world.

MARGARET: There's a quote from Jung: 'Image is a concentrated expression of the total psychic situation' (p. 171).

CLARE: And Milner says: 'I had tried to kill fear with the sword instead of the mirror shield that I had now found expression to be' (p. 218).

MARGARET: That's the other thing that is very important in this book, the importance given to expression itself.

Eternity's Sunrise

Milner began writing this book in 1958. This was the first of her psychoanalytical books written after her psychoanalytical training, but it was not published until 1987.

ALEANA: It felt like her purpose was stretched. She is literally going to other places.

CLARE: Yes, moving on from the expression of the image, to its impact on her. In this book, she explores her notion of the 'answering activity'.

ALEANA: And it is the first time that she uses the word 'beads'.

CLARE: I thought of rosary beads, the sorrowful, joyful associations ...

ALEANA: ... and worry beads. The beads are active things. They are working. Then she brings us back to her memory of getting clay and making and painting beads.

VERONICA: And how they came out different ...

MARGARET: ... transformed by putting them into the kiln.

ALEANA: She says that she appreciates the Parthenon when she goes inward. The idea of it can get in the way of the experience of it.

VERONICA: ... your mind knowing something. She's trying to keep that spontaneity of associations.

ALEANA: The trips to Greece were organised. She avoids the input of a knowledgeable academic source. She is intent on her own hunt, trying to forget what she has been told.

MARGARET: She has a visceral response to buildings, and she mourns its absence in the Parthenon.

CLARE: In Chapter 4, she talks about the need to reflect on the 'beads of experience' to form concepts, seeing this as part of the upward thrust of things in nature, a movement from one level to another, becoming more complex (p. 29:2). She sees this philosophical idea through the lens of nature

VERONICA: ... and science, Darwinism.

MARGARET: It's amazing to me that landscape and buildings, the physical characteristics of where she finds herself, and her own physicality have such an impact on her, and the absence of it has a different impact on her.

ALEANA: It's through recollection as well. She's burrowing more deeply because she's looking back at these beads.

CLARE: These beads call up the 'answering activity'. When it is absent, she has to call up her own inner life (pp. 56–58). This idea is hard to grasp.

MARGARET: Perhaps she was so familiar with her answering activity that she didn't feel the need to explain it. She was just telling you what *she* did.

CLARE: I think the notion of the 'answering activity' is a primordial image, and it has a lot of parallels, lots of extensions. That was one reason why it was difficult for her to articulate.

MARGARET: In Chapter 5, 'The Gypsy and the Soldier', she talks about the excessive split between work and play, keeping the logical from the non-logical (p. 41:3). The benefit is primary narcissism. It starts with your connection, your enjoyment. Your bodily enjoyment helps your enjoyment of the world. Your connection to the world helps you connect to yourself (p. 42).

CLARE: Perhaps transference and countertransference work similarly. Transference and countertransference form connections through a kind of answering activity, so they are a two-way process.

VERONICA: Yes, I got the sense of that too. It brought me back to Christopher Bollas, *The Shadow of the Object* (1987), her visual images of the buildings she saw, and the countertransference from her own imagination. You can feel her psychoanalytical training coming in more in this book than in the other two.

CLARE: In *An Experiment in Leisure*, her Jungian analysis was influencing her, and now she's taken on another kind of ...

VERONICA: ... lens.

MARGARET: But even when a Jungian analysis is at play, other things were not left out. She seems to be able to be herself, take this here, find that there, and *she* pervades everything.

ALEANA: ... and her training doesn't inhibit her.

VERONICA: She recalls Freud saying that there were people who thought in visual images, and she came to accept that she was one of them (p. 153).

MARGARET: She may have paid a price for being a person who thought in images. She felt she missed a greater credibility and esteem. Certain of her colleagues and friends said she didn't have standing. She may have thought that she didn't have the kudos she might have had if she had chosen to speak in the languages of psychoanalysis.

CLARE: It tells us how she valued esteem and standing. They are not where she is aiming.

MARGARET: Her gaze is inward. That's where her interest is.

CLARE: I compare her with Jung who reached out into the esoteric and was criticised for writing about alchemy and about philosophical and religious ideas. She knew that, and I think she trod a very careful path that kept her protected.

VERONICA: I sensed that she was somewhat deliberate in her path.

CLARE: She takes a clear theoretical position, but she is not putting it out into the psychoanalytical world for critical scrutiny. It's as if she is saying 'I am going to talk directly to artists and to ordinary people who might be interested in what you can do if you keep a diary'.

MARGARET: Later she asks, 'When is the inner voice to be trusted?' (p. 51). It is only out of the mud that the new image comes. Going into confusion, lowness, into the mud is where clarity is ultimately to be found (p. 53).

CLARE: When I read the A-Z of jottings. I felt I was ploughing through it.

ALEANA: If something wasn't holding me, I would read a bit of it and then go on.

VERONICA: I found myself attracted to certain headings. I'd delve in there, and free associate.

CLARE: Perhaps it's because they are so much her own, and these are just little jottings. She was trying to empower and encourage people to feel that anything they write can be of value to them.

MARGARET: ... that the process will be of value to them.

Bothered by Alligators

This book was written by Marion Milner when she was in her nineties. It was published posthumously in 2012.

MARGARET: Milner had been a diarist since the age of eleven. This is her diary of 'loose ends', working through these in preparation for death.

CLARE: She didn't know when she started it that it was going to be about aspects of herself as a mother and a wife.

ALEANA: ... and as a daughter realising her mother may have been depressed.

VERONICA: In the last part of the book, 'Towards wholeness', there is a sense of her encapsulating and trying to reach wholeness. There is something very driven here. She is on a mission, *her* mission.

CLARE: The message for us from her discovery that she was writing about herself, not about her son, John, might be that we need to think about what is revealed of us and reflected in the process of our work and in everything we do.

VERONICA: In this book she addresses her personal relationships throughout her life.

MARGARET: I was struck by her honesty and her courage about the exposure of herself as a parent, her horror and regret that she didn't answer John then ... and she didn't notice the distress.

ALEANA: She was away, and she got this from John, and she didn't answer. I found going back over her interpretations of his drawings interesting. His pre-occupation with hooks, as he is fixing on nautical apparatuses. The hooks are wonderful, and the wet and the sand, and the words being part of the picture.

CLARE: And she moves from putting interpretations on the pictures to seeing them with her whole self.

VERONICA: It's a privilege to have that insight into her long life, with her courage to put her errors out there as well as her blessings. There's a sense of her talking out loud ... to herself.

MARGARET: And this is the book where she breaks her silence about Winnicott. She used to say to her students to keep a note of their misgivings. This is her diary of misgivings, her doubts, and misgivings about her life.

ALEANA: Winnicott put her in a difficult position.

MARGARET: She might have been forgiving herself for having agreed to have an analysis on the basis she did. She says that people suggested that it was really his need of her, wanting the comfort of regular contact with her, and wanting her to know about his sufferings. Perhaps it took the writing of all the other books, all her attention to her own process, and her expression of that over all those years, for her to speak about her closest relationships. I wonder too if she always felt a conflict between 'not letting your tongue give offence' (p. 174) and her knowledge of the importance of expression.

CLARE: Part Five 'Using my own pictures' (p. 171 onwards) is perhaps a kind of retrospective art therapy on herself.

ALEANA: ... and she called them 'my old failed paintings' (p. 189).

CLARE: She remembered her father saying that, when you've written a poem, you should tear it up. Then you will have to find a new way of expressing it *Experiment in Leisure*, (p. 234).

MARGARET: It puts the emphasis on the process of producing, not on the product. Yet she was proud of her paintings and had them all over her house, inviting people to respond.

CLARE: She uses her paintings as a means of finding the unconscious in herself. Can it be seen in them by another person who isn't oneself?

ALEANA: Sometimes she is quite literal. When she says something is a shape, she can't just leave it at that. It has to be something else.

VERONICA: A shape representing something.

ALEANA: But her writing is very abstract. I feel she felt freer in her writing, that she wasn't as comfortable to break out of things in her painting, perhaps because she describes herself as an amateur.

CLARE: In both she shows us how, at the back of our eyes, we can see the self that is responding to what we are seeing, that looking out is looking in.

VERONICA: Yes, looking back over her son's diary, and pulling things together for herself, … I am thinking about the phrase remembering, forgetting, and letting go. There is a sense of being at peace and preparing for death. Acceptance and integrating the experience in one's being as authentic … It is what it is, and that's OK.

CLARE: She shows us how to die.

ALEANA: She speaks of being 'ready for being dead' (Intro pl:1). She won't be dead, but she'll be being dead.

VERONICA: She creates a sense of continuum, pointing out the continuous ebb and flow of the universe.

ALEANA: … and of the unconscious.

CLARE: There is also continuity with her father's death. She learned from reading her father's last letter to her about how to die (pp. 216–217) and then approached her own death serenely as her father did, with total acceptance that she is part of nature.

ALEANA: Yes, it feels like she was very in tune too, as she got older, with being a small child. Those feelings of laying things out. I see my two-year-old laying things out and ordering things. She was enjoying that process.

VERONICA: It's interesting too that she had the skills and will to experiment in that late stage of her ageing process. It *was* an experiment.

Looking back at the four books

ALEANA: Reading the four books in chronological order, at the end everything comes back full circle.

CLARE: You see each book in the light of the last one, and the last one in the light of the other books.

VERONICA: I wonder what kind of person you feel comes through these books?

MARGARET: A woman with an above-average amount of self-possession, who became more and more herself. Her essence concentrated. She remained in possession of herself throughout her life through her focus, through her studied consciousness.

VERONICA: My sense of her is her wonderful, observational, analytic way of examining her experience, although her feelings are not made explicit.

CLARE: Perhaps they are hinted in the words she uses to describe each image.

ALEANA: I feel that she is …. focussed on the heart.

MARGARET: I was thinking of the warmth in the aliveness of her language, its immediacy, and from her generosity and honesty. Winnicott did not tell us about his own experience. She gives us her own experience and her own life.

VERONICA: She is also pragmatic. She wants to change how she feels when she is with people. And the cultural norms of the day emphasised not sharing emotions.

MARGARET: What do you feel is characteristic of Milner's thinking and writing?

VERONICA: That she consistently observed her experiences and tried to understand and transform them in a way that is unique to her.

ALEANA: She's trying to see what stops you, what dampens natural creativity, not only in *On Not Being Able to Paint* (1957). She does this in all four books concerned with diary writing.

CLARE: She defended the right of women to work on their individuation.

MARGARET: She seems to have made unprecedented inroads into the idea of working on being herself. The conditioning of her social environment could have demanded that she go in an opposite direction. This may have been why she called the chapter on Winnicott, 'the difficult chapter'. She had always been courageous about herself, but here she was talking about her relationships which put her right up against the dilemma of being yourself and not giving offence in the social environment.

CLARE: Her dilemma was the struggle of women at that time.

ALEANA: Back to Virginia Woolf ... she was saying that everyone is an artist ... and it's not just painting. It's being able to put out something. It's about who is an artist and about validation, about who sees it. I am thinking about the artist Pearl Blauvelt (1893–1987),[1] who did thousands of drawings, of buildings, of interiors and objects, and no-one knew she did drawings until she died. It didn't really matter to Pearl Blauvelt who saw her drawings. It was the doing of it that mattered. And, is there not some creativity in being a therapist?

CLARE: I think the connection with therapy is the practice of widening and opening that she talks about.

MARGARET: The widening of consciousness.

CLARE: Yes, and the two-way transformation in the eye-to-eye encounter, where something transformative happens to both people.

ALEANA: After that it is being expressed ...

CLARE: ... in both people ...

ALEANA: ...because you've changed, whether you like it or not ...

MARGARET: She talks about her body, putting her physical body into the experience, feeling things in her feet and in her body. That itself was pioneering.

CLARE: She demonstrates to us what we can gain by alternating experience and analysis.

VERONICA: ...and the general with the micro and the minute.

MARGARET: What's also personified in her is the cross-fertilisation of various kinds of psychology and being both a scientist and an artist.

ALEANA: It wasn't about them being separate.

CLARE: Isn't what has always been recognised as one of her greatest contributions the way she integrates those two things?

Note

1 Note on Pearl Blauvelt (1893–1987)

American Cubist artist whose drawings of things she wanted, and of things in mail order catalogues, were not discovered until after she died. https://www.outsiderartfair.com consulted 31/03/2020.

Chapter 30

'What Sort of Therapist Are You?' Reflections on *The Suppressed Madness of Sane Men*

Carolyn Coburn, Wayne Featherstone, Anne Jeffs, Allan Shafer

(Melbourne, Australia Reading Group)

Our title aims to capture the innumerable leitmotifs that Marion Milner's writing evoked in each of us individually and collectively as a diverse group of child and adult psychoanalytic psychotherapists from Australia. It was also stimulated by a provocative question a child patient once asked her, 'What sort of a Mrs Milner are You?' As we read, and spoke, and wrote to one another, the group appreciated that we were all creating a very different Mrs Milner in our minds. Many connections and much divergent thought flowed about Milner as the group slowly gathered up the threads of individual associations and transformed them into something we could frame as a whole piece of writing. The more we engaged, the more the group came to appreciate the kinds of therapist Milner might have been and, alongside this task, the group's gaze shifted from the narrow focus of ordinary, singular attention to a wider gaze; a process Milner emphasised is at the heart of creativity.

Eventually the tributaries of individual thought began to pool in the group and our responses began to transform in the group's mind. Feelings emerged of Milner having inspired us towards a wish to respond with unbounded spontaneous gestures: a poem, an art work, thoughts about sustaining life-giving eco systems, and wonderings about what went into crafting sacred spaces. We became a group with a symbolic developmental paradox; how to listen and read with an attuned mind that would capture and acknowledge exceptional responses to Milner's writings, while also preserving our sameness and our marked differences in our lived experience of her work?

The group came to recognise, with relief, that Milner had migrated from her adopted Kleinian tongue through the process of her formidable personal analysis and her experimentations with her own creative process to find her unique voice. Although the passage through reading her work was not an easy migration for some of our group, we came to parallel her voyage of discovery of new possibilities in theory and technique in child and adult psychoanalysis.

The group paralleled an aphorism of Milner's; that a new idea can emerge from simultaneously holding contradictory positions. The group held to its framed task, as Milner recommended, and exercised the freedom to talk in our personal native tongues and analyse what new totality emerged. This chapter is an amalgamation of our personal contributions.

Milner created something new by fashioning original ideas out of what might have once been considered madness or a mess through her dedication to the process of analysis. There was some apprehension in the group as to how to collect our thoughts, but her example indicated that anxiety is inherent in the creative process and is not something to be retreated from.

DOI: 10.4324/9780429433535-38

The inner brushstroke: Wayne Featherstone

After hearing a vivid narrative, it is difficult to 'un-see' the mental images you spontaneously generate. Similarly, it is difficult not to approach Milner's thought through the lens of later writers' ideas. In some respects, Milner anticipates Meltzer and Harris Williams; Matte Blanco; Ogden; Winnicott; and, especially, Bion. She acknowledges that she overlooks her Freudian forbearers (Milner, 1988b, p. 297) in her endeavours to define her own distinct way of seeing. Her project is to find her own way of making something of the '... silence that is the background to all noise...'; '... to discover the nature of the forces that bring order out of chaos...' and to establish 'how psychic creativity works...' (Milner, 1988b, p. 216).

Several interlocking themes recur in her work: a focus on the body and the nature of attention; the framed gap and the notion of emptiness; the creative gesture and its genesis; the nature of madness; personalisation and the question of pre-verbal symbolism. When Symington recently asserted, 'The core of the personality is a creator' (Symington, 2019, p. 14), he followed the trajectory of Milner's thought.

There were occasions when she clearly broke new ground for her time. In asserting that creativity, and even construction of the self, derives from the 'capacity to make a symbol' (Milner, 1988b, p. 217), she doesn't simply equate symbolising with the capacity for discursive language. She cites Suzanne Langer 1951 regarding pre-verbal symbolism, arguing that it constitutes the essence of art, particularly painting.

Embodiment, especially, is pivotal: both in its relevance to the creative impulse, and also in its centrality to the analytic endeavour. Milner claims that it is from a state of quiet, inwardly focused attention on the body, and on the world, that the spontaneous, creative gesture arises, leading to the most productive interchanges between analyst and analysand, whether as interpretations or as silent communion.

Her title, which she borrowed from the philosopher George Santayana, implies that a wide unfocussed gaze, directed both inwardly and outwardly, creates a state where normal logical distinctions are suspended: a state where symmetrical logic (Matte-Blanco, 1988) prevails and one is 'mad' conventionally. However, she emphasises the need for an oscillation between sanity and madness such that it constitutes a way of '...being mad with a shelter around one and a rope back to the usual way of being' (Milner, 1988b, p. 290).

As a snorkeler instinctively orients herself to her boat and alarm intrudes when the swell obscures it, so the analyst orients herself to received concepts and wisdom and she must be brave to surrender such quasi-certainties. Then, only a tenuous thread of memory and the uncertain evidence of the senses maintain contact with reality while intuition, a non-sensual 'probe', leads away from the familiar. As Bion said, the analyst needs faith that she can return, and also faith that she will be able to breathe in the rare atmosphere of whatever new situation arises. Milner has faith.

Finding my mind/minding my find: Allan Shafer

The parallel processes that emerge when reading psychoanalytic writing intrigue me. Marion Milner's book evoked mindlessness – soporific states. I wondered about parallels with the states of mind that produce creativity which Milner explores. I struggled mindlessly through the book. Ultimately, a central proposition about the creative process materialised.

Communication – verbal, somatic, psychic, artistic – is central to her work, especially creative communication of the ineffable, so fundamental to the psychoanalytic endeavour. Yet I often found her work opaque.

Milner highlights the failure of esoteric psychoanalytic terminology to meaningfully engage with the non-psychoanalytic world. I have struggled with this. The language of her early interpretations and some explanations – especially material that was heavily influenced by Melanie Klein – often seemed remote from ordinary understanding.

Her early work with young children frustrated me. Despite my own formative Kleinian education I was astonished at the meanings attributed to early childhood psychic experience and the related interpretations. Was the intensity of my response my own fear of the primitive? Having worked with powerful psychotic and 'primitive' dynamics in many settings, I concluded that this was an unlikely source.

Acknowledging that Milner is indeed deeply and profoundly engaged in exploring primitive unconscious dynamics, I was nevertheless left with misgivings about the value of what often felt like abstruse sense-making or non-sense-making. As her work developed over the years, this seemed to diminish.

Yet I was intrigued and fascinated by her exploration of creative processes, especially the capacity to allow a unique symbol or idea to emerge from simultaneously held contradictory positions. My understanding of her ideas about the crucial function of reverie and absent-mindedness in making space for ideas to emerge and be given symbolic expression in words and in drawings was profoundly useful and confirming. Symbol formation is fundamental to her work and her contribution in this regard is significant.

Symington's ideas about creativity and reverie resonate strongly with my understanding of the creative process in art and in psychoanalysis. I have been impressed by his description of 'a state where the mind of one person is engaged with the mind of another in such a way that there is space for imaginative reconstruction…in the observer' (Symington, 2005).

The impact of Milner's work on my emotional state diminished my capacity for a close reading of her work. I read parts carefully and could only skim others, hoping – in the spirit of the book – to find a state of mind where unexpected ideas could emerge despite the immense gravitational pull to sleep. Consistent with what I have alluded to, I was struck by her reference to 'A place for absent-mindedness' seeing that my mind often felt absent:

> … it requires a mental setting and attitude … a tolerance of something which may at moments look very like madness. … can we, in our so objectively-minded culture, come to recognise them as something to be used, in their right place?
>
> (Milner, 1988)

Dear Murray Darling: Anne Jeffs

In January 2019, in Victoria, Australia where I live, the life force that sustains us – the Murray Darling river – became a killing field. Hundreds of thousands of fish – perhaps up to a million of them – and some at least 100 years old, spontaneously went belly up. They floated – white, bloated, dead – on the surface of the water. Soon they lay – accusing, rotting, stinking – on the stunned banks. No jury system needed. The river killed them. We killed the river.

Soon after, a cartoon, in the form of a letter addressed to the river from 'us', appeared in our state newspaper (Leunig, 2019).

This is the letter:

Figure 30.1 Cartoon: Michael Leuing (*The Age*, 12 January 2019).

I have no doubt that Marion Milner, whose work I barely knew prior to involvement in this reading group, was a custodian of rivers. She knew of the existence of the ancient, timeless, hidden, essential, life-sustaining elements of the unconscious/primary process 'river'. And she knew how essential it is to be in good, respectful relationship with it – allowing it to nourish, sustain and transform her. She also facilitated this process in her patients.

Milner's orientation and life's work is the antithesis to, and antidote to, what her training supervisee and life-long friend, Christopher Bollas, has called 'normotic illness' (Bollas, 2011) and revisited as 'subjecticide' (Bollas, 2018), which he describes as '...a particular drive to be normal, one that is typified by the *numbing and eventual erasure of subjectivity* in favour of a self that is conceived as a material object among other man-made products in the object world' (my italics).

The pulsing heart that draws together the twenty-one papers in Milner's book, *The Suppressed Madness of Sane Men*, is a commitment to the subjective world and to grappling, both in her patients and in herself, with the problem of how to truly 'trust the unconscious, trust the emptiness, the blankness, trust what seems not to be there' (Milner, p. 5) or, to follow my metaphor, to be in good relationship with the river. Milner seems to have been, by inclination, a champion of what Winnicott coined the 'true self', long before she encountered Winnicott, who was her analyst as well as close collaborator. Her early work in occupational psychology shows her awareness of the profound damage that is done to a psyche by 'an impinging external environment that attempted to force...[it]... into a mould of personality quite foreign to...[its]... nature'

(p. 4). It seems to me highly likely that there was a fruitful, bi-directional influence flowing between these two creative minds.

Milner's writings indicate a life-long commitment to the 'river', and to genuine dialogue and openness to be transformed through engagement with the arts, the cultural space and other theorists. It is impressive and inspiring.

What sort of a Mrs Milner are you? Carolyn Coburn

Like Winnicott, Milner is virtually impossible to paraphrase, and one seems only able to absorb much of what she writes 'into one's bones', where her profound contributions to psychoanalysis can be found to be of immeasurable help in one's thinking and practice. Milner had an easy discourse working with creative mediums both inside and outside the consulting room. She was in possession of a mind with a Winnicottian home at its heart. Reading Milner's tantalisingly titled book left an experience of something approximating truth, as truth is always heard fresh and anew every time one hears it, no matter how many times one might think one might have read and heard and understood something. Milner's writings left an affection for a woman who was a Psychoanalytic Artisan. She crafted her skill and knowledge through painstaking and unflinching inquiry and practice over a lifetime. Milner undertook a personal, poetic and scholarly examination into notions of 'madness'. She experimented in her practice with the healing effects of what she called the 'spontaneous creation' in psychoanalysis. This seemed possible because of her openness to using and thinking about a wide variety of artistic and imaginative mediums for children and adults in the hope of creating the potential for symbolisation.

Milner charmingly illustrated how psychoanalysis sets about its aims to strengthen one's hold on reality through utilising the essential method of the frame,

> to mark off what's inside from outside, ...[T]he psychoanalytic session is framed in both space and time, ...and that a longed for 'losing oneself in in an activity' requires a safe setting, that will still be there when one emerges again into ordinary self-awareness.
>
> (1952: The Framed Gap, p. 81)

Milner's papers also stimulate greater acceptance of the fundamental notion that patient and analyst alike suffer the barrages of madness at one point or another, be we sane children or sane adults. Through her courage and capacity to examine her perceptions in minute detail and couple this with her artistic creativity, Milner offers a unique voice that takes the reader on a journey into profound, sacred and liminal spaces that offer psychoanalysis an essential life force. These spaces are often experienced as off limits to all but the initiated, and not often considered suitable for general consumption or critique.

The reader has an experience of being taken into the heart of the matter with Milner's patients and with her own self-examinations. Milner is unafraid to examine what she finds in both patient and analyst. One such unflinching moment is given in Milner's detailed account of her first three-year-old child training patient, Rachel, who germanely asked, 'What sort of a Mrs Milner are you?' Milner reflected, 'as if Rachel was trying to cling to the reality of me in the external world and get away from the idea of what she was doing inside' (1944: A suicidal symptom in a child of three). The reader is privileged to witness a meeting of two ferociously inquiring minds at work, and their explorations about each other's minds. The question of 'Who are you?' as a part of a mutual question and dialogue is, one reads, refreshingly apparent and at the heart of Milner's artistry in the field of psychoanalysis.

In the context of wartime England, Milner reveals a fearless capacity to dive deeply into uncharted waters (Symington, 2005) demonstrating her faith that recovery from the bombardments of madness is possible if the depths of one's mind can be plumbed. Three-year-old Rachel was reported by Mrs Milner to be in the grip of an internal cruel dominating force, which was enacted in her life-threatening symptom of a refusal to eat anything. This reader noted that Rachel's birth coincided with WW2. Madness was in ascendancy and thinking was under siege on an unprecedented global scale with the obdurate forces of fascism taking hold over Europe. Milner realised her patient was at the mercy of what one might call a 'fascist self', an internal annihilating self, as Rachel set about to starve herself to death. The reader can vividly see Milner's acceptance of her little patient's desperate need to have the reality of a loving, thinking mind open and available to her as a form of refuge from the self-imposed cruelty of segregation, isolation and starvation. With Rachel's ability to ask the pertinent question, 'What sort of a Mrs Milner are you?' the reader observed evidence of what Milner had set out to do; to create a space for what she calls a 'spontaneous creation' in the analysis. With relief, one reads of the dawning realisation for Rachel of the emergence of reality, as her Mrs Milner comes to be seen as her ally, and life-giving food no longer her enemy.

Conclusion

The brushstroke, or poem, or cartoon, or interpretation, falls uniquely from the hand of its creator. Whatever is produced is unique to the person who speaks, or writes, or draws. Our group came to realise that our challenge in reading and responding to Milner's writings was something akin to the experience of viewing a painting or travelling up stream. It brings the critic and the admirer together in hard work and necessitates holding the paradox of the simultaneous wish to pull and push against the other, and to hold onto, and let go of, one's madness, one's grip, or one's preconceived ideas, so that with a wider gaze on the task, and the comforts of a solid frame, something new has the possibility of emerging into being. This something new, the group contended, is the space for the quintessential question to emerge; 'What sort of a therapist are you?' It is still as fundamental a question to the philosophy and practice of psychoanalysis with children and adults as it was when Milner first documented her incredible journey of discovery over eighty years ago.

Chapter 31

'Letting oneself be breathed'—*On Not Being Able to Paint*

Joan Raphael-Leff

for

Cape Town Reading Group (of IPA Psychoanalysts)

Carol Richards; Jeanine de Villiers; Cathy Rogers; Melanie Silove; Nicolette Jordan; Joan Raphael-Leff

In an experiment worthy of Marion Milner, a group of busy clinicians came together near the parched Camp Ground in Rondebosch, Cape Town (such a contrast to Milner's own verdant Primrose Hill). As we had no agenda other than exploring our reactions to *On Not Being Able to Paint*, this necessitated tolerating the uncertainty of not knowing what would emerge in our newly assembled group. Several participants ascribed 'taking the plunge' in joining this group to the book's title, which had sparked off a host of resonating meanings, inviting access to greater personal freedom of expression.

Struggling to dispense with barriers of ordinary expectations and niceties, our self-composed group was struck by Milner's tenacious persistence and ongoing courage in trying to 'give in' to temporary chaos while striving to expose and interrogate some of the 'unknown and uncontrollable forces' by which she felt lived.

During our open-ended discussions, we ourselves came to appreciate the difficulty of sustaining this form of receptivity—of staying in an unstructured process without rushing to foreclose with intellectual critique or trite appraisals. We recognised how the wish to explore tensions in creativity ranging between wariness and trust, idealisation, and a disillusion could be derailed by disparagement or even lead to destruction of the end product.

Some participants found that on its second reading over the (December/January) African summer break, the dense text of *On Not Being Able to Paint* yielded extra richness as simple concepts were seen in a deeper, more profound way. Indeed, inspired by Milner's way of letting go sufficiently to glimpse the 'secret germination' of 'moving, alive' colours and 'dim tangled roots' as she put it (pp. 55, 65), several of us ventured towards our own forms of experimental 'transfigurations', whether in writing, art-making or listening to music in a new impressionistic way. This inadvertent incorporation—a process of imaginative digesting and reflective reviewing—seemed pertinent to both art and psychoanalytic work.

Although the group was composed of psychoanalysts, members varied bristling with palpable differences in conditions of upbringing. Yet we were united in our willingness to try and abandon caution in this endeavour. We found ourselves striving like Milner herself, towards a less 'deliberative' approach while aware of relapses and the precariousness of our achievement.

One participant, an art-maker, found it helpful to think about Milner's pointers to underlying fears that block creativity and interaction. Citing Milner, she agreed that

DOI: 10.4324/9780429433535-39

both anger and experiencing a lack of separateness from the object can pose internal dangers. The threat of immersing oneself in an open-ended way, where rationality and separateness between objects is lost in the imaginative process of making the thing one's own. And when anger feels dangerous, it succeeds in curtailing free expression 'in case aggression comes to the fore', due to fear of damaging the other in the process of incorporating him or her.

Another participant was struck that for Milner, taking the risk to share not only her own doodles but also her interpretation of them was ground-breaking for her time. Today it still constitutes a courageous act for any psychoanalyst, given the constraints of the fine line straddled between self-disclosure and patient confidentiality. While we felt grateful for Milner's gifting us the exploratory process rather than a polished product, we were also aware that in the name of education, she risked exposing herself to hazards of ridicule and other forms of criticism.

One contributor felt that by extending the meaning of *reverie* while drawing, listening to music or helping a patient towards a deeper understanding of preconscious expression, Milner takes us beyond slips of tongue, to beyond the spoken and written word, even beyond the symbols of dreams or culture, towards new free association techniques (e.g. doodles). She expressed her hope that one day, such preconscious expressions via all the expressive arts will be granted more value (possibly even including financial support by Psychoanalytic Associations and a place for exhibiting or performing at conferences).

Another participant noted that as a newly qualified psychoanalyst (barely two months ago), she, therefore, found it doubly gratifying and inspiring to read the musings and meanderings of a maverick psychoanalyst, such as Marion Milner. The invitation to journey into the innermost recesses of one's mind and dare to get in touch with one's creativity, whatever that might be, felt timely, promising, and appealing. Especially since in her own case, such a journey now feels daunting but previously felt 'treasonous'.

As a child of Apartheid South Africa classified 'Coloured', this contributor said she had been taught to internalise and suppress her dreams and aspirations in exchange for survival. This, in turn, had created vast and crippling internal inhibitions within her. Now, accompanied by Milner's narration of her own expeditions, she felt better equipped and more enabled to continue her own journey of self-analysis, and to experiment with different ways to uncover and discover aspects of herself, especially those that feel forbidden and treacherous.

Finally, a Jungian candidate singled out Milner's contrasting descriptions of logical 'thinking in the public language of words' comprising detachment and analysis—versus intuitive 'thinking in the private language of one's own subjective images' which seeks fusion, wholeness, and 'becoming one with what is seen'. As Milner noted, encompassing both ways of being in psychic integration leads to 'a solider, deeper-rooted kind of knowing' (pp. 123, 126). While science privileges the first, the second remains obscure, far less well understood.

This contributor suggested that notwithstanding recent developments in attachment theory and neuroscience, the disappointing bias towards primacy of words, reason, and analysis remains *de rigueur* in traditional intellectual academic education and continues to dominate contemporary psychoanalytic publications, meetings, and case discussions. Milner's courageous insistence on a *union of opposites* that melds logic and intuition, and according legitimacy to free-style drawings, raises hopes for the future. That ultimately, psychoanalytic discourse may similarly demonstrate a willingness to confer upon the *nonverbal* products of both analyst and patient the same gravitas and consideration as that traditionally accorded to verbal expression and interpretation.

In sum, participants in this group expressed gratitude for Milner's allowing us to see the *exploratory process* itself, rather than a finished product. In particular, her exposure of the tension of 'disjuncture between wariness, and the thrill of trusting' that what comes to mind will indeed be creative, in bringing alive what is dead/inanimate and produce something new.

Chapter 32

'The insides of solid things' – *On Not Being Able to Paint*

Penny Busetto

For
Cape Town Interdisciplinary group
Elisa Galgut (*philosopher*); Coenie Hattingh (*neuropsychologist, neuroanatomist*); Andrea Palk (*philosopher*); Anna Dreyer (*neuropsychologist*); Roelien Theron (*editor*); Theodor Van der Merwe (*art teacher*); Penny Busetto (*writer*)

Surrounded by a colourful [English country garden] in a leafy Cape Town suburb, an interdisciplinary group of several years' duration dedicated three meetings to discussing its responses to reading *On Not Being Able to Paint*. Comprising a variety of fields of interest ranging from Philosophy of Mind, Psychoanalysis, Neuropsychology, Neuroanatomy, Literature, and Art Education, members of this group tended to be more critical than the clinical group who came together elsewhere in the same city to read the book.

Without context or any preconception of Milner, several members of the group found reading *ONBATP* 'a difficult and confusing project' and searched for clarity in her ideas. They had a sense of something profound hidden in the stream of consciousness but felt it remained avoided, and undeveloped. They found it difficult to classify the genre of the book – neither a psychoanalytic exploration of creativity, nor an exploration of the psychoanalysis of art – it felt more a narrative of Milner's personal journal of creative self-investigation.

Some thought that in the context of current theories of creativity, Milner's hypothesis of the exploration of unconscious affects seemed dated in its simplistic dichotomy between subjective/objective, inward/outward vision, and loving and aggressive impulses. Nonetheless, artists within this group tended to champion Marion Milner's depiction of the *sensory process* of art-making, and her 'brave' blurring of boundary 'outlines' in an imaginative search for the 'insides of solid things'.

The group discussed whether the doodle exercise met the criteria for art (i.e. 'work must stand by itself'… 'expressing the ineffable') from the perspective of the Philosophy of Art. One member wondered whether Milner had possibly been influenced by Husserlian phenomenology (which also raised the interesting query whether MM's Library has remained intact?). On page 16, for example, Milner describes the way in which sensory perception requires an act of imagination. Given that one cannot perceive all aspects of an object at the same time, perception and understanding require the imagining, and thus, the reconfiguring of all past experiences of an object into a coherent whole. This description is highly reminiscent of Husserl's recognition of the

DOI: 10.4324/9780429433535-40

dimension of our experience that has been 'forgotten' or 'skipped over' in daily life. Our awareness presupposes a constant interaction between the perception, recollection, and anticipation of objects (and their unseen parts) and the mental processes and structures of understanding.

Similarly, in their responses some participants expressed annoyance with the 'rough and unformed' nature of the drawings, while others took a more charitable view of it as an experimental work-in-progress, 'an early beginning of a larger theory', yielding interesting 'nuggets', such as the idea of obedience as self-defence against disillusionment with authority, and ways of breaking the inhibiting tyranny of states of mind and bodily restrictions that can block the experience of painting. It struck the group that for an analyst to be publishing a book of such self-revelation was itself an act of courage on the part of Milner, and that at the time of writing it would have been a relatively ground-breaking work.

In retrospect, it was felt that many in the group had been overly quick to criticise Milner, considering the novelty of her project and her brave presentation of unformulated ideas, albeit initially under a pseudonym. There was a sense of respect for Milner's bold quest into uncharted territory (begun on the very brink of World War II!).

Of some interest was Milner's emphasis on the 'emotional achievement' of distinguishing between 'thought' and 'thing' while maintaining an illusion of unity. The idea or mechanism of illusion and disillusion in understanding fusion and separation, and its role in the suggestion of a bridge between logical thought and lived experience, was found to be interesting.

Despite the diversity of opinions, there was some agreement on the book's provision of a 'truthful' account of *an empirical examination of the artistic process.* Albeit some found it 'hard to follow' because the writing style 'irritatingly links then changes topic', emerges yet 'skirts away', and returns chapters later to plumb new discoveries in an old doodle. In fact, the 'angry parrot' and various 'monsters' lurking in these doodles provided some group merriment (e.g. figure 13 as a 'primal scene complete with window to peep through'). To some the 'confusing experiment' – of using art to uncover unconscious feelings implied projecting unconscious feelings on to it. But 'faux naïve' descriptions, the underpinning fears of chaos, madness and disintegration, and 'surprise' findings in the crude line drawings themselves were seen as sometimes contrived.

However, the title 'On Not Being Able to Paint' was noted as 'catchy' – indeed, so much so it had inspired at least two other psychoanalytic writers (Thomas Ogden and Jaqueline Rose on the inability to dream and to sleep, respectively) but also strange, in containing a negative.

The book was deemed potentially beneficial in relation to art-making and art teaching. Milner's writing process does return to, and address, or at the very least, tries to flesh out, the 'demons' of her creative process. Admittedly, this does require the reader to have insight into the creative process (and its temperamental and effervescent qualities).

As one participant expressed it in writing: 'I found the MM book interesting as an exploration of what emerges in the complex process of art-making (painting, drawing), which, unlike other creative work such as writing or singing, is mostly non-verbal and therefore seemingly, more demanding of intuition, imagination and spontaneity. In

MM's book, the drawings are followed by introspection and analysis, delivered by means of words, to help make sense of the form and meaning of unconscious desires, fears, rage, destructive feelings, etc. expressed from "the inside out" in the art. In the language of the imagination (and of psychoanalysis), she finds a way – through the act of drawing and by means of the drawings themselves – to discover what is unknown, following a rich seam of relationships between the internal world (as emotional/feeling world) and the external world of objects, logic, imposed restraint, and of the relationships between the "elements" of painting/drawing – lines, colours, images, bodily experience, imagery and so on. The rich metaphorical meanings attached to lines, colours, images – e.g. to keep things in or out; to provide opportunities for melding/fusion; to dissolve boundaries (as when different paint colours dissolve into each other at their edges on the canvas); to invest lines and shapes with emotional life or liveliness; to draw on the imagination; etc. – made me more curious about the complexity and dynamics at play in the hope for a less inhibited and restrictive way of viewing one's own internal life and how one lives in the external world'.

In time, it was generally felt that a second reading made the text seem less meandering and tangential, revealing some threads that come to the fore.

Chapter 33

Q&A with Marion Milner on *The Hands of the Living God*

James William Anderson

In the Fall Quarter of 1988, I, James William Anderson, taught a course in the clinical psychology PhD program in the medical school of Northwestern University. In that course, we read Marion Milner's book, *The Hands of the Living God: An Account of a Psycho-analytic Treatment*. I asked Milner in a letter whether my students and I might ask her some questions that came to mind as we discussed the book, and she agreed. I wrote her the questions, and she answered in a handwritten letter dated 4 December 1988. Here are the questions and her answers.

Could you provide an update on Susan? Do you know anything about what she has done in the years since her treatment ended? Incidentally, the students were tremendously impressed by your years of devoted work with her.

MILNER: She managed to keep on working (in a Museum) till pensionable age; she is still living with the man mentioned in the book (not married). Together they went to life drawing classes, but she needed something freer and has just started with a painting.

Do you think she would be considered schizophrenic or manic-depressive according to today's definitions of these diagnostic categories? Do you think she suffered from what we now call formal thought disorder? If this question does not seem relevant to you, please do not hesitate to say so.

MILNER: No, no formal thought disorder.

As you think back, what were the circumstances involved in your taking 8-week vacations? Was that simply something that everyone did in that era? From our current perspective, it would seem unusual to be separated from such a troubled patient for that long, but I believe thinking about vacations has changed a lot.

MILNER: Afraid I can't remember, I usually took four weeks.

Do you have a record of how much Tofranil Susan was taking?

MILNER: No record.

We all appreciated your openness about yourself in the book. What do you think the function of your smoking was? You comment that you did not feel a need to smoke after her "awakening." Did you smoking have to do with anxiety or with

DOI: 10.4324/9780429433535-41

the difficulty of paying attention to her? Was it hard just to be with her in the same room?

MILNER: No, I don't think the smoking was especially with her.

Do you recall anything about Winnicott's suggestions about the case or comments about Susan?

MILNER: No, only about the essential role of what he calls "holding" rather than clever interpretations.

Who was your therapist when you were in Boston (the Jungian who later received psychoanalytic training)?

MILNER: Irma Putnam, married to Tracy Putnam.

Could you clarify the title of the book? We read with interest your passage about the line of poetry from D. H. Lawrence, but we did not find it entirely clear just how you thought of it in relation to Susan, to her mother, and to yourself.

MILNER: No, I am afraid that to try and put it into rational, cerebral language would distort the meaning!

Perhaps it would help your students if they look for clues to this question in Chap I & Susan's "breakdown into reality" when working on the farm, and discovering the source of her own weight – that is, joining up (temporarily) her body-mind split and that all this happened when her friend Jackie was, for a time, behaving like the good mother she never had. I hope this helps.

Chapter 34

'The Play of Opposites' – Milner's last book

Bothered by Alligators

Angela Joyce and Tessa Dalley

This posthumously published book is Milner's last and in many ways could be said to be the culmination of her life's work: very much in line with how she has represented herself in both her previous diary writings and her profound contributions to psychoanalysis. She sets out to use this story book written by her son John when he was seven years old, for a particular purpose:

> to show parents some of the ways in which a child can struggle with the interplay of his parent's problems and how he can do this by using his poetic intuition long before he can express the problems in direct logical speech.
>
> (pp. 1–2)

She had found John's book in one of her drawers, unremembered, as she was, in her nineties, clearing the way towards her eventual death. Her purpose is subverted by her own immense propensity for introspection, acute honesty in her ability to follow her associative processes, in words and in images. This text is a tribute also to the classical psychoanalytic method of free thinking – free association; following one's mind to where it might lead, and, thus, discovering what we might not have dared to know about ourselves.

It is also a book very much out of our time. Eschewing her goal of writing a kind of help book for parents, Milner attends to what lies in the shadows of her mind and finds herself, again and again beyond what she had planned to do. In many ways, it is a book which exemplifies the potential depths to which a well-honed capacity for self-analysis can take one; making friends with, confronting what we find so difficult to know about ourselves. And as she was in her nineties when writing, it is a testimony to how life goes on until it stops.

The title "Bothered by Alligators" is an oxymoron: or at least the idea of being simply *bothered* by alligators seems not to grasp the sheer terror one might feel when confronted. Perhaps, this is a metaphor for what is there lurking in the shadows, the alligators in one's unconscious mind that can seem just a little bothering when the full experience of a full-on confrontation seems beyond daring. Milner is courageous as it slowly dawns on her that her first accounts of John's book and her diaries from his earliest years are an attempt to analyse him, whereas what she is faced with is herself, reflected in his "poetic intuition". Her meditations on what bothers her (her alligators?) in John's book take her to guilt feelings about her son's early life; guilt not of the persecutory kind; rather restorative. The kind of healthy guilt that parents might access as they contemplate the inevitable limitations of their parenting and its experience and impact upon their children. The areas that "good enough" doesn't quite touch, the failures

DOI: 10.4324/9780429433535-42

that have to be endured and have consequences. This is the territory that Milner takes us through, to the delicate recognition that our children see us, see through us and if we are lucky, we can learn more about ourselves by being open to their communications.

Written from 1934 to 1942 when her son John was between the ages of two and nine years old, the diary records everyday life simply and perceptively, by closely observing details of his early play. As a working mother, she notes her own frustrations and his growing anxiety about her absences and attachment to different carers/nannies. In this anecdotal way, his internal musings and thinking aloud to himself capture magic moments of a child's own wonderings. The title for the book came from overhearing John talking to himself about one of his carers to whom he was devoted. "Poor Sara are the alligators bothering you?" (p. 18).

It is fascinating to read how the relationship with his mother subtly changes as John acquires language. Also the development of aggression as a little boy, working through Oedipal issues with a father who is quite absent and unwell and a mother who notes there are very few recorded rows due to her later understanding of her own "compulsive agreement tendency".

There are several breaks in the diary. The first, in 1936, Milner moved to Spain where she wrote *An Experiment in Leisure* under the name of Joanna Field (1937). She reflects on her urge to have her own space and to write, "a kind of continuation of what had driven me to keep the 1926 diary" (a nature diary she kept as a young girl for over ten years published in 1934 as *A Life of One's Own* also under the pseudonym of Joanna Field) "The experience was a very deep journey". commenting on "wiping out her self-image" to experience the enormous expansion of perception "I know nothing, have nothing, want nothing" (p. 27).

On her return, John's move into latency is clearly documented but another long gap in the diary follows in 1939 due to the father's illness. It is unclear if this inspired the story book in the same year because at this time, there was other considerable disruption to family life with war looming, evacuation to the country and his parents' failing marriage. Milner gives a frank and honest account of this turbulent time as, in this last section of the diary, she realises her blindness to the intensity of his anger over separations. John later reflected on his own sense of unease and that life at the time was "difficult".

During her absence in Spain, John, aged four, had sent her a chaotic picture letter of a wrecked train and a dragon, to which she admits her failure to respond. Thinking his drawings were just "scribbles" she completely missed his anger and distress, Milner considers the story book as an elaboration of this attempt to communicate through his images. The story book is comprised of thirteen imaginative illustrated stories, each of which involves a central character, an animal or a person and their encounter with the world, and demonstrates his remarkable drawing ability. Underlying themes reflect tensions between an anxious internal desire for safety and comfort and an interest in an adventurous outside world. The predominance of various houses provides a secure base in relation to dangerous events such as fire, killing, death (the fox kills the chickens and the rabbits are caught in snares). As the stories progress in length, detail and depth, the narrative and imagery become more complex as the central elements involve moving containers such as caravans, trains, and the emergence of bridges suggests linking aspects of the different worlds, between the characters playing out in his own mind.

After her discovery some fifty years later, Milner explores the meaning of the different stories, paying particular attention to the detail in the images and focuses on

John's developing sense of maleness and potency and his expression of guilt about rivalry with his father. Milner's astute and careful commentary is remarkable in her exploration of John's lively mind and how his internal world is communicated through his images. She also reflects on how she learnt so much about herself seen through the "eye of common sense" (p. 13) "as if I were a mother who had accepted the idea of there being psychic processes that are unconscious but letting my psychoanalytic ear have a rest" (p. 13). The growing recognition that her purpose in writing about the story book was to use his images "for my own needs for more self-awareness" as she comments "no it is his images analysing me, helping me to find out what had been left out of my own couch analysis" (p. 158). She goes on to explore further her own responses by experimenting with drawing using her left hand, when the "jaws of an alligator" appear and developing these free associative techniques by cutting up and tearing her failed paintings and reassembling them as collages. She allows her mind to wander and work into the unconscious meaning of the resulting images that appear by giving them a framework for thought. There is poignancy in the openness to this freedom of expression and the self-analysis that follows which allows us into the powerful process of using unconscious imagery in psychoanalysis which formed the bedrock of her pioneering work throughout her life.

Perhaps, a surprising referent that runs from time to time through the book, from the early diaries, the imagery that appears in John's story book and then Milner's later writing, is the bible and concerns about God. She is very interested in the appearance in John's drawing of crosses and their significance in Christian imagery. She had read him stories from a book called "The childhood of Jesus" and this seems to have stimulated John to ask many questions about God. Her own background was in an Anglican family, but she seemingly was doubtful from an early age (p. 154) and by her account when John asked these questions she was far from sorted in her mind about God and such matters. Milner's creative associations around these crosses and memories lead her to contemplate both the aggressive, destructive aspects of the cross-pain, suffering, death and also compassion, care, healing (the Red Cross). And then the other meaning of cross – anger, cross feelings and expressions. She wonders if both she and John have not faced "the stone-thrower" in themselves. But she wryly comments that John may well have done so more than herself – at least he had drawn a house with smashed windows! (p. 146)

Suffering on the cross and suffering cross feelings bring her to other imagery, associated with the body, and she spends extended time thinking about how the sense of the body is established and represented in our minds; and how, using John's drawings, this might become apparent. She notices that many of his depictions of people are without arms, and she associates to her memory of swaddling him too long as a baby, but also then wondering about injunctions against using arms for disapproved of purposes, like masturbation. John seemingly had been very content with his "Albert" – no signs of guilt – but Milner, ever alert to hidden, unconscious meaning, remembers his reference to lying atop her and wonders about his Oedipal rivalry emerging now as images of little men with no arms.

The second part of the book moves away from John's book and her diaries, but not entirely, as using free writing and free drawing she contemplates her life, returning to her parents, the limitations of her analyses, her stubbornly-held-on-to reluctance to express her anger, her aggression, her compliance; her compulsion to "think more about the different things I have done". These doings are her artistic creations – doodles, drawings, poems; her recollections of what she has written before now seen through the prism of her approaching death. Her concern with "the spontaneous inner force making for wholeness" or in different words, "the divinity that shapes our ends, rough hew them how we will" is challenged by the cracks belying the possibility of such protection. But she observes ruefully that the cracks let the light in – "But a crack can also be something through which light can penetrate in a pitch-dark place" (p. 198).

Some of what she explores through the cracks that let in the light are aspects of her own early life in her family, which she must have thought about, mused about, associated with (as we all perhaps do) for many years. Her work as a psychoanalyst, her diaries, her constant seeking to be herself, inevitably must have taken her over this ground again and again. But this account has a freshness to it, a revisiting to find again, anew, her origins. We hear about her parents – her father's "breakdown" following a severe head injury; her protectiveness towards her mother for whom her "long-ago alligator kind of love had produced pain in her eyes" (p. 218); her siblings. She realises that in this book which she is now writing, she uses "hate" very little and wonders what she is avoiding, now remembering her hatred for her sister, expressed in a game of Milner pretending to be a cobra rising fully to face her head on – "doing the cobra". Her migraines disappeared after she left home but she remained inhibited with regard to expression of anger and hatred and even speaking in public. She explores not only the injunctions to be good as she grew up, but more poignantly perhaps the recollections of loss – much loved nanny, her father through his injury, her brother on his marriage after an extremely close relationship in her teens. We get the sense of how her enormous difficulty in recognising the effects on John of her absences had its roots in these early unprocessed experiences of loss.

Her reminiscences about her analysis with Donald Winnicott, which took place long after she had qualified and following her sensing there were areas in her training analysis that hadn't touched her "bit of madness" (p. 233), suggest something perhaps a bit mad in the whole process. When she decides to approach him she is seeing a patient "Susan" who at that time is actually living with the Winnicotts. Because of this DWW suggests that he analyse Milner in her consulting room, her lying on her own couch! All a bit mad! She gives the impression in this memoir that Winnicott is himself a bit all over the place and indeed it is the period during and just after the war, when his father died, he himself became ill with his heart condition (which eventually killed him); he left his wife and was planning to marry Clare Britton. The setting for Milner's analysis with Winnicott then carried severe impingements and in apparent support of her description of herself as far too compliant, she stayed in that analysis for four years. There is a curious detail that she remembers, of Winnicott leaving a tiny crucifix in her consulting room and which she links with his poem The Tree, which uses the metaphor of the crucifixion. She wonders if this enactment in *her* analysis suggests something that was left out of *his* analysis, of a hidden suffering, linked to his mother, who in a covert, hidden way, suffered from depression, that nobody noticed but emerged in this act in her analysis. Given that she is always concerned with the hidden, what is in the shadows in herself, her own not-owned depression (during John's early years), her candour about this experience of Winnicott to whom she was close, perhaps idealised (p. 236), is admirable. It is also a caveat for all of us who endeavour to do the work of this impossible profession.

The book ends with a chapter entitled – "*Towards bringing bits of one's self together*" – perhaps her life-long pursuit. Milner died whilst writing this book, a testimony to her immense creative capacities.

Section V

Recollections and reflections

Introduction to Section V

Reflections and recollections

This final section brings into the book a highly personal flavour of Marion Blackett Milner's ways of being, adding to our appreciation of the multifaceted person she was, by means of memorable anecdotes and endearing everyday experiences shared here by some of those who knew her well.

In **Chapter 35**, Marion Milner's grandson Giles Milner recounts his experience of enjoyable meetings with his 'Granny plasticine' at family occasions during his childhood and later, their stimulating conversations when he made regular Thursday evening visits to her home.

In **Chapter 36**, psychoanalyst David Tuckett conveys his impressions of Marion Milner with whom he edited the only volume of her collected papers (*The Suppressed Madness of Sane Men*). He also helped with Milner's third diary-type book with the Blake-inspired title, *Eternity's Sunrise*. He brings to life a Marion Milner for whom he had very obvious affection.

In **Chapter 37**, Bice Benvenuto writes of the profound effect of an unexpected early morning visit – or visitation – from a rain-sodden Marion, creating an enigmatic experience in waking life that took on the quality of a dream.

Chapters 38–40 are fond and distinctive recollections from three British psychoanalysts – Michael Brierley, Donald Campbell, and Jennifer Johns. The first two were Milner's neighbours as well as colleagues and depict a spontaneously playful side of Marion on the street where she lived. Jennifer, whose analyst parents were contemporaries and friends of Marion Milner and Winnicott, leaves us with an image of a very vibrant, fashionista Marion who brought a light touch even to the issue of her immanent demise.

In the penultimate **Chapter 41**, psychoanalyst Vincenzo Bonaminio tells the story of discovering Marion Milner when gifted a visit to her by his friend, her Italian analysand.

The very last **Chapter 42**, by Anne Karpf, journalist and academic, describes feeling blown away in her youthful newspaper interview by the gale force of some of Marion Milner's 'shocking and wildly attractive' ideas.

Finally, in her Epilogue, Joan Raphael-Leff concludes this volume with a subjective overview of Milner's own developmental line from her earliest years to her last days.

DOI: 10.4324/9780429433535-44

Chapter 35

'Granny Plasticine' – my grandmother Marion Blackett Milner

Giles Milner

(Giles Milner speaks about his Grandmother, Marion Blackett Milner with Margaret Boyle Spelman [*Extracts from a Skype conversation on 5th January 2021*])

M: So, Giles, will you tell me a little bit about your experience of Marion, as her grandson.

G: She was always known to us in the family as Moll … and it's only much later that I've got to know her as Marion …[S]he was christened Nina Marion but we've always known her as Moll. I was born in '62 so I guess my first memories of her are around late '60s, 1970, going down to her sister Winn's cottage in Kent which was an old labourer's cottage that was substantially unmodernised,…but it was certainly beautiful, the garden and a beautiful bit of Kent and not too far from Cranbrook. And I remember just walking through the orchards and the woods with Moll looking for butterflies, particularly. She used to come out and sketch and paint and at that time I got into fishing so I would go and fish in the local ponds and often she would come and draw many pictures of the ponds. We saw her in London at family occasions. But I perhaps got to know her better about twenty years later when I was in my late twenties and living in Camden Town, not far from where she lived in Chalk Farm and I used to go, I think it was Thursday evenings, I used to go and see her after work and we'd drink whiskey and smoke cigarettes and just chat about the world and things and she was curious and interested in all sorts of things from politicians, humour to environmental things. She was interested, she had an enquiring mind.

M: As I understand it neither yourself nor your dad, nor your brother are working in the area of psychoanalysis, so Marion spoke to you about other things.

G: Yes, I mean we chatted, I knew one or two of the psychoanalyst friends so I knew a bit about the world that she inhabited but I didn't know the professional details. We would just chat about other things, we'd chat about what I was working at as a management consultant in London then. So we'd chat about that, she was interested in computers and business, she had absolutely no idea how either of them worked and that was something that I was working in so we chatted about that. She was interested in humour and what made up humour.

M: I was thinking when you were talking about computers because I wrote about her book that's only available as an e-book now which is Marion's account of the research that she did in educational psychology with secondary schools.

DOI: 10.4324/9780429433535-45

G: I've got a hard copy of that I'm sure.

> [*Giles kindly went and got his hard copy of the book and showed it to me. It looked like quite a substantial hardback volume*]

M: [A]ctually what I was going to say is that she has charts in there but obviously it's in the time before computers ...I speculated about what she would have done – with her visual and artistic abilities – in terms of graphs and images if she had SPSS (Statistical Package for the Social Sciences) software or something like that because her charts in the book are quite clever.

G: Yes. I've no idea how numerate she was, we never really discussed that but she was obviously interested...I think she must have been pretty numerate, she understood and could make sense of things. Patrick was obviously enormously numerate.

M: Did you know him?

G: Not really. He died in seventy-four and I remember meeting him and my sense as a young boy then was that he was tall and slightly severe and imposing, a slightly distant man. I knew his daughter Giovanna much better and I know his grandchildren who are my equivalents...And I think he probably was very motivated and he and Moll had a pretty competitive relationship which probably drove them both on to succeed.

M: Yes. In Emma Letley's biography I read that Marion didn't consider her own artistic abilities to be as good as her sister's or her mother's – because they all painted?

G: They all painted. I have a couple of their mother's watercolours and they were all the time very much, the Victorian lady's nature watercolours which are entirely competent and I don't know that she was a great painter, I think Winn was a better painter. And probably Dennis, her husband, my grandfather, was a better painter in a painting sense but in terms of art and creativity they're just different that's all... Winn and Dennis were probably better technical painters from the paintings I've seen but I think that Moll's creativity and imagery and ideas, I think Moll was more interested in some of the imagery and ideas and things like the collages she produced.

M: Yes, when she was older she chopped up her paintings.

G: Yes, I remember during the latter part of her life when she was producing them. When I would go and see her, I remember her with the table covered in bits of chopped up paintings and moving things around and just discussing – I'd forgotten about it until you mentioned it – but I remember a couple of evenings where we sat moving pieces around the collage telling stories, discussing what the story might be.

> *Here I asked Giles if he knew anything about Marion's plates of her own paintings or her idea of having her paintings published in book form which I had just come across from Brett Kahr's chapter for this book. But this was the first that Giles was hearing of the existence of the plates and that is as far as we could take that. In that moment we were both aware of the 'as yet to be decided' complexion of so many aspects of Marion's contribution and legacy.*

M: It sounds like you enjoyed Marion's company and it sounds like she enjoyed yours and looked forward to your Thursday evening visits.

G: Yes, we always had interesting conversations. Yeah, I think it took me until I was old enough to perhaps have a better sense of who she was and how to engage with her. I don't know that she was necessarily a typical traditional Granny, but that was fine. She was known as 'Granny plasticine' – it's a name that my parents' friends gave her.

M: Granny plasticine!

G: She was 'Granny plasticine' and the other granny was 'Granny sweets'.
(Both laughed)

M: Is that what you got from her, plasticine?

G: Well yes – and books; all sorts of interesting and obscure books from her. Sometimes copies of her own books, sometimes copies of other books which she liked. And yes our other grandmother tended to provide sweets; It was friends of my parents who christened them 'Granny plasticine' and 'Granny sweets'.

M: Very good (laugh). And of course, she had little figurines made of plasticine in her house?

G: They were clay… It started off, there were sets she built, she was hugely interested in William Blake and she would create these strange clay heads, some of which were slightly disturbed and there are a set of them that I'm not entirely clear what they represent but they were ways for her to express something. I have one here behind me actually. A very strange creature.

M: Do you think it's a representation of something of Blake's, oh my goodness…

Giles showed me a tiny head/bust (2 by 1.5 inches approx.) – a little like a gargoyle – It had a face on one side and something etched into the back of the head (like an alternate face/fantasy). I said 'It's like the conscious and the unconscious.'

G: Yes I think so. They were …very metaphorical, strange imagery that I knew she was interested in but I didn't pretend to understand it.

M: You have just reminded me of something …[W]hen I was interviewing Andreas Giannakoulas, a long time ago now, he said that he made a film.

G: I'm not sure, I knew Andreas many years ago but I don't know about it.

I explained that Andreas said that he had made a film with Italian television; the film came about because Marion had given a lecture in Rome in 1994 where she was talking about Blake's Job and the audience could not properly see the slides of the plates nor therefore get the best out of Marion's lecture. Andreas had wanted some way of representing the pictorial material that Marion was speaking about. He suggested that he was to give a private showing of the film to his colleagues in London at some stage soon after we talked in July 2009.

G: I haven't been in touch with him since way, way before then…My father would have been alive then. Whether Andreas would have got in touch with him I don't know…But John would have been an old man then so perhaps he wasn't in touch… [John] was eighty-one [when he died]…Marion died in ninety-eight and he died in 2013, fifteen years [later].

M: Would you like to say something to describe their relationship or do you feel they were different kinds of people?

G: I think they had quite a complex relationship. I know that Moll started some of her analysis [by] doing analysis on her son, John. I accept that it was a different era and that sort of behaviour was considered acceptable. I don't think it would be now. I think it damaged John, actually. I mean he had a difficult childhood growing up in the war, being evacuated. His parents had split up. I don't think that I think Moll conducting her own analysis on her son, probably sums her up quite accurately. But I don't think it was good for John.

M: And unlike you he was an only child.

G: He was an only child, he had a half-sister but he was an only child, he had an older half-sister from Dennis's first marriage, so yes I think it would have been very difficult for him and I appreciate that it was a different time and different standards. But I think it would be considered pretty un-maternal now. I accept that times were different.

M: Yes and so many children… [T]he evacuation itself caused so much trouble with so many children being separated from their parents.

G: Yeah. And a very difficult time. We still have the cottage that John was evacuated to in West Sussex. And he told some quite funny and rather touching stories about watching the Battle of Britain from Harting Downs in glorious technicolour with no real appreciation of just how dangerous it was.

M: Just as if it was some kind of light display…

G: Yeah, he said it was like a ballet, a dance being played out in the sky and he would have been just eight then. But I think, I mean I think he had a difficult childhood for lots of reasons, clearly his parents separating when he was young, being evacuated out of London… [H]e made the best of it, I mean he was quite reserved but that was also of that generation.

M: 'Reserved' is a word that people use about Marion as well. It's funny because they say 'warm' and 'reserved'; people's experience of her was both.

G: Yes, yes. [T]hat would be fair yes. I mean she could be, yes I think once you got to know her you always got the sense that she was only telling part of the story. And she was always very interested in other people and how they worked and how things worked but slightly, got used to the fact that there was always this slight sense of being, not quite interrogated under caution but you were being watched.

M: It's almost as if there was a sense of her mind working.

G: I remember a couple of times when I was young and I was angry about something or upset about something and she wanted me to explain why I was feeling that and I had no idea, just I was… I remember being angry, I've no idea now what I was angry about but it was something I was angry about or upset about and she wanted me to explain. I don't think I felt that was the response I wanted. But anyway…

I was going to say …after John died I started reading *A Life of One's Own* and I would say to anyone who wants to know what she was like [that when]I am reading that I can hear her voice, very, very clearly…I've read a bit [of Marion's work], *A Life of One's Own* and a bit of *Experiment in Leisure* and my sense reading them was that I could hear her voice, absolutely…[*On Not Being Able to Paint*] was given to me by my friend Jim Lynch in March 1992. I have a whole collection of her books that I've been given by people…One day perhaps I'll read them.

M: It sounds like you've got your own very busy life in a different area.

G: It's in a different area. I have two teenage daughters and my wife is a public health doctor so she's so busy at the moment, too busy at the moment.

M: I can only imagine.

G: It's interesting, quite by chance Emma Letley got in touch and said she'd spoken to you and you got in touch and a couple of other people have got in touch all seeking permission to use pictures or quotes. So there's quite a lot going on in various places…

Here, Giles told me details of the people who were contacting him in the course of pursuing their interest in Marion Milner's work. They were attached to English universities and elsewhere. We discussed this phenomenon that Giles was noticing and I suggested that these people and others mentioned to me in the course of this study might, – if they were identifiable to each other or congregating in a single dedicated forum – might be the people who would be called 'Milnerian/Milnerean' if such an adjective were considered useful in locating Milner's continuing and evolving influence.

G: Yes, it's not a subject I'm any way an expert in but it is quite interesting reading. It's interesting and quite strange reading articles about someone who was my grandmother and seeing her in a completely different light.

M: And of course a hope for this book is to set the beginning of answering such questions; about her personal characteristics but also her clinical and technical characteristics; to say 'what is the contribution that Marion Milner gave to psychoanalysis – and to her other fields of interest?'

G: Yeah, I mean it's great that people are interested. I guess some of my interest in her and her brother and sister is to consider 'what caused those 3 – in their different ways extraordinary people – to come out of an otherwise very ordinary family?' Just their extraordinary intellects: So Winn, the younger sister was one of the first women to become a Fellow of The Institute of Architects and was a very technical draughtswoman and illustrator. And Patrick who went to Dartmouth [Naval College] because the family ran out of money and then ended up in the First World War serving on HMS Barham, he went to Dartmouth Naval College… – [t]he family didn't have enough money to send him to private school – where you could sign up and get an education… So I think he'd obviously qualified. My understanding was that he went to Dartmouth Naval College…and so this would have been just before the start of the First World and then he was I think a junior midshipman at the battle of Jutland on the flagship HMS Barham. And then at the end of the First World War as part of mobilisation there was a university expansion and he ended up at Cambridge…It was just the 'demob'…at the end of those wars there were a number of young people, obviously mostly men with nothing to do. So a lot of them ended up at university as a way of just keeping them occupied. So my understanding is that at the end of the First World War a lot of the brighter soldiers were offered the chance to go to university that perhaps they wouldn't have had otherwise. So Patrick went to Cambridge. Moll had, I don't know the full story of Moll's going to The Slade [Art College] and I think she had a benefactor, a sponsor.

…

M: Yes, but Marion also had a degree in psychology and physiology from Cambridge?

G: I think that was later, I don't know the full story of that, I think that came later…I think she went to art school first…But again I'm not sure, it's one of those things that I never thought to ask at the time.

…

M: I know that you're the person that let Emma [Letley] know that sadly Margaret Walters (Milner's friend and original Literary Executor) passed away last April.

G: Yes.

M: So I wonder where things are now in practical terms with Marion's work. Is there an archive?

G: I believe that Emma had set up an archive at The Psychoanalytic Society (BPAS) and that there is a Milner archive that's been set up [there]...I saw Margaret's partner Jerry a little while ago and he didn't know whether they [Jerry Badger and Margaret Walters] still had many of Moll's papers. I probably have some of her papers and her pictures in London and my brother probably has boxes of the papers and pictures. I know that he and I both have some of her pictures that we like to have on the wall and there's a collection of her other pictures and drawings – and the collages, some of which I have. So my connection has been that based in London it was easier for me, when John died it was easier for me to take over the administration of the stuff with the Marsh Agency and so I got to know them, because I'm in London more than my brother Quentin. I knew Margaret and Gerry and I knew Emma and so [it was] just a lot easier for me.

...

I think [Jerry Badger] was an architect and a photographer. But I mean I saw him a couple of months ago for the first time in probably nearly twenty-five years. I've spent more time in London since we left home than my brother has so I know some of the people involved more than he does, which just makes it easier for me to pick up on those relationships.

Giles explained that he and Emma Letley were aware through their contact with The March Agency that [Margaret Walters] was ill.

...

So effectively I've been acting as Literary Executor; nothing very complicated, just signing the forms for the royalties and granting permission to use quotes and pictures. In answer to your question where is it all now and where is it going, I'm not quite sure...

I suspect that [the archive Emma mentioned in the BPAS] would be a suitable place for lots of things. And a lot of stuff will go there. Obviously some of the pictures and the collages and things have sentimental interest to Quentin and I, so we'll keep those; and probably copies can go into the archive.

We discussed the idea that an art college or an artist interested in Milner's work might be helpful in realising Milner's wish (expressed to Brett Kahr) for a published book of plates of her paintings and drawings. We speculated about how much easier it might be for interested individuals and artists now that her books are in print again.

M: So I imagine that things will be a little more straightforward for anybody who is interested in her work now.

G: Yes and I guess the fact that the books are in print and [with the use of] the internet, that there are more resources available.

I showed Giles some paper made by Aleana Egan based on a detail of one of Marion's drawings. And I told him of the lovely images of some of Marion's paintings that Aleana made for her lecture in the Winter Lecture Series in the Gallery where she has her studio.

G: Yes, I couldn't tell it was Marion's print but it is beautiful.

M: Isn't it. Aleana, who has a chapter in this book, is a really good artist and she thinks that Marion was a really good artist and sees the merit in her art work.

G: I think she was. You know, I think she was and there's a couple of pictures that my brother has got that are really very, very nice pictures. I would say that she and Dennis and Winn were all very different, each very different artists in their own way.

M: Of course, Dennis was an artist as well.

G: Yes, yes he was a painter, psychoanalyst [sic], philosopher, inventor, an eccentric... he died ten years before I was born...Dennis died in fifty-four, eight years before I was born...It's a shame, I would love to have met him, I think he was an interesting character.

...

M: So, have you got ideas about what you think it is important for people to know about Marion or to realise about her as a person or about her contribution?

G: I don't think I have...I know that as a grandmother I understand some of the family dynamics; and that there's a whole range of interesting people who were interested in her and her ideas but I don't work in that space so I don't think there's anything that I can usefully contribute.

I asked about family resemblances to Marion and if he or his brother, Quentin, were considered to be like Marion.

I don't think [Quentin and I] were... It's interesting that we have a portrait of two [sisters] of our ancestors _ Constance Maynard, the first Principal of Westfield College and her sister – who look exactly like my daughters ...a portrait of the 1850s of two sisters who look exactly like my two children at [about] the same age.

...

But no, I don't think that there was a sense that my brother and I were more or less like either of them... obviously my mother wouldn't have met Dennis as he had died before they met.

M: Were either of you supposed to be more or less like your dad?

G: I'm not sure, I suspect we both have bits of him. I think Quentin and I would recognise bits of John in us. Going further back, it's harder to see similarities just because it was a different time and people behaved differently, they spoke differently...

I suspect that there's a fair amount of John in both of us and clearly a bit of influent genes and potentially influence of Moll going through that.

M: And could you see things in him that came from his mother. Did he look like her?

G: Well he looked a bit like Patrick...I don't think he particularly looked like Moll but he did look like Patrick. As my brother does... I take after my mother more, looks wise... I digress slightly but a while ago somebody sent me a copy of a picture of Moll when she was young asking if I could grant permission to use the copyright. I was struck that she was very beautiful when she was young.

M: It seems that she was very beautiful always. I am struck by the number of people who say that she was beautiful, including people meeting her in her nineties – the word 'beautiful' is used repeatedly.

G: Yeah, she was very stylish in her own iconoclastic way. I'm reminded of a very funny story about her that she had a whole collection of slightly eccentric fur coats and she managed to look very grand. And a long, long time ago she was in Harrods shopping and the shop assistant clearly thought she was a very rich foreigner and commended her on her English and she was absolutely furious! (both laughing)

That she had been mistaken for a rich foreigner. But she had a whole style; yeah, she was very stylish in a slightly eccentric, avant-garde way.

M: What about Winn? Had they different or similar styles?

G: I don't know at all...Winn married Burg and they didn't have children. I only remember meeting Winn once when she was [elderly], just before she died. She was living with Moll and I guess it was in the late 1960s, I was just a little boy, I remember meeting her.

M: So your Grand-aunt, Winn, was living with Marion.

G: Win was living with Moll. Marion had a big house in Chalk Farm and Marion lived there with a housekeeper, a whole succession of housekeepers. And she was, I was six or seven, it's a long time ago. But my understanding was that Winn was living with Marion, Moll and I think she died shortly thereafter. I'm not sure what she died of but she was obviously much younger...

Yes she married Burg (George Burger), I don't know anything about Burg beyond the fact that he was older than Winn and was a civil servant who collected a whole series of Gilroy prints (19th-century Punch-type satirical cartoons) and Toby jugs and slightly weird, eccentric Punch cartoons and such.

...

[Y]es Winn was Winifred Burger. And Burg was just, that, Burg. It was his nickname from school or something...

M: You'll have to excuse me because I don't think I've generated very many good questions for you but at the same time you've managed to tell me a lot, so thank you.

G: I hope it will be useful...I really haven't thought about a lot of it for a very long time. So I hope it makes some sense.

M: Yes. And I think that it is good that you're speaking also about the practical end of things; where people can find stuff or who they can contact. But at the same time I can hear that a lot of your already very busy life is taken up with being the custodian of Marion's legacy in a very practical 'hands-on' way.

A: It is something that needs doing and the Marsh Agency have been very good at helping with that...But I think gradually – because John managed that until he died – we track things down and there have been all sorts of loose ends that have taken quite a while to tie up. Probably the common thread there has been Emma (Emma Letley), who I haven't seen for a while but now I've caught up with her...

M: Well nobody has seen anybody except on a screen for a while.
G: I know, yes, but it was longer ago than that.

Giles explained that he had had a lot of life changes (including email address) that caused people (myself included) to lose contact with him.

G: I'd be very interested in seeing a copy of your book when it's done.

I gave Giles a news update on the book and asked if he might have any photographs of Marion for the book cover

G: That's a very interesting question. I suspect I don't have very many but I'll have a look…you have just got me thinking, I will have a look and see…I'm not sure what I have – very few photos of her actually. I'll ask my brother, he might have some.

I spoke about other hopes I had for photographs of Marion

G: Yes I'd love to see that.
M: I'm so happy to meet you and talk to you today. I'll be in touch.
G: Ok, very good talking to you.
M: Bye, bye.
G: Yes. Bye.

Chapter 36

'Words made flesh...'

On editing Marion Milner

David Tuckett

Marion Milner was an extraordinarily wise, creative and intelligent woman whom it was a pleasure to be with. I knew her principally because I helped her publish two books. Both had been lying around on flimsy and slightly yellowing typescript for some time but were published as a result of our conversations in 1987.

The first, which I directly assisted with, became one of the founding volumes of the New Library of Psychoanalysis, published as *the Suppressed Madness of Sane Men.*

The second, *Eternity's Sunrise* was about keeping a diary, of which she kept many, and she was both incredibly well read and informed and a rigorous observer – of herself and others. I managed to recommend it to Carmen Callil of Virago Press – who was a publishing sensation at the time.

Looking back, I must have met Marion perhaps half a dozen times to discuss these books.

When I first went to see her, I had already read *On Not being Able to Paint* and the extraordinary and moving *Hands of the Living God* – a touching account of a long analysis with a very ill young woman done through her drawings.

Probably, I was introduced to Marion by Pearl King, who had long before been analysed by Marion after the sudden death of John Rickman. Pearl and the Publications Committee were looking for manuscripts as we tried to revive the old International Psychoanalytic Library published by the Hogarth Press. It had become defunct through very conservative and negative editorship and had published only a very small number of books in the previous ten years. The new idea was to find engaging work that could be published in hardback and paperback and make a wider impact – the New Library of Psychoanalysis, as it became.

In any case, one day I found myself knocking on the front door of the slightly Gothic house Marion had inhabited for many years in Provost Road. I have no idea if this is accurate, but I recall being ushered through a hall and slightly darkened kind of treasure trove of rooms and fabulous objects into a room overlooking the garden. This would be the first of a series of quite long and regular chats as she handed over, and we discussed, the manuscripts and a great deal of her life, as well as the two books, which, of course, were both rather personal. Marion was quite deaf by then so one sat very close to her as she talked with intensity, precision, loveliness and modesty.

There were some very intelligent people in and around her family including a Nobel Laureate for Physics and she herself had gained First Class honours – at UCL in fact, where I was to go myself ten years later [as Professor and Director of the Centre for the Study of Decision-Making Uncertainty]. I remember her talking about her

DOI: 10.4324/9780429433535-46

husband, Dennis, who had been an interesting and distinguished economist or social scientist with whom I recall she spent some time at Harvard. He was interested in the issues which would become the Welfare state. Marion and he were greatly influenced by Elton Mayo, whose lectures she attended in Boston. He played a leading part in organizational and industrial psychology (today it would be management psychology) in which they had both been very involved.

She also told me about her quite extensive social life with Melanie Klein, which included dressing up, impressive hats and parties.

I say all this to convey my impression that she was part of a generation and a group of the utmost brilliance and creativity, very far from being locked into their consulting rooms. They were linked into the most exciting intellectual, artistic and social developments of the time.

All that made talking to her a huge pleasure. I wish I had had more time. By then she must already have been eighty-seven, and one was acutely aware of her liveliness, curiosity, lovely mobile face, intense gaze and thoughtfulness. Despite our age difference, she was deeply respectful to me, who at the time knew little. She was very easy to work with and responded to suggestions and edits with gratitude and no trace of resentment.

I wish I could remember more.

My last memory of her was in about 1996, two years before she died. I had written a paper (which became "Mutual Enactment in the Psychoanalytic Situation") and it was my turn to present to the "52 Club" – a rather exclusive private group of independent psychoanalysts set up to have real discussion by people like Marion, Pearl King, Adam Limentani, Masud Khan and Charles Rycroft. As I recall, Kit Bollas and myself had been asked to join shortly after qualifying as two lucky and privileged "youngsters".

By then in her late nineties, Marion sat very attentively in the chair next to me that evening and when I had finished was utterly enthusiastic: "I wish I was seeing some patients tomorrow morning", she said, "I would really like to try out these ideas and see what I think of them!"

Her deep curiosity and enthusiasm for learning from another, no matter how relatively ignorant that other might be, will always remain with me.

Chapter 37

'The Visitation'

Bice Benvenuto

An email exchange with Margaret Boyle Spelman during the Autumn of 2018

Dear Margaret,

It was really lovely to have met you in Dublin yesterday.

...As for the uncanny encounter I had with Marion Milner in the mid-eighties, I can give you some more details that may be indicative of her personality (as well as mine, I'm afraid!):

One morning I was woken up by a peal of thunder and a knock at the door simultaneously. There she was, at my doorstep all dripping and with my typescript in her hands. I was half asleep and the whole encounter still seems like it was a dream. I was in my pyjamas, speechless, in the middle of my kitchen that was in utter chaos. She was oblivious of all this (while I was hardly managing to make her a cup of tea) and was speaking, standing in the middle of plates, mugs and crumbs, of her new thoughts about women's Oedipus complex. I barely managed to make some appreciative comments, while spilling tea over the table! Then she disappeared out in the pouring rain again leaving me with my typescript in my hands, feeling I had behaved like a fool for having missed such a great opportunity to discuss psychoanalytic issues with her and honour her in a more appropriate way!

Dear Bice,

Thank you so much for sharing this wonderfully interesting encounter. It has an atmosphere of the supernatural about it, and indeed I think we are both agreed that Milner was an extraordinary woman!

Dear Margaret,

...The truth is that I have repressed most of how all that came about. It is still a puzzle to me, of the quality of a dream indeed.

Dear Bice,

It is like what Milner called a 'bead memory'!

* * *

I have reported this brief correspondence with Margaret Spelman so that the exchange of emails can stand for bead memories the way Marion Milner conceived them: written notes whose significance resonates with the one who wrote them. Bead memory also describes well the uncanny phenomenon Milner herself had incarnated for me in her visitation. It was one of those bizarre or enigmatic moments of our waking lives

DOI: 10.4324/9780429433535-47

that take on the quality of a dream, first as for pointing at those knots and cracks that keep disturbing the daily flow of our minds, then for needing to be noted down, even if only into a corner of our memory, and then deciphered.

Milner's visitation did not take place while travelling abroad, when she usually took care of her beads.[1] Instead it took place as a sudden awakening right inside the very kernel of my home. With her knock at the door the tempest without burst within my sleep. It has always taken me a long time to wake after getting up in the morning, so I was in a sort of semi-conscious state throughout the visit. I will never know why she went out into the rain that early morning to return to me a typescript I couldn't remember having given her and which happened to be the first I ever wrote.

Who had given it to her? Perhaps a common friend? So I assumed at the time, though I will never be able to know what the visit meant for her. As for me, I noted it down in my memory-book for a long time until I could retrace it back, almost forty years on, thanks to the emails exchanged with Margaret. All I can wonder about now is what Marion Milner's visitation meant or still means for me.

The memory was triggered by talking to Margaret after a lecture I gave in Dublin a few years ago about a feminine melancholic disappointment which followed the great expectations of the eighties of women's new intellectual and sexual explorations, of a new feminine way of being, of dreams of subversion or ecstasy!

One of Milner's beads from Greece concerned her second visit to the Acropolis, when ants fighting over a crumb came between her and the Parthenon, distracting her from admiring it. Also my crumbs were lying between us, between the naïve hopes of my youth and her new thoughts on feminine sexuality. She stood there as my Parthenon, with the weight and the size of those *pillars that are maidens*. How not to be tongue-tied in front of the grace of her strong speaking body, apparently oblivious of the chaos of my kitchen. Or were her words attending to the experience of *benign chaos* I was going through?

Still a chaos though. So I could hardly hear her views about the feminine Oedipus. She was holding the manuscript, which I felt as an alien foreign body, whereas my own body was crumbling and pouring tea over it. Is it not in line with Milner's thought that writing, as well as painting or thinking, requires sensing one's own body, entails phases of descent into the mud or even further back into the primordial stirring of our cells? We find a similar experience in ancient rites concerning women's initiation.

It was as if we were enacting such an initiation, a symbolic transmission of knowledge from woman to woman, from a great freethinking psychoanalyst and writer to another woman, the initiate. By way of pouring rain and spilled tea, a baptism was being performed on the manuscript, just born from feminine flesh and already a separate entity, *same and other at the same time*, which I was as yet so ambivalent in acknowledging. Maybe that's why at times we feel like a fool, because of consciousness' inaptitude at taking up an earthly redemption of the body. This entails a process of descent into archaic uncanny territories before re-emerging. I could not focus on this message; consciousness was in the way with its unredeemed state of inertia, of incredible slowness.

But when Marion Milner left, I had the manuscript in my hands, as if my body had sank *right down to the bottom of things* and resurfaced with words spilling from my cupped hands, from Milner's dripping clothes.

Note

1 This text is inspired by Marion Milner's book *Eternity's Sunrise. A Way of Keeping a Diary*, 1987, Routledge. I have italicized some words I have used from her book.

Chapter 38

'Marion on the Swing'

Michael Brearley

The first book I read by a living psychoanalyst was Marion Milner's *On Not Being Able to Paint*, on the obstacles to freedom in painting, many of which lie in not trusting the unconscious, in trying to over-control outcomes with care, consciousness and conscientiousness. I went on to read other books by her. I have learned a great deal from her, including her ideas about the need for two forms of thinking: on one hand for rigorous, separate, secondary-process logical observation and rationality, and on the other for a more fluid, less focused, more intuitive, sometimes body-based way of orienting oneself towards inner and outer worlds.

When I had become clear that there were strong reasons for me to have an analysis, as well as having decided to train as an analyst, I contacted Marion to ask if she would consider being my training analyst. Having invited me to visit her at her home in Provost Road, she listened; she told me she was unable to take me on, as she was too old (she was, in 1976, 76). She then said she had a question to ask me. Her grandson was playing cricket at school. He had done something that was clearly a good thing. He had taken a 'hat-trick'. But what, she asked, *is* a hat-trick?

As it happened, a few years later we became neighbours, and friends. My family and I were very fond of her. She was to the end curious about life, modest about her achievements, sometimes irreverent; always beautiful and elegant. In her eighties and nineties, she would sit on the stairs to chat with small children. At ninety-six, she noticed the long swing we had hanging from a high branch of the ash tree that used to stand in the corner of our garden. She hadn't been on a swing, she said, for sixty years. I asked her if she'd like a go. She would. I picked her up and she swung with child-like pleasure.

Marion said more than once that she wished she could have benefited from recent advances in psychoanalysis. She felt her aggression had not been analysed sufficiently. She was open to ideas from any source. She was a truly independent mind, once saying that there were two kinds of independent analysts, those who wanted a group to belong to other than the Kleinian or Contemporary Freudian ones, and those who wanted to *be* independent. She was in the latter group.

It is a privilege to have known her.

DOI: 10.4324/9780429433535-48

Chapter 39

'Marion on the Drums'

Donald Campbell

Marion was more of a friend and neighbour than a colleague. She lived on my street and passed our house on her way to and from the underground or the corner grocery store. Sometimes, as she got older, she would sit on our front wall to catch her breath, or the sun.

Marion had a kind friendly look. A luminous face. She was always lean and trim and had an eclectic and, some would say, eccentric way of dressing. She favoured calf-length dresses and blouses, sometime with a layered look of waistcoats and cardigans. I was always impressed by the subtle combination of colours and pattern. A bohemian look.

I always admired Marion's work with her child patients. As she was elderly when I got to know her, I asked her when she decided to stop treating children. She quickly said, 'When I couldn't get off the floor.' I smiled to myself and followed Marion's advice when I found it difficult to get up off the floor during an assessment interview.

I was always impressed by Marion's interest in our family.

She remembered the names of our two children Chris and Cath, and always asked about them with genuine interest in what they were like and what they were doing. My guess is that it was not just our family, but that was the way Marion was, interested in her friends as people with lives.

My most enduring memory of Marion occurred when she heard my son Chris playing the drums up in his room. Marion said that she had always wanted to play the drums. So, we moved Chris' drum kit from his room on the top floor to our living room, and invited Marion for tea and to play on Chris' drums. Marion banged away on the drums with gusto. I can still see the wide grin on her face.

DOI: 10.4324/9780429433535-49

Chapter 40

'Marion Milner, Shakespeare and fashion'

Jennifer Johns

Despite growing up with parents who trained and practised as psychoanalysts, and who knew Marion, I did not meet her until after I had become an analyst myself.

I knew about her, of course, and had read *On Not Being Able to Paint* during my adolescence, having picked it up because it seemed to address some of the questions I had about feelings of inhibition, feelings which eventually led me to my own analysis.

I learned more about Marion during the psychoanalytic training when several of my fellow students were supervised by her, and what struck me then was their mixture of respect and affection when they reported her interventions, and their enjoyment of the freedom she gave to use and explore their own responses in the clinical situation. This contrasted a great deal with those colleagues who seemed anxious to find the "right" interpretation to satisfy their supervisors and whose style seemed to me rigid and fearful of disapproval, the very things I was trying to deal with myself.

I did not attend the 1971 Vienna Congress, but on hearing about it, Marion became even more intriguing to me, and for an apparently unpsychoanalytic reason. That Congress was a historically important one in the psychoanalytic world, as it represented the return of psychoanalysis to the birthplace it had fled before World War II. I was told by my parents, who were part of the London delegation, about the powerful and mixed emotions experienced by those of their colleagues who had been part of that terrified and tragic pre-war exodus, and who had suffered personal losses and so much pain. It was while describing to me the immense courage of Anna Freud, in coming back to a place, for her, of such grief and darkness in order to attend the triumphant inauguration of the Sigmund Freud Museum in her old home, that my mother paused, and as if to lighten the dark mood of her recollections, said in a tone of amazement, "And do you know, Marion Milner was wearing a *trouser suit*! At 83!" (In 1971, trouser suits were controversial, somewhat rebellious, worn only by the fashionable and challenging youth, and not at that time permissible at the Opera, or at Ascot. They only became legal attire in the US Senate in 1993.) My mother's mixture of amazement with a strong tinge of admiration emphasised to me that here was someone free to live as she wanted, not be constrained too much by convention, and who as well as being a senior and respected psychoanalyst could please herself in the enjoyment of lovely and dramatic clothes.

I got to know Marion for myself, much later. In 1991, Sadie Gillespie, a South African analyst, an old friend of mine and a neighbour of Marion's, invited a small

DOI: 10.4324/9780429433535-50

group of analytic colleagues to form a Shakespeare reading group. We met on Sunday for tea, about every four to six weeks, and chose a play to read for each meeting. Whereas most of us brought heavy Shakespearean tomes to read from, Marion brought her beautifully bound individual volumes, with quite small print, that cannot have been easy to read from at ninety-one. From these, she read her parts quite beautifully, once inhabiting the role of Juliet and interpreting the words of a young girl caught up in the turmoil of love, sex, fear, excitement, desperation and despair in a way that showed her ability to make that temporary identification and communicate it in an incredibly moving way.

I met Marion at Sadie's and also at the 1952 Club, a group of Independent Psychoanalysts founded in 1952 to hold monthly meetings to complement the British Psychoanalytical Society's meetings and allow development of Independent thought without the acrimony sometimes attendant in the wider Society at the time. Marion had been one of the earliest members of the Club and was a regular attender. She mostly sat quietly listening, making few interventions, but when she spoke, demonstrating a deep understanding of the work or topic under discussion and almost always providing another angle to see it from, another way of thinking about it, an opening up rather than any sort of dogmatic closing down. It was after such a meeting, and shortly before her death that I had a brief but memorable conversation with her, that showed something of a wicked sense of humour.

I had been involved in some of the various events celebrating the centenary of Donald Winnicott in 1996, and it must have been about a year later that Marion asked me whether the centenary was over. I replied that it was, and realising that she was now approaching the age of ninety-nine herself, said that probably the next centenary to celebrate would be her own. She demurred and said that she didn't think she'd last that long. When I pointed out that she was actually nearly there, she looked at me with some amusement and admitted "Well, I have been wondering what to wear!" And as she got into the car taking her home, she asked another quiet but slightly unsettling question, as if to underline her doubt about survival – "Jennifer, do you think they make designer shrouds?"

It was not very long after that conversation that Marion did die, and Pearl King, an analysand of Marion's who had been asked to say something at her funeral, asked me if I would read her contribution at the service, as Pearl did not feel up to it herself. So I did and then accompanied Pearl with others to Highgate Cemetery, where Marion was then interred. The East part of the cemetery is full of notable graves, and Marion lies not far from Karl Marx and many of those whose thinking and actions have influenced the world. It felt like the proper place for her.

There is one other place that always reminds me of Marion, and my own speculations about our personal development. If you go to a concert at the Albert Hall, or maybe the Royal College of Music, and park your car in Queen's Gate, you walk round a corner into Prince Consort Road. The Imperial College building on the corner houses the Blackett Laboratory, with its Epstein bust of Marion's Nobel Prize-winning physicist and socialist brother Patrick, later Baron Blackett, who in 1921 gave her a copy of Freud's Introductory Lectures. I can never pass that corner without remembering Marion, and all that might have developed from that gift – or would she have made her own way?

Chapter 41

'Getting to know Marion Milner'

An unexpected gift from the late Andreas Giannakoulas

Vincenzo Bonaminio

My contact with Marion Milner was rewarding. One day, knowing that I would be travelling to London within a couple of weeks, her ex-analysand Giannakoulas asked me whether I would do him a favour and deliver a letter by hand her. I replied that the letter would have been delivered sooner if he sent it by post. His response was that the postal service was no longer what it used to be.

Once I arrived at my destination, having telephoned ahead, I was welcomed like an old friend into Marion Milner's home. She was an elderly lady with a pale and smooth complexion. I realised that this was a gift from Giannakoulas. He wanted me to meet Marion Milner in person. She had been his third analyst after the death of Masud Khan. She offered me tea and showed me paintings by her most famous patient, Susan, of *The Hands of the Living God* (1969). Seeing the originals left a great impression on me.

We talked for over an hour, discussing her relationship with Winnicott and Klein. Then, as I was about to leave, she called me back: "Ah, one last thing". She led me into a room where one of her paintings was displayed. It depicted a mother hen with chicks around her – bright colours with a pastel background. She asked me whether I understood its meaning. I replied that I did not know. She explained that the mother hen was Melanie Klein and the chicks were her followers waiting for birdseed. Realising that she had perhaps said too much with this disclosure, she added: "I appreciated her, and I still do, but our paths separated. Then I met Winnicott, an exceptional individual".

Giannakoulas, whose generosity cannot be praised enough, subsequently invited Marion Milner to his home in Rome [see Chapter 12]. He showed her around Rome at a pace that took into account her advanced age. He invited her to attend a memorable conference on Blake's illustrations of the Book of Job, with slides of the illustrations. Giannakoulas later made a film on this theme, which is a cornerstone in our tradition. He maintained links with the British Psychoanalytic Society where he had trained as a psychoanalyst, and in addition to Marion Milner, invited other senior analysts to contribute to the training in Rome (e.g. Paula Heimann, Francis Tustin, Adam Limentani).

I am grateful to Andreas Giannakoulas for many things other than this "gift" introduction to Marion Milner. He was my teacher for over thirty-five years, my mentor. He treated me like a son and considered me as his heir. Sadly, he died on the 30th of April 2021 at the age of eighty-five, before he could see my forthcoming book which I dedicated to him.

DOI: 10.4324/9780429433535-51

Chapter 42

'It Thought Me' – on interviewing Marion Milner

Anne Karpf

Before

When *The Observer* asked me to interview Marion Milner in 1987, I had no idea how eminent she was – indeed I'd never heard of her. It was relatively early in my experience of psychoanalysis, personal and academic, and I hadn't quite shaken off the idea that most psychoanalysts were forbidding figures with Mittel or Eastern European accents and not a tall, elderly and very British woman.

Then I began reading *A Life of One's Own* and *An Experiment in Leisure*. I found both books rather alien at first – a little awkward in style, quite old-fashioned. I couldn't properly make sense of the extracts from Milner's diaries, staccato notes on daily fantasies (almost in real time) from deep within another person's life. It seemed odd to log fleeting thoughts, wisps of ideas, passing sensations in a medium that to me was about permanence and record. But then, I came upon two passages that struck me with such force that it was like being knocked to the ground by a sudden gale.

The first, in a chapter entitled 'The Coming and Going of Delight' in *A Life of One's Own*, was about a gestalt switch in attention from Milner's mind to her body, and the resulting change in consciousness which such a small shift could bring about. It led her to experiment with not trying – doing things intentionally without effort, without frowning or tightening muscles, by restraining her head's tendency to interfere and by standing aside instead. As an inveterate, dogged trier, someone who imbued trying with almost magical powers, I found this shocking and wildly attractive. When, a year later, I learned the Alexander Technique for the first time, I recognised Milner's internal gesture as a cousin of Alexander's encouragement to stop 'end-gaining' – a challenge indeed for a virtuoso end-gainer like me.

The second illuminating moment arrived in the chapter called 'Two Ways of Looking', on narrow versus wide attention. This, the difference between looking selectively and looking as a whole, I got immediately. I remembered an instance when I'd been at university, rushing to the hairdresser to have my hair done up in a Chekhovian chignon in preparation for a nightly performance as Masha in *Three Sisters* at the Playhouse. I looked up and suddenly noticed the tops of the buildings, and they shocked me – I'd forgotten that they existed: I was so tightly bound up in my little pod of business that everything outside of it had been erased. I glimpsed, at that moment of looking, how transactional my engagement with the outside world was – that I riffled it for what I needed for the task in hand, rather than allowing it to envelop and suffuse me.

Both those passages revealed how Milner was putting into words aspects of experience and perception that had mostly existed beneath the radar of language – tiny

DOI: 10.4324/9780429433535-52

corporeal habits of mind and being. Pierre Bourdieu identified *habitus* as our acquired, embodied systems of perception. In a sense, Milner was capturing a psyche-body *habitus* that was so intrinsic, personal and unconsciously produced that it escaped both recognition and discussion. I immediately wanted her to save me.

I arrived at her house, not far from mine, and she took me into a very small study, strewn with papers. I seemed to recall sitting slightly uncomfortably close to her. My interviewing of her was steeped in idealising and longing: I wanted what she had and I wanted her to give it to me, right there and then. When I think back on it, what strikes me now is how contained she was (no 'great woman' grandeur), how calmly she resisted my stabs at projective identification, as she told me of her frustration in not having enough time to paint. It's only now, all these years later, that I realise that she was offering me something more valuable than the idealised analyst I was craving – an image of herself as a woman with struggles of her own.

Here's what I wrote about her at the time (Figure 42.1).[1]

EKEND

THE OBSERVER, SUNDAY 8 FEBRUARY 1987

INTERVIEW

Experiment in leisure

If at first you don't succeed, let go. ANNE KARPF meets Marion Milner, who learned to stop striving.

MARION Milner is a balm to our self-improving culture, where pundits—from Samuel Smiles to Shirley Conran—urge us to try harder and do more, where determination and will-power are prized, and time-wasting thought sinful. Magazines describe in military detail superpeople's lives, each moment purposeful. In this ambience of striving and self-driving, Marion Milner speaks for the richness of acceptance and trust in one's hidden resources, and dares to substitute 'is' for 'ought.'

At 26, in 1926, motivated by a vague feeling of dissatisfaction, she started keeping a diary noting when she was happy and why. Her search launched her on a personal journey which, at 87, she's still on. Virago has recently reprinted Milner's classic first book 'A Life of One's Own,' published in 1934 by Chatto & Windus to enthusiastic reviews by Spender and Auden ('as exciting as a detective story'), and its companion volume 'An Experiment in Leisure.' Both are more pertinent today than ever.

Milner was shocked by the unbecoming traits her self-observation threw up — her dependence on other people's approval, and the way contemplation of spiritual matters would be rudely interrupted by coveting a frock or another woman's success.

Delving deeper, she came upon a dark and violent side of herself, all rage and fear of retribution. Her books were published under the pseudonym of Joanna Field, to avoid frightening the teachers she was interviewing for her research on girls' day schools, which later became her third book, 'The Human Problem in Schools.'

But then she began to make contact with something she called 'a still small voice' or her 'inner fact'—an alive and intuitive part, which seemed to express her real, deep needs beneath the noisy clamourings of her will and social norms. She started to note down, 'I want a chance to play, to do things I choose just for the joy of doing, for no purpose of advancement.' She realised that the more she crammed her life with activity and experience, the more frustrated she felt. And the less she strove after happiness and contentment, the more she seemed to find it.

She recounts honestly and vividly the fear of engulfment she felt when she began to let go, and the extraordinary rewards. 'Why had no one told me that the function of the will might be to stand back, to wait, not to push?'

When she did let go, she found the simplest tasks meaningful, and the hardest, simple. She eloquently describes how darning her stockings, usually a boring chore clumsily executed, became fluid and satisfying when she restrained her interfering brain and allowed her arm to do it. Similarly with ping-pong: having been brought up to believe that trying was the only way of overcoming difficulty, she'd concentrate, frowning with effort, even though it only stiffened her body. When she experimented instead with bodily relaxation, again her arm seemed to know what to do by itself.

Marion Milner today is a distinguished psychoanalyst, a painter who's exhibited in the West End, a prolific writer, a grandmother living in a vine-fringed Hampstead home, yet there's a direct continuity beween the 26-year-old and 87-year-old. She says, 'I've been working on the same things all these years.' A slim, elegant, still woman, she's a self-styled introvert, hankering to return to her painting (her fourth book, in 1950, 'On Not Being Able to Paint' was based on a study of her own drawings), and 'a passionate gardener—I'm grateful to the flowers when they come out.'

Receptive

Her life has been rich and fully lived. At the age of 11 she wanted to become a naturalist (her books are informed by her love of nature). Later she took a degree in psychology and physiology at London University and worked as an industrial psychologist. Her late brother Lord Blackett, made a peer by Harold Wilson, won a Nobel prize for work on the atom.

Her husband, Dennis Milner, was a polymath, a man before his time in many fields. He was an inventor (he built a catamaran in their back garden, trying it out on a lake in north-west London); and

Psychoanalyst Marion Milner wanted 'a chance to play.'

a writer (advocating a citizen's income, an idea later referred to in the Beveridge Report). He discovered a book which he wanted to turn into a play, but he couldn't get the copyright: someone else later managed to, and it became the film 'Kind Hearts and Coronets.' He stood for Parliament as an Independent, but didn't get in. When she first met him, he was planning to walk to Constantinople. He died in 1954.

They had one son, and Milner began writing 'A Life of One's Own' after her son's 6 a.m. feed. He's now a physicist, and one of three pro-vice chancellors at the City University.

Following the publication of her first three books, Marion Milner trained as a psychoanalyst. Having stumbled on her unconscious by herself, she learned professional skills to unlock it with others. She still practises, and her work has been widely published in psychoanalytic journals. Two more of her books will be published over the next six months: a collection of her writings on psychoanalysis, 'The Suppressed Madness of Sane Men' (Tavistock, July), and 'Eternity's Sunrise' (Virago, 6 August), a continuation of 'An Experiment in Leisure.' There will also be a Hogarth paperback reprint, due out next year, of 'The Hands of the Living God' (presently available in hardback, Chatto & Windus, £17.50), her study of the psychoanalysis and the drawings of one of her female patients, illustrated with the patient's drawings, and with a foreword by the eminent psychoanalyst D. W. Winnicott.

Milner remains fascinated by the body-mind relationship. 'At school, you sit and listen, and then you have games, and they're separate. I'm very interested in trying to join up that split. At school we used to sing a hymn "On the Resurrection morning soul and body meet again" — well, you can have that resurrection on any morning.'

And her work speaks directly about gender. She believes that, in a culture which overvalues 'male' qualities, we've forgotten that each of us has male and female aspects. ('It seemed that my male side, unwilling to let go its purposes, had not dared give in to receptiveness, for it feared the loss of its own identity.')

She stresses that we need both, in balance with each other. 'A lot of my work as a psychoanalyst has been with men fighting against their femininity.' In this maelstrom age, Marion Milner gentles us back to equilibrium.

01-236 1231

Figure 42.1 Experiment in Leisure (Interview with Marion Milner), by Anne Karpf, *The Observer*. February 3rd, 1987.

After

I bumped into Marion Milner at least once – or perhaps twice? My memory fails – after my article was published, outside the local greengrocer's. We chatted and she told me about a family matter that was vexing her. I wasn't ready for this – I still needed her to be perfect and, once again, the notion of her wrestling with a domestic problem unsettled me. It was only when I wrote her obituary for *The Guardian* eleven years later (Karpf, 1998) and spoke to the writer Margaret Walters about her that I learned of her astonishing capacity to make new friendships, including with a number of younger people, throughout her life. And so I entertained another, this time retrospective, fantasy: that I might have become one of them.

Later, when I took up an academic post, I read *On Not Being Able to Paint* and used it in my teaching: it helped me to look and see better. And when I read Winnicott, it was clear that Milner shared not just a professional realm with him but also an imaginative one – both of them so curious, so delighted in discovering ways of living as creatively, zestfully and openly as possible, but so very English too.

Perhaps, the most powerful thing that Marion Milner said to me in the interview was her description of having an idea: 'It thought me', she said. This completely startled me, although I knew exactly what she meant – the way that ideas arrived almost of their own volition, so that it seemed hubristic to claim ownership of them: all one needed was to create the right conditions, in which they could flourish. In *The Suppressed Madness of Sane Men*, this was rendered as 'it thinks you', part of a reflection on creative surrender.

OBITUARIES 21

Journey to the centre of the mind

Figure 42.2 Journey to the Centre of the Mind, Marion Milner Obituary by Anne Karpf, *The Guardian*, June 8th 1988 (photo by Brenda Prince).

All this time later, I understand more why I was discomfited by Milner's ideas, even while I found them seductive. With so much family trauma still to work through, surrendering – creatively or not – felt to me not just impossible but indeed dangerous: there were unexploded bombs from the second world war lying in wait that needed to be carefully detonated first. 'The capacity to bear the tensions of doubt and of unsatisfied need' – I was a long way from that then but, over time, Milner's ideas became a part of my emotional grammar and my own way of looking.

Now, nearly thirty-five years after I met her, I'm starting to write about how trauma and trying are linked, about how the wider vision can get constricted and attenuated in the process. And in some small part of my being, I'm hoping that Marion Milner can think me.

Note

1 Karpf, A., February 2, 1987. 'Experiment in Leisure'. *The Observer;* Karpf, A., June 3, 1998. 'Marion Milner: Journey to the centre of the mind'. *The Guardian,* https://www.newspapers.com/clip/45758312/the-guardian/. With thanks to Guardian News & Media Ltd 2022 for permission to reproduce these newspaper cuttings.

Epilogue

Marion Milner: 'A mind becoming more aware of itself'

Joan Raphael-Leff

The book you hold in your hand celebrates Marion Milner's 'marks on paper'.

The many chapters have illustrated her particular 'Lines of Development'—the flexible evolution of her ideas, theory, and practice 'over the decades'. The psychoanalytic, artistic, and literary legacy of Milner's interdisciplinary 'gifts in word and imagery' is exceptional. No Milnerean school exists but as interest burgeons since revival of her books the hallmark of this budding tradition is surely *receptivity*—openness to the unexpected.

These forty-two chapters, written by over fifty readers in response to Marion Milner's pioneering work, reverberate across a spectrum of professional fields—psychoanalysis, educational, and organisational psychology, management theory, art therapy, and art criticism, mindfulness and spirituality.

As you read these final pages, you will have come to know Milner well, having accompanied her over almost ten-decades of her personal journey from self-admitted compliance to authenticity—laboriously devising investigatory experiments to rediscover what she called the joys of 'primary madness' while tenaciously working to shed her tendency to 'compulsive' agreement with an ascribed identity that inhibited her spontaneity.

Her scrupulously honest self-examination means that unlike more reticent writers, we readers also have been party to Marion Milner's struggle - doubts, eccentricities and whims. Undoubtedly, her candid self-questioning and generous exposure of self-referential findings is doubly courageous within a profession that guards its privacy so closely.

And it is a rich-veined and lively exposure!

Reading about her daily 'finds' while psychically beach-combing, we readers can actually watch her desires and foibles wriggling in the ingenious methodological 'nets' she casts. Her determination to capture and string together those 'beads' of emotionally charged salient moments runs like a multicoloured thread from her earliest childhood notebooks through her diaries and scientific papers, monographs and many books—self-reflection fuelled by an unquenchable curiosity and incessant striving to tap that 'force by which one is lived'.

Marion Milner's eight volumes and many essays are thus consistently inscribed with her own singular signature—what I might term an 'unwavering wavering' driven by her questioning spirit and adventurous capacity for open-ended research. Remarkably she both maintains the frame yet transcends it, always intent on unfettered expression of interpenetrating differences. And always pushing the boundaries.

Early explorations

How do we do justice to her spectacular capacity for self-discovery?

From childhood she always wrote and researched. Having begun a new diary in her twenties, as a young woman in her thirties she produced an account of the break she took from mothering to seek 'a life of her own'. She found to her surprise that the netting of 'each day's catch of happiness' actually enhanced her fine-tuned capacity for observation, thereby increasing the sensorial experience of embodiment by providing 'a multitude of ways of perceiving it' (1934, p. 47). Three years later, still under the pseudonym Joanna Field, she published more about the 'inner fires' she discovered during her experimentations with leisure. Through automatic writing she not only dug deep, enlisting 'the voice of the blood and the bones' but came to tap the 'song' within them.

But paradoxically, what was to become a lifelong reappraisal of her 'finds' ultimately yielded a contradictory discovery—awareness of her mind's pluripotentiality, but also the sobering realisation of its 'navel' of un(re)capturable existence.

Thus, to some readers, Milner epitomises the paradox of a psychoanalyst's rigorous self-analysis, beginning with Freud's own. Yet she persists with her courageous attempts to systematically ensnare (and publish) the inaccessible in her internal world, while all the while simultaneously aware of the tenaciously unknowable and incommunicable core of unconscious life.

Some readers may have found the driven nature of her relentless efforts irksome. Her innovative yet repetitive endeavour to challenge the insubordination of the Unconscious. Her commitment to make it manifest itself, and to waylay its incomprehensibility, which also necessitated subversive attempts to evade the anxieties this investigative process unleashed in her.

Other readers may have felt caught off-balance by some of Milner's high vaulting. The imaginative leaps of retroactive free-associations in pursuit of unknown connections of her innermost life.

But it is Milner's inventiveness that most readers admire. Sharing her fascination with solving the elusive mystery of the mysterious forces that propel us they identify with her desire to find 'the familiar in the unfamiliar', and relish her ever-new ingenious tricks to ambush hidden meanings, to generate something fresh through a process of psychic creativity. Many hope like her, to 'slough off' an obsolete 'skin' of family ascriptions, and the contorting influences of education and mass-produced ideals .

So, this book you hold is not one but many books—resonating with the personal 'answering activity' of many readers. But in common, all contributors and readers agree that Milner *pushes the limits.*

Middle age

Her consistent integration of opposites is apparent when once again, in middle-age, she re-adjusts her previous methods to break down 'old patterns in order that new might come' (1950, p. 87). Now she employs the 'contemplative action' of free drawing while using 'every bit of willpower' to *stop* using willpower (p. 83). Again, she is cognisant of the 'unfree' aspect of even 'free'-association, while trying to free her hands to communicate-at- random even as she doodles—while the analytic part of her mind watches, making 'running comments' (p. 84).

But Marion Milner does not minimise the dangers of hacking into the unconscious. Aware of her own 'terror of the unknown', she realises she fears not only the discovery of her hatred but also the 'primitive ruthlessness of love'. Her doodles conjure up both magically-fulfilled destructive cannibalistic wishes, and intolerable guilt/remorse/pain. Nonetheless, she makes an effort to avoid explicit and permanent branding, sensing that such an act of 'cowardice' may lead to her *premature naming.* She fears that such a 'desperate attempt to impose a rhythm and coherent pattern on a chaos of feeling' (1950, p. 150) may promote 'a sense of false certainty, a compulsive and deceptive sanity, a tyrannical victory of common sense' (1950, p. 89) [akin to what her supervisee Christopher Bollas was to term 'Normotic illness'].

And so she waits as she wavers. To my mind these 'unwavering wave-ring' machinations in her many-layered exploratory books create an oxymoron I am tempted to term 'solid spray'. *An arrested dynamic*—a freeze-framed 'splash' seized by her many imaginative 'non-planned, non-willed' efforts to expose a 'spontaneous ordering of forces' (1950, p. 83).

Later

Moreover, in her sixties, while writing up the very long analysis of her patient 'Susan', and encouraged by emotional resonances to Susan's many hundreds of drawings, Milner is increasingly aware of drawing as 'a base for communication' (1969, p. 240). It can serve as a 'bridge' and a reparative, placating means of expression as well as a defensive sublimation of an urge to kill, with the potentiality for fertilising creative interplay between these (1969, pp. 241–242).

Having long facilitated opportunities for her patients' expression of their rage, eventually, aged eighty-three, Milner begins to regain access to her own 'stone throwing' self. In her old age she ascribes the inhibition of her aggressive inner voice to her six-year-old self's compliance with her mother's injunction: the warning not to let her tongue speak its truth 'lest it offend'.

As time passes, overcoming this self-imposed reserve necessitates disentangling conflated 'me and not-me', inner and outer. In addition to the secondary self-surrender she has chosen as a ruse, Milner now strives to undo her obedient-self's submissive 'compulsive agreement tendency'. Finally, she can cajole her unknown 'satanic rebellious self' to emerge.

Once again she reworks an 'impotent and boundless rage' against the distorting power of the imperious education which she feels wiped out all sense of her own authentic identity ('off with her head!'). Rather than teach her how to know what she herself 'really wanted' it schooled her to accept what others wanted, believing it was her own wish (1987a, p. 152). No wonder she explored both sides of the argument when studying 'the human problem in schools' (1938). But now, contrary to her previous conclusion that fundamentally the battle is between accepting the conventional view of reality and an injunction on her own favourite occupation of 'remaking' it to have it under her control (1950, p. 156), as an octogenarian Milner discovers one of the most salient facts of her defendedness: *her own idealised remaking of her controlling mother.* My reading is that this revelation seems to release her as once again, through novel forms of free-floating states of non-attentive attention, she braves internal terrors to probe this new unknown—speaking her unspoken rage.

Beyond constraints of time and clucking queen hens, she can suspend old equilateral anxieties—both her earlier 'panic dread of being overwhelmed by the boundless sea of what was not myself' (1934, p. 165)—and the fear of discovering what *was* herself, later defined as 'terror that a split-off and angrily rebellious bit [of myself] would emerge with disastrous results' (2012, p. 266).

Henceforth, in her last years of life she is freer to unleash the 'wildness of the waves' of her imagination more fully by overcoming the fear of annihilation – of being submerged and drowning or pulled out of her depth into alien domains.

Wildness of the waves

Her brave tenacity is what we readers so admire in Marion Milner.

A relentless resolve to evoke what she does not yet know in herself, her commitment to listen to the unheard in the polyphony/cacophony of voices within, to feel unknown passions and become aware of the untameable dissonance of inconsistent secrets, unruly chaos, wily concealment…

Back in her middle years, Marion Milner's declared mode of combatting fear of the regressive 'plunge' into the void of non-differentiation (which posed a threat to herself as a 'known entity') resided in a submissive gesture of silently saying: "I know nothing, have nothing, want nothing". Remembering how in 1957 Ehrenzweig had called her technique 'creative surrender', thirty years later, in her last book she acknowledges that it led to an 'enormous expansion of perception and of spirit' (2012, p. 664). But fearful she will die on its completion, superstition prevents her from bringing 'Bothered by Alligators' to an end.

Later still

As a nonagenarian, she finds another technique.

Re-discovering forgotten in a drawer, the old diary she had kept during her son's childhood (ages 2–6) and his own handwritten book of stories and accompanying illustrations now inspire her try and access her own 'darkly hidden powers' through left handed doodling.

Mother-Marion notes John's own 'special kind of surrender'—the four-year-old's preoccupation with water and immense joy at *letting* 'a wave just do what it liked with him' (p. 290).

Examining his story book she wonders:

> …could it be that he already knew about the source of life, *the water of life*, which lies, for each of us, deep down below our common-sense everyday awareness?
>
> (p. 178, my italics).

But curiously, she fails to recall how when she was a little girl, she herself wrote an even more daring underwater narrative, about 'the beautiful land where the sea nymphs play' not *in* the waves but *below* them, right down at the bottom of the sea (The Golden Cockle-Shell story written at the seaside because the sea always made her 'want to write stories').

So, in her late nineties, after everyone before her has gone, Marion Milner refinds/finds out about the originairy and restorative aspects of *water*.

In the later years of her painstaking analysis of Susan, Milner had assiduously traced her patient's preoccupation with the theme of water. Now, she finds her own redemption in a *watery homecoming*—wallowing in the prelapsarian womb's amnion before the breaking of waters, and greeting the splash of babtismal 'living water' at the 'innermost being' of religion…

She stops recycling.

Having sucked on the inexhaustible teat of her son's nursery-school book and retrospectively examined her own past doodles, and having torn and cut up her old paintings to create new collages—redemption is no longer ascribed to the blade ('sword of a bullfighter'). Henceforth, the instrument of 'true fertility of the imaginative mind' sought since her thirties is reframed as *a liquid*. She recalls how in August 1930, she sat in a German forest: 'Draining sensation to its depths, wave after wave of delight flowing through every cell of my body' (2012, p. 222).

She now feels freer to go beyond the experience of waves. She is ready to trawl dangerous waters, and to encounter momentary annihilation while basking in the safety of a Red Sea gap on the ocean floor. An intermittent borderlessness of potential *self-obliteration* that oscillates with *self-finding*, the essence of exploration in all her books.

So, sixty-seven years later, far from the sea, Marion lies supported by the floor in her landlocked Provost Road home in London, trusting herself to the 'hidden force' beneath her floorboards, naming her body-parts while doing her 'words made flesh' exercise. In this, her penultimate year, she fully experiences the non-differentiating interchange as 'the bottom of the sea comes to the top' [the caption she'd given part three of *An Experiment in Leisure*].

Having worked through maternal-guilt regarding her son, and released herself from the spectre of her own infantile 'cannibalism' at the breast, she seems to gain strength through her newfound aggressive energy, no longer in the restraining grip of her mother's disapproval,. Despite failing vision and hearing, feeling free to relish aloneness at the end of cherished companionship, Milner plans her funeral ('no God') imagining a death embraced, not inflicted.

Her last breath was drawn, sitting upright in bed working to complete the unfinished manuscript of *Bothered by Aligators*.

'Answering activity'

We book-readers each resonate with what is salient to ourselves.

As you end this book, you too will have gleaned your own conclusions about Marion Milner's extraordinary voyage of self-discovery.

Mine stem from a lifelong attraction to the wonderous-perilous ocean. The metaphorical underworld pull of the sea and revealing nature of braving its unpredictable waves: My own way alternates inactive wonder with confrontation. Relishing both the sustained stillness of prolonged coral-reef-gazing and the challenge of plunging through formidable crashers by thrusting my body just above the powerful undercurrent.

Intuitively, I see Milner's way as *simultaneous navigation of water and shore*, seeking creative 'fusion' in immersion, while yet remaining separate—'chilling' within the drained inter-tidal space of emptiness between contrary forces of recurrent high tide and low.

Reading her written 'splashes' from amniotic womb unto watery end, it seems to me that her life's voyage—seeking, learning, forgetting, and re-finding—harbours a secret:

Unbeknownst to her Marion Milner was part fish—a 'sea-maid'.

To me it is implied from her earliest 'memory' of hanging naked off the hook of her father's fish-weighing scale suspended from the ceiling; through unremembered identifications with the protagonist of a story she herself wrote in childhood about cockle-sized Mossie 'able to swim and to breathe underwater'; to her adult narratives of curious 'shoals of fishes' 'following their noses'; her late negotiation of infested waters all the way to reconnection of a 'civilised' part of herself with the 'water magic' of a wild split-off lake-sprite 'Undine' self.

Her life's quest ended, Milner's near-death breakthrough brings her full circle releasing an eternal oceanic feeling within the primordial 'gap'.

I believe that it is on this 'sea-shore of endless worlds' where 'children play' that she finally regains her gills.

Bibliography

Alvarez, A. (1976). The clinician's Debt to Winnicott. *Journal Child Psychotherapy*, 22(3): 377–382.

——— (2018). *The Role of Emotion in Thinking: The Problem of Deficits in the Internal Object*. Paper presented at Northern Ireland Association for the Study of Psychoanalysis, Belfast (October 13th 2018).

Anderson, W. J. (1981). (Unpublished) transcript of Anderson's interviews with Marion Milner.

——— (2014). How D. W. Winnicott conducted psychoanalysis. *Psychoanalytic Psychology*, 31: 375–395.

——— (2015). D. W. Winnicott's constant search for the life that feels real. In: M. B. Spelman & F. Thomson-Salo (Eds.), *The Winnicott Tradition: Lines of Development—Evolution of Theory and Practice over the Decades* (pp. 19–38). London: Karnac Books.

Augenfeld, F. (1974). Letter to Hans Lobner. 8th February. Cited in Michael Molnar (1992). Notes and References, p. 278. In Sigmund Freud, *The Diary of Sigmund Freud: 1929–1939. A Record of the Final Decade*. Michael Molnar (Ed. and Trans.) (pp. 271–308). New York: Charles Scribner's Sons, and Toronto: Maxwell Macmillan Canada, and New York: Maxwell Macmillan International / Maxwell Publishing Company, Maxwell Communication Group of Companies.

Balint, A. (1933). Une forme spécifique de la peur infantile. *Le Coq-Héron*, 147(1): 40–42, 1997.

Bates, M. J. (Ed.) (1990). *Wallace Stevens: Opus Posthumous*. New York: Vintage Books.

Benjamin, J. (2004). Beyond doer and done to: An intersubjective view of thirdness. *The Psychoanalytic Quarterly*, 73(1): 5–46.

Bertolini, M. (2016). Essere nel lavorio psicofisico presimbolico. In: A. Giannakoulas & F. Neri Bertolini (Eds.), *Continuità dell'essere, crollo e oltre il crollo*. Milan: FrancoAngeli.

Bezoari, M., & Ferro, A. (1992). The oscillation meanings <---> affects in the analytic couple at work. *Rivista Di Psiconalisi*, 38: 380–402.

——— (1999). The dream within field theory: Functional aggregates and narrations. *Journal of Melanie Klein and Object Relations*, 17(2): 333–348.

Bion, W. R. (1962). *Learning from Experience*. London: Heinemann.

——— (1967). Notes on memory and desire. In: C. Mawson (Ed.), *The Complete Works of W.R. Bion* (vol. VI, p. 203). London: Karnac, 2014.

——— (1977). Learning from experience. In: *Seven Servants: Four Works by Wilfred R Bion*. New York: Jason Aronson, Inc.

——— (1990). *Brazilian Lectures: 1973 São Paulo and 1974 Rio de Janeiro/São Paulo*. London: Karnac Books.

Birksted-Breen, D., & Flanders, S. (2010). General introduction. In: D. Birksted-Breen, S. Flanders & A. Gibeault (Eds.), *Reading French Psychoanalysis* (pp. 1–51). London: Routledge.

Bleger, J. (1967). Psycho-analysis of the psycho-analytic frame. *The International Journal of Psychoanalysis*, 48: 511–519.

Bloom, H. (1973). *The Anxiety of Influence: A Theory of Poetry* (2nd ed.). New York and Oxford: Oxford University Press.

——— (1997). *The Anxiety of Influence.* Oxford: Oxford University Press (Original work published 1975).

——— (2011). *The Anatomy of Influence: Literature as a Way of Life.* New Haven and London: Yale University Press.

Bollas C. (1987a). *The Shadow of the Object.* London: Free Association Books.

——— (1987b). 'The transformational object', In: *The Shadow of the Object: Psychoanalysis of the Unthought Known.* New York: Columbia University Press.

——— (2011a). Normotic illness. *The Christopher Bollas Reader.* New York: Routledge.

——— (2011b). The destiny drive. In: *The Christopher Bollas Reader* (pp. 37–56). London and New York: Routledge.

——— (2015a). *When the Sun Bursts: The Enigma of Schizophrenia.* New Haven, CT: Yale University Press.

——— (2015b). *A Conversation with Christopher Bollas.* Yale Books Podcast.

——— (2018). Psychoanalysis in the age of bewilderment: On the return of the oppressed. *International Journal of Psychoanalysis*, 96: 535–551. doi:10. 1111/1745–8315. 12352

Botella, C., & Botella, S. (2005). *The Work of Psychic Figurability. Mental States without Representation.* Ed. Dana Birksted-Breen. London and New York: Routledge.

Bourdieu, P. (2014). *The Logic of Practice.* Trans. from the French by R. Nice, 1992. Cambridge: Polity Press.

Bowlby, J. (1960). Separation anxiety. *The International Journal of Psychoanalysis*, 41: 89–113.

Caldwell, L. (Ed.) (2000). *Art, Creativity, Living.* London: Karnac books.

Coltart, N. (1993). *Slouching Towards the Bethlehem...And Further Psychoanalytic Explorations.* London: Free Association Books.

Coltart, N. (1986). 'Slouching towards Bethlehem...or thinking the unthinkable in psychoanalysis.' In: *Slouching Towards Bethlehem and Further Psychoanalytic Explorations.* London: Free Association Books, 1993.

Collovà, M. (2018). The setting as a locus of possible transformations. In: A. Ferro (Ed.), *Contemporary Bionian Theory and Technique in Psychoanalysis* (pp. 1–43). Abingdon and New York: Routledge.

Davies, Bryony (2019). *Sigmund Freud's Collection: Highlights from the Freud Museum London.* London: Freud Museum London.

Davis, M., & Wallbridge, D. (1991). *Boundary and Space: An Introduction to the Work of D. W. Winnicott.* London: Karnac.

Derrida, J. (1978). *The Truth in Painting.* Chicago/London: University of Chicago, 1987.

Di Benedetto, A. (2005). *Before Words: Psychoanalytic Listening to the Unsaid Through the Medium of Art.* New York: Free Associations.

Donnet, J. (2001). From the fundamental rule to the analysing situation. *The International Journal of Psychoanalysis*, 82(1): 129–140.

Dragstedt, N. R. (1998). Creative illusions: The theoretical and clinical work of Marion Milner. *Journal of Melanie Klein and Object Relations*, 16: 425–536.

Eigen, M. (1983). Dual union or undifferentiation? A critique of Marion Milner's view of the sense of psychic creativeness. *International Review of Psycho-Analysis*, 10: 415–428.

——— (1993). *The Electrified Tightrope.* Ed. A Phillips. London: Routledge.

——— (2016). *Image, Sense, Infinities and Everyday Life.* London: Routledge.

——— (2017). *The Therapy Womb.* Karnacology. New York and London: Routledge.

Eliot, T. S. (2002). *Collected Poems: 1909–1962.* London: Faber and Faber.

Ellmann, M. (2011). "New introduction, the thing that lives us", In: Marion Milner (Ed.), *An Experiment in Leisure.* New York and London: Routledge.

Ehrenzweig, A. (1967). *The Hidden Order of Art*. London: Weidenfeld and Nicholson; Berkeley: University of California Press, 1971.

Ehrenzweig, A. (1971). *The Hidden Order of Art*. Berkeley: University of California Press.

Emde, R. N. (1981). Changing models of infancy and the nature of early development: Remodeling the foundation. *Journal of the American Psychoanalytic Association*, 29: 179–219.

Ernaux, A. (2020). *The Years*. Fitzcarraldo Editions.

Everett, G. (1988). Hopkins on "Inscape" and "Instress". Retrieved from *The Victorian Web* website: victorianweb.org/authors/hokins/hopkins1.html

Feit Diehl, J. (Ed.) (2005). *On Louise Glück*. Ann Arbor: The University of Michigan Press.

Ferro, A. (1992). Two authors in search of characters: The relationship, the field, the story. *Rivista Di Psiconalisi*, 38: 44–90.

Ferro, A. (1999). *The Bi-Personal Field: Experiences in Child Analysis*. London; New York: Routledge.

——— (2002). Narrative derivatives of alpha elements: Clinical implications. *International Forum of Psychoanalysis*, 11(3): 184–187. doi:10.1080/080370602760392737

——— (2004). *Seeds of Illness and Seeds of Recovery: The Genesis of Suffering and the Role of Psychoanalysis*. New York: Brunner-Routledge.

——— (2005). Which reality in the psychoanalytic session? *The Psychoanalytic Quarterly*, 74: 421–442.

——— (2006a). *Psychoanalysis as Therapy and Storytelling*. London; New York: Routledge.

——— (2006b). Trauma, reverie, and the field. *The Psychoanalytic Quarterly*, 75: 1045–1056.

——— (2009a). *Mind Works: Technique and Creativity in Psychoanalysis* (P. Slotkin, Trans.). Hove and New York: Routledge.

——— (2009b). Transformations in dreaming and characters in the psychoanalytic field. *International Journal of Psycho-Analysis*, 90: 209–230.

——— (2011). *Avoiding Emotions, Living Emotions* (I. Harvey, Trans.). London and New York: Routledge.

——— (2018). Dream model of the mind (I. Harvey, Trans.). In: A. Ferro (Ed.), *Comtemporary Bionian Theory and Technique in Psychoanalysis* (pp. 44–148). Oxon and New York: Routledge.

Ferro, A., & Basile, R. (Eds.) (2009). *The Analytic Field: A Clinical Concept*. London: Karnac.

Ferro, A., & Bezoari, M. (1992). From a play between "parts" to transformations in the couple: Psychoanalysis in a bipersonal field (J. Denton, Trans.). In: L. Nissim Momigliano & A. Robutti (Eds.), *Shared Experience The Psychoanalytic Dialogue*. London and New York: Karnac.

Ferro, A., & Civitarese, G. (Eds.) (2015). *The Analytic Field And Its Transformations*. London: Routledge.

Fichtl, P. (n.d.). Personal communication to Jack J. Spector. n.d. Cited in Jack J. Spector (1972). *The Aesthetics of Freud: A Study in Psychoanalysis and Art* (p. 15). New York: Praeger Publishers.

Field, J. [pseudonym of Marion Milner]. (1934). *A Life of One's Own*. London: Chatto & Windus. London: Virago, 1986.

——— (1950). *On Not Being Able to Paint*. London: William Heinemann. 2nd edition: London: International Universities Press, 1957. Los Angeles: Jeremy P. Tarcher, 1983. London: Virago, 1986. Second edition: Routledge: London & New York 1987 (Foreword by Anna Freud). Reprinted London & New York: Routledge, 2010, The New Library of Psychoanalysis Teaching Series, (Series Editor, Emma Letley; new introduction by Janet Sayers).

——— (Marion Milner) (1986). *An Experiment in Leisure* (First published 1937 Chatto & Windus). London: Virago.

Fielding, J., & Newman, A. (1988). Editorial. *Winnicott Studies*, *3*: 3.

FLa Fontaine, J. (1678). Les animaux maladies de la peste, Fable 1, *livre VII dans le deuxième recueil des Fables de La Fontaine.*
Follett, M. P. (1924). *Creative Experience.* London: Longman.
Freud, A. (1950). Foreword (pp. xiii–xv). In. Milner, 1950.
——— (1967). About losing and being lost. *The Psychoanalytic Study of the Child*, 22: 9–19.
Freud, S. (1896). The letter to Wilhelm Fliess dated December 6, 1896. In: J. Masson (Ed.), *The Complete Letters of Sigmund Freud to Wilhelm Fliess 1887–1904* (p. 207). London: The Belknap Press of Harvard University Press 1985.
——— (1900). *The Interpretation of Dreams*, ch.7, SE 5, pp. 538–549.
——— (1909). *Analysis of a Phobia in a Five-year-old Boy*, SE 10, pp. 3–152.
——— (1914). *The Moses of Michelangelo*, SE 13, pp. 211–238.
——— (1912). *Recommendations to Physicians Practising Psycho-Analysis*, SE 12, pp. 109–120.
——— (1914). *On Narcissism: An Introduction.* SE 14, pp. 76–77.
——— (1915a). *The Unconscious*, SE 14, pp. 161–215.
——— (1915b). *Instincts and their Vicissitudes,* SE 14, pp. 111–140.
——— (1923). *The Ego and the Id*, SE 19, pp. 3–63.
——— (1938). *An Outline of Psycho-Analysis*, SE, 23, pp. 139–208.
Fuller, P. (1988). *Art and Psychoanalysis* (2nd ed.). London: Hogarth Press. Original edition 1980.
Gamwell, Lynn (1989). The origins of Freud's antiquities collection. In: Lynn Gamwell and Richard Wells (Eds.), *Sigmund Freud and Art: His Personal Collection of Antiquities* (pp. 21–32). London: Thames and Hudson, and Binghamton; New York: State University of New York, and London: Freud Museum.
Giannakoulas, A. (2015). Creative processes and artistic creation. In: G. Saragnano & C. Seulin (Eds.), *Playing and Reality Revisited.* London: Karnac.
Gillespie, S. (1988). Marion. *Winnicott Studies*, 3: 61–62.
Gillespie, W. (1988). Mrs Marion Milner. *Winnicott Studies*, 3: 60.
Glover, N., (2009). *Psychoanalytic Aesthetics: An Introduction to the British School.* London: Karnac Books.
Gombrich, E. (1954). Psychoanalysis and the History of Art. *The International Journal of Physoanalysis*, 35: 401–411.
Green, A. (1998). The primordial mind and the work of the negative. In: P. Bion Talamo, F. Borgogno & S. A. Merciai (Eds.), *W.R. Bion: Between Past and Future* (pp. 108–128). London: Karnac.
——— (2011). The bifurcation of psychoanalysis: Lacan and Winnicott. In L. Kirshner (Ed.), *Between Winnicott and Lacan* (pp. 29–50). NY: Routledge.
Harris Williams, M. (1985). The Tiger and 'O'. *Free Associations*, 1B, 33–56.
——— (1998). The aesthetic perspective in the work of Donald Meltzer. *Journal of Melanie Klein and Object Relations*, 16(2): 209–218.
——— (1999). Psychoanalysis: An art or a science? A review of the implications of the theory of Bion and Meltzer. *British Journal of Psychotherapy*, 16(2): 127–135.
——— (2005a). The three vertices: Science, art, religion. *British Journal of Psychotherapy*, 21(3): 429–442.
——— (2005b). *The Vale of Soul Making: The Post Kleinian Model of the Mind and Its Poetic Origins.* London and New York: Karnac.
——— (2009a). Genesis of the 'aesthetic conflict'. Retrieved from http:// my web. tiscali.co.uk/ megharriswilliams/hmt/ DonaldMeltzer.htm
——— (2009b). An intoduction to the work and thinking of Donald Meltzer. Retrieved from artlit.info - writings and artwork website.
——— (2009c). Psychoanalysis as an art form. *British Journal of Psychotherapy*, 25(3): 381–392.
——— (2010a). *The Aesthetic Development: The Poetic Spirit of Psychoanalysis. Essays on Bion, Meltzer, Keats.* London: Karnac Books Ltd.

——— (2010b). *Bion's Dream: A Reading of the Autobiographies*. London: Karnac.

Hart, M. (2003). Conversations at the frontier of dreaming By Thomas H. Ogden. Northvale, NJ and London: Jason Aronson, Inc. pp. 255. 1st edn. 20. *International Journal of Psycho-Analysis*, 84(3): 769–772.

Heaney, S. (1996). *The Spirit Level*. London: Faber and Faber.

Heimann, P (1950). 'On counter-transference', *The International Journal of Psychoanalysis*, 31: 81, 84.

Hernandez, M., & Giannakoulas, A. (2001). On the construction of potential space. In: M. Bertolini, A. Giannakoulas & M. Hernandez (Eds.), *Squiggles and Spaces* (vol. 1, pp. 146–163). London: Whurr.

Hopkins, L. (1998). D. W. Winnicott's analysis of Masud Khan: A preliminary study of failures of object usage. *Contemporary Psychoanalysis*, 34: 5–47.

Hopkins, L. B. (2004). 'Red shoes, untapped madness, and Winnicott on the cross: An interview with Marion Milner.' *The Annual of Psychoanalysis*, 32: 233–243.

Hopkins, L. (2006). *False Self: The Life of Masud Khan*. New York: Other Press.

Hughes, J. M. (1989). *Reshaping the Psychoanalytic Domain: The Work of Melanie Klein, W.R.D. Fairbairn, and D.W. Winnicott*. Berkeley: University of California Press.

James, M. (1991). Lecture on "Has Winnicott Become a Winnicottian? The Importance of Psychiatry". The Squiggle Foundation, Primrose Hill, London, at the Primrose Hill Community Centre, Primrose Hill, London, 16th February.

Janet, P. (1889). *L'automatisme Psychologique*. Paris: Felix Alcan.

Jones, E. (1916). The Theory of Symbolism in *Papers on Psychoanalysis*. London: Bailliere Tindall & Cox, 1948.

——— (1918). The theory of symbolism. *British Journal of Psychology*, 9: 181–229.

——— (1980). *Sigmund Freud. Life and Work*. London: Hogarth Press.

Karpf, A. (February 2, 1987). 'Experiment in leisure'. *The Observer*.

——— (June 3, 1998). 'Marion Milner: Journey to the centre of the mind'. *The Guardian*. https://www.newspapers.com/clip/45758312/the-guardian/

Kahr, Brett (1985a). Interview with Marion Milner, 16th February.

——— (1985b). Interview with Margaret Little, 25th May.

——— (1994). R.D. Laing's Missing Tooth: Schizophrenia and Bodily Disintegration. *Journal of the Society for Existential Analysis*, 4: 64–79.

——— (2021a). *Winnicott's* Anni Horribiles*: The Creation of 'Hate in the Counter-Transference'*. London: Routledge / Taylor and Francis Group, and Abingdon, Oxfordshire: Routledge / Taylor and Francis Group. [In Press].

——— (2021b). *The Musical Psychoanalyst: From Freud's Ambivalence to Winnicott's Embrace*. [In Preparation].

Keats, J. (2002). *Selected Letters*. Cambridge: Harvard University Press.

Khoroche, P. (2008). *Ben Nicholson: Drawings and Painted Reliefs*. Aldershot, Hampshire; Burlingtin, Vermont: Lund Humphries.

King, P. & Steiner, R. Eds. (1991). *The Freud-Klein Controversies 1941–45*. London: Routledge.

Kite, S. (2009). *Adrian Stokes: An Architectonic Eye*. London: Legenda.

Kleimberg, L. (2018). Illusiory dramatization. The fiction between material truth and historical truth. *Bulletin of The British Psychoanalytical Society*. Spanish version, Revista Peruana de Psicoanálisis N0 24, 2019 Sociedad Peruana de Psicoanalisis.

——— (2019). Illusiory dramatization. The fiction between material truth and historical truth. *Bulletin of The British Psychoanalytical Society*. Revista Peruana de Psicoanálisis N0 24 Diciembre 2019 Sociedad Peruana de Psicoanalisis

Klein, M. (1926). Infant analysis. *International Journal of Psychoanalysis*, 7: 31–63.

——— (1930). The importance of symbol-formation in the development of the ego. *International Journal of Psychoanalysis*, 11: 24–39. In: M. Klein, P. Heimann, & R. Money-Kyrle (Eds.) (1955). Reprinted 1985. *New Directions in Psychoanalysis*. London: Karnac books.

——— (1932). *The Psycho-Analysis of Children* (Alix Strachey, trans.). London: Hogarth Press and the Institute of Psycho-Analysis.

——— (1946). Notes on some schizoid mechanisms. *The International Journal of Psycho-Analysis*, 27: 99–110.

——— (1948). *Contributions to Psycho-Analysis: 1921-1945*. London: Hogarth Press and the Institute of Psycho-Analysis.

——— (1961). *Narrative of a Child Analysis: The Conduct of the Psycho-Analysis of Children as Seen in the Treatment of a Ten Year Old Boy*. London: Hogarth Press and the Institute of Psycho-Analysis.

Klein, Melanie, & Riviere, Joan (1937). *Love, Hate and Reparation: Two Lectures*. London: Leonard and Virginia Woolf at the Hogarth Press, and the Institute of Psycho-Analysis.

Kohon, G. (1986). *The British School of Psychoanalysis: The Independent Tradition*. New Haven, CT: Yale University Press.

Laing, Ronald D. (1961). *The Self and Others: Further Studies in Sanity and Madness*. London: Tavistock Publications.

Laing, Ronald D., & Cooper, David G. (1964). *Reason and Violence: A Decade of Sartre's Philosophy. 1950-1960*. London: Tavistock Publications.

Langer, S. K. (1951). *Philosophy in A New Key: A Study in the Symbolism of Reason, Rite, and Art* (2nd ed.). New York; Toronto: The New American Library.

Larkin, P. (1988). *Collected Poems*. London: Faber and Faber.

Lawrence, D. H. (1929). *Pansies*. London: Martin Secker.

——— (1950). *Selected Poems*. London: Penguin.

Letley, E. (2014). *Marion Milner: The Life*. London: Routledge.

——— (2015). 'People who think in pictures': The continuing dialogue between Marion Milner and Donald Winnicott in Bothered by Alligators. In: Margaret Boyle Spelman & Frances Thomson-Salo (Eds.), *The Winnicott Tradition: Lines of Development. Evolution of Theory and Practice Over the Decades*. London: Karnac.

Leunig, M. (12th January, 2019). Dear Murray darling, letter. *The Age*.

Little, M. (1985). Winnicott working in areas where psychotic anxieties predominate. *Free Associations*, 3: 9–42.

Luepnitz, D. A. (1990). Unpublished transcript of Luepnitz's interview with Marion Milner.

Maclagan, D. (1992). Between psychoanalysis and surrealism: The collaboration between Grace Pailthorpe and Reuben Mednikoff. *Free Associations*, 3: 33–50.

MacNeice, L. (2015). *Collected Poems*. London: Faber and Faber.

Marks, L. (2014). Creative surrender: A milnerian view of works by Y. Z. Kami. *International Journal of Psychoanalysis*, 95: 67–81.

Matte-Blanco, I. (1988). *Thinking, Feeling, and Being: Clinical Reflections on the Fundamental Antimony of Human Beings and World. The New Library of Psychoanalysis,* vol. 5. (pp. 336).

Maxwell, P. (2006). On reading and speaking with Antonino Ferro. *Australian Journal of Psychoanalysis*, 25(2): 1–10.

Mayo, E. (1924). Revery and industrial fatigue. *Journal of Personnel Research*, 3: 273–281.

——— (1933). *The Human Problems of an Industrial Civilization*. Cambridge, MA: Harvard (Reprinted by Routledge, 2004).

Meltzer, D. (1967). *The Psycho-Analytical Process*. London: William Heinemann Medical Books.

——— (1979). *The Psycho-Analytical Process*. Perthshire, Scotland: Clunie Press.

——— (1984). *Dream-Life A Re-examination of the Psychoanalytical Theory and Technique*. Reading: Clunie Press.

——— (2010). In M. Harris Williams (Ed.), *A Meltzer Reader: Selections from the Writings of Donald Meltzer*. Chapter 10. Location 1637–1787 of 3256. Kindle.

Meltzer, D., & Harris Williams, M. (1988). *The Apprehension of Beauty: The Role of Aesthetic Conflict in Development, Violence and Art*. Strath Tay: The Clunie Press.

Miller, A. (1979). The drama of the gifted child and the psycho-analyst's narcissistic disturbance. *International Journal of Psycho-Analysis*, 60: 47–58.

——— (1981). *Prisoners of Childhood*. Trans. Ruth Ward. New York: Basic Books.

Milner, M. see entries below

Molnar, M. (1992). Notes and references. In: Sigmund Freud, *The Diary of Sigmund Freud: 1929-1939. A Record of the Final Decade* (Michael Molnar, ed. and trans.) (pp. 271–308). New York: Charles Scribner's Sons, and Toronto: Maxwell Macmillan Canada, and New York: Maxwell Macmillan International / Maxwell Publishing Company, Maxwell Communication Group of Companies.

Montanaro, L. A., & Stefana, A. (2023). *Surrealism and Psychoanalysis in Grace Pailthorpe's Life and Work*.

Ogden, T. H. (1985). On Potential Space. *International Journal of Psycho-Analysis*, 66: 129–141.

——— (1994a). The analytic third: working with intersubjective clinical facts. *International Journal of Psychoanalysis*, 75: 3–19.

——— (1994b). *Subjects of Analysis* (2nd ed.). London: Karnac Books.

——— (1996). Reconsidering three aspects of psychoanalytic technique. *International Journal of Psychoanalysis*, 77: 883–899.

——— (1997a). Listening three frost poems. *Psychoanalytic Dialogues*, 7: 619–639.

——— (1997b). Some thoughts on the use of language in psychoanalysis. *Psychoanalytic Dialogues*, 7(1): 1–21.

——— (1997c). Reverie and metaphor: Some thoughts on how I work as a psychoanalyst. *International Journal of Psychoanalysis*, 78: 719–732.

——— (1998). A question of voice in poetry and psychoanalysis. *Psychoanalytic Quarterly*, 67: 426–448.

——— (1999). 'The music of what happens' in poetry and psychoanalysis. *International Journal of Psychoanalysis*, 80: 979–994.

——— (2002). *Conversations At The Frontier Of Dreaming* (2nd ed.). London and New York: H Karnac (Books) Ltd.

——— (2003). On not being able to dream. *International Journal of Psychoanalysis*, 84: 17–30.

——— (2004a). The analytic third: Implications for psychoanalytic theory and technique. *Psychoanalytic Quarterly*, 73: 167–195.

——— (2004b). On holding and containing, being and dreaming. *International Journal of Psycho-Analysis*, 85: 1349–1364.

——— (2005a). *This Art of Psychoanalysis: Dreaming Undreamt Dreams and Interrupted Cries*. London and New York: Routledge.

——— (2005b). This art of psychoanalysis: Dreaming undreamt dreams and interrupted cries. In: *This Art of Psychoanalysis: Dreaming Undreamt Dreams and Interrupted Cries*. London and New York: Routledge.

——— (2007). On talking-as-dreaming. *International Journal of Psycho-Analysis*, 88: 575–589.

——— (2010). On three forms of thinking: Magical thinking, dream thinking, and transformative thinking. *The Psychoanalytic Quarterly*, 79(2): 2317–2347.

Olson, N. (2013). Marion Milner: Unventing psychoanalysis. *Journal of the American Psychoanalytic Association*, 61(5): 1003–1022.

Parsons, M. (1990). Marion Milner's 'answering activity' and the question of psychoanalytic creativity. *International Review of Psycho-Analysis*, 17: 413–424.

——— (1999). Psychic reality, negation, and the analytic setting. In G. Kohon (Ed.), *The Dead Mother. The work of André Green*. London and New York: Routledge.

——— (2000). 'Psychic reality, negation and the analytic setting', chapter 10 in *The Dove that Returns, the Dove that Vanishes.* London: Routledge.

——— (2001). Marion Milner 1900–1998. *International Journal of Psycho-Analysis*, 82: 609–611.

Pater, W. (1980). *Studies in the Renaissance.* Berkeley: University of California Press.

Phillips, A. (2010). Introduction to *The Hands of the Living God.* London: Routledge.

——— (2017). *'Playing and Reality' and Reality: Discussion.* Paper presented at New Center for Psychoanalysis, Los Angeles (October 28th 2017).

——— (2018). *The Cure for Psychoanalysis: Discussion.* Paper presented at Confer Symposium, London (December 1st 2018).

Podro, M. (2000). On imaginary presence. In: L. Caldwell (Ed.), *Art Creativity Living* (pp. 63–74). London: Karnac.

Raphael-Leff, J. (2013a). 'The Intersubjective Matrix': Influences on the Independents' growth from 'Object relations' to 'Subject relations', chapter 3. In: S. Dermen, J. Keen & P. Williams (Eds.), *Contemporary Independent Psychoanalysis.* London: Karnac Books.

——— (2013b). 'The affective life of five generations of Baboushkas': The British independent tradition. Commentary. In: B. Huppertz (Ed.), *Psychotherapy in the Wake of War: Discovering Multiple Psycho-analytic Traditions.* New York: Jason Aronson, pp. 85–159.

——— (2023) The core question - what is mind? In: Antonis, B. and Wolf, E. (Eds.), *The Independent Women*, London and New York: Routledge

Raphael-Leff, J., & Perelberg, R. J. (1997). *Female Experience: Four Generations of British Women Psychoanalysts on Work with Women* (New Edition). London: Anna Freud Centre, 2008.

Rayner, E (1990). *The Independent Mind in British Psychoanalysis.* London: Jason Aronson; London: Free Association. 1991.

Read, H. (1951). Psychoanalysis and the problem of aesthetic value. *International Journal of Psychoanalysis*, 32: 73–82.

Rodman, F. R. (Ed.) (1993). *The Spontaneous Gesture: Selected Letters of D. W. Winnicott.* London: Karnac.

——— (2003). *Winnicott: Life and Work.* Cambridge, MA: Perseus.

Roussillion, R. (2010). Winnicott's deconstruction of primary narcissism, In J. Abram (Ed.), *Donald Winnicott Today* London and New York: Routledge, 2013.

Ryan, M. -L. (2001). *Narrative as Virtual Reality: Immersion and Interactivity in Literature and Electronic Media.* Baltimore and London: The Johns Hopkins University Press.

Rycroft, C. (1968a). *Anxiety and Neurosis.* London: Allen Lane/The Penguin Press.

Rycroft, C. (1968b). *Imagination and Reality: Psycho-Analytical Essays. 1951-1961.* London: Hogarth Press and the Institute of Psycho-Analysis.

Safán-Gerard, D. (2018). *Chaos and Control: A Psychoanalytic Perspective on Unfolding Creative Minds.* London. New York: Routledge.

Sandler, J. (1960). The background of safety. *International Journal of Psycho-Analysis*, 41: 352–356.

Sayers, J. (2002). Marion Milner, mysticism and psycho-analysis. *International Journal of Psychoanalysis*, 83: 105–120.

——— (2010). Introduction: *On Not Being Able to Paint.* East Hove: Routledge (first published by Heinemann London, 1950).

Searles, H. (1970). An epic struggle with schizophrenia: A review of Marion Milner's. 'The Hands of the Living God'. In: *Countertransference and Related Subjects.* Madison, CT: International Universities Press.

——— (1979). The patient as therapist to his analyst. In: *Countertransference and Related Subjects.* Madison, CT: International Universities Press.

Sklar, J. (2011). *Landscapes of the Dark: History, Trauma, Psychoanalysis.* London: Karnac.

Solms, M. (2015). What is the mind? A neuropsychoanalytic approach. In: M. Solms (Ed.), *The Feeling Brain* (pp. 40–49). London: Karnac.

——— (2020). *Mark Solms in Lock-Down.* Retrieved from https://mark-solms-in-lock-down.teachable.com/courses/enrolled

Spelman, Boyle, M (2013a). *Winnicott's Babies and Winnicott's Patients.* London: Karnac.

——— (2013b). *The Evolution of Winnicott's Thinking: The Growth of Psychoanalytic Thought over Three Generations.* London: Karnac.

——— (2013c). *Winnicott's Babies and Winnicott's Patients.* London: Karnac.

——— (2013d). *The Evolution of Winnicott's Thinking: Examining the Growth of Psychoanalytic Thought Over Three Generations.* London: Karnac.

——— (2019). 'Milner and Winnicott' in *eWinnicott*, online journal of The International Winnicott Association (IWA).

Spelman, Boyle, M & Thomson-Salo, F. (Eds.) (2014a). *The Winnicott Tradition.* London: Karnac.

——— (2014b). *The Donald W. Winnicott Tradition: Lines of Development - Evolution of Theory and Practice.* London: Karnac.

Spitz, E. H. (1985). *Art and Psyche.* London: Yale University Press.

Stefana, A. (2011). Introduzione al pensiero di Marion Milner. *Psicoterapia e Scienze Umane*, XLV: 355–374.

——— (2014). Marion Milner e il passaggio dall'oggetto primario all'oggetto secondario. *Richard e Piggle*, 22: 288–301.

——— (2017a). *History of Countertransference.* London and New York: Routledge.

——— (2017b). *History of Countertransference. From Freud to the British Object Relations School.* London and New York: Routledge.

———(2018). From Die Traumdeutung to the squiggle game: A brief history of an evolution. *American Journal of Psychoanalysis*, 78: 182–194.

——— (2019). Revisiting Marion Milner's work on creativity and art. *International Journal of Psycho-Analysis*, 100(1): 128–147.

Stefana, A., & Gamba, A. (2018). From 'squiggle game' to 'reciprocity game'. For a creative co-construction of a working space with adolescents. *International Journal of Psychoanalysis*, 99: 355–379.

Steiner, J. (1993). *Psychic Retreats: Pathological Organisations in Psychotic, Neurotic and Borderline Patients.* London: Routledge.

Stevens, W. (1951). *The Necessary Angel: Essays on Reality and the Imagination.* London: Vintage (1965).

——— (1990). *The Collected Poems of Wallace Stevens.* New York: Vintage Books.

Symington, N. (2005). Where is the medicine of healing in psychoanalysis? *Australasian Journal of Psychotherapy*, 25(2), 6–22.

——— (2019). *The Growth of Mind.* London and New York: Routledge.

Tagore, R. (1912). On the seashore. In *Gitanjali.* Digireads.com.

Tate Gallery Archive {TGA 8717.3.1] Ben Nicholson correspondence.

Townsend, P. (2019). *Creative States of Mind: Psychoanalysis and the Artist's Process.* London: Routledge.

Tuckett, D. (1997). Mutual enactment in the psychoanalytic situation. In: J. Ahumada et al. (Eds.), *The Perverse Transference and Other Matters. Essays in Honor of R. Horacio Etchegoyen.* New York and London: Jason Aronson.

Turner, J. F. (2002). A brief history of illusion: Milner, Winnicott and Rycroft. *International Journal of Psychoanalysis*, 83: 1063–1082.

Tustin, F. (1988). A personal reminiscence. *Winnicott Studies*, 3: 57–59.

Wagner, A. M. (2013). *The Threshold: Language and Vision in the Art of Anne Truitt.* Matthew Marks Gallery.

Walsh, N., & Wilson, A. (1941). The observation of infants in a set situation. *International Journal of Psycho-Analysis*, 22: 229–249.

——— (1945). Primitive emotional development. *International Journal of Psycho-Analysis*, 26: 137–143.

——— (1949). Mind and its relation to the psyche-soma. In *Through Paediatrics to Psychoanalysis, collected papers*. London: Reprinted in 1984 by Karnac.

——— (1951). Critical notice of *on not being able to paint* by Marion Milner. In: C. Winnicott, R. Shepherd & M. Davis (Eds.), *Psychoanalytic Explorations* (pp. 390–392). London: Karnac, 1989. Also in L. Caldwell (Ed.), *Art, Creativity, Living* (pp. 117–120). London: Karnac, 2000.

——— (1953). Transitional objects and transitional phenomena—A study of the first not-me possession. *International Journal of Psycho-Analysis*, 34: 89–97.

——— (1955). Metapsychological and clinical aspects of regression within the psycho-analytical set-up. *International Journal of Psycho-Analysis*, 36: 16–26.

——— (1998). *See Sluice Gates of the Mind: The Collaborative Work of Pailthorpe and Mednikoff.* Leeds: Museums and Galleries.

Walters, Margaret (2000). Lecture on "Marion Milner". Series on "The Pioneers of Psychoanalysis". *Confer, London, at Fifth Floor Lecture Theatre, Tavistock Clinic, Tavistock Centre, Tavistock and Portman N.H.S. Trust, Belsize Park, London, 19th July.*

Welter, V. M. (2012). *Ernst L. Freud, Architect: The Case of the Modern Bourgeois Home.* New York: Berghan Books.

Winnicott, D. W. (1941). The Observation of Infants in a Set Situation. *The International Journal of Psychoanalysis*, 22: 229–249.

——— (1945). Primitive Emotional Development. *The International Journal of Psychoanalysis*, 26: 137–143.

——— (1947). 'Hate in the countertransference', chapter 15 in *Through Paediatrics to Psychoanalysis*. London: Hogarth Press, 1987.

——— (1951). Critical notice of on not being able to paint by Marion Milner. In C. Winnicott, R. Shepherd, & M. Davis (Eds.), *Psychoanalytic Explorations* (pp. 390–392). London: Karnac, 1989. Also in L. Caldwell (Ed.), *Art, Creativity, Living* (pp. 117–120). London: Karnac, 2000.

——— (1953) Transitional objects and transitional phenomena. In: *Playing and Reality 1971.* Routledge.

——— (1955). Metapsychological and Clinical Aspects of Regression within the Psycho-Analytical Set-Up. *The International Journal of Psychoanalysis*, 36: 16–26.

——— (1956). Primary maternal preoccupation, in *Through Paediatrics to Psychoanalysis, collected papers*. London: Reprinted in 1984 by Karnac.

——— (1960). The theory of the parent-infant relationship. *International Journal of Psycho-Analysis*, 41: 585–595.

——— (1963). The development of the capacity for concern. *Bulletin of the Menninger Clinic*, 27: 167–176.

——— (1965). *The Maturational Processes and the Facilitating Environment.* London: Hogarth rpt. London, Karnac, 1990.

——— (1966). The location of cultural experience. In: L. Caldwell & H. T. Robinson (Ed.), *The Collected works of D.W. Winnicott, Vol.7 1964–1966.* London: Oxford University Press.

——— (1969a). 'The use of an object and relating through identifications', chapter 6 in *Playing and Reality*. London: Tavistock Publications, 1971.

——— (1969b). Foreword. In: Marion Milner (Ed.), *The Hands of the Living God: An Account of a Psycho-analytic Treatment* (pp. ix–x). London: Hogarth Press and the Institute of Psycho-Analysis.

——— (1971a). *Therapeutic Consultation in Child Psychiatry.* London: Hogarth Press.

——— (1971b). *Playing and Reality.* London: Tavistock Publications.

——— (1974). *Playing and Reality.* England: Penguin Books. Original edition, 1971.

——— (1975) Chapter XIX. Mind and its Relation to the Psyche-Soma [1949]. *Through Paediatrics to Psycho-Analysis*, 100: 243–254.

——— (1984a). *Maturational Processes and the Facilitating Environment*. London: Karnac.

——— (1984b). *Through Paediatrics to Psychoanalysis*. London: Karnac.

——— (1986). *Home Is Where We Start From*. London: Norton.

——— (1988). *Human Nature*. London: Free Association.

——— (1989). *Psycho-Aanalytic Explorations*. Ed. C. Winnicott, R. Shepherd & M. Davis. London: Karnac.

Winnicott, D. W. (1991) *The Piggle*. London: Penguin

——— (1996). *Playing and Reality*. London: Routledge.

Yeats, W. B. (1950). *Collected Poems*. London: MacMillan.

Milner. M entries

Milner. M. (1934). (aka Field, Joanna) *A Life of One's Own*. London: Chatto & Windus. (Originally published under the pseudonym of Joanna Field.) London & New York: Routledge 2011, (Series Editor, Emma Letley; new introduction Rachel Bowlby)

——— (1936). (aka Field, Joanna) *A Life of One's Own*. London: Chatto & Windus.

——— (aka Field, Joanna) (1937). *An Experiment in Leisure*, London: Chatto & Windus; Los Angeles: Jeremy P. Tarcher, 1987. Routledge: London & New York: Routledge 2011. (Series Editor, Emma Letley; new introduction by Maud Ellman).

——— (1938) *The Human Problem in Schools A Psychological Study carried out on behalf of the Girls' Public Day Schools Trust*. London: Methuen & Co Ltd. Revival: Routledge: Oxon & New York, 2018.

——— (1944). A suicidal symptom in a child of three. *International Journal of Psycho-Analysis*, 25: 53–61.

——— (1945). Some aspects of phantasy in relation to general psychology. In: David Tucket (Ed.), *The Supressed Madness of Sane Men*, London: Routledge, 1987.

——— (1950a). 'A note on the ending of an analysis,' *International Journal of Psycho-Analysis*, 31: 191–193.

——— (1950b). *On Not Being Able to Paint*. London: Heinemann, 1957; Los Angeles: Jeremy P. Tarcher, 1983; London: Routledge, 2010.

——— (1952a). The framed gap, chapter 8 in *The Suppressed Madness of Sand Men Forty-Four Years of Exploring Psychoanalysis* (p. 79). London and New York: Routledge, 1988.

——— (1952b). 'The Role of Illusion in Symbol Formation', chapter 9 in *The Supressed Madness of Sane Men*, London: Routledge, 1987. Also published as 'Aspects of symbolism in comprehension of the not-self'. *International Journal of Psychoanalysis,* 33: 181–95, 1952.

——— (1952c). Aspects of symbolism in Comprehension of the Not-Self. *International Journal of Psychoanalysis*, 33: 181–95.

——— (1954). Vote of thanks for Professor Gombrich's Ernest Jones Lecture. *International Journal of Psycho-Analysis*, 35: 411

——— (1955). The role of illusion in symbol formation, in Milner *The Supressed Madness of Sane Men* (pp. 83–111). London: Routledge, 1987.

——— (1956a). 'The communication of primary sensual experience—(The Yell of Joy)'. *International Journal of Psycho-Analysis*, 37: 278–281.

——— (1956b). Psycho-analysis and art. In M. Milner (Ed.) (1987b).

——— (1957). *On Not Being Able to Paint* (2nd ed.). London: International Universities Press.

——— (1987). 'Psycho-Analysis and art'. In J. D. Sutherland (Ed.), *Psychoanalysis and Contemporary Thought*. London: Karnac. Original edition, 1958.

——— (1960). The concentration of the body, chapter 14 in *The Suppressed Madness of Sand Men Forty-Four Years of Exploring Psychoanalysis* (pp. 234–240). London and New York: Routledge, 1987.

——— (1969). *The Hands of the Living God: An Account of a Psycho-analytic Treatment.* London: Hogarth Press and the Institute of Psycho-Analysis. (Foreword by D.W.Winnicott). Reprinted 2010. New York: International Universal Press, INC. The New Library of Psychoanalysis Teaching Series, 2010 (Series Editor, Emma Letley; new introduction by Adam Phillips).

——— (1972). 'Winnicott and the two-way journey', chapter 16 in *The Suppressed Madness of Sane Men*, London: Routledge, 1987.

——— (1973). Some notes on psychoanalytic ideas about mysticism. In: *The Suppressed Madness of Sane Men.* London: Institute of Psycho-analysis, 1987, Chapter 18, pp. 258–274.

——— (1978). D. W. Winnicott and the two-way journey. In: S. Grolnick & L. Barkin (Eds.), *Between Reality and Fantasy: Transitional Objects and Phenomena* (pp. 37–42). New York: Jason Aronson.

——— (Joanna Field) (1984). *On Not Being Able to Paint.* Reprint Edition. London: Heinemann London / William Heinemann Educational Books.

——— (1985). Personal communication to the author, 5th January.

——— (1986a). *An Experiment in Leisure.* London: Virago Books.

——— (1986b). Letter to Judith M. Hughes. 8th April. Cited in Judith M. Hughes (1989). *Reshaping the Psychoanalytic Domain: The Work of Melanie Klein, W.R.D. Fairbairn, and D.W. Winnicott*, p. 202, n. 89. Berkeley: University of California Press.

——— (1986b). *A Life of One's Own.* London: Virago Press.

——— (1986c). Personal communication to the author, 27th October.

——— (1987a). *Eternity's Sunrise. A Way of Keeping a Diary* (begun in 1958). London: Virago. Routledge. London & New York: Routledge, 2011 (introduction by Hugh Haughton).

——— (1987b). *The Suppressed Madness of Sane Men: Forty-Four Years of Exploring Psychoanalysis.* Ed. David Tuckett. London: New Library, Institute of Psycho-Analysis; New York: Brunner-Routledge. Tavistock 1987. Reprinted Routledge, 2011.

——— (1987c). Personal communication to the author, 24th October.

——— (2002). *A Life of One's Own* [introduction by A. Karpf]. London: Virago.

——— (2010). *On Not Being Able to Paint.* In E. Letley (Ed.). London: Routledge.

——— (2012). *Bothered by Alligators.* London and New York: Routledge. (New introduction by Margaret Walters).

——— (n.d.). Letter to Donald W. Winnicott. 25th September. PP/DWW/B/A/21. Donald Woods Winnicott Collection. Archives and Manuscripts, Rare Materials Room, Wellcome Library, Wellcome Collection, The Wellcome Building, London.

Milner's Papers collected in *The Suppressed Madness of Sand Men Forty-Four Years of Exploring Psychoanalysis.* London and New York: Routledge, 1987:

Milner, M. (1942) The child's capacity for doubt, Chapter 1, pp. 12–15 (lecture given to the Institute of Education, University of London, 7th February 1942).

——— (1943) Notes on the analysis of a 2.5 year old boy, Chapter 2, pp. 16–20 (from her notes for supervision with Melanie Klein).

——— (1944) A suicidal symptom in a child of three, Chapter 3, pp. 21–38 (written in 1943 as her membership paper for the British Psychoanalytical Society.

——— (1945) Some aspects of phantasy in relation to general psychology, Chapter 4, pp. 39–62 (read before the British Psychoanalytical Society 24th January 1945 and published in the *International Journal of Psychoanalysis* 26: 144–152).

——— (1947–48) Some signposts - blackness, joy, mind, Chapter 5, pp. 63–65.
——— (1948) An adult patient uses toys, Chapter 6, pp. 66–72.
——— (1949) The ending of two analyses, Chapter 7, pp. 73–78 (The first part of this paper was read on the termination of psychoanalytic treatment at a British Psychoanalytic Society meeting at the Tavistock Clinic on March 2nd 1949 and published in 1950 in the *International Journal of Psychoanalysis* 31: 191–193.
——— (1952a) The framed gap, Chapter 8, pp. 79–82 (two unpublished papers).
——— (1952b) The role of illusion in symbol formation, Chapter 9, pp. 83–113 (previously called: 'Aspects of Symbolism in Comprehension of the Not-self' published in an *International Journal of Psychoanalysis* in a festschrift issue in honour of Melanie Klein).
——— (1955) The communication of primary sensual experience, Chapter 10, pp. 114–167 (writing further about patients Ruth, aka Miss A and 'Susan').
——— (1956) The sense in nonsense (Freud in Blake's Job), Chapter 11, pp 168–191 (similar to her paper in *The New Era* January (pp. 1–13).
——— (1956) Psychoanalysis and art, Chapter 12, pp. 119–215 (published in J. Sutherland (ed.) *Psycho-Analysis and Contemporary Thought*. London: Hogarth and British Institute of Psycho-Analysis, 1958.
——— (1957) The ordering of chaos, Chapter 13, pp. 216–233 (written in 1957 as an appendix to the 2nd edition of *On Not Being Able to Paint).*
——— (1960) The concentration of the body, Chapter 14, pp. 234–240.
——— (1967) The hidden order of art, Chapter 15, pp. 241–245 (based on paper read at the Institute of Contemporary Art, London June 21st 1967).
——— (1972) Winnicott and the two-way journey, Chapter 16, pp. 246–252 (contribution to a memorial meeting for Winnicott given to the British Psychoanalytical Society). Also, Chapter 3 in S. Grolnick (ed) *Between Reality and Phantasy: Transitional Objects Phenomena.* London and New York: J Aronson, 1978.
——— (1972) The two-way journey in a child analysis, Chapter 17, pp. 253–257.
——— (1973) Some notes on psychoanalytic ideas about mysticism, Chapter 18, pp. 258–274 (written for a festschrift for Paula Heimann's 75th birthday)
——— (1975) A Discussion of Masud Khan's paper. *In Search of the Dreaming Experience.* Chapter 19, pp. 275–278.
——— (1977) Winnicott and the overlapping circles, Chapter 20, pp. 279–286 (published in *Winnicott and Overlapping Circles.* L'Arc 69, 1977 issue devoted to Winnicott).
——— (1986) Afterthoughts, Chapter 21, pp. 287–297.

Marion Milner's Lifeline [Credit To E.Letley; H.Haughton]

1895 Parents married – Arthur Blackett to Caroline Maynard.
1900 Nina Marion Blackett born February 1st in London (weaned at 4 months).
1904 Family moved house from Kenly, Surrey to Working. Lost her nanny.
1904 First annual summer holiday at Bamburg Castle, Northumberland (rock pools).
1911 Father's breakdown.
1917 Family moved to Beacon Hill; Marion left school.
1918 Student at Montessori nursery school training institute.
1921–23 Psychology & Physiology at London University.
1924 Graduation with first class degree.
1924–27 Work as an industrial psychologist under Cyril Burt.
1926 Pelman mental training course & beginning of diary keeping.
1927 Married Dennis Milner, dramatist and 'inventor by temperament'.
1927–29 Rockefeller fellowship to work with Prof. Elton Mayo (Hawthorne experiment) in Boston, therapy with Irma Putman and travel in US.

1932 Birth of her son John in London.
1934 Publication of *A Life of One's Own* (as Joanna Field).
1933–39 Study of educational system of the Girls' Public Day School Trust.
1936 'Sabbatical' in Malaga, Spain.
1937 Publication of *An Experiment in Leisure* (as Joanna Field).
1938 Publication of *The Human Problem in Schools.*
1940 Psychoanalytic training at the British Institute [Analyst: Sylvia Payne. Case supervisors: Ella Sharpe; Joan Riviere; Melanie Klein (child case)].
1942? Second analysis with Winnicott.
1942–44 Controversial Discussions in the British Psychoanalytical Society.
1943 Marion Milner qualified as an adult and child psychoanalyst.
1944 Full membership of the British Psychoanalytical Society.
1946 Marion Milner became a training analyst.
1949 Third analysis with Clifford Scott.
1950 Publication of *On Not Being Able to Paint.*
1951–54 Annual Summer School at Brazier's Park, Oxon.
1955 Painting trip in Palinuro, Italy.
1956 Trip to Canada.
1957 Painting trip in Catalonia, Spain.
1959 Trip to Greece & Venice (Hellenic Cruise).
1960 Trip to Athens IPA Congress (Hellenic Cruise).
1961 Trip to Greece (with rucksacks).
1962 Trip to Camargue, France.
1964 Trip to Corsica.
1967 Trip to Greek islands.
1968 Trip to Ibiza, Spain.
1969 Publication of *The Hands of the Living God.*
1971 Trip to Kashmir, India. Winnicott died.
1974 Summer School in France (Chateau de Mons).
1975 Trip to Israel.
1987 Publication of *The Suppressed Madness of Sane Men: Forty-Four Years of Exploring Psychoanalysis*
1987 Publication of *Eternity's Sunrise. A Way of Keeping a Diary.*
1998 Died on May 29th [*Bothered by Alligators* published posthumously 2012].

Index

Note: *Italic* page numbers refer to figures and page numbers followed by 'n'denote endnotes.